Pastoral Conventions

Pastoral Conventions

Poetry, Language, and Thought in Seventeenth-Century Nuremberg

JANE O. NEWMAN

The Johns Hopkins University Press
Baltimore and London

© 1990 The Johns Hopkins University Press
All rights reserved
Printed in the United States of America

The Johns Hopkins University Press
701 West 40th Street, Baltimore, Maryland 21211
The Johns Hopkins Press Ltd., London

The paper used in this book meets the minimum requirements of American National Standard for Information Sciences—Permanence of Paper for Printed Library Materials, ANSI Z39.48-1984.

Library of Congress Cataloging-in-Publication Data
Newman, Jane O.
  Pastoral conventions : poetry, language, and thought in seventeenth-century Nuremberg / Jane O. Newman.
      p.   cm.
  Includes bibliographical references.
  ISBN 0-8018-3996-3 (alk. paper)
  1. Pastoral poetry, German—Germany (West)—Nuremberg—History and criticism. 2. German poetry—Early modern, 1500–1700—History and criticism. 3. German literature—Early modern, 1500–1700—Societies, etc. 4. Nuremberg (Germany)—Intellectual life. 5. European literature—17th century—History and criticism. I. Title.
PT3807.N8N48 1990
831'.509321734—dc20   89-49002 CIP

Frontispiece: From G. P. Harsdörffer, *Playful Colloquies for the Ladies* (Nuremberg, 1642, 1657), 2:329. Universitätsbibliothek, Tübingen.

For John and Julian

Contents

Preface	ix
Acknowledgments	xiii
1 Interpreting Conventions: History, Literature, and Textual Institutions	1
The New Historicism: Literature, History, Meaning	4
Textual Institutions	13
Convention and the Text	23
Language, Meaning, *Différance*	28
2 Academic Conventions	32
The Fairest Flower: The European Academies, 1430–1700	33
Pastoral Conventions: The German Academies in Köthen and Nuremberg	52
3 Redemption in the Vernacular: From the Garden to Society Texts	69
Institutiones Linguae: The Origins of Language and the Original Language	71
The Doctrine of Contextualism in Nuremberg Language Theory	83
True Stories 1: German as Original Tongue (*Ursprache*)	89
True Stories 2: German as a Natural Language (*Natursprache*)	100

viii Contents

The Loss and Redemption of the Vernacular	104
Common Speech and Society Usage: Finding/Inventing High German	109
Textual Foundations: The Dictionary and Translation Projects of the Nuremberg Order	113

4 *Institutiones Poeticae:* A Defense of Vernacular Poetics — 132

Art, Nature, and Inspiration in the Tradition of Technical Poetics	138
Art Creates Nature: The Nuremberg Poetics as Institutions	145
Invention and the Imagination: Logic, Method, and the Representation of Truth in Vernacular Poetry	157
"Inventing" Vernacular Poetry: The Theoretical Origins of Texts and the Origins of Theory in Texts	166

5 Some Versions of Pastoral — 186

The Poetics of Pastoral: Textual Conventions in Theocritus, Virgil, and Opitz	191
Textual Monuments: The Institutions of Poetry of Praise	211
The Nuremberg Pastorals: "Inventing" Origins in the Local Grove	214

6 The Limits of Institutional Practice and the Resistance of the Text — 249

The Nuremberg Institutionalization of Textuality	250
The Limits of Pragmatism and the Resistance of the Text	252
Conclusion	260

Notes	263
Bibliography	285
Index	305

Preface

This study began a number of years ago as an attempt to save the Order of Flowers on the Pegnitz, a German language society founded in Nuremberg in 1644, from the judgments of both its best friends and its worst enemies. The first, those familiar with the language society, found its texts "hardly worth being freed from the dust" that covers them (Klaus Garber); the second did not even know that such a phenomenon had ever existed at all. My goal at the time of this initial study was to read and analyze three groups of texts published by those associated with the Order of Flowers—language theory, poetics, and pastorals—in the hope of finding a consistent intellectual program. Although such a program was nowhere developed explicitly by the order, I sought to locate an underlying theme or textual strategy that would explain the "historical fact" of the Order of Flowers, the reasons why, that is, a group of bourgeois poets banded together in an academy-like endeavor, took shepherd names, chose flower emblems, and wrote massive collective texts at a time when the incredibly destructive Thirty Years' War (1618–48) was raging across Europe.

What I found was that the few isolated references in the texts of the order—and in those of other language societies as well—to military and political events of the time could not provide the principle that shaped the statements made about the German language and vernacular poetry by members of the group in their texts. Nor was there any unambiguous network of references to the chaos of events "on the outside" of the texts. Rather, the uniting principle that emerged from my analyses was one concerned primarily with asserting that the spectacularly uniform vernacular texts written by members of the Order of Flowers could serve as sources of poetic power and norms in a post-classical—indeed, post-Renaissance—age. For lack, then, of any more explicit statements about their historical genesis or potential contextual reference, I was forced to conclude somewhat speculatively that in the face of the chaos of war, the Nuremberg "shepherds" had fallen back on their own communal standards and regulated *textual* practices to structure what was otherwise an unstructured *historical* world.

Since concluding my initial analysis, the combined questions of community formation, historical reference, and textual power have led me to consider the issues of collective thought, formal conventions, and textual identity on a theoretical as well as historical level. When, why, and how do communities fix their practices in formalized codes of behavior? When, why, and how do such codes—precisely as texts—take on normative force? What is the relationship, finally, between these texts and the context in which they are produced? These questions were originally elicited by the very form of the Nuremberg writings. Always lengthy in their insistent attempts to persuade, always highly structured and explicit concerning their exemplary nature, always conscious, finally, of their own conformity to specific ("historical") social expectations, the Nuremberg texts were both allegories of and producers of historical communities insofar as they created the conditions of possibility for standardized communal behavior. As texts, they thus produced the very conventionality that they also described.

Numerous literary theorists have addressed the role of collective or community behavior, especially the establishment of interpretive schemes, in the production of meaning. Numerous theorists have also addressed the relationship of "history" and textuality, of context and text. It was to these theorists, among them reader-response critics, structuralists, poststructuralists, Marxists, pragmatists, and feminists, that I turned in my efforts to understand the structures and production of community in and by textual forms; I review and critique some of these theorists in chapters 1 and 6.

These theoretical considerations of collective behavior and its production in and as text allowed me, in turn, to address the question of how these writings of the Order of Flowers could be considered historically significant despite their limited explicit references to the war that had affected Nuremberg—and presumably the members of the order who lived in or near the city—so deeply. For me, the question became how could I analyze these highly stylized texts and the pastoral phenomenon of the order as "history" without referring explicitly to the political, social, and military context in and out of which they developed and which they must, at some level, represent? How, in other words, could I locate "history" in the text, the history that was the text? It was in response to this question that I developed the concept of the *textual institution*.

My search for a new concept and terminology with which to talk about the relationship of text and history grew out of my readings in literary theory and criticism, in which questions of referentiality and representation—in connection with concepts of community and codification—are primary. A viable alternative to the "reflection theory" method of criticism, in which texts are seen as "mirroring" events (a method that in any case was of little use for my texts), has developed recently. This alternative now goes by the name of the "new historicism"; its theoretical implications are the focus of chapter 1. What has become increasingly clear to me is that the essential questions about texts and history and about their relationship are themselves really a matter of a collective understanding of exactly what those terms are supposed to mean. Thus my examination of theories of community understanding and textual functions has led me to formulate solutions to the methodological problem of how texts can "be historical," "be history," when they are not explicitly referential. My solutions are based on a new terminology and conceptual apparatus concerned with the text as institution. The question of representation—of thought in language, of history in texts—is one that is central to contemporary literary theory. My effort to understand the significance of both the collective in the texts of the Nuremberg group and the "historical fact" of their material existence was thus related to questions about the status of "meaning," about the relationship between "the thing itself," its textual representation, and the reception of that representation, and thus about the interconnectedness of ontology and language.

The thesis of the following study is, then, that communally derived and contextually described standards can function, when they appear in textualized form, both as the origins of historical identity, truth, and behavior and as the absolute standards against which they can be measured within the collective or community. When texts claim to function in this way—as both productive of history and creative of orthodoxy—they may be interpreted as *textual institutions*, as texts that do instituting and institutionalizing work. The texts of the Nuremberg Order of Flowers on the Pegnitz exemplify this institutional identity.

My purpose in discussing theoretical concepts and methodological alternatives first in the present study is twofold. I hope to provide a new reading of some German Baroque texts in light of developments in recent literary theory, particularly issues involving the relationship between history and the text. At the same time, I hope to address the contemporary theoretical debate from a different historical point of view. The German Baroque is (in)famous for its conventionality and for the monumental aspect of its texts and thus offers an appropriate historical field for employing (and modifying) certain theoretical models and terms. In chapters 1 and 6, I explore the background and implications of the theoretical apparatus with which I work in my analyses of the Nuremberg texts. For those more familiar with the theoretical models and terms than with the historical period, the overview of the tradition of language academies in early modern Europe in chapter 2 will provide an introduction to the phenomenon of the language society itself. Chapters 3 through 5 consist chiefly of analyses of the Nuremberg texts. By means of this combination of discourses, the institutional analyses (and the analyses of texts as institutions) that form the substance of *Pastoral Conventions* will contribute to ongoing discussions of strategies of textual representation in the early modern period, to the debate about "history" and textuality, and to the theoretical debate about the historically and ideologically bound (and thus implicitly provisional) status of all meaning.

Acknowledgments

The research for this book would not have been possible without the generous financial assistance of the German Academic Exchange Service (DAAD), the Graduate Division of the University of California, Irvine, and the School of Humanities, University of California, Irvine. I am indebted to Professors Hans Aarsleff, Alban Forcione, and David Quint (Princeton University), Wilfried Barner (University of Tübingen), Klaus Garber (University of Osnabrück), Karl Otto (University of Pennsylvania), James A. Parente, Jr. (University of Illinois, Chicago), Richard Schade (University of Cincinnati), and Blake Lee Spahr (University of California, Berkeley) for encouragement, criticism, and direction in many forms. Blake Spahr was particularly helpful in assisting me in checking my translations of the flowery prose of the Nuremberg writers, much of which appears here in English for the first time. Of course, I alone remain responsible for their final form. The tireless efforts of my research assistant, Gary Campbell, to provide me with even the most obscure information and to check details of the manuscript with the utmost care are most deeply appreciated. I am most grateful for the excellent work done by Joel Reed (University of California, Irvine) in compiling the index. Last, but certainly not least, I must express my gratitude to Benjamin Bennett (University of Virginia), whose insightful reading of this book while it was in manuscript challenged me to clarify its conceptual framework in an extraordinarily productive way.

I would like to thank Eric Halpern of the Johns Hopkins University Press for his efficiency and especially for his commitment to this somewhat unorthodox project, and Pamela J. Bruton, whose editorial skills have helped clarify some of the complex issues addressed in the book.

The extraordinary support provided by the following colleagues at the University of California, Irvine, cannot be adequately acknowledged by thanking them all here: Joan Ariel, Steve Barney, Dan Brewer, Ellen

Broidy, David Carroll, Mike Clark, Anne Cruz, Bob Folkenflik, Vivian Folkenflik, Alex Gelley, Linda Georgianna, Betty Guthrie, Wolfgang Iser, Murray Krieger, Juliet MacCannell, Penny Maddy, Hillis Miller, Bob Montgomery, Alex Morales, Bob Newsom, Dayle Nunez, Pat O'Brien, Spence Olin, Mark Poster, Leslie Rabine, Richard Regosin, Rick Rentschler, John Rowe, Ed Schell, Gabriele Schwab, Martin Schwab, Guy Sircello, Aliko Songolo, and Gary Watson. Special thanks go to Leslie Millerd and to Lynn Hammeras and Kathy White. Colleagues at other institutions should not go unmentioned: Mária Brewer (University of Minnesota), Anthony Grafton (Princeton University), Stephen Greenblatt (University of California, Berkeley), Robert Holub (University of California, Berkeley), Susan Jeffords (University of Washington), Bruce Kieffer (Williams College), Alice Kuzniar (University of North Carolina at Chapel Hill), Tim Murray (Cornell University), and Rainer Nägele (Johns Hopkins University).

Due the most thanks is of course Professor John H. Smith (University of California, Irvine), who, as a community of one, made the completion of this text possible.

1 Interpreting Conventions

History, Literature, and Textual Institutions

> Contemporary literary theory focuses on two questions: the question of reference and the question of reading. Both are posed as investigations of representation, seen alternatively as the relationship between a literary work and the other structures of social life, and as the intellectual and social practice of reading.
> —Susan Wells, *The Dialectics of Representation*

Increasing attention has been paid in recent years to the study of representation in early modern literature and culture, particularly during the Elizabethan age. But more often than not, scholars have addressed only one side of the representational act that Susan Wells describes, namely, the ontological, epistemological, and possibly political relationship of language and texts to "history" as a referent, and have downplayed the other, namely, the critic's interpretive role as a "reader" who gives texts (as both linguistic and nonlinguistic sign-systems) meaning. In particular, recent influential discussions of representation in Elizabethan England by the so-called new historicists Jonathan Goldberg, Stephen Greenblatt, Richard Helgerson, Louis Adrian Montrose, and Steven Mullaney claim to employ a methodology explicitly designed to efface the very borders between history and the text traditionally thought to divide them; and yet, these critics often fail to address the major role that they, as reader-critics, play in constituting meaning by setting the boundaries of where and what is "history" and where and what is "text." Although these new historicist studies deal primarily with a period somewhat earlier than the period with which this study is concerned, they are pertinent here insofar as they provide a basis for measuring the importance of the question of representation and of the relationship between history and textuality for the phenomenon of the seventeenth-century language society in Nuremberg, the Order of Flowers on the Pegnitz, which is the focus of this book.[1]

What I would like to suggest in these opening pages is that the new historicism does not deal adequately with both sides of the question of representation precisely because of its unquestioning acceptance of a single location for the frame that distinguishes between history and the text. In so doing, it ignores the fundamental issues of the reader's horizon or perspective, its circumscription and predetermination of that frame, and the reader's role in determining how (i.e., in which direction) movement between history and the text occurs. As a result, the new historicism ultimately relies upon the quite traditional division between history and the text that it intended to overcome. A specific consequence of the new historicist decision to allow the distinction between text and history to persist is that *the power of the text to itself be and do the work of history* is underrated. Because new historicist analyses are based on a method that continues (perhaps inadvertently and as a result of the very terms used) to assume that history is "other" than and outside the text, the text is interpreted in these analyses only within the framework of a predetermined and predetermining "other" (as history is in general understood to be) rather than in and on its own terms. It is this exclusion of the work of history from the text that, I will argue, the material existence of the Nuremberg texts as texts ultimately refuses.

The language theory, poetics, and pastorals written by members of the Nuremberg language society reject any easy categorization as texts that "merely" reflect history and are thus separate from it. The critique of the new historicism upon which my own method is based takes this rejection seriously and attempts to provide an alternative understanding of texts as history. Like the new historicists, I address the question of representation. But I argue, differently from them, for the importance of recognizing the hermeneutical assumption at the center of all studies of the concept, namely, that the text as writing and as concrete *object* by definition both transcends (its own) history and is different from (the reader's) history in its very presence as text and as object of reading and interpretation. As a written document, it thus constitutes an independent moment of history. Hans-Georg Gadamer writes: "It is in the form of writing that all of tradition [i.e., history] has equal presence for every 'present.'" In the very fact of textual presence, he continues, "there is . . . a unique coexistence of past and present,"[2] of that which is both other than the text being read (by a particular reader) and other than its origin (in a particular author, period, or context). This definition of the ontological status of texts has important ramifications for interpreting the work that they do. Recognizing the text's otherness, its difference—in the most concrete sense—from any particular (referential or reception) history frees the text to itself be and make history because it liberates the text from overdetermination by either the author or a specific audience. The meaning of the text is thus located in the fact of its existence.³

The interpretive model with which I work in the following pages is based, then, on recognizing the power of the text. It calls for an analysis of texts as *institutions*, as themselves capable of both *beginning* and *structuring* history. I argue that this philosophical reassessment of the status of the text in general (a redressing of the fundamental asymmetry of most historicist methods of literary criticism, even those that claim to be "new" because they address issues of representing) can have a significant effect on the interpretation of specific texts, here those associated with the collective enterprise of the seventeenth-century language society in Nuremberg. And I maintain that since just such a concern with texts, history, and the creation of meaning informed much Nuremberg writing, we can interpret the *institutionalization* of the text (its *beginnings or origins as having been written* within a collective context and its *continued existence* in the form of a textual monument to an ongoing orthodoxy of literary form) as evidence that history, textuality, and the historical work of the text are fundamentally inseparable events.

Finally, I suggest that recognizing the text's fundamental ontological difference from any specific predetermining history (and thus its fundamental indifference to that history) in the specific case of the Nuremberg group will have far-reaching consequences for interpreting the texts of every period insofar as it throws into relief the space that the text offers for the constitution of (alternative) histories. That is, because it can itself make a space for history and is thus itself a historical space, the text, both as concrete object and as rhetorical event, can be understood as resisting any forces (including conventionally defined "historical" ones) that seek to (over)determine its meaning or enforce interpretive closure. At the same time, however, the text's (and language's) power *as history* (as conventionally understood) is problematic, since it is based on the capacity of the text to refuse its textuality and thus to resist history in a number of ways. I explore this ambiguity and the importance of maintaining its complexity in more depth below.

My goal in formulating the phrase *textual institution* is to accomplish what the new historicists claim to do—that is, to get beyond the text-context dyad by interpreting texts "representationally." My discussion in the present chapter of the questions raised by the new historicism and my conclusion that meaning is always already both textual and historical precisely as a *result of being institutionalized in texts* provide, in turn, the terms with which I discuss, in chapters 3–5, the argumentative strategies internal to the Nuremberg texts and the significance of the historical work they did. I thus begin with a critical overview of the new historicism and of some traditional historical studies. I then define what I mean by institutionalization in texts and describe how the study of the historical work that texts do can circumvent some of the problems associated with both traditional and new historical methods. I also investigate how one may study textual institutions by analyzing conventionality both as a textual structure and as a theoretical concept because precisely in becoming textualized, conventions claim superior authority for their historically bound norms. Understood this way, institutions are a community's conventions hypostasized in textual form.

The New Historicism: Literature, History, Meaning

Following both Vico's groundbreaking hypothesis that everything "made" by Man, including history, can be understood (as a consequence of this "made-ness") as a "made" event and Auerbach's Vichean analyses of all forms of culture as moments in the history of "expression," the new historicists hope to understand all of human activity, both texts and contexts, both literary and extraliterary achievements, as mediated in and as a system of signs.[4] They call for an analysis of what has been christened the "poetics of culture" of the early modern period that would combine hitherto-separate analyses of history and literature by focusing on both as representational acts, as acts that can be "read" with reference to the "world." The new historicists argue first that since language is a "collective construction," it must be interpreted within and as the same kind of system of "public signification" as other, more traditionally defined public acts in the sociopolitical sphere.[5] These public acts, in turn, although conventionally thought of as "determining" the significance of (literary) culture during this period, must also be analyzed as structured or "fashioned," according to the new historicists, since these acts too are "made," discursive events, not unmediated existence. The result of this representational analysis is allegedly the liberation of the text from its literary confines, the freeing of the text to be "socially and culturally instrumental" in history.[6] Both texts and history become complex, rather than simple, phenomena.

The charge has been made that the new historicism is not a method but is merely anecdotal and narrative in nature.[7] Alternatively, it has been accused as a method of being immobilized by its essentially Foucauldian assumption that all acts—both literary and literal—are caught in an all pervasive, all-determining discourse of power. Even as the new historicists characterize some texts as subversive of a dominant discourse about Queen Elizabeth as monarch, for example, they must admit (and often fail to do so in their analyses, according to critics) that this very subversiveness is itself produced by and thus ultimately remains subject to that dominant discourse instead of actually disrupting it. Within this model, the text cannot be said to be "free" at all.[8] As a result of an uncritical indebtedness to Foucault, the new historicism has been accused, finally, of being a form of historical-textual criticism that remains unaware of its limited (even uncritical) use of the very terms *text* and *history* in spite of the very crucial role that the status of these terms plays in its analyses.

In response to such criticism (or perhaps as part of an inevitable self-criticism and self-situating in a critical debate), some scholars associated with the new historicism have attempted to formulate principles by which their methodology could be defined. One of its most eloquent formulations comes in Louis Adrian Montrose's essay "The Elizabethan Subject and the Spenserian Text," in which he describes the new historicism in the following way:

> The new orientation to history in Renaissance literary studies ... may be succinctly characterized, on the one hand, by its acknowledgement of the *historicity of texts:* the cultural specificity, the social embedment, of all modes of writing ... On the other hand, this new orientation is characterized by its acknowledgement of the *textuality of history:* the unavailability of a full and authentic past, a lived material existence, that has not already been mediated by the surviving texts of the society in question.[9]

The chiasmus of the "historicity of texts" and the "textuality of history" calls for a method that is interested in a complex identity for literature as social production, a method that understands that "any particular text" is not only "socially produced" but also "socially productive," as Montrose writes. Thus the new historicism "challenges the assumptions that guarantee a secure distinction between 'literary foreground' and 'political background' or, more generally, between artistic production and other kinds of social production."[10] It is based on what Lynn Hunt has called the "discursive model of culture," which has been most explicitly formulated by anthropologists critical of conventional anthropology's "unspoken assumptions about interpreting and writing." According to Hunt, this model asserts that "culture is inscribed in and through rhetorical and narrative, as well as semiological means."[11] Although some may object that the model relies on a certain kind of "discursive determinism" that ignores empirical "reality," Hunt argues simply for a recognition that "all social reality is in fact culturally constructed (and discursively construed) in the first instance." (10–11) There is thus a "reciprocal relationship between the literary and the social," as Montrose says (305), that challenges the notion of an "autonomous aesthetic order" (306), on the one hand, and of a nonfashioned cultural "reality," on the other.

Thus, the new historicism has addressed its own project of combining the previously separate discourses of history and textuality and, in so doing, has attempted to disrupt the conventional practice of understanding them as separate categories of analysis and interpretation. Nevertheless, as a result, perhaps, more of the terms in which the discussion about history and literature has traditionally been framed rather than anything else, even some of these innovative critics continue to accept a certain duality between texts and contexts in their critical practice even as they seek to overcome it in statements about the textualization of culture and politicization of literary artifacts. Greenblatt, for example, explains the project of cultural poetics by declaring that critics must be prepared to investigate "both the social presence to the world of the literary text and the social presence of the world in the literary text."[12] Similarly, Goldberg's thesis rests on the assertion that politics and language are "mutually constitutive," with the term *politics* designating the "social processes in which relationships of power are conveyed" and *language* referring not just to writing but to public discourse in general.[13] Thus both recall the previously dissolved distinction between the "real" and the "imaginary"[14] (through the back door, so to speak) in order to explain the primacy and thus "presence" of social and political power to and in the representational, textual sphere. "Writing represents authority," Goldberg continues (xi), thereby (perhaps unintentionally) assigning writing a secondary status by means of the *re-*. Greenblatt's explanation is more elaborate:

> Social actions are themselves always embedded in systems of public signification, always grasped, even by their makers, in acts of interpretation, while the words that constitute the works of literature that we discuss here are by their very nature the manifest assurance of a similar embeddedness.[15]

The first part of this statement makes clear that the (social) sphere of action and the (textual) sphere of representation or interpretation cannot be separated given their common embeddedness in and debt to wider systems of signification ("language"). Yet the second part nonetheless relegates literature to a position of indebtedness to the social, whereby it can only "manifest," "assure," or, in short, *merely* re-present in literature "historical facts" that are "real."

Thus, the new historicism succeeds in "de-center[ing]" the text, as Peter Erickson writes, by locating it in a "novel cultural context."[16] But it does not complete its project, because it does not succeed in decentering history as well. Indeed, it continues to invest a specific set of predetermined, literal sociopolitical events with an ontological status superior to that of representational (figurative) language use. As a result, the discourse of historical power comes, in a circular fashion, to serve as the social (Greenblatt uses the term *anthropological*[17]) phenomenon that is simultaneously before, above, and after (but never *in*) the text.

History thus serves as the background, "origin," and ultimate goal of textual expression. Along the way, History also becomes a monolithic, "transcendental signifier," as Edward Pechter writes, and is never textual at all.[18] In an attempt to avoid the unidirectional trajectory (from social into aesthetic, from context into text) lurking in some of his own earlier assumptions, Greenblatt's most recent work is based on the fascinating concept of "circulation," transfer, and "negotiation," whereby social life (the "real") and literature exchange "materials" and "discourses."[19] Here too, however, literature appears in a lockstep relationship with the world; the text becomes a player in the "real" game of politics and society only insofar as it is produced by and produces that world.

The new historicism is valuable because it has caused renewed discussion of the relationship between texts and contexts, between literature and history. And yet it remains caught in the original dichotomy both terminologically and methodologically. As a result, it restricts its applicability and usefulness to those cases of literature and literary history in which a specific, historical discourse of power and public purpose is manifestly present in literary texts, as, for example, when Shakespeare's plays can be said to "be about" power relations at the Elizabethan court, early imperialism/colonialism, and so on. But texts from this same period without such implicit references to the "outside" seem to have no "history" in them at all.[20] In spite of their desire to liberate textuality, then, these critics' separation of the world from the text—even if another kind of world is said to exist "in" the text that is very much like the "real" one—leads to a devaluation of the power of artistic or textual representation and suggests that history is only ever really "on the outside."

The notion of *poeisis* upon which this devaluation is based does not escape the dangers inherent in the belief that the only possible relationship between art and the "real" is a mimetic one, a belief that originally led Plato to his philosophical critique of art. The Platonic condemnation of the mimetic object resulted from a "metaphysical conception of the world in which the idea or Archetype [was] a nodal point" that by definition could not be reached by objects in any other sphere.[21] Embedded in this kind of "metaphysical" construct, art cannot help but be *merely* mimetic and thus inferior precisely as representation, since it is never any more than a reference to some "higher" or prior state.

Plato's dismissal of all art as mimetic provided a logic whereby it became difficult to understand the nonliteral (textual) realm as an origin (of meaning or history), since the very fact of mimesis robs that realm of the possibility of autonomy. In subsequent mimetic theories of art, the aesthetic object took on the status of a mere illustration of, reaction to, or conditioned response to some prior "conditioning order,"[22] thus necessarily idealizing that prior order (paradoxically so, in fact, in those cases where the order was allegedly historical). In turn, this reduction implicitly identified that prior order as nonfigurative by suggesting that there were some realms of human activity (such as history) that are not "made" but that simply exist. Such an argument represents a philosophical stance that Vico and the new historicists would have to reject (at least in theory), since it implies that human history as one possible, referential "outside" is as timeless and absolute as nature or the sacred, an assumption that (again paradoxically) universalizes, transcendentalizes, and has the effect of shutting history down, as Heidegger wrote, by rendering it static.[23] And yet it is precisely this stance that even the most careful of the historical critics have inadvertently come to adopt.

Existing studies of the Nuremberg Order of Flowers on the Pegnitz have been limited by theoretical stances related to the new historicism primarily in their acceptance of the status of the text as secondary. Because they assume that the phenomenon of the language society (*Sprachgesellschaft*) was a fundamentally "historical" one (in the least complex understanding of the term), they argue for an interpretation of the order based on the following logic.

In 1644, a number of bourgeois poets gathered to celebrate a double wedding involving members of three leading families in the imperial city of Nuremberg. The text in which the event is related, the *Pegnesisches Schäfergedicht* (Shepherd poem of the Pegnitz) by Georg Philipp Harsdörffer and Johann Klaj, and Sigmund von Birken's *Fortsetzung der Pegnitz-Schäferey* (Continuation of the Pegnitz pastoral) (1645) contain an elaborate narrative of the ritualistic founding of the Order of Flowers on the Pegnitz, so called after the Pegnitz River in Nuremberg. In keeping with the customs of learned academies in Renaissance Italy, the order prevailed upon its members to take society names (here, the names of shepherds), to choose symbolic emblems (here, flowers, hence the "*Blumen*orden"), and to follow certain conventions in the composition and publication of texts. The result was a pastoral poet society that still exists to this day.

What we know about those involved in the Nuremberg language society and about the context in which the order thrived depends, to a large extent, on interpretations of portions of texts they themselves wrote as well as on descriptive accounts of Nuremberg and central Europe at the time. The society was modeled after the academies flourishing in Italy since the late fifteenth century. Its membership consisted primarily of citizens of Nuremberg belonging to the bourgeoisie. The order was founded during the late years of the Thirty Years' War (1618–48), a conflict that raged across central Europe, destroying the populations and property that lay in its path. Nuremberg, in particular, suffered greatly from the war; the city was besieged more than one hundred times.

Studies of the seventeenth-century pastoral language society in Nuremberg have chosen to emphasize the "historical background" of the order based on such data, thus locating its "meaning" primarily in events external to the massive number of texts authored by those affiliated with the group. This methodology involves seeking out those portions of these texts that can be said to "reflect" or "refer to" the "historical" (political, socioeconomic) conditions that existed at the time. Studies that analyze the formation of the order as an escapist response to the Thirty Years' War fall into this category.[24]

More complex is the work of Klaus Garber and of Max Reinhart. In his study of the order, Garber focuses on the pastoral texts exclusively "as the medium of self-representation of the learned bourgeoisie." The choice of flower emblems by society members—primarily wild flowers rather than exotic plants—reflects, he maintains, the "sociological makeup of the order" out of the ranks of the bourgeoisie rather than the nobility. The role of the Nuremberg texts in Garber's analysis is thus limited to reflecting a "masked articulation of the sociocultural self-understanding" of the "learned bourgeoisie" ("bürgerliche Gelehrtenschicht"). Reinhart has argued for understanding the pastorals of the order as "transformational" of the "life world" of their authors and thus as "reciprocally" involved in the "history" of their moment of origin.[25]

Analyses such as these assume, first, an interrelatedness (but also a dichotomy) between what "actually happened" ("wie es eigentlich gewesen ist") in Nuremberg during the second half of the seventeenth century and literary events and, second, a method of reference or correspondence that sees in literary artifacts only sources for knowledge of sociological, military, and political events of a given historical period. Although they implicitly pledge allegiance to a kind of ideological criticism, these analyses do not in fact question the nature of the representational relationship of such texts to the contextual "facts" associated with them precisely because even more straightforwardly than in the work of Greenblatt et al., extraliterary events are considered the "origin" of textual "meaning." Texts are treated as mirrors of historical conditions "on the outside." Knowledge of context is implicitly understood as unproblematic, as transparently rendered in texts. Interpretation can thus be more or less identified with diligent "detective work."[26] As a result, textuality can be considered no more than a "feeble form" of "reality," the overdetermined offspring of a historical moment. Its meaning becomes located in its ability to reflect and respond to literal, contextual events, whose meaning, in turn, is limited and can also thus be discovered in unambiguous textual form.[27] To study the texts of the Nuremberg language society thus means decoding the figurative into an actual (literal) reference.

The argument that the "meaning" of the texts written by members of the Order of Flowers on the Pegnitz lies in their reflection of specific historical, political, and social events is difficult to maintain since only isolated sections of a limited number of the many texts associated with the order can convincingly be asserted to unambiguously "refer" or "respond" to an "outside" of developing class consciousness. Moreover, such an argument does not admit that the texts themselves and their existence could constitute independently meaningful acts. Even as an approach to "history," finally, the method must be considered "monological," as Greenblatt would say, in that "it is concerned with discovering a single political vision" in a historical era and set of texts.[28] Texts are rendered static as they are reduced to mouthpieces; "history" is locked into the role of a mechanism that can do no more than articulate the rise and fall of a single, homogeneous class.

Returning to the more general questions about representation that opened this chapter, we can challenge the assumptions about texts and contexts, literature and history, upon which analyses like Garber's and Reinhart's and, ultimately, those of the new historicists are based by recasting the relationship they describe between texts and history as one of *figuration*.[29] Precisely as a result of the influential Platonic notion of mimesis as the sole mode of representing, a limited concept of the figure has, up until now, been used to explain the mechanics of representation as applied not just to the text-context debate but to the notion of "meaning" in literature in general. David Carroll summarizes a number of different forms that this relationship has been understood to take:

> Literature is considered to be representational when it produces a *figure* of either a particular and recognizable historical, social or psychological reality or, in a more abstract manner, a *figure* of an ideal, mythical, metaphysical "reality"—when it presents or makes visible the "essential" or "characteristic" traits of some "outside," of a space or context other than the "strictly literary."[30]

The problem here, Carroll explains, is not merely the terminological one of defining the "inside" of literature and language as distinct from some "outside," either real or ideal. It is also one of the critic's potential blindness to the "real," ontological status of the figure as such. In methodologies that rely on this or a related definition of figure, Carroll writes, the "outside" is always "assumed to exist before its representation . . . to be present in itself before it is represented in literature" (201) and is thus excluded from and outside the figure, or text. In dictating that "truth" always be "present" on the "outside," such methodologies define all "art" as always already figurative or re-presentative and thus derivative, since art depends for meaning on some other "literal" code, act, or event. The strictly literary sphere is thereby deprived of the ability to either mean or be the origin of meaning independently of its referents in an outside, nonliterary sphere.

Thus, even if the act of textual representation is contextualized and granted greater significance in both old and new historical approaches to early modern texts by being understood as either produced by or productive of a certain context or discourse (as opposed to being described only formally, as existing in an ahistorical vacuum), there is the assumption of a prior presence, of an idealized "reality" (either historical or metaphysical). The assumption of this presence permits, validates, and itself actually constitutes the text's meaning and necessarily leads to a hierarchy in which art is automatically secondary, deprived of the possibility of itself ever being an origin and thus of ever resisting or being influential in history at all.

As Carroll has argued in a more recent discussion of the relationship between "theory" and art, the very separation of the two terms *theory* and *art* necessarily "frames" art as the "object *of* theory" and thereby has the effect of a "theoretical predetermination" of the object.[31] Carroll maintains that this kind of theoretical predetermination has always led to a return to and heeding of the "call of the 'object'" (131) as a means of resisting that totalizing predetermination. I would add that "historical" predetermination will inevitably lead to a similar return to the text whenever the text becomes the "object of history" and is prevented *as object* from *being and doing the work of history* as a result. Varying Carroll's terms, I would argue that we can "displace the frame" (as Carroll argues that Derrida does in his *La vérité en peinture*) by showing that the "inside" of art and literature cannot be separated from any "outside" of history (132). We can do so by heeding the call of the object, by looking to the text's identity in and as both history and itself.

My interest in reassessing the terms in which the debate about literature and history has been conducted is indebted, then, to the challenge to the implicitly and explicitly hierarchical relationship between text and context found in many contemporary approaches to the notion of representation and to this challenge as it is articulated in the new historicism in particular. The text-context debate has once again reached an impasse, however, and not surprisingly, in view of the fact that the terms used and the structure in which they appear are ultimately themselves so overdetermined. The asymmetrical nature of the debate—the fact that the narrative of a transcendental "history" that is the "Other" of meaning and its origin and goal is still so often in place—never really permits texts to be other than that "Other," never really allows them to resist either that monolithic history or the critical act.

However, we can go beyond such referential or "reflex theories"[32] of the "historical significance" of culture and textual representation if we treat texts not as reproductions of and thus the same as "history" but rather as, so to speak, the same as themselves. We can do so by employing a new concept, namely, that of *texts* as *institutions*, as the *beginnings (of history) in textual form*. When viewed from the perspective of textual institutions, the apparently ontological and epistemological distinction between history and literature, outside and inside, must break down. Without solving, then, the "problem" of the text-context dyad once and for all, we can enter into and work to maintain the fruitfulness of a difficult chiasmus rather than try to arrest its play.[33] As a result (and perhaps paradoxically) of resisting the notion of a text's "sameness" to history, we can understand texts as resisting the notion of history's "otherness," since they too are and make history on their own. Not "merely historical," not figures of some historical ground, literary texts have the power to *be* and *make history* in the same way that other kinds of texts do (the Constitution, the Bible, and, indeed, any contract).[34] The texts of the Nuremberg poet society in particular perform an institutionalizing function because on an ontological level, they do not reflect some other moment "on the outside." Rather, as textual institutions, as the beginnings of a new and pure poetic tradition in forms specifically appropriate to the German vernacular, they create a space for and constitute a historical moment of their own.

Understanding the institutional coincidence of the originary moment in and of the text with actual beginnings (of a particularly German poetic voice) in time allows the relationship between history and the text to stay alive and well. Much along the lines of Hegel's argument that the *res gestae* and the *historia rerum gestarum*, the "that-which-has-happened" ("das Geschehene") and the "telling of history" ("die Geschichtserzählung"), necessarily coincide in the "historical" text, I would propose that the historical gesture that is the "being written" of the text and its continued presence in this textual form constitute the history that is the text.[35] It is to an exploration of the combined inaugural and monumental nature of textual institutions that I now turn. By means of an institutional analysis of texts as well as an analysis of textual institutions, a fruitful balance between texts and history can be maintained.

Textual Institutions

Much work has been done recently on institutions, specifically on the institutions surrounding and constituting the production and reception of both literature and literary criticism and theory. Peter Uwe Hohendahl and Jeffrey M. Peck in particular have analyzed the problems studied by the Group for Research on the Institutionalization and Professionalization of Literary Studies (GRIP). Hohendahl focused on the social models historically guiding and controlling criticism, the universities, and the press. Peck studied contemporary practices such as the examination, the seminar, and the scholarly convention.[36] Jonathan Culler has explored similar questions on a broader level in his "Criticism and Institutions: The American University," as has Gerald Graff in *Professing Literature: An Institutional History*. Both Culler and Graff use the term *institution* in a way similar to Hohendahl and Peck to refer to the disciplinary facts of the academic profession and to the histor(icit)y of those facts, that is, their rootedness in specific socioeconomic and political practice.[37] Following

Heidegger, all of these critics implicitly see the dangers of institutionalization so understood because of its tendency to reduce the study of literature to a business, to a process of "dealing in" knowledge.[38]

As interesting and important as Culler's, Graff's, Hohendahl's, and Peck's analyses are for assessing the state of the discipline today, they all fail to pause over the concept that is at the center of their investigations, namely, that of the *institution*. Given that all four critics "profess" literature professionally, it is ironic that the term's powerful *textual* resonance goes unmentioned in their work. Were they to seek to articulate the understanding of the term implicit in their work, it would in all likelihood be to the discourse and definitions provided by social scientists and political theorists that they would turn.

Maurice Hauriou, for example, the leading legal philosopher in what has been called the school of French institutionalists, which emerged in the decade before the outbreak of World War II, defined the term in the following way in his essay "The Theory of the Institution and the Foundation: A Study in Social Vitalism":

> [A]n institution is an idea of a work or enterprise that is realized and endures juridically in a social milieu; for the realization of this idea, a power is organized that equips it with organs; on the other hand, among the members of the social group interested in the realization of the idea, manifestations of communion occur that are directed by the organs of power and regulated by procedure.[39]

In a study of academic institutions, the organs of power might then correspond to such formations as the university or the press; the regulated, communal procedures would refer to explicit and implicit codes about performance in seminars, publication of theory and criticism, adherence to guidelines for academic peer review, and so on—in short, the "business" of ideas of which Heidegger writes.

Hauriou's definition becomes more complex, however, and the question of the text's role in the institution's "history" is implicitly raised as he goes on to explain where the "idea" that is the institution is located, how it comes into being, and how individual subjects (moral persons) can be conceived of as acting with free will within the "constituted" or "corporate body" of the social group or milieu formed around (and as) the instituting and institutionalizing idea (100–101). His description of the "life cycle" of an institution as one that is juridically determined points out that there is history and human agency in the institution. The act of foundation must be textual, moreover, although Hauriou never says so explicitly; it is the legalistic moment establishing procedures, a program of action, and so on. Individuals play a role in the life of the institution, including its birth and death, by being the agencies (authors of texts) that bring the institution into existence in this way (and that can terminate that existence by altering the code that describes the procedures, for example). Nevertheless, the institution is also above and beyond its beginnings precisely as text, because the program continues to be enacted by others not present at the founding moment. Thus institutions "live a life that is both objective and subjective" (100), both begun by individuals and beyond the instituting act.

Subsequent social theorists have focused on the interactional aspect of the definition of the institution, on the question, that is, of the ongoing relationship between the institutional structure and the individual rather than on the question of the beginnings of the institution's history in and as text. Anthony Giddens, in developing his structuration theory of social action, for example, focuses on structure and subject as mutually constitutive during the life cycle of the institution:

> Institutions, or large-scale societies, have structural properties in virtue of the continuity of the actions of their component members; but those members of society are only able to carry out their day-to-day activities in virtue of their capability of instantiating those structural properties.[40]

English-speaking social scientists "see the structural properties of institutions as like the girders of a building," Giddens explains (162). But this objectivist understanding must be supplemented—indeed, even made to coincide—with the subjectivist theory of social action, he claims, in order to take into account that it is after all individual persons and actions that instantiate and thus continually constitute these structures in their everyday social behavior and occurrence. By addressing neither the foundational moment of the institution nor the establishing of that moment's authority in and as text, nor even the ongoing presence of the founding text to any number of individuals, however, Giddens is surprisingly unrealistic about the power of the institution over the individual. He underestimates, for example, the power that a legal code can have over those who must submit to it, both as enforcers and as criminals, indeed, the power that the code has to give individuals those identities in the first place.

Hauriou's definition of institutions implicitly poses the question of the textual nature of their historical beginnings even as his use of organic metaphors obscures and elides it. Giddens ignores the role of the text in institutionalization altogether as he focuses on the ongoing, interactive nature of the relationship between institutions as they already exist and the individuals within them and not on the role of the regulatory code in this interactive behavior. When Culler, Graff, Hohendahl, and Peck use the term *institution* and refer to their work as analyses or histories of institutions, then, they probably mean some combination of Hauriou's and Giddens's definitions. They probably conceive of the institution as a historical product (of either a juridical act or of its constitutive members' behavior) that functions as a transpersonal "structure of behavior of relative permanence." Such a structure relieves individuals of the necessity to act in an original and originating way each and every time they seek to structure their social, spiritual, intellectual, moral, and emotional behavior.[41]

Society as a whole is made up, then, of various institutions (discourses) within which individuals locate themselves and their activities. These institutions clearly have a history and are susceptible to adjustment. What goes unmentioned in all of these discussions, however, is the fact that *texts* are inevitably associated with and crucial to the existence of these institutions. These texts, in their identity either as founding documents or as codifications of behavior (the two are not mutually exclusive), become naturalized and act as more or less transcendent, semipermanent, and objective reference points for individuals not present at the institution's historical origin. In terms of social behavior, the *institution* is thus not unlike a textualized *convention*, which Lawrence Manley has defined on a conceptual level as "an order of objective rules . . . [that] possess[es] the atemporal qualities of pattern and form" even as it "paradoxically express[es] changing social values."[42]

By not explicitly addressing the *textual* nature of the institution, these approaches avoid crucial questions about the validity of the standards imposed by institutions and about the conditions under which they become enshrined in (textual) codes. Indeed, they do not address the question of the power that must be present in the text to bridge the gap between the institution's historical origin and its normative role. To address this and other questions requires investigating the relationship between the historical moment of origin of the institution as code and its ongoing (atemporal) functioning as objective standard or rule, the relationship, that is, between the inaugural and the ongoing identities of the institution.

Whereas each invocation of a code constitutes a kind of reinscription of its origin in the here-and-now, it is the very *nonpresence* of that "bounded" (limited, specific, "historical") origin that endows the institution with an ongoing, current, and "unbounded" power to inaugurate, regulate, and guarantee.[43] And, as I discussed in the previous section, the nonpresence of the (historical) origin together with the presence of the text follows from the *textual* nature of the institution and from the freedom of the text to be itself rather than anything else. Raymond Williams has written that the term *institution* was originally a "noun of action or process" that "became, at a certain stage, a general and abstract noun describing something apparently objective and systematic."[44] It is the moment of transition between these two stages, between action and object, and the role of the text in effecting the transition to which we must turn.

In a recent essay that appears as the afterword to Samuel Weber's *Institution and Interpretation*, Wlad Godzich points out in Weber's work the crucial distinction between two aspects of the institution: the institution consists of both a historical "instituting act" and ongoing, "institutionalized functioning."[45] The act of instituting, Godzich writes, is a "trailblazing one" that subsequently "becomes a moment of odd standing in the now constituted institution":

> [T]he instituting moment, which endows the entire institution with signification and meaning, is held within the institution as both proper to it and yet alien; it is its other, valued to be sure yet curiously irrelevant to immediate concerns. (156)

Godzich highlights that with reference to Paul de Man's work, Weber understands the moment of instituting as "blind," whereas institutionalized functioning has the effect of "error-correction" (155–57). That is, instituting is a historical shot-in-the-dark that is then gradually adjusted by institutionalized functioning as origins take on a more permanent institutionalized form.

And yet, as far as the life cycle of the institution is concerned, I would suggest (in contradistinction to Godzich and Weber) that it is in the act of institutionalized functioning (rather than in the instituting moment) that blindness occurs, because *as text*, the institution transcends—in its day-to-day functioning—the moment of historical "otherness" that was its origin. This original moment of historical otherness may be understood as not at all blind but, rather, as very self-conscious of its historical task of providing the regulating institution with an origin in a text that will function as transcendental beyond that context or history. The splitting off or self-differentiation of the ongoing functioning of the institution in textualized form (as law or code, for example) from its historical moment of origins, or "first causes," nevertheless has the effect, as Godzich points out, of rendering both those first causes and the institution transcendent, "inaccessible to human intervention or tampering" (159) *precisely through the combination of their nonpresence and continued presence in textual form*. Paradoxically, then, the instituting moment (which, we remember, Hauriou called a juridical moment, which involved human agency) becomes "excluded" from its origin, from the realm of historical or social beginnings, even as that origin comes to function as a transcendent guarantor of new forms of behavior, a guarantor whose standards are now enshrined, indeed immobilized, in textual form. Those involved in the institution are left with the sense that the "existing order is the only possible one and should be left alone" (159), because its beginnings seem not historical but rather absolute and codified in a text. Confronted with this text, it is the individuals who become blind to the historicity of (the beginnings of) their institutionalized behavior, holding that behavior to reflect the transcendent norm present in textual form.

All of this discussion of the nature of institutions, instituting moments, and institutionalized functioning is crucial for offering a fruitful terminological and methodological alternative to the debate about texts and contexts, literature and history, discussed in the beginning of this chapter. As becomes clear in Godzich's focus on the dyad contained in the term *institution*, it is precisely the holding in balance of the two sides that gives the term—and the practices it describes—significance and effectiveness. And yet, it is with the utmost care that we must use his valuable distinction, since Godzich does not point out that the "excluded" (and thus idealized) "origin" of an institution nevertheless continues to be present *in a text* that coexists with and thus provides the origin of subsequent (historical) practice even as its own (historical) origin fades away. If we remember the (originally) textual nature of the term *institution*, the fact, that is, that since Quintilian, throughout the Renaissance, and into our own period, the location of instituting moment and institutionalized functioning alike—both "historical" in their own way (the first as originating behavior, the second as dictating proper ongoing behavior)—has been in and as textual object, we have a term that is historical and textual at one and the same time. Both instituting origins and institutionalized practice are copresent, I would argue, and thus cohistorical insofar as they are present in texts. It is to the nature of institutions as textual objects and to a description of the historical work that they do that I now turn.

The classical usage of terms based on the verb *instituo* ranged from activities associated with literally "setting up" (a building or military force, for example) to those associated with establishing ceremonies, standards, customs, precedents, and so on.[46] The most familiar usage of the term is in association with *rhetorical* education, however, with training or forming the intellect or character of the student to perform effectively in a specific civic situation. This usage depended on both the more literal and the more figurative meanings of the term at one and the same time, since it signified "setting up" a kind of practice that "created" (formed) new individuals by inculcating routinized public behavior in them. This practice was, in practice, primarily textual.

This double understanding of the term *institution* and the coincidence of its two poles in textual practice dominates Quintilian's well-known *Institutio oratoria* as well as Cicero's treatises on the "formation" of the orator. You must instruct or form your students, Quintilian writes ("institeris," 1.3.6), according to the best principles ("optimis institutis," 1.1.16). The education must be complete ("universam institutionem," 5.7.6); one's personality can be indelibly marked by one's education in youth ("ab illa institutione puerili," 1.1.9). What is central, and yet, to Quintilian, perhaps so obvious that it does not seem worth emphasizing, is that this rhetorical education, this formation, occurs by means of texts, more precisely, according to the principles set forth in *his* text, his *Institutio*, which he refers to as "our method" or "system" ("nostra institutio," 4, Pro., 1) and as the method professed or taught by us ("nos institutionem professi," 10.1.5). It is the text, in other words, that provides the space for the beginning and formation of the orator. Not coincidentally, of course, as becomes obvious in the famous book 10, this institutionalization in fact consists mainly in recommendations to the student to "ingest," or process, other texts in addition to the *Institutio* and following the plan set out by the master-text of the *Institutio*, as the means of producing future texts.[47] Locked into a specific understanding of individual activity in a civic context, the instituting and institutionalization of the orator—his origins, formation, and subsequent behavior—are primarily textual.

The textual nature of institutions and institutionalization was manifested not only in the sphere of rhetoric in the classical period but also in that of law: Gaius's *Institutionum commentarii quattuor* (ca. A.D. 161) and Justinian's *Institutiones* (A.D. 533), for example. This nature was bequeathed to the Renaissance. Although most dictionary-type definitions of the verb form continue to be based on the rhetorical/educational usage ("to ordaine, to appoynt, to teach"—de Sainliens, 1593; "doceo," "instituo, id est paideuo"—Budé, 1557), noun forms most often make the textual implications of the original terms explicit by referring to specific textual events ("Precept; Ordinance, Decree, Statute"—Cotgrave, 1611).[48] Many books entitled "institutions" were published during this period: Budé's own *De studio literarum recte et commode instituendo* (1532), *Institutio compendiaria totius grammaticae* (1540), *Institutions, or Principall Groundes of the Lawes* (1543), *Institutiones piae, or Directions to Pray* (1630), *Institutionum logicarum libri duo* (1637); an English version of Galen, *The Institucion of Chyrurgerie* (1567); Calvin's *Institution de la religion chrétienne* (1536), which formed the basis of a renewed religion in a textual form; and many more.[49] Texts were to become the means by which deliberately new, postclassical beginnings could be made in all fields; institutionalizing those beginnings meant both marking and masking the (historical) rootedness and belatedness of the gesture in an inaugural *textual* moment that would in effect create the new period by initiating and providing new guidelines for future practice.

To understand the texts of the Renaissance as institutions thus means, above all, understanding them as historical events in a maximally concrete sense. The text is a material phenomenon[50] that comes into existence at a given moment and testifies to that moment; however, the text also hides that moment by separating itself (as text) from it and by embedding it in a rhetoric of transcendence. As a result, the text comes to be defined by a prescriptive identity and thus by its service as a point of origin for subsequent behavior.

The material conditions of texts in the early modern period were of particular importance in this instituting gesture. As Anthony Grafton has pointed out with specific reference to Italian humanism, the invention of printing made possible a "new level of precision in textual scholarship" after the mid–fifteenth century; the existence of "generally uniform copies of most classical texts, and, within a few years, of commentaries on many of them as well" created, among other things, the possibility of collective debate among humanists all over Italy at the same time. This collective debate was crucial to opening a (literally textual) space for the construction of a new, generational identity for subsequent humanists, who worked to distinguish themselves not only from the Ancients but, as Grafton points out, from one another as well by means of elaborate commentaries on classical works.[51] The conditions of possibility for this new identity and thus for the "historical reality" of Renaissance humanism were thus defined precisely by the production of texts.

Grafton explains that not only did the "detailed commentary" of the humanists revive the ancient genre of the line-by-line commentary (Servius on Virgil, for example), illustrating that the Moderns could keep up with the Ancients at their own annotative game, but the technique had become both so refined and so pedantic by the late fifteenth century that the actual text of the modern glosses gradually overwhelmed the "small island" of the original, ancient text on the page.[52] Thus the beginnings of the postclassical tradition occurred in the very presence of the past as well as in the literal competition of the present with the past for textual space. Moreover, Grafton argues, precisely as a result of the drawbacks of this system, namely, that one modern commentary became more or less indistinguishable (both typographically and in content) from the next, a new kind of annotative genre of a more prescriptive nature emerged, that of the short treatise on selected ancient passages and philological questions. The short treatise gave individual humanist commentators a greater chance to distinguish themselves from both the Ancients and their contemporaries by highlighting their own polemical points about other commentators instead of "burying the pearls" of their own insights in the "mudbanks of a full-scale commentary" on an ancient text (19). Moreover, by often failing to identify (by means of a footnote or some other mark) what in their texts was a citation, a paraphrase, or merely an invention on the part of the commentator (22), the authors of these treatises had the chance to render their own textual interpolations indistinguishable from and thus equal to the ancient texts upon which they were based. Any position of dependency on the Ancients could thus be made invisible in and by the text in all of its concrete presence, as new words literally "stood in for" old ones, creating beginnings for vernacular traditions out of traditions whose presence in the new text was testified to but also literally rendered invisible and transcended by it.

It was this genre that developed into the celebrated method books of subsequent periods as sets of editorial rules for correcting and explicating the texts of the Ancients (which included discussions of Latin dependence on Greek models, for example) gave way over the course of the late fifteenth and early sixteenth centuries to sets of rules for the "arts," including the composition of modern texts equal, sometimes even superior, to their ancient predecessors. Eventually a plethora of treatises on method flooded the market. Designed to teach the fundamentals of a discipline to students quickly and efficiently and thus to provide for textual futures of all kinds, these method books came in practice to replace the massive tomes of commentary on the Ancients as well as, at least in some cases, the reading of the ancient texts themselves.[53] By the mid–sixteenth century, method books existed not only for the *ars poetica* but for other fields as well; often called "institutions," the method books served as textual "beginnings" and provided rules for ongoing practice of the "new," postclassical disciplines. Ramus's *Dialecticae institutiones* (1543) and Johann Sturm's *Institutionis literatae* . . . (1586) are but two examples of this popular genre.[54] These texts by no means rejected study of the Ancients or a reliance on earlier works. Precisely the opposite. And yet, as short-hand versions of a more extensive, text-based program of education and training, as textual institutions, that is, in their most concrete sense, these volumes both literally and symbolically contained the Ancients while also surpassing them. They thus formed the beginnings of modern traditions and functioned as the exemplary standards to which those traditions could refer. The "instituting act" that made room for a new (historical) moment thus masked the presence of the prior models in it even as its very textual presence did those models one better. A text became the origin of new orthodoxies, the rules that were to govern a future of "institutionalized functioning" in a wide range of fields.

To study the institutional identity of a text as well as the function of textual institutions relies, then, on analyzing both the *inaugural function of the text*, its power to be foundational and to provide a historical beginning, and its *monumental function*, the strategies whereby it not only testifies to that beginning but also transcends it by serving as a fixed model for specific future (perhaps not only textual) behavior. These strategies gain their authority by strategically "forgetting" and then recoding in a "monumental" textual form the historicity of the inaugural moment as a moment beyond and outside history.

What makes the concept of textual institutions so appropriate to an analysis of the Nuremberg texts in particular is that they belonged to a collective enterprise (the language society) explicitly designed to be institutional in both the inaugural (foundational) and monumental (testimonial but also codificatory) senses of the term, to provide both authoritative, textual "beginnings" and usable, textual models for the German language and for German poetry. Living in a clearly print-dominated world, the Nuremberg authors were fully conscious of the power of a relatively widely distributed text to fulfill this combined founding and standardizing task. Understanding the Nuremberg enterprise as one of textual instituting and institutionalization explains the simultaneity of the remarkable claims in society texts for the superior accuracy of the German language and for the "originality" of German poetry, on the one hand, and the (for us) astounding conventionality and (commemorative) belatedness of both individual texts and the whole body of texts in which these claims are made, on the other. The concept of the textual institution is based on precisely this coincidence, on the convening of the originary and the orthodox in (and into) concrete (textual) form. It is to definitions of convention and to the power conventions accrue to themselves as origins of norms that I now turn, because it was by means of conventionalizing strategies and claims that the texts of the Nuremberg order did their institutionalizing work.

Convention and the Text

Perhaps the most thorough conceptual analysis of conventions and of the power of a historically circumscribed group to determine normative behavior (the power that defines institutionalization) can be found in the work of Ferdinand de Saussure. Saussure explains the way convention enables language to function as a communicative tool. "The linguistic sign," he writes, "unites, not a thing and a name, but a concept and a sound-image," the signified and the signifier respectively.[55] The bond between the signified and signifier is an arbitrary one, since it is merely representational; the "idea" of "sister," Saussure explains, is not linked by any inner relationship to the "succession of sounds s-ö-r which serves as its signifier in French" and thus "has no natural connection to the signified" (67, 69). The two elements are nevertheless intimately linked and "appear to us to conform to reality" within the boundaries of the language system within which the sign appears (67). This semblance of reality is based on the fact that "every means of expression used in society is based, in principle, on collective behavior or—what amounts to the same thing—on convention" (68). Thus language is the instrument of a historical collectivity, a "product of social forces" (74), a matter, finally, of intersubjectivity. As a result, even though the link between signified and signifier is arbitrary, the signifier is "fixed, not free, with respect to the linguistic community that uses it" (71). Conventions and their codification in language are thus experienced by the historical collective as "natural law." The study of the "life of signs within society," which Saussure christened semiology (16), focuses, then, not on reference to "things" or to nonlinguistic social acts, but on the way the sign code is constituted and understood by a given community of speakers.[56]

Saussure's description of the sign links the concept of the specific, historical collectivity as the "origin" of meaning to the function of convention as both a monument to that collectivity and as the collectivity's effectively absolute "law" in a way that is crucial for understanding the institutional nature of the Nuremberg texts. For Saussure, even though the bond between the signified and the signifier—and thus the very process of linguistic signification—is itself arbitrary (rooted in a historical community of understanding rather than in nature, for example), it can never be experienced as arbitrary by individuals in that linguistic community. Rather, it is perceived as and is indeed part of a fixed code and thus is experienced as and may even be called "natural."

Because language and acts of speech (*langue* and *parole*) are two different kinds of linguistic event—the first, as Jonathan Culler explains, "a system, an *institution*, a set of interpersonal rules and norms," the latter "the actual manifestation of the system in speech and writing"[57] (emphasis added)—the speaker of a language can engage in individual "acts of speaking" while not compromising the collective moment, the institution, the "social side of speech" that is "outside the individual" speaker, who "can never create nor modify it by himself." Language functions "only by virtue of a sort of *contract* signed by the members of a community" (emphasis added).[58] Signification is governed by laws "accepted by a community" (71), laws that exist within time but that are valid because they take on a timeless status. The "particular language-state" is "always the product of historical forces" (72). Language's existence, its "circulation" in the world (76), thus assumes historical change even as it also creates a series of provisional but effective linguistic absolutes that seem organically motivated and thus are able to function as universal "first causes" and rules. These rules take on concrete form as they are enshrined in both implicit and explicit "contracts" (from habitual practice to grammar books) whose *authority* to regulate is derived from their association with "nature," but whose *effective power* to regulate is located in their textual form.

Saussure's drawing of the linguistic facts, as he calls them, indicates that social forces and the action of time work simultaneously and participate equally in the creation of a system of arbitrary (conventional) signs whose relationship to referents and whose functions in acts of communication are nevertheless considered fixed (absolute) by a particular linguistic community (78):

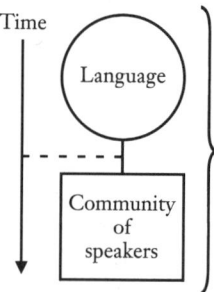

Accordingly, he divides the science of linguistics into two parts, the synchronic study of "language states" and the diachronic study of successive states and their relation to one another (81). The division makes it possible to analyze numerous languages and systems of signs as internally logical, "organic," coherent, and functional without hypostasizing any one of them as an absolute guarantor of linguistic or representational "truth." Within the synchronic analysis, it is *convention* that governs the internal accuracy and effectiveness of signs in a given *context*. The diachrony of *different* systems of signs does not exclude these systems' respective *immutability* within their own limited and mutable frames. Indeed, the validity of the system is defined by its historical origin and proved by its effectiveness as law. Paradoxically, then, diachrony, or history, has the effect of eliminating the need for the frame of reference usually provided by a metaphysical moment. Instead, "contextual absolutes," or conventions, provide the origin of and determine the standard of obligatory behavior of the group, thus producing a stable frame of reference themselves by allowing the historically motivated to seem to be the result of nature.

Steven Mailloux goes beyond the strictly linguistic model in his analysis of how the habitual acts of any given community are transformed into a normative code.[59] He explains that there are essentially three kinds of convention, a term he in general uses to designate "shared practices": the *traditional* ("recognizing 'past' regularities in action and belief"), the *regulative* ("prescriptions regulating 'future' action"), and the *constitutive* ("descriptions determining 'present' meaning") (126–27). Although Mailloux differentiates between traditional and regulative conventions (the "we-have-always-done-it-this-way" attitude versus a law, for example, or the "regular/regulative" and "expected/obligatory" contrasts), he nevertheless admits that traditional conventions easily harden into regulative ones (128). Like institutions, then, conventions are intersubjective structures that hold their (historical) origins within themselves but also easily lose sight of those origins as the conventions take on normative status.

Implicit in Mailloux's argument is of course the assumption that conventions, the "normal behavior" of the specific (historical) group, form the basis of what is to become "binding practice" (129) for everyone else. The root of the word is, after all, the Latin *convenire*, "to come together."[60] The "coming together" of the few produces the rules not only for the few, however, but for others as well. Intersubjectivity (or historical consensus) is thus the basis on which functionally transcendent rules are formed. Mailloux acknowledges but unfortunately downplays the fact that the "rigidification" of the (merely) traditional into the regulative takes place in and through a *text*, in the drafting, for example, of a prescriptive document that redefines traditional behavior (such as standing when the national anthem is played) as obligatory.[61] The text in which this codification occurs must of course mask its traditionalist origins (in the historical collective) in order for the "merely" conventional to become normative for both its community of origin and for others too. The recoding of what is essentially habitual group practice as orthodox creates the "reality" of institutionalized behavior by instituting, or fixing the beginnings of, standard behavior in textual form ("The audience must rise . . ."). The authoring and authorizing of convention coincide.

Mailloux's typology of conventions indirectly underscores one of Saussure's main points: the importance of the moment of codification in the transition from tradition to regulation, the power of the text, that is, to transform collective agreement into obligatory behavior. In his book *Convention 1500–1750*, Lawrence Manley "historicizes" both Saussure's and Mailloux's descriptive models by pointing out the shift during and after the Renaissance away from a rhetoric of natural or sacred models to one of just such consensus-based or conventional codes.[62] Manley traces how, during the period covered by his study, such notions as decorum, aptness, and appropriateness to a particular context (all designed to highlight the role of the historical collective in determining norms even as that historicity became masked in the development of such universalizing concepts as "good taste") came to replace reference to models external to a particular context (such as the Ancients) in the formation of standards of behavior (in art, the law, even in religion). Moreover, in the tradition of normative Renaissance poetics in particular, the notion prevailed that the poet was "every man," his experience everyone's experience.[63] Thus the individual poet could represent the collective because his will simply represented the will of "all good men." In turn, reference to either implicit or explicit collective agreement by and consensus among contemporaries, a consensus that the individual poet could represent, came to regulate vernacular culture in a much more effective way than reference to ultimately absent (ancient, sacred, natural) models. The radical relocation of the absolute into the local, of transcendence (formerly located in ancient practice) into contemporary historical and particular form, was based, however, on no more than the normal functioning of convention, namely, the transformation of familiar, historically conditioned "social values" into "order[s] of objective rules . . . [that] possess the atemporal qualities of pattern and form," in Manley's words.[64]

Like the instituting moment, moreover, this "objectivity," although based on intersubjectivity and the concept of a historical collective with internally coherent norms, necessarily became blind to its own historical origins as it moved into textual form (necessarily since, as a text, it did not reproduce its origin but was, rather, separate from it and ultimately transcended it). Moreover, admitting to the text's own historical rootedness would have compromised its subsequent regulatory (institutionalizing) function. Thus categories like those of right reason, propriety, and natural judgment were established, defined, and came into use as organicized, universal reference points for determining, for example, what kind of text was appropriate to a particular occasion at a specific moment in time, which rhyme scheme was "fitting" to a given genre, and so on. These categories sometimes appeared alongside references to the Ancients ("Nature and Homer were . . . the same," Pope wrote[65]) but more often made marginal reference to them or replaced them altogether. Context-specific catalogues of "proper" poetic forms were drawn up and used to direct poetic composition, replacing *imitatio* as the young poet's guide. Gradually, a rhetoric of aptness explicitly linked to the (poetic, ethical, political) expectations of a particular community replaced even reference to nature. Based on an understanding of historical *difference*, on the recognition, that is, that each generation, community, or group would develop institutions peculiar to its group, "natural" behavior came to be defined as the kind of behavior that grew out of, was effective for, and would persuade (be apt or appropriate to) a particular audience. Only matters of convention could, in other words, be considered binding for a given group.

What Manley does not emphasize but which is clear in his study is that this transformation of the conventional into the normative occurred in the composition, printing, and distribution of the very texts that he so carefully analyzes. The objectification of rules of poetic composition in volumes like Puttenham's *Arte of English Poesie* (1589), for example, gave the power of obligatory form to what had been no more than the common practice of a particular group. The widespread dissemination of Luther's Bible translation in print had rendered his German standard (at least symbolically) in a similar way. Although I am heavily indebted to Manley's study, it is thus an interest in the crucial role played by the *material presence of the text* in the transformation of consensual into normative behavior that guides my analysis of the structures of the Nuremberg texts, since it is in this material existence and in the rhetorical claims these texts are able to make for their own superior authority as a result of their "having-been-written" that this transformation takes place.

Of central importance, then, to an analysis of the self-imposed task of the Order of Flowers on the Pegnitz to create a new and self-regulating, original and orthodox German language and German-language poetry are the following questions: What was the discourse that permitted the Nuremberg texts to claim that they were doing the work of both instituting (beginning) and institutionalizing (regulating) poetic practice in the vernacular? What was the relationship between the monumental or regulatory moment of each kind of text (language theory, poetics, pastorals) and the rhetoric of origins (newness, originality, authority) upon which its authority was to be based? How, in other words, did each kind of text mask its conventional origins (in the "coming together" of a group of bourgeois poets in seventeenth-century Nuremberg) in metaphors of atemporality, thus effecting the transition from normal to normative, from habitual to obligatory, behavior? How, finally, did the rule of linguistic and poetic aptness to a particular circumstance (a particular kind of language or text in and for a particular occasion) function as a guarantor of beginnings for a vital, original (as opposed to imitative), and authoritative vernacular tradition?

The thesis of the present study is, then, that the texts of the Nuremberg Order of Flowers on the Pegnitz were designed to create not only the conditions of possibility for but also the very substance (or historical reality) of a new set of linguistic and poetic conventions in the vernacular.[66] As a result, these texts may be understood as institutions, socially conditioned conventions that both used and masked their historical origin in a collective endeavor to create a new moment of history. In a gesture that was both inaugural (originating and original) and monumental (commemorative and creative of orthodoxy), the Nuremberg texts—like many vernacular texts being written throughout Europe at this time—were history and did the work of history by offering both a literal and an ideological space for the beginnings of an autonomous literary tradition.

Language, Meaning, *Différance*

Returning to the opening discussion of this chapter, we can begin to formulate a response to the question, Where is history if it is "in the text?" This response takes the following shape: History is always in the text when the text generates and serves as the origin of meaning. The very existence of the text dictates that meaning will arise from it precisely because as text it is necessarily "other" than any "Other" on the "outside." In an intellectual endeavor indebted to Heidegger, Jacques Derrida has addressed the question of the "temporalization" of the sign and its inevitable creation of a space for meaning "in history." By way of conclusion, I will pursue Derrida's argument about the sign for the sake of understanding its implications for the present discussion of the presence of history in the text.

Derrida coins a new term—*différence* spelled with an *a: différance*—to designate "the movement by which language, or any code, any system of reference in general, becomes '*historically*' constituted as a fabric of differences" (emphasis added).[67] Derrida's notion of "primordial temporality" is derived from his studies of Nietzsche, Freud, and Saussure. He accepts Saussure's distinction between the signifier and signified and between two signs within a synchronic context but questions the notion of substitution he believes to be crucial to it: namely, that the sign is both "secondary" and "provisional with respect to [a] final and missing presence" (138). The ontic-ontological difference (here the Derridean and Heideggerian discourses coincide) between presence and absence, he seems to suggest, is difficult to locate when dealing with signs because it presumes a reference theory according to which there is an ontological difference between the sign and its meaning. That is, in a theoretical turn that Saussure would seem, at least on the surface, to reject, the latter is *referred to* and necessarily absent where the former "is" (and vice versa). Rather than talking in this way of differences, Derrida proposes going beyond the internal contradiction in Saussure. He suggests that we speak of a "movement" of *différance*, of the "play that 'produces' . . . these differences, these effects of difference" instead of differences as such:

> This does not mean that the differance which produces differences is before them in a simple and in itself unmodified and indifferent present. Differance is the nonfull, nonsimple "origin"; it is the structured and differing origin of differences. (141)

Differance is, then, the precondition and explanation of the sign's ability to exist and mean independently of the referent. Differance is why all textual representation must be conceived of as "historical," not as linked, that is, to a referential "truth" but as itself productive of meaning. Precisely because the Nuremberg texts (like all texts) existed under the sign of differance, they both relied upon and also themselves created conventions of linguistic and poetic behavior in German.

My analysis of the textual institutions of the Nuremberg language society in mid-seventeenth-century Germany assumes, then, a concept of differance because it discusses society texts as institutions, as foundational/originary and monumental/regulatory, at one and the same time. Chapter 2 describes the European academic tradition and the place of the German language societies within that tradition as well as the political situation in Nuremberg prior to and during the Thirty Years' War. As cultural phenomena, the academies were concerned with and understood the ideological power of making institutionalizing gestures and were aware that such gestures could be made most effectively in texts.

In chapter 3, I begin my analysis of three sets of Nuremberg texts as institutions. There I focus on the first of these sets: the massive treatises on language theory written by various members of the order. Of central concern is the attempt made in the language theory texts to legitimize the language of a particular community, namely, German. These treatises are quite literally obsessed with providing an instituting logic for the vernacular; they do so by explaining that the origins of their own (historical) usage lie in a sacred, natural language. Society texts were to be composed in such a way as to produce the standards whereby, by means of institutionalized and carefully policed practice, the vernacular as currently used could be invested with the authority of these origins and thus be rendered capable of serving as a standardized, normative tongue. The language theory texts thus function as monuments to their moment of (historical) origin while at the same time attempting to surpass that moment as the origins of linguistic law.

Chapter 4 analyzes the elaborate technical poetics of the society, which were to institute (begin and oversee) standardized poetic practice in German. They were based on prescribing techniques for both internal and external *aptum*, guidelines for the creation of vernacular texts that would be both reliable and effective and thus both "true" to an objective ("natural") standard while also apt to specific, historical conditions. Vernacular poetry's "originality" and truth could thus be guaranteed if it remained true to these institutions, to descriptive accounts of the order's practice that became prescriptive precisely in their codification in the poetics. The appropriate was transformed into the originary as it was institutionalized in texts.

Chapter 5 describes and interprets the prose-and-verse pastorals (*Schäffereyen*) as texts that both emanated from and literally constituted the very existence of the language society itself as an institution and collective event. The localization of the classical textual forms of pastoral in the here-and-now of seventeenth-century Nuremberg invested a historical present with a transcendent authority formerly associated with tradition alone. According to the logic of the pastoral tradition, it was in the convening of a group of shepherd-poets and in their creation of a community of texts that poetry both originated and could survive. The Nuremberg "prose eclogues" follow this tradition and localize it within the context of a local grove. Thus convention (imitation) produces "new" texts with the power to establish and standardize vernacular poetic practice.

Viewed in this sequence, the texts of the Order of Flowers on the Pegnitz with which I deal here (and there are others) bring the question of institutionalization into ever clearer focus as they concentrate on providing a space for "history" as I have defined it here. By embedding conventional moments—the German language per se, German-language occasional poetry, and a highly localized form of pastoral song—in a discourse of "premature ultimates," the Nuremberg texts enacted the institutional moment whereby historically generated, "made" categories are transformed into "universal and apparently natural" measures of standard behavior.[68] In a concluding discussion in chapter 6, I explain my reservations about what the Nuremberg texts as texts *do* when they assume that convention can determine meaning and that contextually apt or provisional norms and determinations of meaning can function as normative by virtue of their institutionalization in and by texts. Many texts and many critics make similar assumptions about meaning and literature. I argue instead for the importance of remembering the resistance of the text to any such totalizing predeterminations of meaning and thus its potential (precisely as institution and origin of history) to call into question the very concept of a single meaning or universally applicable norm.

2 Academic Conventions

As I have indicated in chapter 1, the German language society project was based on textual institutionalization, on providing the German-language literary tradition with authoritative beginnings based on collectively defined conventions codified in textual form. The (historical) instituting moment of this tradition is contained within, but is also transcended by, the prescriptive codes of linguistic and literary behavior embodied in society texts. The Nuremberg texts thus themselves create the transcendence of these codes as a "historical" act, as do all institutionalizing texts, because without them, the codes and their status as guarantors of orthodoxy would quite literally not exist. Thus the texts themselves are not subject to a predetermined and predetermining history in the general sense of the term, even though there is always some sense in which texts are the "subject" of history. At the same time, texts also participate in the very creation of history by creating a new language and new poetic forms.

The (historical) instituting moment of these texts is the social, intersubjective, and collective moment to which the texts become blind as they seek to take on a kind of timeless authority. At the same time, it is this very moment that is also commemorated as the texts assert their authority to institutionalize, regulate, and control. It is not by chance that the project of standardization and codification of German-language linguistic and literary forms developed at a time when academies across Europe were attempting to relocate classical standards of learnedness, poetry, and linguistic purity as well as scientifically guaranteed knowledge in strictly vernacular forms. The age understood itself as deliberately postclassical, as anchored in the reality of historical difference; reproducing the languages of the past to communicate the knowledge of the present had become a questionable act. The creation and use of new languages and of new forms of legal, social, political, scientific, and literary discourse would announce the onset of the new age, the difference of the present from the past, the appropriateness of the age to itself.

The interdependence of history and textuality becomes clearest here. Renaissance texts simultaneously called for and themselves created the languages of the Moderns and thus the very conditions for existence of postclassical culture. Of less importance, then, than what these texts can be said to have "meant" (in terms of something "outside" them) is the recognition that it was in their very instituting and institutionalizing *existence* that a historical event, namely, the "modern age," came about. Aware of the creative power of the text in an already print-dominated age to bring new discourses into existence, academicians had the production of such textual institutions in the vernacular as their main goal. The seventeenth-century German language societies followed this trend, but with the knowledge of the fundamental difference of their enterprise, namely, that the "renaissance" of their *language* had already been secured by Luther's Bible translations of the 1520s and 1530s. Unlike some other European traditions, the Germans perceived fewer major *literary* texts or literary genres in their past upon which they could base their renewal. Thus the German academies undertook the institutionalization of a literary language and of poetic forms in the service of producing a new era of vernacular culture. The arguments by which both the German and the other European academicians justified the authority of the (historical) instituting moment of their textual institutions are the focus of the present chapter.

The Fairest Flower: The European Academies, 1430–1700

The German language societies of the seventeenth century found their inspiration in the Italian academies established during the previous one hundred or more years. In *Der teutsche Palmbaum* (The German palm tree) of 1647, Gustav von Hille describes the founding of the first German language society, the Fruit-bearing Society (Fruchtbringende Gesellschaft), in the small town of Köthen in 1617. On the occasion of the funeral of Duchess Dorothea Maria of Weimar, numerous members of the local nobility gathered in the small residence at Anhalt-Köthen to mourn her death; their sorrow was allayed by a discussion of the Italian *accademie*, to the most famous of which, the Accademia della crusca in Florence, one of the company, Prince Ludwig of Anhalt-Köthen, belonged:

> The story [Erzehlung] about the Italian societies comforted the duly informed princely and noble assembly [Zusammenkunft] to a certain

extent. Said societies are established to much acclaim to motivate praiseworthy youth to pursue every kind of lofty virtue, to maintain good trustworthiness, and to develop respectable behavior, and especially to practice to a useful end the language spoken by the people of the region [zu nutzlicher Ausübung jedes Volkes Landsprache]. They are found in almost every city in all of Italy.[1]

Prince Ludwig (1579–1650) had visited Italy while on the grand tour customary among even the lesser nobility in Europe and had become a member of the Florentine group of 1600. After three years of active participation in the Crusca academy, he returned to the more inclement clime of Upper Saxony to re-create there what he had seen on his trip. Most of his attempts centered on transplanting the fruits of southern culture to the tiny principality of Anhalt-Köthen; his efforts included an elaborate estate, complete with experimental farms and model gardens based on a Latin treatise, the first Italian translation of which, the *Trattato dell'agricoltura*, was in fact dedicated to Ludwig by his friend and fellow Crusca member, Bastiano de' Rossi, in 1605.[2] The founding of a language society (a *Sprachgesellschaft*) and the sponsoring of programs of linguistic purification and standardization after the model of those undertaken by the Italian academies, identified as "societies" ("Gesellschaften") rather than academies in Hille's description, were to be the final touch in this local re-creation of the grand culture of Italy in parts farther north. Thus the conversation at the duchess's funeral in 1617 is reported to have continued:

> Accordingly it was decided by unanimous vote of the great princely persons present that a similar praiseworthy society was to be begun [beginnen] ... Thus was the so often mentioned society founded [gestiftet] to maintain and reproduce all knightly virtues, to establish and increase good German trustworthiness (as previously mentioned), and, above all, so that our own German motherland, until now abandoned, despised, and left to die, in recovering, could give courage to her desperate children of German blood and soul.[3]

The renewing, defending, and increasing of German prestige associated with the founding of the Fruit-bearing Society was to begin with use of a purified German language. Hille exhorts: "Stop! Hold fast the mother tongue, so pure, so chaste! So rich, so able to express all that is meant!" (13). To reproduce the Italian academy on German soil by definition meant shifting the focus to a defense of local values and the use of the local language. To be the same as the authoritative model thus meant being different from it, meant starting anew (instituting) in one's own time and place.

The founding of the Fruit-bearing Society meant that the paradigmatic Italian academy could be made to reappear in local, German garb. The abundant fruit-and-flower imagery associated with it nevertheless expresses clearly (if perhaps inadvertently) the attempt to transcend both the local and the momentary (or historical) origin of the society by masking both the fact of mortality (so obvious in the duchess's death) and the imitative origins of this first German language society in a welter of botanical metaphors, which are, ironically, highly imitative themselves.[4] Appeals to the virginity of the language associate this organicized inaugural moment ("gestiftet") with a discourse of origins that are not only primal (original and originary) but also untainted, pure, and intact. In the very specific sociopolitical context that was early seventeenth-century central Europe, then, a rhetoric of origins, universalism, and closure was employed to serve the ends of a strictly local, derivative, and fragmented cause. It was a rhetoric designed to endow subsequent regulatory practice proceeding from the group with an untouchable origin before, above, and beyond the historical founding act.

The founding of this first German language society, whose model four others, including the Nuremberg Order of Flowers on the Pegnitz (Pegnesischer Blumenorden), were to follow, was thus both an inaugural and a highly conventional, codified, and ultimately prescriptive act. Not only did members of the German *petite noblesse* resort to storytelling and thus to the conventions of narrative to distract themselves from their loss, but they quite literally convened, or "came together" ("Zusammenkunft"), to define themselves as the corporate moment out of which the absolute norms or "laws" governing both behavior and textual production in German were to flow. As an individual, Luther had already "blessed" the vernacular one hundred years earlier, as Hille points out:

> It should especially be considered that the well-known society just referred to was begun at a time when, just one hundred years earlier, the sacred light of the Holy Scripture had shown through and the Bible was made available in our German language in a distinct (intelligible) way, translated, that is, as accurately and thoroughly as any one man could achieve.[5]

Luther's translations themselves had demonstrated the power of the text to "create" a new language.[6] The group's purpose was to renew Luther's act and extend the authority of his language into other spheres by institutionalizing it in their texts.

Lawrence Manley, we will recall, described convention as "an order of objective rules . . . [that] possess[es] the atemporal qualities of pattern and form but paradoxically express[es] changing social values."[7] It is to the origins of the conventions of the German language societies in the changing social values of the central European *petite noblesse* that Klaus Conermann implicitly refers when he identifies the notion of *conversatio* and the establishment of homogeneous and homogenizing social practice (*maniere convenevoli*) after the Italian model as the "center of the German society's program."[8] But to transform those social values into a semipermanent rather than changing "order of objective rules" above and beyond the actual coming together of the particular, historical group, it was necessary to produce *textual institutions* that rendered the group's linguistic and literary practice both standard and binding. To legitimate this act of institutionalization, the *transformation, that is, of regional standards into textual sources of universal and even sacred norms*, two discourses, one of *timeless nature* and the other of *scriptural truth*, were invoked in society texts and thus convened into the present in textual form. The first is obvious in the elaborate system of botanical imagery, common to both the northern and southern academies. Through it, not only the German imitators but the Italian "originals" characterized historical, consensus-based standards as linguistic and scientific "natural law." The academies could then take on the task of "policing" the learned community, using their texts as a kind of legal code. Hille's chronology—the founding of the Fruit-bearing Society on the centennial of Luther's Bible translation—belongs to the second authorizing discourse, that of the sacred. The reference to Luther is of course peculiar to the German societies but illustrates the same association of the moment of historical beginnings with a moment of authoritative origins beyond time. It was by means of these two discourses—themselves the products of textual events—that the early modern academies sought to endow their historical acts of organization with standardizing force.

To be sure, the phenomenon of the academies by its very nature could not be monolithic, given the commitment of each group to transforming its particular moment of historical origin into a moment of universal proportion (the capturing of the natural and the sacred in a particular vernacular language). There were, for example, a number of material differences, as Conermann has pointed out, between the Italian academies and the Fruit-bearing Society.[9] The German group was not an urban one, as many of the Italian academies were, but had its center at a small, rather inaccessible, court. The Italian academies often included members of the clergy, a group specifically excluded from the Köthen group. Conermann also finds that the German language society had less of an explicit sense of a possible political role, whereas the Italian groups seem to have deliberately included, for example, members of the bourgeois intelligentsia, a class that was to become increasingly influential in urban politics in Italy after the fifteenth century. At the same time, however, there were a number of similarities between the first German language society and the Italian academies, among them the use of society names and emblems (*imprese*) as well as a commitment to translation and to the development of a standard language as the focus of their collective activity.[10] Prince Ludwig was aware of and cultivated the parallels between his society and the Italian academic tradition to such an extent, Conermann argues, that it is appropriate to use the same term, namely, *academy*, to designate both the Italian and the German groups insofar as they all belonged to the larger European phenomenon.[11] I have nevertheless chosen to differentiate between the German societies and the other European academies terminologically, while still understanding both sets of groups as committed to the instituting and institutionalization of vernacular forms.

The indebtedness of both the German language societies and the other national language academies to the Italian *accademie* and to the model of the Accademia della crusca in Florence in particular brings several points into focus. First, the Italian model signified a connection to the intellectual heritage of antiquity. But the Italian academy's geographical location was symbolic above all of the creation of a new order in the very backyard, so to speak, of the Latin tradition taken by some as authoritative and paradigmatic for postclassical literary creativity. The desire to both internalize and move beyond their classical past necessarily led to an implicit rejection of overt reliance on the Ancients as linguistic and literary models not only by the Italians but by other humanists as well. Sometimes associated with "anti-Ciceronianism," this second trend saw modern linguistic practice as at least equally authoritative as ancient practice precisely because it was contextually based, responded to the new and different needs of a modern public, and was thus in general more appropriate to its own historical time.[12] Erasmus wrote in 1528:

[S]ince the whole scene of human affairs has been overturned, who today can talk sensibly unless he uses language very different from that of Cicero? Wherever I turn my eyes I see all things changed, I stand before another stage and I behold a different play, nay, even a different world.[13]

David Quint, following Eugenio Garin, has identified a "new historical awareness" and sense of historical difference of the kind Erasmus expresses here as the source of the peculiar urgency with which writers confronted the possibility of creative originality and individuality in the Renaissance.[14] But, as Erasmus indicates, the championing of a new language (as opposed to a continued and anachronistic use of classical Latin and its literary forms) was not just an *effect* of the era's awareness or understanding of its own "internal coherence," and thus difference from the past, but was in fact ultimately *constitutive of* that difference as national languages developed.[15] The existence of poetry, laws, political treatises, and the very possibility of writing and "talking sensibly" in the vernacular that occurred as a result created new audiences as well as new social and political practice. Quint sees the problematization of the absolute authority of the Ancients during this period as a shift away from a "bookish method of organizing and explaining the world" by means of the written word toward a culture that was to locate authority in "scientific reason and empiricism," which would result in and be proof of superior modern achievements.[16] And yet, he underestimates the role of the vernacular texts he analyzes in ensuring that this very shift away from the past would occur. The Italian academies still belonged, I would suggest, as did the German language societies that followed, to a very "bookish" (in the sense of textual) culture even as their programs produced the reorientation toward the scientific that Quint describes. They saw their autonomy from the Ancients as depending on the existence of a vernacular tongue in which not only the wisdom of the Ancients but also new (scientific) knowledge could be made accessible to the here and now. But this language could be developed and that knowledge made real only in texts authored by Moderns.

Framing this logic of a modern multiplicity of languages and of the contextual authority of any particular language in a naturalizing, organicizing, and even sacred discourse gave vernacular languages the authority they needed to take the place of an outdated ideology of linguistic uniformity and universalism based primarily on ancient models and a false sense of nostalgia. Thus it was precisely in language that the new languages, new knowledge, and new era came to be. Change and the conventional nature of linguistic standards it implied became clear to Renaissance humanists as they investigated the texts of the past as part of their devout editorial work. It was only by producing their own standardizing texts that the threat of relativism could be overcome, as the language of the new period, the new knowledge it needed to distinguish itself from the past, and new, more appropriate "laws" were given concrete form.

"For humanists," William Bouwsma has written, "language was power."[17] And for them, texts became history too. It was thus not by chance that the Renaissance language academies were often affiliated with both regional and national centers of power and prestige, since the authority of that power not only came to be associated with but was in fact constituted by the existence of a standardized language and of regulatory texts in that language. The direct availability of descriptions of uniform behavior of all sorts (military and political as well as linguistic) and the effective rhetorical use of the vernacular by the powerful gave increased weight to expectations of conformity. Ignorance of the law could not be pleaded; indeed, wider audiences could be persuaded of and be expected to conform with the law's truth. All manner of obligatory texts and codes written in the vernacular were possible, and the ideological assumption was that compliance would follow.

The humanistic academies that had existed in Italy since at least the mid–fifteenth century testified, then, to the coincidence of authority and convention, of cultural power and the power that comes from literally "coming together" under the sponsorship of the powerful to create new forms of authority.[18] In particular, the establishment of the Accademia platonica, led by Marsilio Ficino, was made possible by the powerful patron Ficino found in Cosimo de' Medici, who put a villa in Careggi at the disposal of the group in 1462 as a sign of his support for their project of meeting to renew the study of ancient philosophy. This informal intellectual community—founded according to the prototype of the Platonic and Ciceronian academies—was one of the earliest modern academies. Its sponsorship by Cosimo was significant, moreover, because of the commitment of an influential, local personage to the resuscitation of ancient learning in a new time and place. Just as significant, however, was the prestige with which the academy—"his" academy—endowed Cosimo himself. Eighty years later a second, more overtly politicized and more explicitly textual phase developed under the patronage of Cosimo II de' Medici, when the Accademia degli umidi, with its emphasis on the literary aspect of the humanist endeavor, was patriotically renamed the Accademia fiorentina (1540).[19] Ancient learning—conceived of as an "absolute standard"—was given new and specifically Florentine form, with the local academy acting as the collective creator and guarantor of authority in vernacular texts, which were considered certainly equal, if not superior to, the ancient models by virtue of having been generated by a local, learned elite.

The Florentine act of regionalization and the turn to an overt concern with the purification of vernacular languages and with the production of standardized texts were neither spontaneous nor isolated events. Whether the invention of print in the mid–fifteenth century "caused" increased literacy or whether increased literacy necessitated the invention of print is impossible to judge. But according to Eric Cochrane, by 1530–33 a greater demand had begun to be felt by a larger *Volgare*-reading public to be included in the humanist culture that had previously been the domain of a learned, Latin-speaking, and Latin-writing elite.[20] As regional literate classes developed and local presses were established, there was pressure for classical learning and universal knowledge to be made available locally (both literally and linguistically) in textual form—hence the explosion of regional academies at midcentury, as the tasks of humanism were transformed into local projects to cultivate and standardize the dialects in which this knowledge was to be catalogued and disseminated. The Florentine academy was, then, but one example of what Cochrane has called not the "provincialism" but the "adaptability" of the humanist endeavor to local needs and demands.[21] Nevertheless, the statutes of the Umidi make it clear that the academy's adaptability was just as much a move in the direction of a kind of textual "imperialism" as anything else. Indeed, one of its missions was to translate "into our language every worthy science" known, thus acknowledging the aptness of the vernacular and of locally available texts as superior vehicles for the immediate renewal of universal knowledge and poetic forms in the modern age.[22] And yet, translation masked dependency here, allowing (stolen) "foreign goods" to appear naturally and legitimately one's own. While the academies may not necessarily have been subject to direct political pressures by their sponsors, as Cochrane argues, the renaming of the society as an explicitly "Florentine" academy expresses a kind of regionalism that elsewhere in Europe eventually resulted in the consolidation of the nation-state. Local, contextually specific (as opposed to ancient or foreign), but also authoritative texts first offered proof of the parity between local authorities and both ancient and contemporary competition. Arguments about the legitimacy of this local authority, arguments made precisely on the basis of the fact that these new texts could and did exist, could in turn be used to invest the "new learning" with the status it needed to replace ancient models (even as it was partially based on them) and usurp their authority as the origins of naturelike linguistic, poetic, scientific, and ethical norms.

The Accademia della crusca, Prince Ludwig's direct model for the Fruit-bearing Society, was founded in 1582 by five secessionist members of the Accademia fiorentina for whom the court academy had become too preoccupied with the "solemnity" and "pedantry" of its project.[23] Already in his 1564 *Orazione*, Leonardo Salviati had denounced the pomposity of his fellow academicians. By 1580 certain "anarchic" members of the Fiorentina were engaging in *cruscate*, or parodies of the learned activities of the "great academy" at banquets.[24] But by 1582 Salviati had indicated where he thought more serious activity should occur, namely, in the elevation *in texts* of the Florentine language to a position of superiority. The "crusconi brigade," whose games had included elaborate but hardly serious experimentation with the Florentine tongue, should take the name of an academy, he suggests, in order that "by taking the name Crusca and living cheerfully . . . its valor may shine with greater strength" and show "other associations the manner and the way of maintaining academies *by writing and reading* . . . with pleasantness" (emphasis added).[25] Thus what had come to be considered the only symbolically learned activities of the Fiorentina were challenged by those who believed in the far more legitimate task represented by their emblem of a sifter with the motto "the fairest flower" (punning on *flour*), the gathering together and processing, that is, of the chaff ("crusca") of language that would form the essence of a purified Florentine tongue. It was only in the creation of this language that the legitimacy of the new era would become real.

By 1590 the academy's quasi-folkloristic interests had subsided and were replaced by an internal debate on exactly where the sources of this superior language lay and how it could become standard in published texts. Unable to decide whether the Florentine language as currently used or as defined in its "classical" forms by Bembo should serve as a model, the members met and agreed that certain collective philological endeavors, among them providing a standard edition of Dante's *Commedia*, could set the standard for correct vernacular usage. The texts of local authors, the *tre corone* of Florence—Dante, Boccaccio, and Petrarch—were to serve as linguistic authorities;[26] by 1591 plans for a dictionary had begun to be made. It was thus that the texts of three local authors—themselves Florentine, whose writing quite naturally reflected local usage—came to both institute and provide examples for the cataloguing of a lexicographically normative tongue. The dictionary, the *Vocabolario della Accademia della crusca*, was first published in 1612; it was a monument to the academy's origins that also transcended them in its offering of institutionalized vernacular forms. The academy thus entered into the phase for which it was to become known in subsequent years, namely, the phase during which it created a standardized language in and by means of a text. In the dictionary, collectively agreed-upon standards based in local texts rather than in ancient, classical ones took on the power of objective norms, "forgetting," obscuring, but also preserving their "conventional" (historical) origins as they entered into codified form. It was in its identity as a producer of codes—as the originator of lexicographic "legislation" of vernacular "law"—that the Crusca academy became the model for other European academies, including the German language societies.

The subtext of linguistic chauvinism that developed with the Accademia della crusca and the *Vocabolario* represents a moment of considerable ideological importance. The dictionary was not a multilanguage text (Latin-Italian) but was rather an essentially monolingual one, with the local dialect (Tuscan) in the position of the standard tongue in which words were defined. Textual standards were derived, moreover, from texts by major local authors. When the linguistic forms of a single vernacular dialect (Tuscan here in the case of the Florentine academicians and Saxon or Meissen later in the case of the Germans) are gathered together (convened) in dictionary form in this way, the very codificatory act has the effect of elevating a "mere" dialect into a position of equality with Latin and thus, perhaps paradoxically, of transforming it into a norm-setting version of vernacular usage based on usage but also transcending it.[27] The "blindness" to and "forgetting of" the limited contextual origin of a dialect is facilitated, moreover, by appealing to other properties, such as its "natural" purity, abundance, and communicative reliability. Thus the historical origins of the dictionary were simultaneously contained within and obscured by its textualized and regulatory form.

Of course, ancient rhetoricians had used very similar argumentation to establish the superior linguistic authority of a particular language group in classical times.[28] And yet, even though the assertion that a specific form of the *Volgare* was equal to Latin could be understood as an imitative act, as relying on and thus not being free of ancient models, it was the arguments used by the Ancients about the naturelike abundance and clarity of a specific language that were imitated rather than merely their words. Some of the more radical early writers in the Italian tradition, among them Sperone Speroni, for example, in his *Dialogo delle lingue*

(1542), simply asserted that since Latin and Tuscan were essentially equal, Moderns should not waste their time on acquiring the ancient tongue. Texts in the vernacular were equally clear and could contain the same knowledge. Language learning, he wrote, merely diverted attention from the progressive "scientific" projects that could illustrate the superiority of the present over an illustrious past.[29] Thus the symbolic victory of one dialect over another and of a dialect over a national tongue (expressed, for example, in the favoring of Tuscan over "Italian" that emerges in Machiavelli's *Dialogo intorno alla nostra lingua*) was argued on the basis of a proto-Enlightenment interest in "scientific," apparently neutral progress, even as it in fact expressed the gradual ascendancy of specific political powers on the local, national, and international level and thus the "interestedness" of "science" as a historical event.[30] Cosimo II's championship of the Accademia fiorentina after 1541 and of the "pure" forms of Tuscan Italian thus suggests a budding *Kulturpolitik* based on regionalism and a bid for local prestige legitimated on the basis of scientific principle.[31] Demonstrating "natural" linguistic superiority would create the conditions for cultural (and political) preeminence. And at the same time, this preeminence would form the cornerstone of an argument in favor of the obligatory usage of a particular set of linguistic norms.

Perhaps an even more obvious expression of Renaissance concern with legitimizing historical difference as a source of functionally universal norms and thus with the authoring and authorizing of modern texts and languages lies in the French-language example. Here, for reasons of political organization, the desire to demonstrate the prestige of a particular language and the necessity of creating that language in specific texts became evident on a national rather than a regional level. In his *La déffence et illustration de la langue françoyse* (1549), for example, Joachim Du Bellay urges French poets to enrich the vernacular by forcing other literatures into its service to the end of creating new texts; wanton sacking of ancient models and imitative plundering of contemporary sources are encouraged.[32] Du Bellay's treatise itself literally enacts the plundering he advises as he comes into his ancient heritage—Quintilian's rhetorical program—by pillaging a contemporary Italian competitor—Speroni's *Dialogo*— for most of his statements, never identifying either source explicitly.[33] The militaristic language of the treatise in fact suggests the political struggles between Italy and France some twenty or so years earlier even as it claims to guarantee the fertility and natural purity of the vernacular. Thus beneath the surface of a text that calls for the enrichment of the French tongue based on metaphors or organicity and the "natural richness" of the vernacular, a very specific battle for textual space and authority as well as for linguistic hegemony is being fought.

It is not surprising that the group of poets around Du Bellay and Pierre de Ronsard, now known as La Pléiade, had clear affiliations with the center of political power at the Paris court at midcentury. Originally identified with Baïf's Académie de poésie et de musique (1570), this circle of intellectuals, while already associated for many years with royal patronage, only became the official "Palace Academy" several years later under Henry III.[34] The direct affiliation of an academy with the king only made explicit, however, the already clear patriotism of vernacular poets who, although by no means naively uncritical of the policies of the Paris court, produced texts that were instrumental in the enactment of its official cultural code. Similarly, Richelieu's offer of protection to the young Académie française some years later in 1635 turned a community of intellectuals and poets committed to the development of literary and scientific culture in France into an organ of national unity and prestige.[35] By 1672 Louis XIV had transformed the academy into a tool of national culture, and work on a dictionary as well under way. At the same time, then, as France became increasingly visible and powerful in the central European political arena, the Académie française became the standard of academic excellence, almost eclipsing its Italian model; the dictionary, finally published in 1695, became a model for lexicographic standardization for the other European tongues and had the same function as the Crusca *Vocabolario*, namely, the creation of modern authority by means of the creation of a "perfected" vernacular tongue. Texts like the *Vocabolario* and the Académie's *Dictionaire française* were institutions, texts that contained foundations and obligatory codes of linguistic behavior, apparently timeless norms whose objectivity was nevertheless legitimated only by their codification in a text sanctioned by the court. The coincidence in the French and Prussian academies of the late seventeenth and early eighteenth centuries (and I return to the Prussian example below) of a project for linguistic standardization and the coalescence of a sovereign nation-state suggests that where linguistic unity and autonomy could be created and the naturelike, even divine accuracy of the language maintained, arguments about the political legitimacy of that unity and autonomy would also be made.

In England, a similar coincidence of linguistic and political centralization began to occur in the middle to late sixteenth century as a high degree of national consciousness emerged in the wake of the Act of Supremacy (1534). The domination of London and the court was crucial to the consolidation of both literal and linguistic power. The forms of English to be institutionalized and considered as the origin of textual standards often were determined by centers of political influence. Puttenham writes in his *Arte of English Poesie* (1589), for example: "[Y]e shall therefore take the vsuall speach of the Court, and that of London and the shires lying about London within lx. myles, and not much aboue."[36] This attention to the presence of standard English in a particular geographical area and sociopolitical milieu merely echoes John Hart's injunction in 1569 to follow the usage of London and the court, since there resides the "flower" of the English tongue; the botanical reference suggests a parallel to developments in Italy of some fifteen years hence.[37] That this English was perhaps not superior to but was nevertheless capable of being elevated to a level of equality with the classical tongues had already been declared by Sir Thomas Elyot in his *Governour* of 1531 and reaffirmed by Andrew Borde in 1548: "The speeche of England is a base speeche to other noble speeches, as Italian, Castylian and French; howbeit the speeche of England of late days is amended."[38] These "amendments" had come in the form of a purification of English, a process that mandated the exclusion of foreign-based words, for example, and the translation into English of works of great learning similar to the "imperialist" efforts undertaken by the Accademia fiorentina. The new level of knowledge could thus be the same in modern times and in England as in days of old and abroad. The presence of texts in standard English, a language based on the usage of those near or with influence at the court, would prove it. It was thus the very (historical) origins of the language that would be internalized but also transcended by the language's function as textual standard. Ideological capital could be derived by the court from the very existence of such a powerful tongue.

The great number of treatises on the "improvement" of the English language and on lexicographic standardization published in the late sixteenth century undoubtedly made possible Edmund Bolton's idea of an "Academy Royal or College and Senate of Honor," a concept that received royal support for a more explicit literary and scientific imperialism: "that good books might sincerely be turned out of foreign tongues into ours."[39] With the death of James I in 1625, however, plans for this vernacular academy and its program of translation failed to materialize; they remained unfulfilled until the creation of the British Academy in 1902. And yet, in 1662, after the return of the monarchy, Charles II's sponsorship turned a "private society of scholars and amateurs" meeting in London and Oxford since 1645 into the nationally based Royal Society, which, as an institution, was intended to gather "Natural Knowledge" together in an objective and accessible form, namely, in English-language books.[40] In 1664 the society voted to form a committee, with John Dryden and John Evelyn at its head, whose task it would be to improve English by creating just such "exemplary works," on the assumption, akin to the one on which the notion of Enlightenment reason was based, that an identity existed between language and knowledge. The significance of this move toward reason in terms of Charles's personal and political orientation toward France should not be overlooked.[41] Even though these efforts to create an academy-like organization came to nought, illustrating an anti-academic trend (as Woodhouse has called it) in standardization efforts by the British, it is clear that the project of creating a language capable of being a vehicle of modern, scientific (as opposed to imitative or inherited) learning was similar to the agenda behind both the Italian and the French groups. This language and the growth of knowledge it would permit could be evidenced only in the production of standardized and standardizing texts. The appearance of Samuel Johnson's dictionary in 1755, while an individual achievement, may be seen, then, as the culmination of a long-term growth in the cohesion of a linguistic national consciousness in Britain.

The German language societies were established, then, in a context of increasing consciousness of historical and cultural difference, of a kind of regional chauvinism that declared vernacular languages equal to Latin in expressing universal knowledge in a linguistic form accessible and appropriate to the here-and-now. Moreover, this knowledge would supercede that of the Ancients, since "scientific" projects for gathering information could progress unhindered by a prior necessity to learn the classical tongues. The historical and contextual limitations of these projects as well as their indebtedness to the past, primarily in the form of translations, were obscured, first, by their appeal to "nature," to "objective," scientific norms, and, in the case of the Germans, to divine sanction in the form of the achievements of the great predecessor, Luther, and his "blessing" of the German tongue, and, second, by their very appearance in textual form.

The projects of the academies and societies ultimately depended, then, on the production of standardized and standardizing texts in the vernacular (in Italian, French, English, German, and so on) in which both old and new knowledge would be contained and handed on. The translation of "good books" from both ancient and foreign languages into these tongues, together with the lexicographical standardization of each national language so that these works would be comprehensible to all, was to be the first step in what was simultaneously the creation, celebration, and regulation of postclassical culture.[42] Like the Italians, French, and British, those affiliated with both the Fruit-bearing Society and the other language societies in seventeenth-century Germany proposed using translations and dictionaries as their primary textual institutions, as encyclopedia-like sources and reference points for the collection and production of linguistic and technical knowledge and norms.

But in spite of the announced commitment to such projects by some of the early seventeenth-century language societies, to which I devote special attention below, Gottfried Wilhelm Leibniz still found it necessary as late as 1697 to publish a programmatic statement in his *Unvorgreifliche Gedanken, betreffend die Ausübung und Verbesserung der teutschen Sprache* (Timely thoughts on the use and improvement of the German language) suggesting that neither the Italian or French academies nor their dictionaries had been adequately reproduced on German soil.[43] Moreover, even the most recent efforts of the Italian and French groups, a 1691 version of the *Vocabolario* and the 1695 *Dictionnaire française*, are hindered, he contends, by their excessive purism and ignore the technical terms ("Kunstworte") and current usage necessary to develop the vernacular fully enough for it to represent both things and words fully and accurately. Unfortunately, it "is also clear that some of the members of the Fruit-bearing Society and of the other German societies have gone too far in this respect."[44] They limited the scope of their vernacular dictionary by appealing to a certain pedantic localism as the source of linguistic objectivity. The need continues, he concludes, for a rationally ordered dictionary of the German tongue to provide the foundations of and, indeed, to *create* a universally comprehensible and accurate German tongue that cannot be accused of such localism (even as his description of the process of compiling this dictionary goes on to reveal itself as a clearly limited one). Leibniz proposes a three-part project that is to include a catalogue of usage, one of etymology, and one of technical or scientific terms, thus gathering the various impulses for universal coverage and comprehensibility into a single but multifaceted lexicographical task. And the mission of composing such a dictionary should fall, he explains, to "a certain assembly or group at the instigation of an illustrious leader of high [social] standing" (529), to a collective, in other words, that under respectable political leadership would capture an unimpeachable standard of knowledge in intersubjectively compiled and thus consensually derived linguistic forms. The limits of the collective's point of view would be hidden, we might add, in and by the objectified and objectifying fact of the dictionary itself.

Leibniz's call for an assembly or association and for the creation of a dictionary as a textual institution that would both found and regulate standardized vernacular usage recalls the principle of "coming together," or convening, central to the academic tradition. His identification of this potential collective as a group of "scholars well disposed to things German" ("Teutschgesinneten Gelehrten") (553) is reminiscent of the name of one of the German language societies, the Deutschgesinnete Genossschaft (German-minded Association). The term suggests the regionalism, if not incipient nationalism that the dictionary project would both entail and, once accomplished, help create. And indeed, in 1711, Elector Frederick III of Prussia (King Frederick I since 1701) formally inaugurated a Society of Sciences (Societät der Wissenschaften) at Berlin, directing the assembled parties to compile a "complete dictionary" along the lines of the texts created by the Italian and French academies that the Berlin society was to take as its models.[45] The Societät was renamed the Académie des sciences et belles lettres by Frederick the Great, its French title indicating paradoxically that while the status of the vernacular in Germany obviously remained unclear, the regulation of both science and language in German was thought to be able, at least theoretically, to contribute to the glorification of the nation-state's cause.

While the publication of a "complete" German dictionary was not to take place until the mid–twentieth century,[46] the regular meetings of the *académie* in Berlin document the collective pursuit of a standardized language in which intersubjectively verifiable and thus "scientific" knowledge could be accurately created, catalogued, and increased. It should come as no surprise that such an academy was founded in Prussia during the age of absolutism and, indeed, under the sponsorship of one of that political system's most representative figures. The king was to be the specific embodiment of the organic entity of the nation-state, a "concrete universal," in Hegel's terms, that functioned as the agent of the divine and absolute in local, individual terms. The academy, as an agent of scientific knowledge and thus, like the king, the definitive interpreter of nature's laws to humanity, was an institution designed to initiate and guarantee the transmission and growth of this knowledge in locally available textual forms. In both cases, the singularity of the historical moment (Prussia and the German-language dictionary) is foregrounded as the expression of nature's greater and more authoritative force. At the same time, the very specific historical moment out of which this version of "nature" had grown is elided in acts of political and linguistic institutionalization. From the Italian academies to the Berlin academy, then, the result of embedding the linguistic conventions of a specific community in a rhetoric of natural, sacred, and "universal truth" remained the same: it gave the status of institutions, as foundations and guarantors, to the knowledge gathered by members of that community and to the texts in which that knowledge was catalogued and preserved. The programs of the humanistic and Enlightenment academies were thus consistent with one another; in both cases, the appeal to a moment of origins above reproach was made in texts authored within very specific contexts of political consolidation, in the first case in the context of an organicizing Renaissance discourse about regional/national languages, and in the second, in the development of a logic of "natural law" present to and in an accumulation of knowledge in the vernacular languages used in the nation-states of the here-and-now.

It was thus the power of language to "make history" that connected the various phases of the European academic project. The understanding of their own historical difference from the Ancients that had led Renaissance humanists in Italy and elsewhere to develop a new sense of corporate (rather than strictly individualist) autonomy as they cultivated the art of vernacular poetry within the academy setting had not abated and, indeed, became particularly acute in the age of religious wars that followed directly upon it. A desire for a single, uniform language capable of consolidating regional, national, and even international movements was quite logical in the context of the hostilities that became widespread both in England and on the Continent after the break with Rome. Moreover, the increasing "scientific" tendency to consult a universally accessible "Book of Nature" rather than Scripture for knowledge, on the one hand, and the growing preoccupation of visionaries with the immediacy of a divine "Inner Word," on the other, suggest that the arguments for a new kind of language capable of transcending difference emerged in both scientific and mystical religious discourses at a time that coincided not only with the growth of linguistic national consciousness obvious in the earlier academies but also with the fact of external (national/confessional/political) difference at the root of the ongoing political and military strife.[47]

The creation and use in the seventeenth century of a "scientific," collectively agreed-upon, and codified language capable of reflecting nature accurately and objectively would thus reconcile and transcend difference in a way that merely inspired—and thus subjective—discourse could not, as Hans Aarsleff points out. Were this language a truly universal one, moreover, modern knowledge could be accumulated all the more quickly as a collective effort. The obsession in the program of the British Royal Society in the 1660s with the question of objectivity in language and with the development of a "philosophical character" illustrates Aarsleff's point. The creation (instituting) and codification (institutionalization) by the society of a "philosophical" language or "character" whose "very signs [would express] the nature and essence of what is designated" would counteract the notion of a privatized and intersubjectively unavailable "Inner Word."[48]

Aarsleff describes Locke's implicit rejection of Paracelsus and Böhme in his *Essay concerning Human Understanding* (1690); Locke's disagreement with the Germans was based on his suspicion of the potentially divisive aspects of any knowledge based, as they would have had it, on strictly subjective tools of understanding and communication, a subjectivity that the development of a written "character" would avoid.[49] Aarsleff points out that it was in opposition to such "enthusiastic" views of language that attempts were made by John Wilkins and others to develop a philosophical, or objective and mutually verifiable, language based on a system of simple and clear linguistic forms or signs. In this system, words would be "designed to mirror things directly . . . learning the character [language] with its symbols [would be] entirely co-extensive with the gaining of real knowledge of nature."[50] Not only would this language be a useful scientific tool for dealing with the *res ipsae*, the things themselves, in a transparent and thus objective way, but it would also prevent the kinds of disagreements based on merely subjective human opinion that were ostensibly the cause of the religious wars.

Institutionalizing objectivity in language would thus facilitate—indeed, even create—the possibility of the mutual understanding and "universal agreement" so desperately needed in war-torn central Europe; the "Irenic cause" of bringing the period of conflict to a close by invoking mutually agreed-upon norms would be best served by the development of both "scientific principles" and a standardized tongue in which they could be expressed.[51] The society and its texts, in turn—and here the nationalistic impulse behind and in the Royal Society's project becomes clear—were to be the institutions by means of which such bases for consensus would be formed. Because, as the logic of the universal language went, there could be an "isomorphic relationship between language and reality," all peoples could and would agree as long as they spoke or used the same tongue, the tongue "created" by society texts.[52] Thus the convening of a particular set of intellectuals on both a local and an international level, made possible by the availability of a universally comprehensible language, would resist the "dislocation, division, and decline" such as took place in central Europe in particular during the hundred years between 1550 and the end of the Thirty Years' War.[53]

While perhaps not as convinced of a future of both intellectual and religious harmony and concrete social change on a universal scale as the "associations of initiates" and secret societies such as the Rosicrucians that were founded at the same time,[54] European academies like the Royal Society and the "society mentality" they expressed thus do seem to have been designed to re-present (literally, to make present again in local form) the Respublica Literaria and spirit of intellectual fellowship and exchange nostalgically thought to have existed in humanist culture before the outbreak of war.[55]

It was precisely this recognition of difference (of historical, confessional, and linguistic "otherness" as opposed to identity with either the Ancients or contemporaries) that, combined with a concept of natural reason proper to all men (a concept that authorized this "otherness" as a form of the absolute), called both the earlier and the later European academies into existence. Their texts—dictionaries, translations, founding and standardizing texts of all kinds—were self-defined embodiments of universals in particular form. They were proof, so to speak, of the ability of the present to be both other than the past and just as authoritative. The attempts to efface the historical limitations of the normalization efforts made by the academies and societies—by describing these efforts in organic metaphors, for example, or by claiming the "accuracy" of any single language, either a dialect or a "philosophical character," in representing nature—indirectly confirmed the importance of their historicity in an age during which universals could in fact no longer be said to have their foundations in either nature or the sacred but rather in regional or national authorities and political forms. For it was precisely this historical singularity and the institutions of power with which it was aligned that, once enshrined in academy codes, systems, and texts, ceased belonging to the particular moment and took on normative force. It is thus within an age during which the conventions of particular powerful groups had already begun to become equated with and take on the function of ancient authority and natural law that the German language societies' task of providing the vernacular with instituting and institutionalizing texts may be best understood.

Pastoral Conventions: The German Academies in Köthen and Nuremberg

Like their academic models in Italy and the later European societies, the German language societies represent a shift from imitation of the Ancients to convention and to locally based and consensually derived institutions as sources of linguistic and literary "natural law." And, as was the case in many of the other academies, the creation of an interested discourse of universality in connection with the language societies coincided with external political and military events. It was, I would argue, in the texts of the societies themselves and in the language they contained that this shift of authority to the local occurred. This is not to say that there were not German-language texts available prior to 1617. Nor is it clear that political unity developed immediately after this time. And yet, it was during this period that a binding rhetoric of a unified high culture in the vernacular was created.

The fact that the first language society, the Fruit-bearing Society, found its origins in a narrative moment—in a story ("Erzehlung") told in a group context about an Italian *accademia* characterized by its use of botanical metaphors to describe poetic and linguistic endeavors—inadvertently highlights the role of textuality in transforming historically, socially, and politically generated norms into the discourse of a powerful and unified national language. Only in telling a story of origins could the founding moment transcend itself to become the location of a set of linguistic and moral "first causes" that could legitimate both the society enterprise and the actions of local authorities. And yet, it was the power of the historical moment to produce its own origins and binding standards in textual form to which the textual institutions of the society in fact paid homage even as the texts themselves worked to transcend that moment. The literal and figurative conventions involved in the founding and textual self-stylization of the Fruit-bearing Society and the Order of Flowers on the Pegnitz as cultural concepts and literal events are the subject of the following pages.[56]

It is clear in Gustav von Hille's description of the founding moment of the Fruit-bearing Society that coexisting with the drive for linguistic purity was a desire for the preservation of a specific social order as well:

> Thus was the so often mentioned society founded [gestiftet] to maintain and reproduce [Fortpflantzung] all knightly virtues, to establish and increase good German trustworthiness (as previously mentioned), and,

above all, so that our own German motherland, until now abandoned, despised, and left to die, in recovering, could cheer up her desperate children of German blood and soil.[57]

We must analyze the interplay of two discourses—one of social interestedness, the other of organicity—in this passage and in other descriptions of society behavior and goals in more detail in order to understand the process of institutionalization in the German language society project.

In Hille's description, the language heroes or knights ("Sprachhelden") of the society were to defend the purity of a clearly feminized motherland. In so doing, they would be following a code of chivalrous behavior that ensured common, ethical goals. Society members were directed to "preserve and practice our highly respected mother tongue in the most delicate and perspicacious of manners." Primarily, according to the statutes Hille recites, they were to "present themselves collegially and modestly," "act in a praiseworthy and honorable way," and much, much more.[58] Although the language societies were not identical with the knightly (or nobles') academies (*Ritterakademien*) of central Europe— indeed, an early suggestion by one member of the Fruit-bearing Society that the society be turned into a knightly academy was soundly rejected by the prince[59]—the two kinds of institutions did share chivalric metaphors such as these as well as a dedication to upholding a clearly class-based standard of virtue.[60] Thus linguistic and moral rectitude in defense of the motherland were to coincide in the task of establishing the language society community of heroic "knights."

Hille writes here in 1646 of events taking place some thirty years earlier; his description might well have been influenced by historical hindsight. Georg Philipp Harsdörffer (1607–58), cofounder of the Order of Flowers on the Pegnitz with Johann Klaj (1616–56) in 1644, uses a vocabulary in which the discourses of language and class coincide in a similar way in enumerating those aspects of another Italian academy, the Sienese Accademia degli intronati, that he claims to have followed when he instituted his language society in Nuremberg. He cites the model of the Italian academy with which he had become acquainted while in Siena in 1623 as he describes the "founding behavior" appropriate to the order's membership in the foreword (*Vorrede*) to part 5 of his *Frauenzimmer Gesprächspiele* (Playful colloquies for the ladies, 1646):

[The following] is taken from the eminently praiseworthy academy of the Intronati at Siena:

I. Enemies of virtue and of the heroic German language are not to be admitted;
II. Pray devoutly, study diligently, and be of a positive disposition; do not insult anyone . . .
III. Seek honor among those most like you . . . learn from the learned. Inquire about what you do not understand. Be friendly to all.
IV. He who speaks well will have a good reputation. He who does well will be treated well. He who seeks praise must behave himself in praiseworthy fashion.[61]

One hundred years later, Johannes Herdegen, historian of the Nuremberg society, describes the membership code of the group in much the same terms. Members must swear three basic oaths: "To attend to the glory of God, to encourage the practice of virtue, and to maintain the purity of the German language."[62] Van Ingen is correct, then, to emphasize the broader goals of the language society movement when he writes that "it was apparently the goal of the Fruit-bearing Society to pursue not just a linguistic, but equally as importantly, an ethical ideal."[63] The same seems true for the Nuremberg order as well. And in this context, ethics were part of a greater sociopolitical agenda. The injunction to be virtuous, for example, belonged both traditionally and during the seventeenth century to a heavily coded, class discourse that allowed the nonnobility to be "noble in spirit" and thus equal to their class superiors.[64] Thus, with a characteristic penchant for the fictional, the founding members of both societies wrote themselves into the narrative of a medieval epic that had clear social and political implications. Both "orders"—the Order of the Palms at Anhalt-Köthen and the Order of Flowers at Nuremberg, one at the court, one in the city—were associations designed to preserve the values of an anachronistically understood "knightly" world even as, and precisely because, they were engaged in the work of creating a purified and organically superior vernacular in their "heroic tongue."[65]

The linkage of the German societies' program of linguistic standardization with an overtly prescriptive, class-specific social decorum reveals the origins of the Fruit-bearing Society, first of all, in a moment of historical difference; the first German language society found both its roots and the origins of the linguistic and moral absolutes it was to institutionalize in the soil of the central European *petite noblesse*.[66] The sociohistorical interestedness of this moment seems at first deliberately downplayed, even challenged by the discourses of nature and universality that characterize, at least in the case of the Fruit-bearing Society, its founders' plans for a language society of humanist character.[67] But the democratization of learning and universality of membership allegedly represented by society rituals—the fact, for example, that each member was to be known only by his society name and botanical insignia and was to be seated according to date of membership rather than social status[68]—was only apparent. A later historian of the Fruit-bearing Society points openly to the fact that even at the time it was clear that society formalities could not and should not transgress class barriers:

> But the meaning [significance] of this is not that the great gentlemen and illustrious members of the Fruit-bearing Society are to get involved with the lesser members in [a form of] altogether-too-common intercourse that is disdainful. Nor [ought] the lesser members, just because they also belong to the society, approach the distinguished persons of rank in too intimate a way, as some have done with an immodest audacity and foolish delusion. They should much rather persist in humble attendance and fitting humility as circumstances and necessity require.[69]

Thus society conventions could not hide (indeed, they indirectly reasserted) the rigidity of the specific historical conditions and clear sociopolitical hierarchy of the early seventeenth century in central Europe. And associating the fact of the society's existence with a "natural" state of affairs only confirmed the legitimacy of the hierarchy. In spite of the textual mask of democracy present, then, in society rituals and membership books, social status determined standard behavior. Indeed, the rituals and books themselves assimilated the different classes into a single one as the very "knightliness" of society trappings and affiliation identified "normal" behavior within the group with aristocratic, hierarchical norms.

The injunction in society texts to follow a socially defined set of ethical standards and to create (allegedly) objective and universally applicable linguistic and poetic norms and rules of orthography and prosodic forms may be seen, then, as having had its origins in a class-bound movement and mentality—in the nobility, in the case of the Fruit-bearing Society, and in the urban patriciate, in the case of the Nuremberg group. I explore the details of these origins below. And yet, the power of these specific (historical) origins to regulate depended very much on obscuring their presence in a discourse of authority and transcendence. And it was in the texts of both societies that this separation of authority from the (limited) moment of origins could occur. The institutionalization, or formalization and systematization, of a specific group's behavior in easily accessible, textual form thus ultimately usurped the exemplary function of the (historical) group itself, since one no longer had to belong to the society to participate in its class-based program, but had, rather, merely to read and reproduce its texts in order to apply the principles detailed therein.[70] Thus the embedding of the "changing social values" of the house of Anhalt-Köthen both in a rhetoric of atemporality and in textual form provided those who followed not only with the guiding logic of the first German language society but also with the very means of using that logic to transcend the (limited) moment of origins.

The rootedness of the Fruit-bearing Society in the landscape and customs of the early seventeenth-century, central European petty nobility is particularly obvious in much of the language used to describe society activities and goals. The language society, Hille writes, was to function as a "place of honor for German virtue" ("Teutsche Tugend Ehrenort") as well as a "knightly arena for the German tongue" ("Teutscher Sprache Ritterplatz").[71] The chivalric metaphor surfaces again and again as the "language heroes" of the society are called to the defense of a "heroic tongue" ("Heldensprache").[72]

The militaristic undercurrent in the discussion of language emerges in other, much more explicit references to the era of conflict and foreign domination in which the society was founded. Hille writes that the Fruit-bearing Society had its origins "in that year of destruction and death, 1617, a year afflicted with corpses, when the fury of vengeance first thrust the unquenchable fire of proud discord into the jaws of our dear fatherland and scattered our fields with armour and cadavers."[73] Although much of Hille's information on the early years of the Köthen society is based on earlier documents, such as the *Kurtzer Bericht der Fruchtbringenden Gesellschaft Zweck und Vorhaben* (Short report on the purpose and plans of the Fruit-bearing Society) of 1622, from his position, writing in 1647, the year 1617 symbolized the beginning of the Thirty Years' War, a devastating conflict whose innumerable internal power struggles, invasions from without, and confrontations with foreign armies on German soil brought destruction to much of central Europe. The call to return to an ancient or "primeval" ("uralt") German language free of foreign influence could also be read, then, as a call to return to conditions prior to the outbreak of the wars. And language would serve as a means of pacification:

> Our ancient and imperfect German mother tongue, administered in pure form to us, drop by drop, with our mother's milk, and then, at the time of the bloody and lamentable war, watered down and spoiled by

the intrusion of ostentatious foreign words, should be returned to its ancient, customary, and natural German purity, grace, and receptivity, harmoniously pursued, liberated from the foreign linguistic yoke, secured with both ancient and new technical terms, and in this way finally restored to a most glorious throne of honor.[74]

The desire for peace is couched here in a call for linguistic autonomy, even superiority. Homologies between politics and language such as those in Du Bellay's *Déffence* of 1549 thus emerge in the German discourse as well, fixing the project in a context in which a renewed version of the vernacular would be a political event. The task of the heroic language knights was to rescue a "mother tongue" and fatherland in distress.

What began, then, as the project of a very limited group of lower nobility quickly stylized itself as a linguistic mission of grand scope. As a result, it soon became a matter of great prestige to belong to the Fruit-bearing Society; already in 1668, just some fifty years after its founding, Georg Neumark lists the society emblems, mottoes, and names of 806 members in his *Der Neu-Sprossende teutsche Palmbaum* (The newly budding German palm tree), an encyclopedia of society lore. And yet, it was precisely the class homogeneity of the society's initial and continuing membership that allowed a consensus to develop. Expressed in the terms of an organicizing discourse, this consensus was to be just as effective as "natural law" in dictating both ethical and linguistic norms. According to Conermann's calculations, over 90 percent of the 527 members of the Fruit-bearing Society admitted during Prince Ludwig's presidency belonged to various levels of the nobility.[75] The mutual agreement on certain matters by a specific class or group took on a quasi-organic legitimacy as it entered textual form. The language of the society was to become standard and could claim authority on the basis of the class unity of its members. Their texts, in turn, would create and fix linguistic, literary, and ethical norms with which not just this class but all others were to comply.

The power of texts to engage in this work of not just linguistic consolidation emerges in the fact that meetings of members seem to have played less than a major role in the efforts of the Fruit-bearing Society. Rather, the group's texts seem to have been expected to do much of the institutionalizing work. It was largely symbolic action, moreover, that dominated the Köthen group rather than discussion of and agreement upon matters of consequence. Of the six meetings known to have taken place between 1617 and 1658, only two concerned themselves with substantive issues: in 1624, the proper translation of the word *Materie* was debated; in 1645, questions of orthography were discussed. The largest documented gathering of the society occurred in 1651 and was called for the purpose of electing Wilhelm IV of Sachsen-Weimar as the society's second president. And yet, even then, only twenty-four members were in attendance, in spite of the fact that some thirty years earlier there had been a membership of seventy-eight.[76]

Negotiations about the society's literary program and the exchange of texts did allow a sense of community to coalesce, however. The volume of correspondence between members and the president was enormous, even though it was largely a matter of form, confirming the receipt of or requests for manuscripts, for example, and seldom dealing with matters of substance.[77] Conermann conceives of this exchange of letters as itself a form of joint "learned communication" that demonstrated "fruitful" intellectual activity of the kind officially endorsed by the group. And yet, much of the correspondence seems in fact to have been concerned with petitioning the society for membership; contact was initiated for the sake of demonstrating a bond of obligation between the two parties (rather than for discussing any material that books and writings might have contained).[78] Thus even though some of the members of the Fruit-bearing Society were in fact certified as hardly literate (not only had they not attended university, but some could hardly write their own names[79]), the manuscripts submitted and exchanged as evidence of a candidate's interest in preserving the purity of the mother tongue in the years after Prince Ludwig's death functioned as a means of keeping the class-specific conventions of the society alive.

The "spiritual consensus" that the founding of the Fruit-bearing Society was meant to represent seems, then, to have taken its most *concrete form* in the *circulation of texts* among members and in the society's extensive membership list. The overwhelming class homogeneity of that membership—in spite of the representation of various national groups—marked its singularity and rootedness in a moment of historical difference characterized by specific social, political, moral, as well as linguistic codes. But it was the textual versions of this homogeneity that allowed society discourse to present itself as the bearer of "objective rules." Conventionality—in both the original consensus and in its textual extensions—became the dominant society mode.

The discourse of nature that informs the texts of the Köthen language society conveys its founders' conviction of the universality of their particular cause and functions to solidify their claim to authority. In pursuit of this same goal, the Nuremberg Order of Flowers on the Pegnitz chose the equally organicizing and conventionalizing notion of pastoral as its governing metaphor. Pastoral repeats fixed, quasi-transcendent textual patterns even as it accommodates ancient literary traditions to new and specifically vernacular occasions and forms (see chapter 5). As both repetitions and as texts, vernacular pastorals are thus necessarily separate from the past and true to their own moment of origins even as that (authoritative and authorizing) past is contained within them. As a genre, pastoral thus appeals to an atemporal realm (as grove or as literary form) even as it acknowledges social, historical, and linguistic difference as the very reason for not just one but a series of texts.

While the literal pastoral mask of the Nuremberg poets, their shepherd names and local "grove," might thus seem as much, if not more, indebted to fiction as the "democratizing" trappings and ceremonies of the Fruit-bearing Society, their texts may have actually had somewhat less institutionalizing work to perform, since those involved with the Nuremberg society seemed to have actually participated in a more unified group.[80] This group's production of texts whose regulatory intent was clear could more easily testify, then, than the endeavors of the Köthen society to a set of shared assumptions and goals while also commemorating the literal presence of the group. For a number of reasons, the proximity of the Pegnitz "shepherds" (*Schäfer*) to one another played a more important role in the Nuremberg enterprise than in the earlier group. However, it was for the purpose of composing texts that a collective was formed, persisted, and aspired to become an arbiter of norms.[81]

The smaller size of the Order of Flowers on the Pegnitz and its affiliation with the imperial city of Nuremberg and, within Nuremberg, primarily with the learned bourgeoisie distinguished this urban language society from its courtly model, as did the later date of initiation, 1644, as opposed to 1617. The Fruit-bearing Society was founded before the outbreak of hostilities associated with the Thirty Years' War. Although on the brink of strife, those involved had not yet been directly touched by the disastrous conflict. The Order of Flowers, however, was founded on the eve of the conclusion of outright hostilities by a pair of poets, one of whom, Georg Philipp Harsdörffer, belonged to the Nuremberg patriciate and had experienced the loss of property and life brought on by the strife. A number of the order's members, including Birken, Klaj (cofounder of the group), Faber, and Locher, either themselves came from refugee families, exiles from the hostilities of war, or had connections to the large refugee community in Nuremberg. The conflict had clearly touched many of those affiliated with the group.

The refugee status of intellectuals associated with the language society as well as the presence of the university at nearby Altdorf, which many society members attended, may have led indirectly to an additional defining characteristic: many of the members of the Order of Flowers actually lived and worked near or in Nuremberg during the time of their association with the group, producing collaborative theoretical and poetic texts.[82] By 1672, at the latest, the society was well known enough as a distinguishable group with a well-defined poetic style and practice to be singled out (albeit for censure) by the city council explicitly as a "society": "the so-called Pegnitz shepherd society." And by 1716, there seem to have been some measures taken to restrict membership in the group to those who were officially citizens of Nuremberg, perhaps reflecting an earlier trend.[83] Spahr has pointed out that much work remains to be done on the activities of and influences on members of the Order of Flowers.[84] But it nevertheless seems apparent that the community formed by the Pegnitz "shepherds" was more literal than fictional. The homogeneity of background, schooling, and interest took on concrete form in the texts that society members wrote.

The small size of the Nuremberg society (called by some an "association of poets"—"Dichtervereinigung"—rather than a language society—*Sprachgesellschaft*[85]) indicates that actual discussions among the membership (as opposed to correspondence, as in the case of the Fruit-bearing Society) could have occurred. Between the year it was founded (1644) and the death of the first president, Harsdörffer, in 1658, only fourteen members were admitted, thus allowing for direct and ongoing intellectual and literary exchange.[86] Membership grew almost fourfold only later, during what has been called the "organized" period of the society under Sigmund von Birken's presidency between 1662 and 1681.[87] (Birken is said to have made a concerted effort to interest local poets and intellectuals in the group.[88]) But by 1732, total membership had increased to only 117, perhaps as a result of restrictions on the group by the authorities in Nuremberg, perhaps as the result of exclusionary practices by members of the society itself.[89] In any case, although members of the order eventually all took society names, chose emblematic flower insignia, and wore silk armbands in much the same way as the members of the Fruit-bearing Society, the activities of the group began and in all likelihood remained on obviously more intimate and, perhaps for this reason, more than merely formal terms.[90] There is no evidence, for example, of strict guidelines for membership in the Order of Flowers except in terms of the charge to champion the vernacular, nor that it was as socially prestigious an affair to belong (in spite of Harsdörffer's patrician origins[91]) to the Nuremberg group as to the Fruit-bearing Society at Köthen.

The Poets' Corner (*PoetenStüblein*) on Andreas Ingolstetter's estate may have served as an informal gathering place for local members; after 1678, a Poets' Grove (*Poeten-Wäldlein*), later called the Maze (*Irrhayn*), was completed in Kraftshof, a Nuremberg suburb. The "shepherds" thus had a local sylvan setting where members could in fact meet and conduct the discussions that are repeated in many of the pastoral texts.[92] While it is unclear just how often its membership met officially on society business during the years that spanned Harsdörffer's and Birken's presidencies between 1644 and 1681, it seems obvious from the descriptive passages in the pastorals that the Pegnitz "shepherds" often gathered—perhaps in the Poets' Corner, perhaps in the Maze—to exchange information, compose collective texts for various occasions, and discuss events of relevance to the group.[93] After 1681, official meetings are documented as having occurred only yearly, an indication, nevertheless, of regular exchange.

A sense of genuine community thus seems to emerge here and in the society's collective texts as it does not in the case of the Fruit-bearing Society. Membership in the Nuremberg language society was probably more than a formality, then. Moreover, the creation of and general adherence by society members to a recognizable poetical and theoretical program of linguistic and poetic renewal and standardization—to the general goal, that is, of advancing the vernacular in certain, ultimately normative ways—and to what Spahr has called a "spiritual tendency" associated with a pre-Pietistic, "practical Christianity"[94] are evidence that membership in the "Shepherd Order on the Pegnitz" ("Hirtenorden an der Pegnitz") was probably more than merely formal. The production of remarkably homogeneous texts by society members not only testifies to the literal existence of a community but may have contributed to creating that existence as well.

The tendency of many of the early modern academies to find the origins of absolute moral and linguistic standards in their own immediate contexts and, ultimately, to institutionalize (make normative) their own behavior and language use is vividly demonstrated by the texts of the Nuremberg group. Even though the Order of Flowers was a private organization and received no direct support from the city itself, it was in fact Nuremberg and the local membership of the society that moved into positions of authority in the group's texts. Local practice was to dictate which vernacular and which poetic forms were to be considered obligatory, for example, even as references to German as the original and universal language of Adam and German poetry as divinely inspired crowded the pages of society texts. While traditional in academic discourse, as we have seen, this localization of authority, along with its masking, seems to have made particular sense when the status of the imperial city of Nuremberg itself is considered in more detail.

As an imperial city, Nuremberg had been granted religious tolerance in the accords reached at Augsburg in 1555. This doctrine of religious and hence political impartiality brought with it the power of direct recourse to the emperor in political disputes. It nevertheless did not guarantee the city an unproblematic role in the subsequent century of religious war as local and regional powers took sides and tried to force the city to do the same. The absence of an immediate source of political authority and military protection meant that local authorities, in the form of Nuremberg's town council (*der kleine Rat*), were faced with the task of maintaining a neutral stance in political, religious, and military disputes as the sole means of self-defense.[95] It was thus ultimately issues of local authority and autonomy that were of primary political concern.

The complex history of Nuremberg during the Thirty Years' War was in large part the result of the neutrality granted to the imperial cities in Augsburg in 1555. The Reformation had penetrated quite deeply into Nuremberg (and into many of the imperial cities); the town thus continued to have a largely Protestant population in the late sixteenth and early seventeenth centuries in spite of the city's official "imperial" status. The town council nevertheless understood its leadership role defensively and refused to support the radical Calvinist leaders of the Palatinate in the early years of the next century in their attempt to unite the Protestant estates against the Habsburgs, since such partisanship might easily have provoked a reaction on the part of the emperor as well as among more militant Catholics closer to home.[96] As a result of its carefully observed neutrality and desire for self-preservation, then, Nuremberg waited until 1609 to join the Protestant Union, but soon parted company again under pressure from Vienna in 1621 to return to the imperial fold.[97]

This politics of "defensive neutrality"[98] soon became a political and military liability, however, as battles began to be fought locally, and every military engagement meant a potential siege, if not the sacking of the city, by one or the other side. Throughout the Thirty Years' War, Nuremberg was caught in the crossfire and was often unable to act; the city was surrounded and assaulted more than one hundred times. The situation became so desperate at one point that the town council was forced to attempt to buy off the invading army of Tilly and the Catholic League under the leadership of Maximilian of Bavaria by offering the general the city's cultural patrimony in the form of a number of Dürer's paintings.[99] When, in 1630, Nuremberg joined the Protestant Union under John George of Saxony, the wrath of the emperor was felt once again; the town was forced to withdraw from the union in 1631. Soon thereafter, however, Gustav Adolf of Sweden challenged Nuremberg once again to show its Protestant loyalties by joining the very active and apparently successful Swedish campaign. Gustav Adolf set up his camp in Nuremberg in 1632 and remained there until Wallenstein provoked him into battle at Lützen, where the Swedish liberator fell. The Peace of Prague (1635) found both Saxony and Nuremberg in the imperial camp once again. But the Swedish general Wrangel continued to do battle with Maximilian of Bavaria; as a result, Nuremberg saw conflict up through the last years of the war.

During this entire period, the imperial city of Nuremberg tried to protect itself diplomatically by forbidding its citizens to speak out for one or the other side. The cofounder of the Order of Flowers on the Pegnitz, Harsdörffer, was among those who felt the impact of the city's strict censorship laws during the crucial year of 1648.[100] This neutrality and the fact that Nuremberg was more or less forced to rely on its own resources to assert independence in the context of competing claims for allegiance suggest that it may have become a matter both of local pride and of necessity for the imperial city to become its own agent of survival, to use its own resources, that is, to transcend the military and political conflicts threatening to engulf it. Indeed, the celebrations of peace in Nuremberg in 1649/50, held in honor of the arrangements made in Münster and Osnabrück in 1648, were dedicated, indirectly, just as much to the city's survival strategies as to the "end" of the war. Although not commissioned by the town council, the celebratory festivities at Nuremberg—designed in large part by members of the language society—reproduced *in nuce* the policies of the city. On the one hand, Johann Klaj choreographed the Swedish celebrations at the request of Count Carl Gustav of the Palatinate, later king of Sweden. On the other, Sigmund von Birken was instrumental in staging the banquet arranged by Octavio Piccolomini, the imperial representative.[101] The desire to maintain impartiality made it necessary to use such opportunities to draw opposing forces together in the interest of producing peace. And, indeed, the texts of the celebration quite literally staged the creation of political and religious harmony both within and just outside the city walls, thus allowing a local context to serve as the space of universal accord.

There was a second consequence of the neutrality of the imperial city, however, that proved beneficial to Nuremberg's literary reputation in a more direct way. A policy of religious tolerance in an era of religious war meant that the town attracted large numbers of the homeless—exiles and refugees—who had been forced to leave areas of mercilessly enacted religious persecution. Particularly important to Nuremberg was the great influx of Bohemian Protestants after 1629, when Emperor Ferdinand passed the Edict of Restitution, which returned estates and properties held by Protestants since 1552 into Catholic hands. These refugees often came from well-to-do and well-educated families; many flocked to Nuremberg as a "tolerant city" and center of cultural as well as business activity. On the crossroads of the great north-south trade route and thus a center of commercial exchange, Nuremberg had gained a reputation as a kind of intellectual and economic melting pot.[102] Many of the figures prominent in Nuremberg's cultural affairs at this time belonged to this group, among them Johann Klaj, Catharina Regina von Greiffenberg, and Johann Beer.[103] Also attracted by the city's status since the sixteenth century as a center of the publishing industry, intellectuals from all over Europe could feel comfortable settling there. A certain kind of conformity may have been expected of this population. In any case, the community that formed was itself a fairly homogeneous one, with similar class affiliations and educational backgrounds; it seems to have been able to legislate its own activities informally in a way that the town council could, in most cases, support. Although the relationship between this community and the language society founded in Nuremberg toward the end of the war must still be investigated in greater depth, it is not surprising that the group saw itself, its membership, and its texts as vehicles for the realization of a series of idealizing doctrines in local form, since it was precisely in this context that its origins in the antagonisms of war could be shut out.

Thus both the composition of the membership of the Order of Flowers and its location in Nuremberg distinguished it from the Fruit-bearing Society at Köthen. The urban, rather than courtly, setting, like that of two other language societies, Zesen's German-minded Association (Deutschgesinnete Genossschaft, 1643) in Hamburg and Rist's Order of Swans on the Elbe (Elbschwanenorden, 1658) in Wedel, resulted in a high percentage of membership in the Order of Flowers coming from the bourgeoisie. Nobility was represented only by a very few members of local families whose titles were either very low or newly purchased.[104] Nevertheless, as Hirschmann has made clear, the patrician class in Nuremberg had already begun to stylize itself as equal to the nobility by such strategies as the purchase of estates (*Landgüter*) outside the city walls.[105] The effect of a possible class consolidation among the bourgeoisie both in Nuremberg and elsewhere upon the formation of a literary self-consciousness has been the subject of much debate.[106] The membership of the Nuremberg language society in any case reflects a certain social and intellectual homogeneity that could have been both created by and used as a source of authority for the society's linguistic and poetic practice. Harsdörffer, for example, was a member of the Nuremberg patriciate. While pursuing a career as a civil servant, he translated texts from the Spanish and put together anthologies, collections of fables, an epistolary pattern book, and countless other texts. Harsdörffer became a member of the Fruit-bearing Society in 1642 and cofounded the Nuremberg language society two years later with Johann Klaj.[107] Klaj was born in Meissen and studied in Leipzig, but was forced by political and confessional circumstances to leave his homeland for Nuremberg in 1644.[108] Klaj taught at the school (a *Lateinschule*) connected with the parish of St. Sebaldus in Nuremberg and wrote several spoken operettas (*Redeoratorien*) based on religious subjects as well as a vernacular poetics and a series of celebratory texts in honor of the peace ceremonies in 1649/50. He seems to have been less active in society affairs after 1650, however, when he received a position as rector in Kitzingen.

Sigmund von Birken, the second president of the order, was an émigré like Klaj but shared more with the patrician Harsdörffer in terms of intellectual commitment. Birken came to Nuremberg with his family in 1629, when his father became a Protestant minister there. He studied law, theology, and philology in Jena and returned to Nuremberg in 1645, when he joined the newly formed language society. Although himself originally a member of the bourgeoisie, Birken had the reputation of being a social climber;[109] he had many connections to both noble and aristocratic circles, serving as a tutor to the Wolfenbüttel court between 1645 and 1647 and spending time at Bayreuth in the late 1650s. He was enobled by Ferdinand III in 1655.[110]

Justus Georg Schottelius (1612–76), one of the most influential of the nonresident members of the Nuremberg order, was also a member of the learned bourgeoisie. Born in the town of Einbeck in Lower Saxony, he studied in Leiden, Leipzig, and Wittenberg and then returned to his homeland as a tutor to the sons of nobility. He became a member of the

Order of Flowers in 1645. Like Birken, Schottelius mixed with the nobility, then, although somewhat more successfully than the Nuremberg poet; his influence in Brunswick and Wolfenbüttel, first as tutor, then as consistorial councilor and assistant in the duke's famous library at Wolfenbüttel, created useful links between the Nuremberg language society and the house of Brunswick-Lüneburg.[111]

The other two noteworthy figures in the early history of the Nuremberg group were Johann Michael Dilherr (1604–69) and Johann Hellwig (1609–54). Dilherr, although not officially a member of the Order of Flowers, seems to have been very influential both in promoting the society's members and in influencing the spiritual direction of their thought.[112] He was originally a professor at Jena and came to Nuremberg in 1642, where he taught at the St. Sebaldus school and later helped Klaj to secure a position there. He became minister of St. Sebaldus in 1646, was in charge of the library, was influential in the Nuremberg schools, and sat on the city's censorship board.[113] Hellwig was a Nuremberg doctor who also participated in literary activities. He studied at the nearby university at Altdorf as well as in Strassburg and Montpelier before returning to Nuremberg in 1645, when he became a member of the group.[114]

In 1662, Martin Limburger (1637–92), who had studied medicine and theology at Altdorf and become a "crowned poet" in 1656, joined the order. It was Limburger who was primarily responsible for establishing the Maze in Kraftshof. He became the third president of the society in 1681. Like Harsdörffer and Birken before him, Limburger belonged to a bourgeois learned class with high visibility in Nuremberg.

The uniformity of purpose represented by the society and present in its texts was well served, then, by its rootedness in the culture of Nuremberg. And yet, even as the astounding homogeneity of the social background of the order's membership found expression in society texts, it was nevertheless also hidden by the very universalizing discourses in which the group's linguistic and ethical norms were created and codified. In these texts, then, the (historical) instituting moment is contained within but also masked and transcended by its ongoing, institutionalized (textualized) forms.

The German-language texts sponsored and written by members of the Nuremberg Order of Flowers on the Pegnitz engaged in the work of shifting the location of authority from the absence of the Ancients to the presence of specific conventions, the work to which the early modern academic enterprise as a whole was committed. The Nuremberg texts functioned as institutions in the sense that they provided authoritative origins and an ongoing orthodoxy of structure for the German-language literary tradition. Their arguments about the great age and "natural" authority of German words and poetic forms both highlighted and hid the contextual rootedness of their claims in a discourse of accuracy and authenticity. The Nuremberg texts, while clearly monuments to a local enterprise, to local poetic and linguistic usage, and to a local sociopolitical cause, became separate from their local origins precisely as texts that took on the task of providing linguistic and poetic "law."

In the systematic treatises on language theory and poetics, for example, the German vernacular is described as linked to ancient, naturelike linguistic forms. Contemporary (language society) usage could legitimately be treated as normative if it could be said to reflect these original forms. It became the self-proclaimed job of the Nuremberg language theory texts, then, to catalogue and document the presence of these forms as they survived in the usage of the group, thus literally creating a new version of the ancient, perfect tongue in accessible form. German-language poetic practice, in turn, even as it in fact adhered to a strictly delineated set of socially coded genres, formulaic expressions, and patterned rhyme schemes with their origins in the practice of the group, is said in the society's technical treatises on poetics to be as close to divine inspiration and natural talent as art can be to nature without being nature herself.

These juxtapositions may seem paradoxical. And yet, precisely when linguistic forms, genres, and rhyme schemes become separated from their social origins as they enter textual form, they function not just as products but as productive of absolute (sacred and natural) compositional norms. It thus becomes possible—and, indeed, more effective—for others not present to the specific origins of these textual orthodoxies to consider them laws with which to regulate and authenticate their own (new) composition. The historical moment of origins is thus transcended precisely because of its realization in institutionalized (textual) form.

The lengthy prose-and-verse pastorals (*Schäffereyen*) that many members of the Nuremberg society composed reveal most clearly the mechanics of instituting and institutionalizing, of preserving and surpassing specific conditions of authority in texts. These pastorals locate scenes from the classical pastoral tradition in what are, for the most part, recognizable Nuremberg landscapes. As texts, they illustrate the reality of difference by demonstrating that the "eternal forms" of the genre can only ever be created in and by a specific, historical time. The moment of (past) origin and authority is thus necessarily absent from and yet also always present in the (new) pastoral text. Conversely, the historical specificity of the new grove is automatically transformed in textualization into a moment beyond itself.

These are the three sets of texts—the language theory, the poetological treatises, and the German-language pastorals—that I examine in more detail in the following chapters. Their commitment to the institutionalization of the German language and of German-language poetic forms in a collectively agreed-upon, historically based program and in the transformation of that program into normative behavior in their texts both produced and was produced by the historical event that was the vernacular language society in Nuremberg. Designed, like the British, French, Italian, and other German academies, to gather a community of learned members together to elevate the vernacular to the status of one of the ancient tongues, the program of the Nuremberg Order of Flowers on the Pegnitz both called for and enacted the development of a competitive modern tradition alongside, even in place of, the universal culture of earlier times. On the verge of the Enlightenment and of a notion of human reason that declared that all men had equal access to the "laws of nature" (an access that allegedly "democratized" knowledge and culture), the phenomenon of the German language society was based on the premise that the collective (rather than an individual) would establish where and what exactly these laws were and would communicate this knowledge to and expect the acquiescence of the rest. The origins of the "rational state," a potentially dangerous construct on both the theoretical and the material levels, may well be located here. Representing the need for an internally coherent cultural system based not on reproducing the Ancients but on producing themselves and their historical place in and mark on the world, society members authored texts that demonstrated that their standards were equal to the "truths" of ancient practice and natural law. Historical circumstance and consensus took on concrete, textual form and, in so doing, claimed to be able to act as a source of functionally absolute linguistic and poetic norms.

3   Redemption in the Vernacular

From the Garden to Society Texts

Most accounts of the language theory of the Order of Flowers on the Pegnitz begin by attempting to locate the "origins" of its accounts of the original and orthodox forms of the German vernacular in one of two prior discourses about the nature of language. The first combines the Judeo-Christian and the mystical traditions to posit an "Adamic" or "natural" language capable of naming divine or immanent essences, a "true language" against which the forms of all future, "fallen" or "corrupt" tongues must be measured. The second stems from the Graco-Roman philosophical discussion of the "natural" versus "conventional" origins of linguistic meaning (*phusei/thesei*), a discussion that centered on the debate about whether names inhered in objects or were posited by humans, whether language was characterized by metaphysical necessity, in other words, or whether it came into being and was established as a human (historical) act.[1]

There has been considerable controversy as to which of these traditions formed the "true" basis of Nuremberg language theory.[2] What emerges from the texts themselves, however, both the lengthy "histories" of German told in works such as Schottelius's massive *Ausführliche Arbeit von der teutschen HaubtSprache* (a detailed account of German as a principal tongue; cited hereafter as *Account*) (1663) and from the many translation, dictionary, and cataloguing projects called for and undertaken by members of the Order of Flowers on the Pegnitz, is that both of these discourses were influential in defining Pegnitz language theory *as a process of institutionalization* whose goal was to found and organize the future of linguistic practice in German. Both discourses located the origins of the vernacular in a privileged, sacred, and natural sphere; thus both provided a clearly historical language with solid foundations and first causes in a transcendent realm.

On the basis of such authoritative origins, the language theory texts,

texts in which these origins were to be catalogued by society members for the first time, could in turn regulate and provide models for ongoing practice. At times, the two traditions are so interwoven in Nuremberg writings as to be indistinguishable, not surprisingly so, given the eclectic nature of the language theory of significant predecessors and the encyclopedic approach that Schottelius, Harsdörffer, and others took.[3] At other times, one or the other of these strands of thought is strategically highlighted in the context of a particular concept, as Kayser and others have shown, in the interest of making the strongest case possible for a superior German tongue.[4] And yet, of central importance to an analysis of Nuremberg language theory texts as institutions is the manner in which they located themselves *as textual events that could "make history"* in these two discourses and how as a result they were conceived of as capable of founding and codifying the pure forms of the German tongue.

Much Nuremberg language theory is concerned, then, with constructing and situating the society project for linguistic purification and standardization within an elaborate foundational narrative based on locating the origins of human language and specifically of German in the Garden of Eden and in Nature herself. The narrative is heavily indebted to the Judeo-Christian "story" of the *lingua adamica*, the original tongue of man, and is designed to endow the (historical) instituting moment of the language society with the authority to serve as the origin of a new, standardized tongue. At the same time, the regulatory texts of the society (such as the dictionaries and the models for future German-language poetry in translations produced under society sponsorship) and the very discourse of authority that the theorists developed for themselves as authors of these regulatory texts functioned as examples of this standardized tongue as it was used by the language theorists themselves. As (historical) monuments, the regulatory texts of the society thus testified to their own origins in the conventions of a particular group while at the same time transcending those origins both as texts and as law.

It is not by chance that the figure of Martin Luther plays an important role in both the foundational and regulatory discourses. As we shall see, his translation of Scripture into German in the early sixteenth century was perceived as a textual event with great explanatory value. Nuremberg language theory may be understood, then, as working to provide a space for the creation of a new historical period by creating a new and renewed German language. It did this work in and as these two kinds of textual events, the narrative and the monumental/regulatory. By both instituting and institutionalizing a purified and standard vernacular tongue, Nuremberg language theory demonstrated the power of the text to be historically creative, to "make history" as it created a new stage of the foundational narrative, a role for the language theorists in that narrative, and a new set of vernacular norms.

Institutiones Linguae: The Origins of Language and the Original Language

In 1644, the year in which the Order of Flowers on the Pegnitz was founded, Georg Philipp Harsdörffer, its first president, wrote to another German poet, Philipp von Zesen, in response to a letter from Zesen asking Harsdörffer to join his new language society, the German-minded Association. Harsdörffer's words are exemplary of Nuremberg language theory. He explains that although he is not yet familiar with the statutes of Zesen's society and thus is unable to comment on them specifically, he is sure that the project will be worthy of his approval and membership

> insofar as I understand the goal of this association to be the following, namely, that German, as a principal language [die deutsche Hauptsprache], ought to be elevated from its [her] foundations [Gründen] to its [her] majestic throne of honor by means of the steady [strong] hand of a trustworthy assembly [Zusammensetzung].[5]

Harsdörffer's words sketch the parameters of his own society's language theory at the same time as they describe what he assumes are the standards of Zesen's group. They do so by highlighting several stages in a complex narrative about the identity of the German vernacular, a narrative that, like the "history" of national languages being told across Europe at the time, told the story of the sacred and timeless perfection of the mother tongue, on the one hand, and of its aptness to its particular, historical context, on the other. This narration was an instituting event in two senses: it provided German with a transcendent origin even as it called into existence the very language whose past it claimed to explain. The vernacular language whose story is told in much seventeenth-century language theory is thus said not only to participate in sacred history by being defined as a new sacred tongue but even to improve upon that history precisely by defining its transcendence as unbounded rather than as bounded, as capable of expanding into the present in the form of the language used in the texts of the Nuremberg group.[6]

The assumption of the instituting power of the *written text* behind Harsdörffer's words must be emphasized here. In counterdistinction to

Plato's apparent suggestion in the *Cratylus* that the most authentic human language was a spoken one, the language theorists of the seventeenth century believed that the creation of new beginnings and standards for an authentic German language would be achieved in vernacular texts written under the direction of an elite group of learned men such as those organized in both Zesen's and Harsdörffer's groups. The production of such texts was one of their main goals.

This shift to a belief in the power of texts to create authenticity in language is not as directly contradictory of Plato's argument as it may initially seem, however. For the seventeenth-century language theorists, the suggestion that texts could contain an authentic form of language merely reformulated one hundred years later Luther's claim to have captured the "true" Word of God in his translation into German of the Bible, a translation based, as he claims, on the vernacular as spoken "in the streets," but which he explicitly defends as a textual event in his "Sendbrief vom Dolmetschen" (Letter on translating) (1530).[7] For subsequent generations, Luther's translation of Scripture provided a textual milestone, proof that a German Bible, in all of its concrete specificity in easily reproducible printed form, could in fact create and disseminate a divinely sanctioned form of the vernacular. This form of the vernacular would in turn become standard precisely because it was widely available in print (this argument is developed in detail in the section "Textual Foundations: The Dictionary and Translation Projects of the Nuremberg Order").

In imitation of Luther, the language theorists of the societies sought to institute and institutionalize an authentic form of German in and as not one but two different kinds of explicitly textual events. The first consisted, as I have indicated, in the telling of a foundational narrative about German implicitly based on reference to Luther and on an argument that describes the "first causes" of the vernacular as part of a (divine and organic) realm beyond time. After explaining the terms of this narrative as they are used in Harsdörffer's letter to Zesen, I will discuss the background of his call for concrete regulatory texts, the second kind of textual institution, at greater length.

Harsdörffer's assumptions about the goals of the vernacular language society revolve around the claim that only a unified German language—rather than one of the numerous local dialects that were in fact spoken in central Europe in the sixteenth and seventeenth centuries—can provide the mother tongue with instituting and institutionalized forms. His claims for the power of this (if not mythical, then at least anachronistic) uniform language become clear as he describes it. In his *Poetischer Trichter*

(The poet's funnel) he defines the German with which the society is to be concerned as a "principal tongue" (*Hauptsprache*), one of the main languages of humanity that, in the imagination of the language theorists of the sixteenth and seventeenth centuries, originated in biblical times. Identifying German as a principal tongue already endowed it with foundational authority because in the logic of historical linguistics of the period, contemporary language groups were said to find their paradigmatic origins in the "principal" scriptural tongues of Greek, Hebrew, and Latin, which were theoretically just as capable of fulfilled representation as their precursor, model language, spoken by Adam, had been.[8] Luther's Bible translations of the 1520s and 1530s were said to have created a "new" principal tongue in German. Thus, the material existence of a German Scripture demonstrated that a further stage of sacred history had been made possible, another principal tongue added and made part of the original, divinely sanctioned triad.[9]

When Harsdörffer writes, then, of German as a principal tongue in his letter to Zesen, he endows it with "founding" power based on textual events that had transpired some one hundred years prior to the establishing of the first German language society. His words nevertheless indicate that there is still recovery work to be done, since the German principal tongue does not currently exist. The vernacular had, it seems, "entered history" by lapsing into disuse and becoming corrupted after Luther's time. The task of the language society would be to take this "historical" language and re-create its "original" identity as a principal tongue, thus inaugurating yet another sacred phase in the here-and-now. Hence the society's "strong hand" in achieving vernacular renewal was necessary. German's "foundations" ("Gründe") must be elevated to their proper position of prestige, the vernacular restored to its status as one of the blessed languages of humanity by "founding" it anew. This redemptive work was to be accomplished by a committed, collective effort on the part of the language society to "convene" and define its own linguistic conventions, now posited as divine, as "new" absolute norms to be codified in society texts. It would be a "historical" effort, in other words, to both make and transcend "history" by making the sacred present in a new and authoritative textual form.

The narrative about the identity of the vernacular implicit in Harsdörffer's words not only created the possibility of a new moment of linguistic history but also institutionalized (created orthodoxies) in this sense: it linked the divine origins and essential purity of an authentic, German principal tongue with standardized vernacular usage as it was to be established by the language society in a particular time and place. On the basis of this link with the sacred, society usage was thus able to define itself as exemplary, standard, and correct. The call for the codification of German as a principal tongue in texts was crucial, then, both to its definition as an original language (in association with Luther's German) and to its ongoing regulatory power, since texts by society members, written in a sociohistorically specific language, were to be not just monuments to their own moment of origins (as Luther's translations had been) but would also transcend it precisely as texts and as providers of linguistic norms. Identifying German as a principal tongue—and suggesting that it could be both divine and historical, both transcendent and immediately available in society usage at one and the same time—meant that the existence and authority of the sacred were no longer limited to unchanging patterns and a timeless sphere but could, rather, also become real in changing historical contexts, in new language formations, and in their very capacity to be produced in and as a new (historical) textual event.

The implications for Nuremberg language theory of the narrative about German embedded in Harsdörffer's words may be best explored by examining the narrative's origins in the more familiar Judeo-Christian discourse about the origin, corruption, and restoration to perfection of the language of humanity.

The biblical account of the origin of language provided the most significant framework for the language theorists of the German Baroque in articulating their narrative of a language that was both transcendentally accurate and historically powerful. It is referred to explicitly in the Nuremberg texts. According to this account, both man and his language originated in the Garden. "Yahweh God planted a garden in Eden, which is in the east, and there he put the man he had fashioned" (Genesis 2:8–9). "Yahweh God said, 'It is not good that the man should be alone. I will make him a helpmate.' So from the soil Yahweh God fashioned all the wild beasts and all the birds of heaven. These he brought to the man to see what he would call them; each one was to bear the name the man would give it" (Genesis 2:18–20) ("Denn wie der Mensch allerley lebendige Thier nennen würde/so solten sie heissen").[10] In the Christian history of language, this first act of naming represents the origin of all human language. The *lingua adamica* was *the* first and original tongue (*Ursprache*). As such, it provided a standard of linguistic perfection.

Adam's words are defined here as possessing authority because they are divinely sanctioned. At the same time, however, the description of their origins in the human act of naming makes clear that the accuracy and fitness of any language are measurable only against the standard of effective representation and thus only in terms of language's function as a communicative tool. The road to a nationalist language theory, to the assertion of vernacular languages as sacred tongues, is opened here. God may have "fashioned" the beasts and the birds, but their existence for humans was realized only in language. Adam in effect created the beasts, the birds, and the world for humanity as he named them; the origins of human language as rhetoric and thus the necessity to create a new language in every new historical context are thus located in the biblical account. Accurate not because it was divinely inspired nor even because it reproduced God's work, the *lingua adamica* was an original—an originating and creative—language because it endowed God's work with existence by naming it in language apt to the sublunar realm.

The story of Adam's language plays out a fiction of origins that, in its claim for the original duty of linguistic signs not to re-present but to present essences to Man for the first time, was read by those involved in the language society project as a moment that legitimated their own foundational effort to establish norms. By associating German with Adam's language, they were able to locate the origins of their own (contextually apt) language in a realm of first causes other than the context of the here-and-now precisely by appealing to a biblical story that argued in principle for the contextual accuracy of language and thus for its ongoing power to "re-found." Moreover, they found in that narrative not only a logic upon which to base the prestige of vernacular languages but, perhaps more importantly, the sacred "otherness" that could provide their own project with an authoritative origin beyond time.

The story of the sacred, Adamic "original" or "originary" tongue (*Ursprache*) thus held within itself a surprisingly "historical" standard of absolute linguistic aptness. On the basis of this standard, the originating function of Adam's language—its creation of the meaning of the Creation for Man for the first time—could be made to account for the legitimacy of linguistic diversity so crucial to theorists of vernacular tongues in the humanist era, since the ability to communicate in a language appropriate to a particular context of reception (rather than represent prior essences) could be understood as defining linguistic authenticity in the biblical tale. The power of the original, sacred tongue to do precisely this kind of creative work reemerges, moreover, in a subsequent stage of the biblical narrative about language, namely, the story of Pentecost, a stage read by theorists of vernacular languages as strengthening the link between a realm of origins (whose authority was based on its being "other" than any particular historical moment) and the originality and legitimacy of each new, historical language group. The story of Pentecost highlights the importance of the ongoing need to "create" the reality of God's Creation for Man in language by embedding in the divine plan itself the reality of different languages and thus the necessity of different linguistic formations of the divine.

In the Fall, Man lost access to the perfection that characterized both his Edenic existence and the prelapsarian tongue. At the same time, however, he gained an awareness of his own temporality and the crucial role that linguistic difference had to play in releasing the sacred from the garden and in making it available in postlapsarian time. The story of the Confusion of Tongues at Babel (Genesis 11:3–9) recounts this linguistic "Fall" and thus accounts for the presence (albeit initially a negative one) of linguistic variety. But the concept and, indeed, even postfigural reality of linguistic difference are redeemed by the Gift of Tongues. Legitimated by the Holy Spirit, a pluralized form of the universal language of the Garden thus supersedes the fallen linguistic diversity at Babel. Its authority is defined, moreover, by its extension of a collectively agreed-upon version of the divine message beyond the confines of the original apostolic group, by its ability, that is, to extend the (atemporal) authority of the original Word beyond its moment of origins into historical time:

> When Pentecost day came round, they all met in one room [waren... alle einmütig bey einander], when suddenly they heard what sounded like a powerful wind from heaven, the noise of which filled the entire house in which they were sitting; and something appeared to them that seemed like tongues of fire; these separated [zerteilet] and came to rest on the head of each of them. They were all filled with the Holy Spirit [vol des heiligen Geistes], and began to speak foreign languages as the Spirit gave them the gift of speech. (Acts 2:1–4)

The link to a privileged origin is maintained here through the reference to the visitation of the Spirit. And yet, it was only in the group's unanimity ("einmütig"), in its convening and conventions, and in the ability to establish for itself in its own time the "truth" of God's Word that the divine could become real in human form. The necessity of human cooperation in producing the divine thus emerges at Pentecost, as the Apostles "perform" a collective *imitatio Christi*, their words reproducing the Word in multiple forms and thus "beginning" (indeed, creating) the universal message of Christ. Both the authority of the original collective and the subsequent division ("zerteilet") of that collective from its original moment made it possible for that moment to function as an authoritative (because absent) point of reference in the spreading of the Word.

That the Pentecostal division did not "reflect" but rather itself actually "created" the universality of God's message by allowing it to "become real" in multiple tongues becomes clear as the message is spread:

> Now there were devout men living in Jerusalem from every nation under heaven, and at this sound they all assembled, each one bewildered to hear these men speaking his own language... "Surely" they said "all these men speaking are Galileans?... [W]e hear them preaching in our own language about the marvels of God" [Wir hören sie mit vnsern Zungen/die grossen Thaten Gottes reden]. (Acts 2:5–12)

Thus both the consensus of the original group ("einmütig bei einander" [of one mind together]), defined by the group as the "true" understanding of God's works, and the rendering of that consensus in multiple languages are as instrumental in making God's marvels universal as the marvels themselves, since it was literally the various linguistic renderings of the marvels that produced a unified understanding of the original spiritual message (itself produced by convening) in a variety of nations. The universal community of believers thus came into existence only when "truth" was accommodated to the conventions of new language groups. The "separation" of the Holy Spirit into diverse tongues at Pentecost reinscribes Adam's original act of naming into a larger arena of cultural and linguistic difference by defining the accuracy of God's message in language as a matter of rhetoric, in terms, that is, of its efficacy in the context in which it was used.

In concluding this section on the biblical narrative that formed one part of the background of language society linguistic theory, I would argue, then, that for the vernacular language theorists of the early modern period, the Gift of Tongues at Pentecost represented a doctrine organized around the concept of *contextualism* in language, a doctrine that permitted the existence of "naturally" pure and linguistically accurate vernacular tongues. This concept and its incorporation in language society texts will become central in the analysis of Nuremberg language theory below.

The Gift of Tongues reconfirmed the standards of linguistic accuracy set by Adam's tongue, namely, that the presence of the divine for humans can be created only in language. At the same time, however, this very first standard of linguistic accuracy depended on human comprehension and thus on the possibility of extending the sacred into the sublunar realm. The (historical) recuperation of that divine moment in the convening of the Apostles and in the Gift of Tongues made it possible for a postfigural, historical collective like the language society to function as yet another context that could describe its own establishing of the terms of the divine message as accurate, authoritative, and "true." While commemorating this context in their use of particular (their own) linguistic forms, language society texts also in fact transcended it precisely by identifying the vernacular as a new, sacred language capable of originating norms.

The Judeo-Christian tradition provided early modern language theorists with a narrative structure that explained the fall of human language from a state of singularity and perfection into a realm of legitimate and even necessary linguistic diversity. It also provided a logic that defined both the original Adamic language and the Pentecostal tongues as themselves constitutive of God's message rather than as dependent on its preexistence. Much Nuremberg language theory was concerned with situating German in this narrative. It was the *classical* tradition of language theory, however, that provided the implicit philosophical framework within which the society project of institutionalization, the rational construction by society members of guidelines for the composition of dictionaries and other exemplary texts, can best be understood.[11] It was the logic of this second tradition from which the strategies of establishing a standardized German tongue in language society texts were derived, even as the authority to standardize found its source in reference to Judeo-Christian ideas.

For many, the discussion of linguistic fitness that occurs in Plato's dialogue *Cratylus* stands at the beginning of a philosophical tradition that attempts to explain the presence of discontinuities in language and to provide for the possibility of correcting them by establishing rational and collectively agreed-upon patterns of stability and control.[12] Both Plato's and Aristotle's theories of language are framed in the terms used in the *Cratylus* and are referred to explicitly in the language theory texts of the Order of Flowers on the Pegnitz. Plato's and Aristotle's discussions about the natural versus conventional origins of language are interwoven with the Nuremberg assertions of German's relationship to the language of the biblical narrative.[13] The *Cratylus* in fact encodes much the same story as the Christian narrative of a perfect tongue that falls into history and difference but whose original accuracy can be redeemed—indeed, re-created—in the here-and-now. The privileged moment of collective activity in the biblical narrative is replaced here, however, by a "legislative" act.

And yet, in both cases, it is precisely the authority of a set of contextually based linguistic laws that is at stake.

As Plato's *Cratylus* opens, Hermogenes asserts that "there is [no] principle of correctness in names other than convention and agreement [syntheke kai homologia]" (384d). "There is no name given to anything by nature; all is convention [nomos] and habit of the users" (384e). Hermogenes' statements initiate a wide-ranging discussion of correctness in language that ends by describing categories of convention that, in the absence of a "true" language, can be substituted for natural accord. Socrates, unwilling to accept the Protagorean relativism of standards implicit in Hermogenes' stance, namely, that "man is the measure of all things" (386a), forces the younger man to admit that there are real (that is, not merely rhetorical) distinctions between, for example, the wise and the foolish. If essences are permanent, Socrates argues, in "the relation prescribed by nature" (386e) and if naming a thing is an action proceeding from that thing in the "natural way" (387a), then "names ought to be given according to a natural process, and with a proper instrument" (387d) in order to "distinguish things according to their nature" (388b). Thus, according to Socrates, Hermogenes' reliance on convention in naming—if it reflects a doctrine of arbitrary naming—is an untenable strategy with which to guarantee accuracy in language. It then becomes Socrates' task to develop a way of ensuring accuracy in the relationship between nature and linguistic signs. In the long run, it is convention (albeit of a different kind) upon which he comes to rely.

Socrates succeeds in forcing his interlocutor to recant the concept of idiosyncratic naming in favor of name-giving as a "natural process." But he offers a definition of this process that combines the concept of epistemological certainty and philosophical accuracy in language with a doctrine of *contextualism*, or accommodation to external circumstance, in naming. Language is an instrument, Socrates explains. Like any instrument, it does work, but it only does so effectively when handled by the skilled and according to the law. The word for law here is *nomos* (388d), the very same word used by Hermogenes to mean "habit" or convention in 384e.[14] The "maker of names," the "legislator," is a "skilled artisan" (389a), Socrates explains, who "know[s] how to put the true natural name of each thing into sounds and syllables, and [how] to make and give all names with a view to the ideal name" (389d). This legislator, Socrates concludes, must be directed in his task of determining the "ideal name" by the one most able to determine the name that "each thing by nature has" (390e) by following the "law," namely, the "dialectician," or philosopher (390d). Thus, "naturalness," or accuracy, in naming is the result of and will produce epistemological certainty if, and only if, it is the result of the kind of intellectual speculation used by the philosopher to penetrate to the form of the thing named. Reason distinguishes the philosopher's use of language from merely idiosyncratic naming, then. What he posits as natural becomes nature; the dialectician's convention functions, in other words, as law. Linguistic signs are thus neither universal nor absolute; they do not inhere in the object and thus cannot be intuited in a random or unmediated way. And yet, in the crucial Platonic distinction between substance and form, the "law" of proper naming, based on "skill" ("techne," 388d), may be properly said to "be natural, or no less real than nature," only when linguistic signs are not "natural" but, rather, are "products of mind" (*Laws*, 10.890d). Laws and the linguistic norms established on the basis of them are thus also only conventional; but the conventions upon which they are based are closer to "truth" than any nonrational act because they reflect an "art," a *techne*, a set of logical principles.[15] A philosophically correct "art" of naming—even though it too is only conventional—will thus guarantee the production of a "natural" language.

Socrates' theory of philosophical fitness in language defines a new kind of convention different from habit; it is a legislative principle (*nomos*) equivalent to nature. He uses this concept to go on to explain the possibility of diversity, of geographical and historical variety in language, while at the same time taking care not to compromise his assertion of the possibility of epistemological truth. Plato thus offers a philosophical foundation for the doctrine of linguistic contextualism in the dialogue, a doctrine that permits and, indeed, requires variation in language in order for the principle of "natural" linguistic accuracy to be maintained. He does so in the following way: A substantial part of the *Cratylus* consists in etymological exercises concerned with establishing the "true meaning" of a series of Greek names and words; these investigations have the effect of creating the origins or building blocks of a "pure" Greek language in the text. Plato is of course not so parochial as to suggest in the dialogue that only Greek words can represent the "true" nature of things. To the contrary. Like the smith who fashions the instruments of his trade according to an ideally adequate form but not always "of the same iron," legislators will always give names "with a view to the ideal name" even though "different legislators will not [always] use the same syllables" (389d). For the smith, Socrates explains, the "form must be the same, but the material may vary, and still the instrument may be equally good of whatever iron made, whether in Hellas or in a foreign country—there is no difference."

And the legislator, whether he be Hellene or barbarian, is not therefore to be deemed by you a worse legislator, provided he gives the true and proper form of the name in whatever syllables—this or that country makes no matter. (389e–390a)

It is thus possible to establish "true" and "proper" names while also allowing for a concept of difference and linguistic diversity in the form of different "legislators" and "laws." By arguing in this way, Plato anticipates the discourse of Renaissance and Baroque theorists of language. Variety in language "makes no matter." Rather, truth combined with propriety— or appropriateness to context—can yield viable vernacular norms. Plato can thus acknowledge both nature and convention (or law, *nomos*) as means of guaranteeing accuracy in naming (perhaps in spite of himself) as he integrates history and the possibility of difference into his definition of "truth" in language. For Plato—as for the Nuremberg language theorists many years later—arriving at the true names of things in accordance with their nature is based on the notion of rational, "legislated" understanding, of arbitrated, rather than arbitrary, norms.

At the same time as Socrates' reasoning in Plato's *Cratylus* combines philosophical propriety with the legitimately diverse expression of that propriety in different languages, it also uses the doctrine of "natural fitness" and its ultimate reliance on convention to motivate one further aspect of Platonic language theory. Large sections of the *Cratylus* concern a mysteriously indefinite "old language" and its "ancient" and "original forms" (418b–418d). With the "lapse of ages" and the intrusion of foreign words, this old language has become so unfamiliar as to appear to be "a barbarous tongue" (421d). And yet, the second half of the dialogue in fact attempts to recuperate and make textually present whatever possible of this "ancient tongue" on the basis of an investigation of "primary names" (422c) and of the "primitive or first nouns" (433d). These are the closest, save a language of gesture, to "representations of things" (433e). If it is true, as Socrates and his interlocutors seem to assume, that there was a "primitive" or "first" accurate language, which has merely been obscured by time, its retrieval and codification would be the task of the linguistic "legislator," who, with the help of the dialectician, would develop a "law" (elsewhere Socrates calls it a "new" or "higher method"—422b, 425c) according to which the "truth" of these "primary elements" and their "proper forms" could be agreed upon and made accessible once again (422b).

We are reminded here of the Judeo-Christian Adamic language, itself a "first tongue," whose "truth" had to be restored. There must be dialecticians for each language, according to Socrates, whose purpose it would be to ensure the recovery of the "proper forms" of the historical tongues. By implication each language, if established according to the conventions or prevailing law of its legislators, could come to reflect "truth," the "nature" of its own ancient original; classificatory texts like the *Cratylus* would provide "catalogues" of these "truths." It is upon a version of this Platonic logic and upon the kind of textual event that the *Cratylus* itself was that the Nuremberg language theorists based their production of texts in German that would recover and preserve the "ancient" and "original" forms of their own tongue. These texts would be monuments to both these "first forms" and to the very process of recovering them as a historical event. Precisely as catalogues, however, these texts would outlive their moment of origin as they became the first forms of future linguistic orthodoxy.

The Christian narrative of linguistic fitness is an *instituting* narrative; it begins with an "original" moment of normative naming beyond and before time and ends with the necessity of new forms of expression to create, maintain, and extend the authority of those "timeless" origins into the here-and-now. Plato's *Cratylus* explains the simultaneity of nature and convention in language and itself provides a textual example of how to *institutionalize* language by cataloguing the original forms of an accurate language. In both texts, consensus and context—spiritual, philosophical, and linguistic—take over from and take on the power of inspiration and intuition, of the divine and the natural, as guarantors of accuracy in human speech. The arch that both accounts of the origins of language make from nature and transcendence to socially based and constructed linguistic norms marks the path that the language theorists of the seventeenth century followed in producing texts that could serve as founding and regulatory institutions for them. The origins of language in transcendence had to be made (narratologically) absent, on the one hand, so that their foundational authority could be maintained. They had to be made present in the texts of the society, on the other, in order to signal the beginning of and the opening of a space for a new tradition and time.

In the account of Nuremberg language theory that follows, I argue that the texts of the language society deliberately define the pure forms of the vernacular as both absent and present by locating German both within the biblical narrative (and its corollary, the story of German as a "natural language") and within an argument about the establishing of an authentic language rooted in Platonic logic. The fall of an ancient, natural German tongue into confused human form was thus to be rectified by the creation of a pure and accurate vernacular in texts authored by society knights. The telling of the story of German as a redeemed tongue and its "legislation" as standardized High German occurred in and as a series of instituting and institutionalizing textual events. For purposes of clarity, I analyze these various events sequentially, even though they are often simultaneous and indeed mutually reenforcing in the texts themselves. A succession of metaphorical affinities and equivalencies marks the stages in the development of a *foundational discourse* about German that ranges from its affiliation with the original, Adamic tongue (*Ursprache*) to its intrinsic identity as a natural tongue (*Natursprache*). These foundations are then identified as the essential elements of a standardized High German (*Hochsprache*), which is itself to become institutionalized in society usage and, in particular, in the society's explicitly regulatory texts (dictionaries and translations).

The sources for High German are identified, moreover, as being located in society texts themselves as well as in Luther's language, in the language of the imperial court, and in chancery language. Thus contemporary usage gains the authority of the lost German principal tongue and provides the building blocks for a future, standardized vernacular. In the chiastic logic of society conventionality, language theory texts do the work of testifying to and commemorating the usage of a particular (historical) collective (of German speakers) and thus establish a standard of language use that gives historical shape to the divine and transcendent in much the same way as the Adamic, apostolic, and Platonic languages were said to have done.

The Doctrine of Contextualism in Nuremberg Language Theory

Both the story of the Gift of Tongues at Pentecost and Plato's *Cratylus* make the question of the fitness of language for representation in a particular context the center of a debate about the "natural" origins of linguistic legitimacy. It is the construction of a doctrine of *contextualism* in Nuremberg language theory texts and its indebtedness to these two prior discourses about language that I explore first before moving on to an analysis of the foundational narrative about the German vernacular. Explanations of what I call contextualism in fact often coincide in the Nuremberg language theory texts with references to the biblical narrative. But the theory itself is, I believe, in fact conceptually prior to the narrative of divine origins. I thus treat it here first and separately because it provides the necessary precondition for the argument that links language society German with the Adamic tongue and with the legitimate linguistic diversity of Pentecost.

Justus Georg Schottelius, the member of the Order of Flowers on the Pegnitz most often associated with the group's language theory, describes German as rooted in nature, in terms of both reference and reception, at the opening of his *Account* (1663).[16] In a statement that seems almost to animate the organic realm by imputing an intention to it, he writes, "Whatever nature would have us understand [verstehen] we are able to repeat after nature" (*Account*, 1:12). Schottelius's emphasis here may seem to rest on the vernacular as originating in nature. And yet, it is the *context* of human understanding ("verstehen") out of which the "Germanness" of German arises. He continues:

> The firmest and most central foundations [HaubtGründe] of our language . . . thus command us to form words and to express things: moreover, a German disposition [soul] is naturally capable of understanding [vernehmen] such German words easily and, by means of them, also imagining [comprehending] very clearly [gar vernemlich] in his mind [Bildung] the many variations in earthly existence. (*Account*, 1:13)

Here, too, the origins of linguistic accuracy lie in clear understanding; in turn (and tautologically), clear understanding (rather than accurate reference) guarantees that a "natural" form of German has been used. German speakers can thus rest assured about the authenticity of their tongue, because in the very *fact of speaking* a comprehensible German, they represent both nature's will and the "historical fact" of "the many variations in earthly existence." It is thus language's rhetorical power to accommodate itself to changing historical contexts that defines its authority, its power to "create" nature accurately in the speaker's mind.

Underlying this assumption of a rhetorical definition of linguistic accuracy is a *historiographical* theory of contextualism crucial to Nuremberg language theory. It is this theory—structurally indebted to the logic of Pentecost but articulated separately from it in the language theory texts—upon which the foundational narrative associating German with the *lingua adamica* is based. If historical change (the "many variations") can be revealed as evidence of a divine plan, then different (geographical and cultural) contexts can be said to constitute the necessary prerequisites for the human experience of (that plan's) transcendence. The model allows for linguistic diversity to serve as proof of divinity precisely because it demonstrates that the universal truths of revelation must be accommodated to specific, historical contexts (as the Gift of Tongues had demonstrated long before) in order for them to be universal at all.

In terms that allude to the historiographical subtext underlying Schottelius's description of a philosophically accurate and specifically German tongue, Harsdörffer writes, for example, of a prior, divinely ordained plan of geographical difference designed to ensure cultural and historical change. This plan foresaw and provided for diversity in language:

> The most wise Creator of this universe differentiated between the earthly landmasses [Erden] with lofty mountains, separated them with extensive oceans, and divided them with many slender rivers. [And He] wanted to know [that] the inhabitants of these areas [would exist] in unequal [incommensurate] constitution [being] [with one another], this by means of [different] languages and customs. (*Funnel*, 1:123)

According to this narrative of the Creation, geographical as well as demographic discontinuities together with the resulting discontinuities in language are all part of an original plan.

Apparently random reasons for linguistic imperfection do exist, Harsdörffer admits: "The languages became mixed partially because of the victories and defeats of war and partially because of commerce with foreign nations" (*Colloquies*, 2:49). But even this purely human mismanagement of business, politics, and linguistic affairs in fact reflects divine volition. He writes:

> Now since everything that we humans possess persists in a constant state of changeability, it is not at all surprising that with the destruction of the tribes of Man by—at times necessary, at times freely chosen— migration, wars, victories, and defeats, their languages have gone wrong and ended up in all manner of mutation, contamination, and error. If this world itself is so changeable, how is one to maintain or approve any amount of constancy in a single, fleeting sound of a word? (*Funnel*, 2:123–24)

Even the forces of human diversification are the result, then, of the changeability imposed on humanity by God. And the beginnings of all languages, no matter how varied, are rooted in it. "If all national and principal tongues have been subject to such changes, how could then our German language alone have escaped them?" Harsdörffer asks (*Funnel*, 3:3).

Like Harsdörffer, Schottelius admits that there may be what appear to be specifically human reasons for linguistic discontinuity. Yet these are subordinate to larger factors such as the very arrangement of human time:

> There are three main reasons for the disintegration and mutation that usually occurs in every language: The first is the course and demise of time [the ages] itself [themselves] . . . The second main reason is the intermixing and confusion of races and inhabitants . . . The third main reason for the changes experienced by the national tongues is the careless, unreflected, and unobserved uncertainty of common speech. (*Account*, 1:166)

It is a principle of contextualism that lies, I would argue, behind the first two reasons Schottelius gives for linguistic change. But the third reason for linguistic mutability, equated here with the inarticulate habit and uncertainty of common speech, is not part of the systematic or motivated change that contextualism guarantees. Random usage is impermissible because it is incomprehensible even to those within a specific language group; it thus does not fulfill the rhetorical expectations of accuracy in language. Historical variety in language is legitimate, however, when it seeks certainty rather than uncertainty, when it becomes an expression (indeed, a realization) of an original, divine plan of contextual aptness.

According to the preexistent plan that both Schottelius and Harsdörffer describe, both human mutability and linguistic variety are divinely sanctioned events. To initiate a new language appropriate to the here-and-now was to extend this original plan by giving it substance in the present. Explanations of a primal and comprehensive design for human history such as these allowed Nuremberg language theorists to acknowledge their own and their language's historicity while also constructing this very historicity, individuality, and timeliness in such a way that the vernacular could be said to be playing a role prescribed by a timeless script. "This fleeting and vain world consists," Harsdörffer writes, "in unchanging changeability . . . Is it any surprise, then, that Man's language . . . cannot escape [this] constant change, [indeed, cannot escape] change as its fate?" (*Funnel*, 3:1–3). Much Nuremberg language theory is concerned with telling the story of a universe defined by a divinely motivated inevitability of change. By telling this story about German *in German*, moreover, in their own German texts, the Nuremberg theorists could locate their manifestly historical vernacular within a framework of transcendence even as they created that framework and established its validity in those very same texts. Continuity and change, a divine plan and self-empowerment to produce their own future, could coexist and coincide in specifically German linguistic forms.

An additional aspect of the historiographical model that the Nuremberg language theorists articulated for themselves, an aspect crucial to the institutionalizing ability of the language theory texts, was a chronological argument about an original, prehistorical linguistic moment in an ancient, "time immemorial" ("Uraltertum") before God's plan for diversity in human tongues began to take effect. This prior moment is often conflated in society texts with the origin of human language in the Garden of Eden. And yet its chronological priority and fundamental difference from that origin, its difference, that is, even from Adam's language, is crucial. The metaphorics of *Uraltertum* encountered so often in Nuremberg language theory describe a period whose very inaccessibility and thus absence guaranteed its authority for the present. And it was upon a renewal in the present of an apt form of the language associated with this ancient period that the power of society texts to found a new era and tongue would be based.

A clearly distinguishable metaphorical constellation of "ancientness" locates the roots of the German language in an ambiguously defined old, primeval, and "original" ("Ur-") period, a time before (human) memory, perhaps even before the divine plan itself. Johann Klaj, cofounder of the Order of Flowers on the Pegnitz, explains that the ancientness of the German language is itself a "figure of eternity."[17] Prince Ludwig of Anhalt-Köthen, the first president of the Fruit-bearing Society, describes his society's goals in terms so close to the Nuremberg discussion of an ancient Germanic tongue that they might have served as a model for it:

> Admission into the society is free and open to all who prize [love] honor and virtue, above all, however, to those who cherish [love] our *ancient* German native tongue.[18] (emphasis added)

What is crucial about the metaphorics of ancientness here and elsewhere in language society linguistic theory is not just that it is based on a chronology that links German as it is to be used by society members with this ancient tongue but also that this very chronology, in association with a discourse of morality, is clearly embedded in a discourse of contemporary events as well. Such an embeddedness testifies to the language's origin in a particular (historical) context even as it strains, by means of its codification in society texts, to move beyond that history into the realm of law. Schottelius writes, for example, that not only this ancient language but also its ethical equivalent will be the result of philological work by society members; they will "[make] apparent, by means of explaining the piety and courage of German words, also the diligent and austere courage of [our] *ancient* [uhralt] German honesty" (*Account*, 1:5, emphasis added).[19]

Carl Gustav Hille's history of the Fruit-bearing Society, *Der teutsche Palmbaum* (The German palm tree) (1647), written just after the founding of the Order of Flowers on the Pegnitz, reflects the discourse of language theory at the time. He uses similar terms to describe a naturally pure, moral state that was and will be coextensive with the ancient German tongue and its resuscitation in current times:

> [It is our duty] in these days of bloody and lamentable war to take our ancient [but?] imperfect German mother tongue, once fed to us entirely pure along with our mother's milk and later spoiled and diluted by the presence of "splendorous" foreign words, and to return it once more to its ancient, customary, and intrinsic German purity, beauty, and establishment, to perpetuate it in harmony, to free it from the oppressive yoke of foreign languages, to reenforce it with old and new technical terms, and thus finally to place it on the most glorious throne of honor [that it deserves]. (*Palm Tree*, 7)

The prior existence of an "honest" and "brave" ancient German language and ethic is posited, then, as part of a rhetorical response to the contemporary violent war that has "spoiled" the purity of the mother tongue. Ironically, the ancient, pure, and honest forms of the vernacular thus grow out of a contemporary situation; they are generated out of the necessities of a particular historical context of strife, namely, the Thirty Years' War that had devastated central Europe. The rhetoric of ancientness in society texts thus itself *produces* this ancient time—as it produces its morality and language—for the first time. The repeated references here and in Schottelius's remarks to the "purity" and "bravery" of German's original forms, although in part remnants of a sixteenth-century Tacitus reception that located the origins of superior German morality in the values of great Teutonic ancestors,[20] thus suggests that the prehistory of the vernacular served not only as a repository of absolute values but also as a way of overcoming the context of violence and dislocation surrounding the Nuremberg writers.

The narrating in texts of an ancient time of linguistic purity and thus the creation (in German) of that language's (literally) timeless "original" authority provide the present with unassailable foundations that could be used to guide and guarantee the society's (historical) standards. Establishing the authority of this ancient tongue thus depended on the success of the Nuremberg texts in doing the work of making it both absent (as timeless origin) and present (as an ongoing guarantor of norms) at one and the same time. This work was performed first and foremost by the narrative that associated German with a sacred predecessor, the Adamic tongue of Eden, a narrative that declared the forms of that original language "lost" but also capable of being found again in the texts of the Nuremberg order.

True Stories 1: German as Original Tongue (*Ursprache*)

The consistent reference to linguistic and moral norms that are clearly generated out of a historical context and yet, in their identity as ancient and primal elements, are also said to be prior to that context and thus to approach the authority of nature itself is made specific in Nuremberg language theory by linking German, a historically specific vernacular tongue, to the "original," Adamic tongue (*Ursprache*) said to have been the first human language. The development of a narrative that identified the vernacular with the language of Adam provided German with foundations above reproach that, when converted into normative, linguistic forms in the society's regulatory texts, would also serve as the authoritative beginnings of a new, standardized tongue. The instituting gesture in the development of a foundational narrative relied, I would argue, on a doctrine of linguistic contextualism that followed the historiographical model discussed above. As a result of its affiliation with the *lingua adamica*, the German of the language society, as evidenced in its texts, could be defined both as a reflection of divine or transcendent truths and as appropriate to its particular context.[21]

The arguments used to link the vernacular to the original tongue of the Garden sometimes seem contradictory. They oscillate between arguments based on German's *historical* affinity with the Adamic language, on the one hand, and arguments based on *analogy*, on formal elements that the two languages are said to share, on the other. On the one hand, both Adam's tongue and German are ancient, primeval ("uralt"); they are thus said to be linked by chronological proximity. On the other, they share an array of intrinsic properties and are thus also "naturally" (in addition to historically) allied. The fact that these two sets of arguments are so carefully interwoven in the foundational narrative of the group can be explained as the result of a need to accept the Fall of Man and his language into history (and thus into linguistic diversity) while retaining the possibility of an absolute standard of linguistic accuracy that could be used to recuperate and reestablish the lost tongue in the here-and-now. Convention and appropriateness to context could thus be understood as not excluding the sacred but rather as combining with it to produce the present as a new part of divine time.

From an analytic point of view, the Nuremberg language theorists begin their story of the historical affiliation of German with the *lingua adamica* by arguing its resemblance to Hebrew, commonly accepted as the original Adamic tongue. Once again, Hille's *Palm Tree* provides a convenient paradigm of the biblical narrative used by many language theorists at midcentury as a point of departure in their demonstration of German's great age. Hille begins by repeating the opinion prevalent at the time that Hebrew was the original language of the Garden:

> It is beyond all doubt that in the Beginning and directly after the Creation, men in general spoke only one language, namely, the ancient Hebrew tongue. (*Palm Tree*, 79)

The assertion of a single, unified language and of its proximity to the Creation itself points to the foundational function that the argument served. Hille gives a number of collateral arguments to "prove" the identity of Hebrew as the original tongue. First, Hebrew was the original language of Scripture, "the first, learned tongue in which Moses and the prophets described the divine Revelation" (80); second, Hebrew, according to Cabbalistic doctrine, is privileged because of its divine, verbal nature, its capacity, that is, to hold God's wisdom "locked" ("versiegelt") in its elemental forms (80). (The association of the Cabbala with German in the language theory of the Nuremberg language society is discussed below.) Both arguments serve in Hille's logic as proof that Hebrew was indeed "the first and the eldest among all of the languages" (80) and prepare the way for an equally lofty genealogy for the vernacular since in the meantime God's wisdom (in its textualized form in Scripture) had been translated into German as well.

While this argumentation demonstrated that Hebrew was the original tongue, or, as Schottelius calls it, the "very most perfect 'arch' tongue" (*Account*, 1:13), Greek and Latin (explicitly called *Hauptsprachen*, "principal tongues," here) could be granted sacred status along with Hebrew because, in Hille's argumentation, they were the original three languages of the Cross (John 19:19–22). Hille writes:

> These are (as I have indicated above) the three principal tongues in which all knowledge, arts, and divine and mortal wisdom lie embedded and preserved. They are the languages that were consecrated and blessed on (and through) the sign nailed on the Cross of our Redeemer,

the only one to preserve (maintain) the Fruit-bearing Society. (*Palm Tree*, 81–82)

Hille goes on to declare: "In addition to these three principal tongues there are two more principal tongues that are widely used, namely, our aforementioned highly esteemed German language and Slovanic" (85). Because the argument based on the question of age and the existence of the principal tongues of the Cross did not explicitly include German, Hille must backtrack here in order to legitimate his inclusion of the vernacular in this community of sacred linguistic forms. In a narrative that depends on a mythical "postfiguration" of the Fall into history, Hille goes on to use the story of the Tower of Babel to extend the sacred origins of language into the present and thus includes German among the redeemed languages of Man.

The argument begins deductively. German must be the eldest language of its kind since all other Germanic languages—Dutch, Danish, Norwegian, and Swedish—can be derived from it: "These various dialects are originally all German, as can be seen in their radicals and rootwords [Stamm- und Grundwörtern]." But Hille then swerves into "history": [Thus] "there is no doubt that our language of today is precisely that *ancient* one that the descendants of Japheth spread into so many countries and ruined in so many ways" (86, emphasis added). Here the authoritative and absent ancient time has been converted into a specific historical moment; the reference to Japheth's offspring indicates the source of Hille's narrative of the vernacular's legitimacy, namely, the biblical account of the Confusion of Tongues. Noah's son, Japheth, still spoke a pre-Babel and thus pure German; it was only "ruined" ("verstimmet") by those who came after him. Because German can be said to have existed at least as early as "the era of the Confusion of Tongues at Babel" (88), if not before, its original forms must have been nearly as ancient and as unsullied as Hebrew.

Hille does not go as far in his local patriotism as Goropius Becanus (1518–72), who ironically used the very same explanation to assert that his native Dutch was also originally spoken by Japheth and thus was in fact the closest of the vernaculars to the Adamic tongue. In an attempt to validate his mother tongue even further, Becanus argues that the Dutch-speaking Japheth was not present at the building of Babel at all.[22] In his *Specimen philologiae Germanicae* (A model for a German study of words) (1646), Harsdörffer attempts to exempt German from Babel in a similar way by arguing that the ancestral German tongue predated the Confusion: "[T]he Tower of Babel occurred [fell down?] at the time of Eber," he explains, "who was fifth in the line of descendants after Noah, at the time when [there were] already all four generations [as] mentioned above" (*Model*, 41–42). Hille's logic, if not so extreme, is based on a similar notion that German is historically related to a pre-Babel and thus primal tongue. In a lengthy verse paean to the vernacular, he goes on to describe both antediluvian and pre-Babel events as a literal, historical sequence that could explain German's proximity to the sacred and intrinsically accurate tongue of the Garden.[23]

Many others, among them the theorists of the Order of Flowers on the Pegnitz, followed a logic similar to Hille's in assuming the historical facticity of the biblical narrative of the Confusion of Tongues, a narrative that explained both the initial connection of German with the pure Adamic tongue and its separation from it. The chronology of the tale is sometimes used to maintain that German predated even Latin and Greek. Schottelius quotes the Belgian language theorist Adrian von Schrieck (1560–1621), for example: "The Hebrew language was the progenitor, Japheth's actually came second . . . And at the beginning Japheth's language was the universal one, and was altogether more ancient than Greek and Latin" (*Account*, 1:31). More important, however, the scriptural genealogy is made to confirm an uninterrupted, linguistic lineage from Adam through Noah to Japheth, and, most important, from Japheth to Ascenas, the mythical father of the seventeenth-century language society. Schottelius writes:

> And thus one can reckon beginning with Adam: Adam begat Seth, Seth begat Enosh, Enosh begat Kenan, Kenan begat Mahalalel, Mahalalel begat Jered, Jered begat Enoch, Enoch begat Methuselah, Methuselah begat Lamech, Lamech begat Noah, Noah begat Japheth, Japheth begat Gomer, Gomer begat Ashkenaz, and this Ashkenaz (as I said before) is the patriarch of the Germans, who brought with him from Babel the old Celtic or German language, the very language that was spread abroad in the aforementioned nations of Europe by his descendants. (*Account*, 1:34)

Sigmund von Birken recites this same genealogy in his historical panegyric, the *Königlich polnischer Chur- und Fürstlich sächsischer Helden-Saal* (The heroes' gallery of the royal Polish Electorate and Saxon princes) (1677), as does Johann Klaj in his *Lobrede der teutschen Poeterey* (In praise of German poetry) (1645).[24] German as it is currently used by members of the language society is thus linked to an origin in prelapsarian time.

By recognizing the postfigural fall of language into linguistic variety at the Confusion of Tongues, the Nuremberg language theorists explained how modern vernaculars could be related to an originally singular perfect tongue. But they still had to "prove" the superiority of German amid the plurality of these modern vernaculars. Schottelius, while accepting the loss of the "universal" and "unique" Adamic tongue at Babel, nevertheless maintains that only a confused and not a new "dialectus" of that language was the result (*Account*, 1:33). Post-Babel languages like contemporary German thus still hold within themselves the remnants of a more perfect tongue and time; the roots of German in particular clearly lie, he says, in the *lingua adamica*, the universal ("allgemeine") tongue of Man (*Account*, 1:34). And on the basis of these roots—present in the radicals (*Stammwörter*) of present-day German—Schottelius and others believed that a restored version of the original German principal tongue could be derived. The philological task of the society was thus to reclaim these sacred forms in its texts.

The concept of the German radicals made it possible to link arguments about the *historical* relationship between German and Hebrew to an inductive logic designed to demonstrate the *intrinsic* similarity of the two tongues.[25] Here the foundational narrative sows the seeds of an argument about the "natural perfection" of German, an argument that bridges the gap between the Garden and the Nuremberg grove, between the original (instituting) moment of the mother tongue and its ongoing (institutionalized) functioning in society texts, by allowing the authority of a divine (and presumably irrecoverable) origin to penetrate into and take on new form in the present. In spite of the Confusion at Babel, Schottelius reasons, the original units of an "ancient, universal German language" still lie hidden within the vernacular as it exists in post-Babel times:

> It will certainly follow, according to all [that I have said], that just as the Germany of today is the same Germany as existed one thousand years ago, although it is now better developed and more magnificently adorned ... in the same way, the German language of today is the same [as the] ancient and universal German language ... because just as the land remains Germany, so too must the radicals remain German words that have retained their natural properties and their meaning as long as they have been in *rerum natura*. (*Account*, 1:48)

The defining characteristic of German radicals, Schottelius continues, is their "fundamental monosyllabism" ("Grundartige Einsilbigkeit").

And, in a strategically placed explanation that implicitly acknowledges the precariousness of an argument that relies on mere historical coincidence by so clearly attempting to transcend it, Schottelius and others emphasize that the monosyllabic radicals, in spite of the intervention of time, *continue* to be capable of reflecting nature and thus of being philosophically accurate even in their present-day form:

> Suppose we were to look to children for the origins of the natural [nature]: they first learn to control their babbling tongues by producing monosyllabic words. Consequently even nature herself will not be able to approximate [her?] origins [in any other way] than [in the production of] a fundamental monosyllabism. (*Account*, 1:61)

Nature herself creates, Schottelius seems to say, in monosyllables. The basic elements of contemporary German reflect the "origins" of elemental nature and are thus capable of forming origins themselves. This argument allows German to substitute for the ancient Hebrew tongue, since the intrinsic coincidence of vernacular radicals with the *res naturae* themselves legitimates and dispenses with the historical link between the vernacular and the primal, Adamic tongue at one and the same time.

Schottelius, Harsdörffer, and Klaj of course allow that the sheer abundance of monosyllabic root words in German helps demonstrate its affinity to Hebrew (also rich in monosyllabic roots) and thus its great age, since the simplest is always the oldest.[26] But the overwhelming insistence here and elsewhere on the accuracy of the radicals, on their abundance, and thus on their coextensiveness with the natural world signals, it seems, that the full adequacy of the vernacular can ultimately be declared only if its ongoing epistemological accuracy can be established independently of Hebrew. Schottelius declares:

> Without a doubt the irreproachable perfection of the radicals in any language will thus be:
> 1. That they consist in their own, natural characters [Letteren] and not in foreign ones;
> 2. That they sound pleasant and express their referent(s) properly;
> 3. That their number is complete and adequate;
> 4. That they sprout and allow [other words] to be derived from them when necessary in abundance;
> 5. That they provide direction in the combination, doubling, and clever joining [of words]. (*Account*, 1:50–51)

These general principles and the fact that they apply to any and all philosophically accurate languages thus supersede, although they do not contradict, the allegedly historical link between German and Hebrew. Schottelius explains:

> Both I and other scholars have celebrated two properties of Hebrew, namely, a correct and regulated certainty together with a certain and complete number of lovely, short, and clear [deutlich] radicals. These much extolled properties are to be found in our mother tongue [as well]. (*Account*, 1:62)

Harsdörffer agrees: "These and other similar monosyllables [in German] can, with some effort, be identified with the primitive [words] of the Hebrews" (*Model*, 57). But here the alliance between Hebrew and German is based not on a lost historical proximity but rather on a present common property, a common abundance of perfect, monosyllabic radicals that can be catalogued and demonstrated in the here-and-now. Thus even post-Babel German is capable of a kind of prelapsarian proper naming. The authority of a vernacular with origins in the (now absent) Garden can be absorbed into German as it is currently used.

The presence of an abundance of accurate radicals in both Hebrew and German thus argues for the philosophical perfection of both tongues. The presence of these radicals allows contemporary German to transcend its own historical facticity, moreover, by identifying it with elements of natural linguistic fitness that are intrinsic to it, and thus were not lost at the Confusion of Tongues. The Nuremberg story about the similarity of the two tongues is complicated, however, by the acknowledgment of the fall away from the philological perfection of the *lingua adamica* caused by Babel. This acknowledgment appears in a series of complex references to the applicability to German of the Cabbala, the ancient Hebrew system of gaining access to the secret meaning of Scripture that God had encoded in Old Testament Law as handed over to Moses.[27] "Losing" this original linguistic perfection and having to find (and found) it again were nevertheless crucial steps in the Nuremberg foundational narrative, building an authoritative absence into the story of a "redeemed" modern tongue.

According to the Cabbala, hidden beneath the linguistic surface of God's specific commandments lay an even more profound statement of his will. By attributing certain quantities and concepts to the Hebrew letters, people could decipher these messages. By associating German with Hebrew and specifically with the Cabbala, the Nuremberg language theorists created a context in which the vernacular could also contain the secrets of nature. A key had yet to be developed, however, to unlock them from within language's hold. Like Plato's demand for a "legislator" or dialectician, who alone could penetrate to the meaning of things and represent that meaning in language, the language theorists' declaration of the necessity of an *ars cabbalistica* for German presumed the possibility of a perfect vernacular (that they would create) while avoiding the claim that it already existed. The "dialectical" work still to be done to unearth this language belonged to the language theorists; the "cleansing" process would take place in their texts.

The Cabbala was based primarily on equating the letters of the Hebrew alphabet with numeric quantities; secret levels of meaning were thus always present within the very letters and words of a text and had merely to be decoded. Harsdörffer declares "that the letters signify numbers in both Hebrew and Greek, specifically, that they signify numbers according to their place in the alphabet, is beyond doubt" (*Funnel*, 2:25). He goes on to explain the original method in his *Frauenzimmer Gesprächspiele* (Playful colloquies for the ladies) (3:348). Other Nuremberg language theorists attribute a related kind of mystical numerology to their vernacular. Georg Neumark wrote in his *Poetische Tafeln* (A treatise on poetry in schematic form) (1667), for example, that the "number-letters" ("Zahlbuchstaben") are the key to a German Cabbala: "We Germans can use the number-letters in place of the Cabbala of the Hebrews . . . A certain quantity is attributed to the consonants, [for example]" (71). In *Delitiae mathematicae et physicae* (Mathematical and philosophical lessons to delight and refresh), Harsdörffer generalizes the phenomenon to all principal tongues, illustrating that it is the fact of secret but fully adequate linguistic representation that links the main contemporary language groups, including German, to the original, sacred tongue:

> All principal tongues, for example, Hebrew, Greek, and Latin, have associated numbers with the letters. We Germans follow their example in this way, as is proper . . . That secrets of great magnitude are also contained in Latin letters is demonstrated by many, in particular in a small book, untitled, that was printed by George Rhau in Wittemberg in 1532 . . . Now even though it appears that the numbers were [really just] the product of human ingenuity and thus cannot reveal any [great] secrets, this book demonstrates that the majority of numbers that appear to be sealed in Daniel's prophecy and the Revelation of John [may be] decoded and revealed in this way. (*Lessons*, 66–67)

The reliability and legitimacy of the "secrets of great magnitude" hidden in numerical equivalents and letters attest to a language's divine origins, since such numerological patterns are the products not of an "ingenious" human mind but, rather, of divine revelation itself. It does not seem to bother Harsdörffer that it is a book, a man-made, printed text, that he relies upon for assurances about the divine capacities of the written word—precisely the opposite. The availability of this knowledge in textual form adds to its authority and testifies to the reality of divinity present in the German tongue.

The possibility of such numerological manipulations in German gave rise to numerous secret codes and linguistic games of the kind often found in Harsdörffer's *Colloquies* and in other society writings. At the same time, however, it was also possible to use Cabbalistic graphs of the German language to more serious ends, to reveal the intrinsic "magic" of the German radicals, for example, in accordance with a plan to demonstrate both the relationship of German to Hebrew and the vernacular's potential as a philologically and philosophically accurate tongue. Harsdörffer's "Fünffacher Denckring der teutschen Sprache" (Fivefold ring for thinking in the German language) in part 2 of his *Lessons* contains movable, concentric rings inserted in each copy of the book. Inscribed with monosyllabic and thus numerically simple German radicals as well as with all possible prefixes and suffixes, the mechanism could be manipulated in combinatory fashion to produce a virtual encyclopedia of accurate, German words.[28] The *Denckring* discloses German's capacity to reflect the natural universe in both its simplicity and its variety while also providing the means to literally produce that universe in language and in concrete textual form. Although the elaborate system of the Hebrew Cabbala is not reproduced for German in all of its complexity in the Nuremberg writings, textual "gimmicks" like the *Denckring* did allow the language theorists to assume that a kind of magic similar to the Cabbala lay hidden in the letters and words of their mother tongue and to begin to unearth it in their texts with devices such as these. In so doing, what seemed to be no more than the language used by a historical community became an instrument with which not only to communicate but also to create divine truth in palpably German form.

The concept of the "hidden" capacity of the vernacular to reflect nature is sometimes expressed in terms reminiscent of a specifically German tradition of mystical language theory. In *Der teutschen Sprach Einleitung* (hereafter cited as *Introduction*) Schottelius writes, "Something almost celestial lies hidden in language, something that concerns and delights not our senses but, rather, our soul" (106). Elsewhere he refers explicitly to the mystic Ickelsamer: "Ickelsamer writes in his German grammar that under every German letter and word there lies hidden no less [than] a deep secret" (*Account*, 1:59). The association of German with magical forces in terms such as these can be attributed to the so-called inspirational theories of language developed by Paracelsus and Böhme; but even in the absence of explicit connections to these traditions, it serves to emphasize the importance to the Nuremberg theorists of the concept of the vernacular's fitness in representing the secrets of both divinity and nature correctly in a historically apt tongue. While Schottelius entertains the notion that nature is animated by language in general ("[Y]es, the languages run through all the mysteries [secrets] of nature" [*Account*, 1:74]), his disciple Johann Klaj is much more specific about the reasons for German's particular aptness for providing an almost magical linguistic accuracy:

> There is no word in German that does not express that which it signifies, that of which it is a question, that which it desires in and by means of a special secret. We must truly be full of wonder in the face of the unimaginable artfulness that God has bestowed upon our language. (*Praise*, 398)

The possibility of wonderful and magical qualities that a German Cabbala could contain thus complemented the society's discourse about the vernacular's relationship to Hebrew. On the one hand, it accepted that German was appropriate to its context and thus not a truly universal tongue in its post-Babel form. On the other, it attempted to redeem the vernacular from a position of historical belatedness by isolating the intrinsic, "magical" qualities of philological perfection implanted in it by God.

A final, crucial element in developing the narrative of an intrinsic German-Hebrew link lay in emphasizing the "essential monosyllabism" ("Einsilbigkeit") that German was said to share with Hebrew through a historical connection, but in a different way. The argument about monosyllabism made it possible for German to be historically related to Hebrew; at the same time, it allowed it to bypass that link and become a new, "original" and originating tongue by pointing out that German possessed intrinsically (in the present) all the properties that Hebrew had been known to have in the past. As a result, the "original" language could literally become a "lost" one and thereby take on its necessary identity as the absent "first cause" of a new (historical) one. Important in effecting this elision of Hebrew was the concept of a present, natural "copiousness" of vernacular radicals, since in their abundance they approached the unity-in-variety of nature itself. Schottelius writes:

> Moreover, the third necessary property, or indicator of perfection, in the radicals concerns the following: that their number be complete and sufficient. This the German language can prove [as well as] any other [tongue] . . . It is sufficient, as has been indicated here, that this number include several thousand; certainly German will not allow itself to be easily outdone [in this respect] by another language but, rather, will itself be the language to be outdone by others. (*Account*, 1:65)

Both the abundance and the fitness of the radicals prove the affiliation of the vernacular not just with Hebrew but with the divine plan itself:

> The beginning and foundation of German characters [Letteren], of [German] radicals, of its ways of deriving and doubling [words], were the result of special artfulness and experience [and were] not without divine intervention. The internal aptness [appropriateness] and astonishing manner cannot be sufficiently understood. (*Account*, 1:58)

Harsdörffer argues that the abundance of radicals in German proves its great age (*Model*, 57, 141). But Schottelius goes even further by subtly using the very fact of these intrinsic qualities—monosyllabism and *copia*—to demonstrate German's superiority even to allegedly more ancient tongues:

> Simon Stevin has inventoried approximately 2,170 of the monosyllabic radicals alone in German. (This is certainly not the complete number of our German radicals.) This is opposed to approximately 163 radicals in Latin and 265 radicals in Greek. (*Account*, 1:61)

Regardless of its historical relationship to the other principal tongues, then, German possesses greater authority because it possesses a greater number of monosyllabic radicals and thus is probably older and, in any case, intrinsically more perfect than the most ancient of the languages to which it could be compared. Elsewhere Schottelius provides the concluding argument for this logic:

> Rather, what is more enduring, what is more pure, what is more certain than an enduring, pure, and certain unit [one]? The words! So brief and pure! So brief and firm! So brief and fine! So brief and powerful! Yes, the words that are the most abundant because of their brevity! What is lacking in them that one could call or must call richness, vitality, and strength in words?[29]

Thus the perfection of the vernacular and its historical and intrinsic affiliation with Hebrew as the *lingua adamica* are "proved" by German's simplicity and its copiousness. A specific vernacular language (if spoken correctly, that is, in accordance with its own "innate" rules) could thus provide a moment of naturally and divinely motivated linguistic perfection, a renewal of the original, sacred tongue.

True Stories 2: German as a Natural Language (*Natursprache*)

The swerve away from historical and analogical arguments of German's relationship to Hebrew into a discourse that explicitly linked the vernacular to nature makes sense in terms of the overall institutionalizing goal of Nuremberg language theory. What must be clear here is that constructing an argument in their texts about German as a "natural tongue" was, for the Nuremberg theorists, a *rhetorical* act that used the discourse of divine origins and accurate referentiality as a means of establishing the legitimacy of the vernacular in its present forms. Not only did they seek to provide the vernacular with a kind of primal or ancient authority by writing its origins into divine history, they also sought to demonstrate that its "natural" or "intrinsic" properties provided it with power in the present to create "new" origins by providing new standards and valid norms of its own. The main line of argumentation for German as a "natural language" (*Natursprache*) is of course never developed completely separately from that of the vernacular's affiliation with Adam's original tongue; separating the two arguments analytically allows us, however, to understand the structure of the Nuremberg foundational narrative by understanding how it was necessary for the "origins" of the vernacular to be both absent and present at one and the same time.

The identity of German as a "naturally accurate" language lay, the Nuremberg language theorists argued, in the "fundamental correctness" (*Grundrichtigkeit*) of its words (*verba*) in expressing the things (*res*) to which they refer. In a general sense, the rhetoric of the vernacular's philological perfection as a natural language belonged to what has been called the *phusei-Lehre*, a classical doctrine of a fully motivated and naturally perfect system of linguistic signs not unrelated to theories of German as a monosyllabically rich and accurate ancient tongue.[30] Some statements in fact mention German's fundamental correctness in connection with Hebrew. Schottelius writes, for example:

> Upon constant reflection upon and consideration of the essence of language from beginning to end, I have nevertheless [?] finally, after very many dubious forays, tracked down and discovered the astounding relationship and accord between the *essence of nature* and the Hebrew and German tongues. Likewise [I have found] that everything has a

clear significance and meaning as indicated by German and Hebrew words. (*Account*, 1:20, emphasis added)

But the emphasis here on the "discovery" of the accord between the words of the two principal tongues and the "essence of nature" ("natürliches Wesen") of things named indicates where Schottelius believed the importance of his statement lay. Only by demonstrating that German was itself a "natural language" (in addition to demonstrating its relationship to the original human language) could the vernacular be invested with intrinsic properties capable of guaranteeing the reappearance of Hebrew-like epistemological certainty in the here-and-now. The narrative of the *lingua adamica* upon which the language theorists dwell at such length thus gains significance as additional arguments about German as a natural language develop. It does so by becoming the story of an absent origin that guarantees and is embedded in the ongoing "fundamental correctness" of the vernacular in the here-and-now. Schottelius cites Becanus: "The very same language that possesses the most ancient words and the *most proper* [eigentlichsten] meanings of things must be the very oldest language" (*Account*, 1:31, emphasis added). The intertext of the story of Adam's tongue is clear here; the most ancient meanings of words are understood as the most literal, most proper, most real ("eigentlich") ones. In fact, as Harsdörffer writes, even the original language was divinely privileged only because it was fully motivated in just this way:

> It is beyond doubt that Adam dispensed correct [woldeutende] names to all of the animals and creatures out of [according to] their species and real [true] attributes. (*Colloquies*, 4:511)[31]

Since, as Schottelius argues, the German radicals accomplish this very same task, namely, "they have a pleasing sound and express their referent properly [eigentlich]" (*Account*, 1:51), the monosyllabically rich vernacular could be considered not only a "true and legitimate offspring of her 'arch' mother" (*Account*, 1:b v), ancient Hebrew, but also, in the absence of that original tongue, a naturally accurate language on its own.

Crucial to the defense of German as a "fundamentally correct natural language" ("grundrichtige Natursprache") was the fact that the Nuremberg language theorists were able to state unequivocally that their vernacular was both immediate to and fully coextensive with nature. Harsdörffer writes of German's "monosyllabic simplicity" ("simplicitas monosyllabica") and stresses that its words are meaningful only insofar as they "follow the standard of nature" (*Model*, 292). That he and others were so eager to spell out German's "philosophical character," its ability, that is, to express the essence of that which it designated and thus to be effectively coextensive with nature,[32] may indeed have had something to do with a desire like that of their British contemporaries for a protoscientific and intersubjectively verifiable language whose natural accuracy would further scientific investigation. In *Teutsche Sprachkunst* (hereafter cited as *Art of Language*), Schottelius writes:

> The most abundant and best language is the one that most properly [auffs eigentlichste], most clearly, and most purely expresses, articulates, and gives shape to the objects and the characteristics [of the objects] that God and Nature have revealed to the mind; [this language is the best] because its words measure up to nature equally by virtue of their intrinsic [eingepflanzter] aptness and communicate to our understanding whatever nature produces. (16–17)

German's abundance and precision can thus be relied upon, these theorists maintain, to represent nature correctly. It is important to recognize, however, that their demonstrations of German's "scientific" accuracy often relied heavily on a merely metaphorical discourse of naturalization meant to carry the burden of proof. Schottelius's characterization here and elsewhere of linguistic fitness as "intrinsic," or, literally, "implanted" ("eingepflanzt") in German words is but a modest version of a later, more elaborate description of the "artful growth [that is] our principal tongue" ("Kunstgewächs unserer Hauptsprache"). German is an organic creation that extends its roots—by virtue of the radicals, or root words ("Stammwörter")—throughout all of nature (*Account*, 1:68). The root words are the "vital [juicy] roots" that "keep the entire tree of language moist, [and] whose little shoots allow boughs rich in branches and veins to spread out in a most admirable neatness" (*Account*, 1:50). Still elsewhere Schottelius describes the transcendent organicity and divine origin of the radicals, thus conflating the discourses of the natural and the primal tongues.[33] This combination of a metaphorics of organicity with a code of divine origins reveals how central the doctrine of an original, natural fitness intrinsic in their own language was to the Nuremberg language theorists. Independently, and yet also in affirmation of German as historically related to the Hebraic primal tongue, a contemporary, contextually appropriate vernacular could also be considered to conform to—indeed, to instantiate—natural and thus timeless norms.

It is of course in the *textual practice* of the Nuremberg language society that the dyad of German's "natural" epistemological accuracy and its vernacular contextualism becomes concretized at the most obvious level. This practice is the subject of later sections of this chapter. In connection with the discourse of German as a "natural language," however, it is important to point out that the abundant presence of *Klangmalerei*, or onomatopoeia, in many of the lyric texts produced by members of the Nuremberg group may be explained as one kind of textual realization of the doctrine of contextualism, a doctrine predicated on an understanding that the "natural propriety" of a language (even a divinely motivated one) could be "proved" only in the comprehensibility of its "natural," linguistic signs. To demonstrate that the presence of "nature" could be measured only in its reception and thus only as a rhetorical act, the Nuremberg language theorists took care to identify its *sound* as the key ingredient in German's "naturalness." Schottelius writes that "its sound, [heard] in unison, is so astounding and its harmony so superlative in its artfulness that nature [has shown itself] in this [to be] fully and completely worked out" (*Account*, 1:59). Harsdörffer explains, in turn, that the sounds of his own German and that of his fellow German speakers reflect nature: "We speak with the nature of things: whatever the sound that the things in this universe emit, we produce it" (*Model*, 295). In fact, the inner nature of the thing and the sound of the word that represents it in German are one and the same. Thus all those who speak and hear German—the German-language community at large—theoretically have direct access to nature as they speak their mother tongue. Again Schottelius:

> For it is an especially artful achievement in German words that they are related to the innermost nature [of their referents] and that they are able to demand most conveniently the sound, power, and appearance of the nature of the things whose expression they are.[34]

Klaj too makes clear in his *In Praise of German Poetry* that German is capable of onomatopoeia precisely because it is a monosyllabically rich "natural tongue." He uses the language of German's "fundamental correctness" to state his case while also (in an almost untranslatable flourish) "proving" his point by using onomatopoeia to state it:

> Let us then consider our German tongue and recall [its] powerful and brief expression and [how it] allows itself to be heard according to the instruction of the inner character [of things]: it crashes and splashes with great intensity, it boasts and toasts its own greatness, it roars and soars ... it gossips and babbles and knows how to imitate a thousand other sounds of nature in a masterful way. (*Praise*, 402)

The biblical narrative is not neglected, finally, in the discussion of onomatopoeia, since it also confirms that the "truth" of naturally motivated words can be measured only in the hearing. Harsdörffer writes that nature "speaks German": "Nature speaks our German tongue in everything that gives off a sound" (*Colloquies*, 1:357). Elsewhere he explicitly equates onomatopoeia with Adam's original act of naming (*Lessons*, 3:41). He concludes in the *Colloquies* passage, moreover: "This is why some have wanted to imagine incorrectly [wähnen] that the first man, Adam, could not have named the birds and the beasts except with our words." The use of the term *wähnen* may suggest that Harsdörffer doubts the authenticity of the assertion that German itself was the Adamic language; but its complete accuracy in naming, an accuracy measured by comprehensibility, nevertheless justifies the comparison:

> [German] speaks with the tongue of nature in that it expresses in a comprehensible way every sound and thing that makes the slightest peep, noise, or reverberates with sound. (*Colloquies*, 1:355)

The natural sounds of German are, most importantly, "comprehensible" ("wol vernemlich") and thus demonstrably present only in a language that can be understood. The naturally accurate German vernacular was capable, then, of being both intrinsically correct, like Adam's tongue, and appropriate to specific contexts. Linked to a realm of origins and capable of providing standards for contemporary usage, German could thus be absolutely and historically correct at one and the same time.

The Loss and Redemption of the Vernacular

Onomatopoeia, or *Klangmalerei*, was thus of more than strictly theoretical interest to the language theorists of the Order of Flowers on the Pegnitz, because it became a vehicle for giving shape to and even creating the intrinsic perfection of the vernacular in their own (historical) texts.[35] Nuremberg descriptions of onomatopoeia maintain that this perfection is innate in the language; at the same time, it was only the use of German in a "fundamentally correct," onomatopoetic way *in society texts* that would guarantee that the language would be fashioned anew. The final stage of the foundational narrative in society language theory was concerned, then, with locating the "historical fact" of the order and of its texts in a version of biblical chronology and in the discourse of a "natural" tongue that had been lost and corrupted but that could now be redeemed. After exploring the rhetoric of self-situating in this final phase of cleansing and redemption, I deal with the texts themselves as monuments to this foundational moment and as productive of vernacular orthodoxy in the next two sections.

Society theorists completed the "story" of their sacred and naturally correct tongue by writing the society endeavor into it in the following way: the *lingua adamica*, "the unique and universal language" of Edenic times, had become "confused, spoiled, and fragmented," first by Adam's Fall out of the Garden into linguistic imperfection and then by humanity's mismanagement and pride at Babel (Schottelius, *Account*, 1:34, 33). Pre-Babel language, perfect because it was based on a unified understanding, reflected the "natural consensus" among peoples. This language had been destroyed by the Confusion of Tongues:

> The Confusion of Tongues at Babel was the greatest disaster [that ever occurred]. [Because of it] men were cruelly separated from one another; trust, love, and community among them were done away with for the most part. Every race was isolated in a particular location by itself. In this way not only was the natural bond of kinship effectively destroyed, but the proper knowledge of the one, true God also gradually obscured. (*Account*, 1:35)

The foundational narrative of the language society required that its history be written into this chronology as well. Thus yet a third Confusion of Tongues, "the recently rampant polluting of language," was said to have been visited upon German in the all-too-recent past, namely, in the general chaos and confusion that marked the first half of the seventeenth century during the Thirty Years' War.[36] The penetration of eschatological time into the here-and-now of early modern Germany, a penetration scripted, so to speak, by the language theorists themselves, thus enabled the "language heroes" of the society to define their own philological work as part of a historical effort to restore a "confused" vernacular to its "original" pristine state and, in so doing, to originate linguistic perfection once again.

References to current, Babel-like conditions were thus used to locate contemporary discussions of a "lost" linguistic perfection in both an eschatological and a historical context. Such references surface in many discussions of the vernacular contemporary to the Nuremberg theory. Gustav von Hille, for example, describes the current state of the vernacular in a language of both military conflict and of "confusion"; the loss of an original, German "heroic language" ("Heldensprache") harking back to an ancient time is equated symbolically with the current threat to political autonomy. The leader of the first language society, Prince Ludwig of Anhalt-Köthen, had been aware of the similarity of the current (political) crisis to the Confusion at Babel when the society was founded. Hille writes:

> Just so, then, our most capable founder . . . as a defender of reason and god-fearing father of our country, was most likely able to see that the increasing fruits of the persistent and bloody war [were] that the coals

of misery were so stirred up that virtue was melting away, reasonable laws regressing, yes, even the heroic German language being brought, finally, into a state of disregard by the mingling [Vermischung] of the many different languages of foreign intruders [fremden Völker Zungen], or, rather, would [simply just] silently rot away and die. (*Palm Tree*, 14)

Taking random linguistic experimentation rather than war to be the principle (human) reason for the current linguistic confusion, Prince Ludwig himself had also used a discourse of explicitly Babel-like conditions to describe the current state of language use. He writes to the poet Philip von Zesen:

The Nourisher [= Ludwig] deems it inadvisable [that there be] more confusion [verwirrung] in the German language than [there already is] as a result of incorrect orthography and other pointless puzzles, which consist more in self-concocted illusions and other opinions directed [more] toward foreign languages than toward the true *foundation, nature,* and *good usage* [guten gewonheit] that has been introduced.[37] (emphasis added)

The prince explains the current "confusion" and thus the place of his age in a postfigural narrative as the result of having yielded to foreign influences, on the one hand, and to "self-concocted" and thus purely subjective opinion in language use, on the other. Both compromise the "natural" comprehensibility of the vernacular and thus corrupt its ability to articulate the "foundations" and "fundamental correctness" intrinsic to it. Human history, then, and irresponsible usage have re-created Babel in the here-and-now.

Harsdörffer and Klaj use the same logic but refer to their own age as a postfigurative one in more explicit terms. They see the Germans as themselves responsible for "a new Tower of Babel" (*Colloquies*, 4:505), "a new Babel . . . on German soil" (*Praise*, 410). It is only in "good usage" ("gute gewonheit") that the pure "foundations" of a language linked to the Adamic tongue could become real again; that this usage was to be defined as society usage and that society texts would thus come to instantiate a moment of linguistic redemption will become clear below.

Creating a postfigural reality of lost vernacular perfection by defining their own history in Babel-like terms made it possible for the Nuremberg language theorists to construct the possibility of a Pentecostal redemption in the present as well. The necessity for such a redemption is made obvious, first, in a discourse organized around metaphors of *purifying* the "mother tongue," a discourse within which a trajectory of loss and recovery is embedded. There is a tendency, for example, to characterize the original "natural language" as virginal, as an unsullied "mother tongue" free of imperfection, and as the "pure and undefiled virgin" of pre-Babel times (*Praise*, 403).[38] Schottelius uses the same kind of vocabulary:

> It is well enough known that the German language must lose its [her] own words, must have them become meaningless and unknown, must see its [her] own magnificent richness impoverished, and must suffer its [her] own pure body [form] to be alienated, spoiled, and disgraced [verschandflekket] . . . [This is the way that] our so magnificent, splendid, and royal tongue has been transformed into a poor, starving beggar woman. [Under such conditions] the pure, old, clear, and distinct German words [must] sound and appear unpleasant and not so prestigious to the Germans; and, as a result of such an arbitrary addiction to all that is "other," the fine, native essence [of Germanness], innately honorable and honest by custom, has changed into an upstart's fickleness [inconstancy] and a destructive craving and desire for the foreign. (*Account*, 1:137–38)

The task of society linguists is thus to save the mother tongue from both inarticulate habit and foreign influence and to restore it to its original, pristine form. The allegedly virginal, primal state of the German language invests it with a paradisical identity as a pure, ancient, clear, and accurate tongue; the Babel-like intervention of time and history makes redemption at the hands of society "knights" a necessary and timely task. The distinctly moral vision implicit in Klaj's and Schottelius's words and its relationship to ancient, uncorrupted values surfaces again in Harsdörffer's call for the use of "honest" German words: "Words should be courteous and honorable . . . our language has a natural aversion to all that is unclean" (*Funnel*, 1:114). Such formulations are reminiscent of the appeal to timeless ethical standards so clearly stated in language society membership codes and thus associate the society's program of cleansing and redemption, a historically situated task, with a moment of purity "in nature" and thus both before and beyond time.

The need to assume a redemptive role in order to locate their own historical enterprise in the foundational narrative may explain the second and final set of terms that society language theorists used to characterize the purifying work to be done in their texts. The inner essences of the vernacular are said to be "hidden" ("verborgen," Schottelius, *Art of Language*, 47) within German as it is currently used; they must be either mined, extracted from their deep hiding place, or alchemically distilled ("abgesondert," Harsdörffer, *Funnel*, 3:9), as when gold is rendered from common metals.[39] Vocabulary such as this reveals the theorists' preoccupation with identifying their vernacular as part of an "original," organic realm now lost or obscured. Harsdörffer writes:

> Languages can in many ways be compared with metals. Metals lie hidden in their *foundations* [Gründen]; it takes a great effort to bring them to the surface; they must be cleansed, purified, and made useful in the oven of their craft. (*Funnel*, 3:9, emphasis added)

Society theorists must "help," Schottelius writes, "to expose the[se] hidden treasures" (*Introduction*, 143). The repeated use of metaphors of geological and alchemical refinement recalls those elements of the *ars cabbalistica*, which also emphasized that the "hidden" nature of the vernacular's perfection must be "unlocked," and thus also recalls the relationship of German to the "original," Hebraic tongue. The goal of these purification processes is to make the "foundations," the innate, essential elements ("Gründe") of the "natural tongue" available once again. Schottelius writes:

> Every language can come on its own into its own power by means of an exploration of its natural *foundations* [Gründe] and through an investigation of capacities it has acquired . . . This by no means indicates that new, non-German, and unknown words should be created. Rather, the correct knowledge and technique [for doing so] will consist for the most part in raising the German language up out of the German language even further. (*Account*, 1:145, 98, emphasis added)

Such metaphors of restoration reveal that the language that has been reduced by current, Babel-like conditions of foreign intervention and random usage can indeed be restored to its original, intrinsic conformity with nature. That this pure language will not be a new one but, rather, related to its own ancient and primal "foundations" and forms is clear in Schottelius's words. Thus, in a narrative of purification that endows the language society with a legislative role like that of the Platonic dialecticians, the "new" natural tongue will be created by the language knights (*Sprachhelden*) of societies like the Order of Flowers on the Pegnitz.

Given the coincidence, however, of the rootedness of the society in a historical context that had brought on confusion and corruption and of the (historical) effort of the language society to re-create a "pure," divinely inspired, and "natural" language, the status of the language knights had to be carefully defined as part of an institutionalizing discourse that would transform unsupervised habit into systematic routine. This careful distinction was made, I would submit, on the basis of differentiating between spoken and written usage and on the basis of associating the writings of the language society with earlier redemptive textual events. Common usage belongs to its historical moment but is characterized as "blind," inarticulate, and by definition unsystematic, and is thus unrelated to "foundations." Society usage was also indebted to its own historical moment, but it represented a kind of purified usage that could be rendered standard in texts. It was thus capable of both "founding" and regulating anew. In their textual codification, then, the "foundations" of society usage would be appropriate to their context because they would be generated out of collective understanding; they would become standard by virtue of becoming institutionalized in texts. As monuments that created and embodied linguistic "law," society language theory texts would thus both commemorate and transcend their context of origin as a historical moment within the greater foundational narrative.

Common Speech and Society Usage: Finding/Inventing High German

Having defined their own historical period as one caught in a Babel-like linguistic confusion, the Nuremberg language theorists went on to define their role in their narrative of foundations as one of redeeming the vernacular by allowing its true and original purity to emerge in new, textual form. The reliance on the concept of textuality as a vehicle of redemption becomes apparent in a set of claims about *where* the "foundations" of this "new" vernacular were located. A first, important part of the argument relies on defining where these foundations were *not*, namely, in common speech. A second part focuses on locating exactly where they *can* be found, namely, in regulated textual usage, both of certain predecessors and in works authored by society members themselves. It is in the second part of the argument that the power of institutionalization becomes clearest as the conventions of a specific group take on normative status as they enter textual form.

In descriptions of the fragmentation and inauthenticity of the vernacular as it is currently used, the Nuremberg language theorists make clear that the contemporary linguistic "confusion" was not brought on by foreign invasion alone. Irresponsible and arbitrary common usage of the language by its own native speakers was just as responsible for the gradual obscuring of the intrinsic perfection of the vernacular as any foreign force. The emphasis put time and again on the distinction between contemporary common parlance and refined society usage is perhaps the single most revealing moment in the elaborately constructed story of the vernacular's "cleansed" identity. Because the Nuremberg language theorists were aware of the thin line they were treading between random habit and society convention, between asserting that history was at once the culprit in the defilement of language and the agent of its redemption, they waged a systematic battle against mere common parlance and for the "good custom," or contextually defined standards of good (society) usage, in order to define their time as a time of redemption rather than as one of further corruption of the mother tongue.

Schottelius in particular emphasizes that mere common parlance obscures natural fitness in language. Like many others, he refers to common usage as "blind," as incapable of representing things in an accurate way:

> If we wanted to measure our mother tongue against and justify it
> in terms of the way it is used according to many dialects in hundreds
> of ignorant ways and distorted by blind and inconstant usage, we would
> [find ourselves] constructing a language that would be for the most
> part an uncertain [unstable] wreck of a creature. (*Account*, 1:10)

Harsdörffer is more explicit: "May the blind usage [habit] of the ignorant masses stay put where it belongs" (*Funnel*, 1:125). Here as elsewhere, unreliable and arbitrary common usage is associated explicitly with the habits of the common person. "The unfounded usage among the common people is an abusive fraud," Harsdörffer declares (*Colloquies*, 3:329). This uncommonly vehement criticism of the lower classes in the language theory of a group dedicated to promoting vernacular culture may be understood both as a reaction to the potential instability of a doctrine of contextualism that finds absolutes produced by historical circumstance and as the product of a class-bound social consciousness. The linguistic standards of the vernacular language society had to be appropriate to contemporary circumstances, for it is only in such aptness that their "accuracy" would emerge. At the same time, only a rational, philosophically correct, and above all standardized (and codified) aptness would distinguish society norms from random public use. Schottelius explains, "The kind of usage that is at odds with a principal law or *foundation* [Grund] of a language is not [proper] usage but is, rather, an abusive adulteration" (*Art of Language*, 3, emphasis added). Thus it would be only by virtue of laws based on a language's "fundamental" forms that "eyes" would be given, Schottelius writes, to the "blind usage" of the *Volk* (*Art of Language*, 12–13).

Renouncing the use of various local dialects as models for this rationally derived language offered a way to begin to differentiate "good usage" from common parlance. While the dialects of Saxony and the Meissen area often appear individually as preliminary forms of a normative tongue,[40] the notion of a particular dialect as a source or model for a pure, standard tongue is most often rejected in the general statements under consideration here. Schottelius writes, for example:

> Our High German [HochTeutsche] language does not consist in this or that dialect. Rather, it demands no less time and effort as any of the other principal tongues enjoy to [attain] its final fundamental correctness and perfection. (*Account*, 1:bij r)

The use of the term *HochTeutsch* here to designate a correct, standardized tongue may have followed from Martin Opitz's use of the word a generation earlier: "But in order to be able to speak purely, we must make a great effort to approximate [the language] that we call High German and not local speech."[41] Sigmund von Birken makes clear, however, that High German—like the "principal tongue," which is its model—is not yet any more than a theoretical construct: "For there are many dialects, to be sure, but only one German language."[42] The contextualist logic upon which such statements relied demanded that the historical present be emphasized as a possible source of a transcendentally accurate language (rather than exclusively as a moment of linguistic dissolution) but that this present also be clearly distinguished from a general context of random error. Emphasizing the "fundamental correctness," or philological accuracy, of the vernacular as it would be used by society members (in contradistinction to the random linguistic habits represented by multiple dialects) opened up the space from which this "new" language was to emerge.

It was in response, then, to the necessity of defining what High German might be—since it was not yet present in common use—that usage by society members appears so often in direct and explicit opposition to "the incorrect habits" ("die unrichtigen Gewonheiten") of random speech. *Ex negativo* logic converts here to positive statements. Schottelius writes:

> It is thus proper that we should overlook incorrect habits, which neither have any foundation in nor find any acceptance by the [standards] of true and fundamental correctness of the language. [Rather] first of all we should persist in completing an art of [our] language. To be sure, [in so doing] we should persist in all that agrees with general good usage and relies on fundamental law, or in whatever is able to locate its

unmistakable and correct origin and proof in the natural foundations of the language. (*Account*, 1:11)

The explanation that "general good usage" will reflect the "natural foundations of the language" makes it clear that Schottelius is referring not to the "common usage" ("gemeiner Gebrauch") of the man on the street. Common usage of the street is unreliable, even misleading and dangerous, as Harsdörffer writes: "Usage is a tyrannical law."[43] Good usage is to be found in a rationally standardized High German with discernible, legislated norms based on the vernacular's intrinsic capacity for perfection.

The development of an "art of language" ("Sprachkunst"), or philological method, that would systematically "legislate" vernacular "good usage" was thus to be the main goal of the society's language theory. Harsdörffer even goes so far as to suggest that the question of German's relationship to the *lingua adamica* is in fact a pedantic one, "a question for scholars rather than a necessary one." Of much greater importance is the systematic development of High German, the *Hochsprache*:

> It is of greater use to consider how High German, the principal and heroic tongue currently used, how this language could be brought to the level of greatest perfection, to a position of exceeding honor, to a technically correct constitution, and to a fundamentally correct orthography, and how it could be fully established therein. (*Funnel*, 1:124)

Johann Klaj is also more concerned with the work that "still must be done" (*Praise*, 410) in normalizing the vernacular than with the pedantry of proving its lineage. Like Schottelius, he believes that a "technically correct constitution" or legislation ("Verfassung") in which High German will be founded and its continued use guaranteed must be the fruit of the society's work. Schottelius writes elsewhere:

> Language must thus first and necessarily be given a certain technical shape [gewisse Kunstform] and the ways and means thereof must be made popular and commonly known. (*Introduction*, B v)

The plan to create a vernacular capable of fit reference and apt representation by means of correct legislation recalls Socrates' suggestion for a method (*techne*, or *Kunst*) whereby linguistic accuracy could be derived. The method would guarantee widespread (*gängig*) *correct*, rather than random, usage.

"Correct usage," out of which the "foundations" of standard German would emerge, would thus not follow the vulgar German learned "from the wet nurse" or "at the mother's breast."[44] Rather, it would be a "general *good* usage" (emphasis added), as Schottelius writes, judged according to *consuetudo*.[45] Harsdörffer understands *consuetudo* as the "usage that scholars have used and introduced" (*Funnel*, 1:125) and calls it "the most respectable of teachers" (*Colloquies*, 3:324) in the re-creation of a monosyllabically perfect German tongue. And for him, these scholars form the membership of the language society. "An all-benevolent God," he writes, "has aroused great minds to this end . . . They have with a combined effort formed a society [vergesellschaftet], and they will not neglect the continuance of such a fruitful endeavor [fruchtbringendes Vorhaben]" (*Funnel*, 1:124). Thus, in a conflation of the language society project with divine will, Harsdörffer declares that the conventions of the language society (and, in particular, of the Fruit-bearing Society) will establish the rules whereby the "natural" correctness of the vernacular will be restored. Schottelius points out the coincidence of a "natural" and an arbitrated perfection in German, thereby alluding, like Harsdörffer, to the language society's ability to generate standards with an authority beyond that which its (limited) historical origins could have produced:

> Thus both truth and nature must be in the German language, not just what the many have acquiesced to but also that to which the most distinguished of their teachers have simultaneously and unanimously agreed. (*Account*, 1:16)

By virtue of consensus, then, and common agreement among the learned few, the "good usage" of the language theorists themselves could be distinguished from random contemporary speech. Because it would be based in this usage, this language would commemorate its own (historical) moment of origins. And yet it would also transcend that moment by containing the "foundations" of a new German tongue capable of reflecting both "nature" and "truth." It was specifically as a series of *textual concretizations* of this foundational "good usage," a series that included the dictionary projects and the translations of foreign works into "good" German by language society members, that this consensus could be documented as having been achieved.

Textual Foundations: The Dictionary and Translation Projects of the Nuremberg Order

The first act of "legislation" concerned with establishing the "foundations" of vernacular "good usage" in regulatory textual form focused, then, on methodically collecting the "fundamentally correct" radicals into the publicly available form of a *Dictionarium*, or *Wortbuch*. The plan of compiling a German dictionary had originally been Schottelius's. Attempts to write "a lexicon from the foundations of the German language" (*Account*, 1:158) had been undertaken in the past, Schottelius explains, but "no really complete lexicon" (159) had been completed. While he offers examples of how such a dictionary might look (159–70), Schottelius was in fact unable to follow up on his project, and Harsdörffer, as early as 1647, announced that he would take up where The One Who Searches (*der Suchende*), as Schottelius was called in the Fruit-bearing Society, had left off.[46] The language that Harsdörffer uses to describe the dictionary indicates its rootedness in a discourse of redemptive textual forms.

The working title of Harsdörffer's German dictionary (*teutsches Dictionarium*) and his explanatory comments indicate precisely where the origins (both as sources and as new beginnings) of a fundamentally correct German were to lie:

> Title: A Complete Dictionary in Which the Majestic German Principal Tongue Is Raised up out of Its Foundations in an Artful and Proper Way, Established according to Its Innate Characteristics, Embellished by Its Radicals, Derivations, and Doublings, and Explicated by Means of Wise Maxims, Courteous Speech, Metaphors, and Sayings, Brought to Light for the First Time. Of Use and Indispensable to Those in Both Clerical and Lay Professions, Ambassadors, Trustees, Orators, Poets, and Lovers of Our Language.[47]

It is in Harsdörffer's commentary that the *textual* nature of the "foundations" becomes clearest. He glosses the terms he uses in the title in the following way:

> "Out of Its Foundations": That is, out of all German books. To read through all of these, everyone's help will be required, so that one person may extract special radicals, maxims, and sayings from the imperial edicts [Reichsabschieden], another from Goldast, a third from Doctor Luther, a fourth from the poets . . . Whatever is [of] common [usage] may be disregarded. (388)

Writing the dictionary is thus to be a collective act in which precedents will be compiled; they "must be learned and copied from usage" (389). It is clear, however, that this usage must be of a particular sort, namely, of the kind documented in the texts of the authorities cited, and not in common speech. Indeed, the foundations themselves are said to be explicitly textual. The "sayings" to be collected are glossed, for example, as "*phrases* in which the use of the words illuminates [their meaning]; these *phrases* must be taken from the *writers* [Scribenten] mentioned before"

(389, emphasis added). What emerges, then, from the list of guarantors is that each had been responsible for a significant *textual event* in the past. Thus the "correct usage" and "fundamentally correct custom" ("grundrichtige gewonheit")[48] to be catalogued in a language society dictionary would have authority because they would be based on authoritative textual acts.

The choice of standard setters in Harsdörffer's announcement is significant in its preference for written (above all, printed) language. Melchior Goldast had published collections of old German poetry in the early part of the century, texts potentially full of "ancient" vernacular forms.[49] The term *poets* may refer to the authors of these texts or to contemporaries of the language theorists, perhaps even to the theorists themselves who were also authors of poetic texts (and the historical present is thus represented as the source of authoritative foundations once again). Strategically most important, however, in the discourse of origins and authority invoked here are the imperial edicts and "Doctor Luther," Martin Luther, the great champion of the German vernacular whose German Bibles had made printing history. Referred to here as elsewhere in tandem, the great reformer and the language of imperial administration appear as guarantors of German as a revealed, divinely sanctioned language, on the one hand, and as the origin of widely distributed, collective prudence, on the other. Their combined appearance as privileged standards of vernacular usage and their common availability in print made them crucial precedents for the language theorists in their project to provide both the foundations of and the means of maintaining the pure forms of German in textual form.

The symbolic importance of Luther's German was central to the seventeenth-century language societies. The founding of the Fruitbearing Society in 1617 had itself been explained as a commemoration of Luther's Bible translation, thus raising the year 1517 in language society mythology to a moment of origin, to the genesis of the society's redemptive linguistics.[50] Gustav von Hille had written:

> It is especially to be observed that [this] well-loved and very famous society took its start [at a time] when precisely one hundred years earlier the blessed light of Scripture had begun to shine and the Holy Scripture had been pulled out from obscurity and translated in such a comprehensible way [wolvernemlich] and with a technical thoroughness [kunstgründig] into our German tongue as well as one man's skill could achieve. (*Palm Tree*, 9)

The stamp of divinity that Luther's translation of Scripture had bestowed on the vernacular was crucial. While 1517 was clearly not the year that society theoreticians should have chosen, because Luther's two major scriptural translations appeared in 1522 and 1534, the historical miscalculation is revealing of the way the language theorists located themselves in the eschatological narrative. Luther himself had stylized familiarity with classical languages and the ability to translate accurately as proof of a second Gift of Tongues; a "correct" German Bible would thus effect the inclusion of the vernacular in a community of divinely inspired, sacred tongues:

> For just as God desired to have his message communicated to the entire world and gave the Gift of Tongues [to the Apostles] to do so . . . just so now he has done the same thing.[51]

While Luther himself had never argued for the superiority of German as a national language—since his concept of a "sacred language" ("heilige Sprache") relied not on its country of origin but on demonstrating its commensurability with Christ as the Spirit made flesh—his own "blessing" of the vernacular, the "consecration of German [that he] achieved,"[52] had introduced the mother tongue into the community of holy languages in which the Word of God was expressed. It was precisely this Protestant theory of language, the belief, that is, in a vernacular capable of carrying a spiritual message in unmediated fashion directly to its receivers, that endowed German—both in Luther's eyes and in the eyes of those who came after him—with divine status.[53] Thus the emphasis in Hille's reference to the comprehensible ("wolvernemlich") nature of Luther's text. In a Pentecostal gesture, Luther had redeemed the vernacular; the language theorists would find the foundations of a new sacred tongue first in his texts and would then imitate him by integrating those foundations into their own texts in an appropriate way.

While it has been shown that the language of the "Luther Bible" in fact had little impact on linguistic norms at the time, Luther's German began to be cited almost immediately as the epitome of vernacular clarity in its ability to render the divine message of the Spirit in a transparent and unmediated way.[54] Although originally considered normative because, as revelation, it overcame history, Luther's language became embedded *in history* as a precedent, as an exemplary case, "ein gutter exemplar."[55] It may have been the overwhelming presence of his language in print that allowed it to function as the interface between divine and historical precedents. The juxtaposition of Luther's German with the language of the imperial code in the Nuremberg texts suggests that this was so. Luther himself had singled out the chancery language ("Canzeley-Sprache") of Saxon administrative organs as "the most common German language."[56] This idiom was not "common speech" ("Gemeinsprache"), not the language of the *Volk*. Rather, it was "a certain [sure] language" ("eine gewisse Sprache"), a single standardized vernacular comprehensible to all.[57] Like the language of the imperial government, then, the most normative form of the vernacular was the one most widely distributed and thus uniformly understood.[58] The association of Luther's language and the language of the imperial chancery that we see in Harsdörffer's gloss on the "foundations" of the language to be catalogued in his dictionary thus merely highlights the link that print and thus textuality had forged between them.

Many Nuremberg language theory texts find the "foundations" of a new German tongue in Luther's language and in the language of the chanceries. While some of the statements are obviously indebted to similar formulations of an earlier period, the fact that they reemerge here makes clear the redemptive and even political role the language society and its texts had designed for themselves in becoming the legislators of a spiritually sanctioned and contextually apt tongue. It seems that for the sake of the chronological coherence involved in the 1517–1617 one-hundred-year spread, it is the achievements of the Fruit-bearing Society that are emphasized over those of the Order of Flowers on the Pegnitz whenever Luther is mentioned—even in the texts of the Nuremberg group. Johann Klaj, for example, depicts Luther's translation of Scripture as a blessing of the vernacular in the following way:

> With the rising of the sun of Holy Scripture, Luther—may he rest in peace—planted sweetness, dignity, and suppleness in our language, removed all the words that might be rough or grating, and in their place enriched its capacity with a wide assortment of ingenious songs. (*Praise*, 395)

Klaj presents Luther here as an agent of both natural fertility ("implanted") and spiritual correctness in German. On the basis of this correctness, Klaj is then able to interpret the founding of the Fruit-bearing Society as a symbolic commemoration of Luther's heroic, Pentecostal act:

> So is the way of the world; time is consistent with itself and invents a new achievement every one hundred years . . .

> Then came Luther, the pride of German and an honor to it, and lit the light of the pure teachings of the Lord;
>
> He was an unarmed man who disdained the world, just as he wished; he defeated Babylon with a stroke of the pen.
>
> Just one hundred years hence, the well-esteemed brotherhood [guild] of the German Order of Heroes was founded; with its help the German language is thriving now.[59]

The redemption of the vernacular by Luther was thus part of a divine plan that guaranteed the restoration of the German language to perfection every one hundred years in a form appropriate to the time. The errors in language brought on by human usage, indicated here by the reference to the "Babylonian" habits of the Catholic church, had been rectified once. The collective reenactment by the language society (the brotherhood to which Klaj refers) of Luther's redemptive achievement had the power to do so again. The first language society's project of purification and standardization is thus invested by means of juxtaposition with the authority of revelation. Language theory written by those associated with the Order of Flowers on the Pegnitz, in turn, would commemorate the originary moment of both Luther's translation and the Fruit-bearing Society's renewal of the vernacular's sacred forms.

Unlike some of the other Nuremberg writers, Klaj does not juxtapose the language of imperial government to Luther's revealed language directly. Nevertheless, the moral code he insists that the chancery language embodies refers to the same timeless standards that the "ancient" forms of the vernacular had been said to contain

> [g]iven the fact that it [namely, the German language] is the very language that is written in the chanceries and [used] by the City Council, that hovers above the heads of [our] citizens, and that is used by the clergy in the performance of worship services.
>
> [Also] because it is the very same language that is used in the courts, that dominates recommendations, that dispatches communiqués, that calls regiments to order, that conducts wars, that punishes criminals, that rewards the pious, that fills pulpits, that encourages the despondent, and that drives fear into the hearts of the dastardly. (*Praise*, 410–11)

The just language of political administration and spiritual guidance thus seems to follow a divinely inspired "right reason" in its provision of guidelines and laws for all occasions and circumstances. As a result, it appears divinely infallible even as it sentences the guilty and rewards the innocent in a "contextual" way, in a vocabulary, that is, that is clearly rooted in seventeenth-century, urban life. This language is as reliable, then, in contemporary legal and ethical matters as Luther's language was appropriate to the absolute message of the Word.

Countless other theorists of the period, including Titz, Tscherning, Buchner, and Zesen, name the language of "the dear worker of miracles, Luther" as a standard.[60] The land's chanceries are cited, moreover, along with Luther and just as often, as a source of more than merely arbitrary linguistic norms in the Nuremberg writings. Schottelius writes, for example,

> For the chanceries are the correct schools in which the German language, insofar as it concerns civic affairs, has been practiced and often embellished in a most delicate way. (*Art of Language*, unpaginated foreword)

He makes clear elsewhere that it is the public recognizability, comprehensibility, and thus appropriateness of chancery language to its historical context that make it an appealing source of linguistic norms:

> It has taken time, [but] language has finally oriented itself toward High German or the High German "dialect," that is, [language] the way it is used now in Germany in public documents.[61]

These "public writings," Schottelius explains later, are the "publica imperii acta" of the imperial chancery (*Account*, vol. 1, "Dedication," b). Luther's language and "chancery speech" were thus designated as acceptable sources of "foundations," I would submit, because of a widespread acknowledgment among members of the learned community that because they were printed, both provided public, intersubjectively confirmable linguistic norms. It is thus the consensus of the community and accessibility to standards available in textual form that the language theorists implicitly declared coterminous with both nature and revelation in the legislation of linguistic standards. To make the "foundations" of a new and newly purified High German widely available in (society) texts would by definition place the texts alongside Luther's Bible translation and the imperial edicts as initiators and guarantors of linguistic "law."

Harsdörffer's description of the dictionary stops just short of naming individual society members as the standard setters for a pure German vernacular. They are identified only collectively as "the poets." But he prepares the way to be more explicit in his treatise on the poetical uses of this language, *The Poet's Funnel*, where he writes:

> [For instruction in] prose speech [language], we should read the writings of the German Cicero, Doctor Luther, first... Then we can read Aventinus, Goldast, Lehemann, Hordleder, and especially the imperial edicts, in which the purity [pure forms] of our language are to be found again, should they be lost everywhere else. (*Funnel*, 3:52)

Luther's status as a German Cicero was traditional, but Harsdörffer's repetition of the topos here in association with the "imperial edicts" as well as his insistence on the *textual* nature of these vernacular guarantees (they must be "read") signals the direction in which Nuremberg theory was to take the concept of a "method" for deriving High German. If the purity of a naturally fit tongue is no longer to be found in the mouths of the people, it is nevertheless still secure in writing, in *texts*, and in texts written by members of the language society in particular.

The attempt to direct attention to which texts were to supplement Luther's writings and the imperial code as the sources of legitimate contemporary language use is exemplified in the monumental Fourth Tractate in book 5 of Schottelius's *Account*, entitled "A Timely Report on the Well-Known, Learned, and Famous People and Authors Who Have Written, Both in the Past and Recently, on Germany and the Germans, on Germany's Condition, Essence, and Past History, and Especially on the German Language and [on Those] Who Have Written Anything Special and Astounding in German." The "Report" runs some sixty pages and does exactly what its title promises in great detail. It begins with mention of the Germans by Livy, Pliny, and Tacitus, and (proceeding not quite chronologically) names the obligatory standard bearers, Luther, Goldast, and the imperial edicts. It also dwells at great length on the texts and translations sponsored by authors of the Fruit-bearing Society and the Order of Flowers on the Pegnitz, thereby indicating that contemporary texts and, specifically, texts sponsored by language societies can function as "foundations" as well. The Nuremberg language theorists thus did not just refer to instituting and institutionalizing texts other than those they themselves wrote as sources for standardized High German. Rather, *in* the very founding texts themselves (the treatises on language theory and the dictionary prototypes) they invest their own texts (namely, those that had already been published) with foundational authority too.

It is thus to the founding power of the language society's own texts that Harsdörffer refers when he writes:

Among those who have demonstrated their knowledge of the language are the following: Luther, Aventinus, the authors of the imperial edicts, Lehemann, Colonel Opitz, Schottelius. (*Funnel*, 3:19)

As in Schottelius's "Timely Report," the language heroes of the language societies are made to join the community of exemplary authors and texts here and are absorbed as "institutors" into the company of predecessors commonly acknowledged to have foundational status. Opitz, the "father of German poetry,"[62] and Schottelius, the foremost contemporary authority on German, as well as those who follow their teachings—all are to become the new Ciceros and the new Luthers in the seventeenth-century project for developing a divinely sanctioned, naturally fit, and contextually appropriate mother tongue. Society texts could thus serve as institutions, both inaugurating and creating orthodoxy in the production of a "new" and sacred German tongue.

The Nuremberg language theorists may in fact have seen their own regulatory texts as forming new beginnings almost superior to the "foundations" "hidden" in the writings of their predecessors, since theirs was explicitly a project to catalogue, reveal, and disseminate knowledge of the pure tongue in the here-and-now. Their own "word books," or dictionary-type texts, are foundational primarily in two ways. First, although a "complete" German dictionary was not published until the mid–twentieth century, Schottelius and Harsdörffer in particular did engage time and again in various projects to systematically catalogue various elements and examples of the vernacular's "ancient" and pure forms in both dictionary- and encyclopedia-like texts, thus literally providing the building blocks of a new and redeemed German tongue.[63] The Sixth Tractate of book 5 of Schottelius's *Account* is perhaps the best example. It contains, as he explains in the subtitle, "The German Radicals, Complete with Explanations and Other Notes concerning Them." The catalogue is just under two hundred pages in length. Harsdörffer's catalogue of "poetic images" in book 3, part 2 of *Funnel*, although designed to serve as a source book for poets in need of metaphors, witty conceits, and the like, is also arranged alphabetically and contains in its just under four hundred pages of entries a series of monosyllabic radicals that in places is identical to Schottelius's list. Schottelius also creates an inventory over sixty pages long of "ancient German proper names" "out of the true foundations (ex genuino . . . fundamento) of the German language" in the Second Tractate of book 5 of his *Account*, and spends countless pages in book 2 on listing all of the German words that can be formed through either the addition of numerous prefixes and suffixes or a combination of monosyllabic root words. Harsdörffer had probably conceived of his *Denckring*, described in book 3 of *Funnel* (82–84), as a mechanical device that could generate with a turn the lists that Schottelius so painstakingly draws up in his *Account*. The ring is described as consisting of five concentric circles of increasing size, with the radicals, prefixes, and suffixes printed on them; by manipulating it, all manner of accurate German words could be produced. These kinds of Nuremberg texts play a key instituting role in the production of orthodoxy in that they bring the beginnings (foundations) of a purified tongue into existence in concrete form.

The second way in which the Nuremberg regulatory texts performed founding work is by referring to language society usage as standard. In their own texts language society members appear alongside Luther and the imperial code as guarantors of German's "fundamental correctness." An example is found in one of Schottelius's vast lists of "pure" German words, in particular, in chapters 11 and 12 of book 2 of his *Account*. Here, as in a historical dictionary, authors and texts are indicated as sources of the authorized usage of a given word, prefix or suffix formation, or expression derived from a combination of words. In the lists we find repeated reference to the imperial edicts (designated with the initials "R.A.," *ReichsAbschiede*), to Luther, to Goldast, and others. Equally as often, however, the abbreviations, "Harsd." (Harsdörffer), "Johannis Clai" (Klaj), "Dilh." (Dilherr), and "Sigismundus Betulius" (Birken) appear, all members of the Nuremberg Order of Flowers, whose names are given in full at the very beginning of Schottelius's *Account* (together with five pages of other "Authores") as the guarantors of "good usage" whose works have been used and cited as sources ("Gründe") in the composition of his tome. Thus, not only did the regulatory writings of the order themselves prove to be textual concretizations of the beginnings of a new era in their catalogues of radicals and other kinds of "pure" German words, but they also created their own authority by elevating society members to a position of priority within the very (textual) regulatory act itself.

Language society statutes make explicit the premise upon which these word books and lists were drawn up; all texts by members of the societies must serve as vehicles of High German. Hille recalls the duties of members of the Fruit-bearing Society:

> Thus it is incumbent upon society members above all else to maintain and practice our highly honored mother tongue in its [her] fundamental

essence [in ihrem gründlichen Wesen] and correct understanding
in their speeches, letters, and poems, [and to do so] without mixing
in strange [and] foreign patchwork words. (*Palm Tree*, 17)

The "practice" of the vernacular's pure and accurate essences can and must take place, then, in all society texts. Johann Herdegen, the historian of the Order of Flowers, likewise emphasizes that "maintaining the purity of the German language" consists in the textual practice of the group: it is each individual's duty to "further extend the fame of the German language by dint of his learned pen."[64] The emphasis here on written usage rather than on spoken habit reconfirms the distance between the merely random speech so often thought to document authenticity and the "good usage" of the order that—precisely because it was fixed in writing in texts—came to represent a stability equivalent to natural linguistic law.

The communal sanctioning of both a specific kind of poetic practice in the vernacular as well as of methods whereby "speeches," "letters," and "poems" in High German could be produced identified as normative not only the writing and publishing of *original* works by society members but their practice of *translating* foreign and ancient texts as well. In what has been called a "rehabilitation of the verbal arts" during this period,[65] translation, which had earlier been considered merely a preliminary stage in developing independent rhetorical and poetical skills, took on a new role in the purification, development, and enrichment of the national tongues. Harsdörffer considered translation to be related to the original Pentecostal gift of tongues: "It is a great and miraculous gift of God to be able to speak in many tongues" (*Colloquies*, 4:313). Thus the natural abundance and divine perfection of the vernacular could (ironically) be redeemed from its current spoiled state of confusion with the help of challenges from abroad. Schottelius writes, for example, of the necessity

that the true content of the foreign language that has been translated
be made quite obvious in real [eigentlich] and proper German words
and in expressions comprehensible to German understanding. Second,
that the well-being of the German language be promoted by the
translated, or Germanified [verteutschtes], book; that the arts, sciences,
history, and other *realia* be expressed [clothed in] and become known in
a very natural German; and thus that [the vernacular], which [already]
displays an abundance of words, become quite rich in art as well.
(*Account*, 2:1225)

The assertion of German's "natural" ability to produce words that are completely adequate ("real" and "proper") to the things that they designate is the basis for the society's theory of translation. The transfer of foreign words into German was considered an act that accepted and allowed for the historical change that caused surface linguistic differences. At the same time, translation was seen as an activity in which continuity of the translation with the message of the original was the ultimate goal. Although not so very different from classical theories of translation that gave priority to substantial over surface fidelity,[66] the Nuremberg theory of translating thus deemphasized the necessity to "reproduce the original"—indeed, often failed to acknowledge the author of the original text—and instead paid more attention to *producing a new text* whose primary duty would be to render the original in a language adequate to current, contextually oriented needs. The generating of new texts in German, texts linguistically "true" to their models but also as if original with and originating in a new time and place, would produce proof of the vernacular poet's independent ingenuity rather than indicating his beholdenness to voices from the past. Moreover, it would literally bring into existence more of the very monosyllabically rich and pure language upon whose "natural" abundance its success had initially been based by bringing into existence, by publishing, more German-language texts.

The Nuremberg theory and practice of translating were thus based on the notion of linguistic contextualism that lay at the foundation of language society linguistic theory. It would be "a great error," Harsdörffer writes, "and a wrongheaded belief to think that reason was tied to [only] certain languages and that scientific knowledge could not be explained and expressed in German too" (*Colloquies*, 2:57). Human reason, the sciences, and knowledge of both natural and historical events are universal; but their textual presence had to be appropriate to a specific time and place. Again Harsdörffer: "[H]ow could human reason, practically a divine thing itself, be tied to just one land? How could the universal musings of great minds be limited to and restrained in a single tongue?" (*Colloquies*, 1:370). Thus, when Harsdörffer describes three ways of translating into German, it is obvious that only the one that guarantees correct expression of the original meaning in contemporary linguistic forms can be defended:

> There are thus three ways of translating: (1) When one translates word for word, as schoolboys usually do. (2) When one takes hold of the meaning of the words and dispenses with [the words] themselves. (3) When one orients the idea or the understanding according to German

expression and explains the matter in the translation. If we are dealing with trafficking in foreign artworks in our language, no other kind of translating can take place other than this last kind. There is no problem with letting go of the words in the original language, if one is able to render the matter itself comprehensible. (*Colloquies*, 1:393)

The assumption upon which the argument here is based is one of the fundamental, epistemological accuracy of language, an accuracy that can be demonstrated, however, only if language is rhetorically successful as well. Accurate knowledge of "the matter itself" is possible in any and all tongues and thus is not bound to any one set of words. Thus the fidelity of a translation to the original "matter" in contextually appropriate form outweighs a kind of Ciceronian fidelity to the language in which that matter was originally expressed.

The practice of translation to which this preservation of matter rather than medium gave rise allowed for any steps to be taken in translating as long as they guaranteed the creation of a new text appropriate both to the "original" message and to the internal characteristics of the new tongue. Having read texts in a foreign language, Harsdörffer explains,

each [individual] ought to go home and write down the verses [rhymes] that occur therein, and ought to report for each line (1) the meaning of the words, (2) the intention of the author, and (3) how it would be expressed in proper German. (*Colloquies*, 3:79–80)

Difference—what is "proper" to each language—makes it inevitable that surface fidelity will give way to matters of substance. "Just as all human beings differ from one another in their bodily form, mind, voice, and gestures, so too does each and every language possess special characteristics that must be attended to" (*Colloquies*, 7:515). Thus it would be an error to think that translation could (or should even try to) preserve the (linguistic surface of the) original in its entirety. "Translating is not unlike an artful or [even] unartful [inept] [unkünstlichen] painting, which, even if it is characterized by the utmost perfection, can never represent [darstellen] the natural constitution [of the thing]" (*Colloquies*, 3:80). Harsdörffer reasons that "if it happens that the translator wanders from the letter [of the original], but [in so doing] retains its meaning, then his well-intentioned achievement will not lack for praise" (*Colloquies*, 3:80). To translate a text into German according to language society theory meant, then, to create a new (German) text and thus to literally make present (in writing or print) more instances of the pure, redeemed mother tongue.

The "loss" of (the surface of) the original in translating thus indirectly guaranteed the production of a new text and of a new moment of authority in German since the act of translation was understood by the Nuremberg theorists not as a moment of transfer but, rather, as a moment of poetic insight and creativity, of the translator's own understanding and representation of the thing itself.

> Although it is incumbent upon the translator to stay close to the meaning of the original language [words], sometimes the thoughts of subtle minds are so lofty that they cannot be expressed adequately or comprehensibly [by translating those words] into our tongue. This is why one must abandon the sense of the words [*Wortverstand*] and translate just the meaning, insofar as it is more responsible to stray too much from the original language and [in so doing] make oneself understood than to stay so close [to the original] that the reader is not able to grasp or comprehend. (Harsdörffer, *Funnel*, 3:37–38)

The mediation that occurs in translation is thus only superficially between two languages. At a more fundamental level, Harsdörffer asserts, a transfer actually occurs between the "thing" that must be expressed and the translator ("making oneself understood"). Schottelius's rule that the translator must know both languages "fully and in [their] foundations" (*Account*, 2:1221) is based on a similar interplay of understanding and expression, because it is only in and through the mind of the translator that the "fundamental" meaning of a word occurs. The doctrine of contextualism, of maintaining that universal truths could also be "made real" in historically specific form with no loss, clearly also had an impact here.

It should come as no surprise, then, that the measure of correctness in translating for the Nuremberg theorists consisted in being able to mistake a translated text for one written originally in German. "The best translation is the one that cannot be distinguished as such" (*Funnel*, 3:39). The German translator must free himself from the strictures of the language in which the text was originally written in order to create the matter in and of his text in new and adequate form.

> But it is to the enormous credit [of a translation] when it appears practically the same as the original, as if it had been German from the very beginning. This happens when the translator does not tie himself down to the properties of the foreign language in which [the text] was originally written. (Birken, *Art of Poetry*, 179)

In fact, the translator seems almost free to ignore the surface of the original text entirely, since it is the creation of "the thing itself" in German "for the first time" rather than preservation of the original linguistic vehicle that is at stake. Translating is thus no longer considered a crutch to which untalented poets turn in the absence of original ideas. To give adequate expression to thoughts in a text composed in one's own language, regardless of the origins of those thoughts in a prior text, qualifies as original expression: "It may not be less of an artistic achievement, then, to translate something thoroughly [gründlich] than to invent it out of one's own mind" (Harsdörffer, *Colloquies*, 3:81). Thus, it is not merely that the *verbum verbo* theory of literal translation is rejected here, as it had been for centuries. Rather, translating is equated with original textual production, with the production of "original" texts.

Language society theories of translation were motivated, then, by a desire to overcome history—to efface the historical origins of a predecessor text—even as they desired that the translated texts "make history" by making more of a redeemed German language present in textual form. The translations themselves were thus institutions, new and standardizing (textual) concretizations of German's redeemed forms. The activity of translating was no less than an obsession for Prince Ludwig, the founder of the Fruit-bearing Society, as Dünnhaupt has shown.[67] Ludwig's work was exemplary for the members of the Nuremberg group. He was the author of approximately fourteen translations of texts, primarily from the French and Italian, including the works of Bartas, Bec-Crespin, Geslin, Gelli, Malvezzi, and Petrarch. Perhaps even more significant than the translations themselves was the fact that Ludwig, with the help of the famous pedagogue Wolfgang Ratichius, founded his own printing press and shop in Köthen the year after the Fruit-bearing Society began. Ratichius's method of instruction for translation in the schools was based on having students read translations of foreign works first and then the works themselves;[68] the method itself thus necessitated the availability of translated texts, which the prince's "house press" (the Fürstliche Drückerei, as the imprints read) provided. Ludwig's project of translating was supported and extended by others affiliated with the Köthen group. Diederich von dem Werder (1584–1657) provided both partial and full translations of Tasso's and Ariosto's major epic texts.[69] Johann Wilhelm von Stubenberg (1619–63) gained entrance to the Fruit-bearing Society on the basis of translations of works by Biondi, Loredano, and Marini; thereafter, he continued his project, producing German versions of the works of Bacon, Grenaille, Scudéry, and Sorel.[70]

Although it may have been obvious in the case of Ludwig's translations that the prince was their "author," since the colophons show the Fürstliche Drückerei as the place of publication, it is the German language and the fact of the translations themselves that appear to be emphasized in the titles of many of these other texts. Werder's translation of the *Dianea* by Loredano is characterized, for example, as having been achieved by the "majestic German language"; Werder as translator/author is not named.[71] Similarly, Stubenberg's *Eromena* by Biondi is said to have been translated by "our magnificent mother tongue," Loredano's *Scherzi geniali* into "our most honored, High German mother tongue," and so on.[72] And even when the author/translator is identified, as in the case of most of Stubenberg's other translations, it is only with his society name, The Unhappy One (*Der Unglückliche*), that he appears in the titles; thus it is his society affiliation that is emphasized, as is the case in Ludwig's Petrarch and Malvezzi translations too, where the Fruit-bearing Society is said to have officially "approved" ("gutheissen") the translation and thus serves as the primary sponsor of the text. The translations are identified, then, as instances of pure German come into being under society sponsorship rather than as the products of particular authors. It is their textual appearance, then, and the work that the translations do to give the redeemed language shape that demonstrate the instituting power of society texts.

Many members of the Order of Flowers on the Pegnitz—among them, Birken, Neumark, and Schottelius—followed the footsteps of their predecessors in the Fruit-bearing Society (some were members of both groups) in devoting some time to the work of translating. It was Harsdörffer in particular, however, who dedicated himself both to translating and to securing the publication of translated texts in a fashion that paralleled the work of Ludwig and his friends.[73] What is significant about Harsdörffer's translations is the extent to which they too declare their presence as texts published under sponsorship of a language society (rather than as testimonies to Harsdörffer's individual achievements) and thus as instantiations of vernacular abundance made real in printed form. Of all of Harsdörffer's works, it was the translations that seem to have gone through the greatest number of reprintings.

What appears to have been significant for Harsdörffer, moreover, was not *how* he arrived at a translation but, rather, the fact of the translation itself. His German *Diana* by Montemajor provides a revealing example. Here Harsdörffer identifies the original author and also makes clear that he (Harsdörffer) was only the "editor" of parts 1 and 2 that had originally been translated into German by Kuffstein in 1619. He nevertheless does identify himself (with his initials) as the translator of part 3 of the text, which was not written by Montemajor, but by Gil Polo, whom Harsdörffer names. What is significant for the institutionalizing power of this text, however, is that Harsdörffer effaces the fact of an extra step, so to speak, in the translating process. The first translation of part 3 of the *Diana* from the Spanish was in fact that of Caspar von Barth in an earlier *Latin* translation, which is not named. When Harsdörffer writes in the title that part 3 had "never been translated before" ("zuvor nie gedolmetscht"), what he means is that it had never been translated before *into German*. This, the providing of a German-language version, was to be Harsdörffer's task. Suppressing a key predecessor text might not seem crucial here. In other translations, however, such as his *Der grosse Schauplatz/jämmerlicher Mordgeschichte* (The grand theater of lamentable murders, 1649), which is a German version of Jean Pierre Camus's *L'amphithéâtre sanglant*, the title identifies the text as a translation but omits the name of the original author. Harsdörffer does not, however, allow his own name as "editor," for example, to stand in its place (even though he did, apparently, do the work of collating the stories of Camus and others). Rather, he designates as the "author" "A member of the most praiseworthy Fruit-bearing Society" and thus indirectly identifies the translation as the society's work. Although Harsdörffer often does name authors in his translations of texts by Camus, Cornaro, Eustache du Refuge, and others, and sometimes identifies himself as translator (although again, only with his initials after the dedication rather than on the title page), it is not his achievement but, once again, always that of the society that is stressed. It is thus the *concrete presence* of his translations as "new" texts written in purified German that was to be emphasized to a German reading public, not their indebtedness to or origins in foreign places or tongues. The translations were thus to serve as institutions, as texts that founded and expanded the "praiseworthy" German tongue for which society statutes called by casting themselves in the role of "originals" and standard setters in linguistic matters.

Thus, in both the theory and practice of translating developed by the Baroque language societies, appealing to a text's inner substance, or nature, as the measure of accuracy allowed the translator to prove that meaning was not bound to any one time or mode of expression but could always be "made real" "for the first time" in multiple forms as long as it was rendered accurately in every and all tongues. The theory was based on the chiastic logic of contextualism that informed the institutionalizing project of the language society: only by effacing the authority of transcendence as "other" could one's own (historical) authority emerge. In practice this meant giving expression to as much knowledge as possible in texts translated into the society's "naturally" monosyllabically rich, divinely sanctioned language. These texts demonstrated that the vernacular was capable of being "original," of producing philosophically and philologically accurate representations of all things in contextually appropriate words. Proof of German's richness thus came not in a competition with authors of predecessor texts but in an internal test of the vernacular's capacity to render the substance of those texts truthfully in texts of its own. The countless translations produced by society members and their sheer abundance in multiple reissuings in the name of the society thus "proved" German's richness and ability to provide origins. Like the dictionary projects, then, the translations by society members provided the foundations of the new, High German tongue.

The crucial feature of the language theory of the Order of Flowers on the Pegnitz was thus a doctrine of contextualism, a strategy that created "natural" fitness in language by means of historically generated linguistic standards while also maintaining that these standards reflected universal norms. This doctrine was created in and as two kinds of textual events: one, a foundational narrative with its roots in the classical and Judeo-Christian traditions, the other, a set of regulatory writings (dictionaries and translations) designed to call for the creation of and to instantiate pure forms of the mother tongue. The foundational narrative was used to avoid charges of random, historical relativity by describing German's divine and "natural" properties, by commemorating the language of the Garden, and by linking the vernacular to a revealed linguistic precedent that, in its divine motivation, set the standard for a naturally fit tongue. This narrative enabled the language theorists to separate their language from everyday speech. Their own usage—as captured in the linguistic forms of the regulatory texts—could thus become canonical, their own habit naturally fit, and thus their own rule of consensus an origin of "natural law." The High German called for and created in the society's regulatory texts was thus understood as both a sacred (or natural) and a historically apt tongue. Its origins and normative forms were being made present in the (historical) work of society texts.

As a conceptual system, Nuremberg language theory could easily have fallen prey (as it did, some years later) to the accusation of overstylization, to the charge, that is, of too great an efficiency in forcing a collective code of expression upon all individuals and their texts. Language was said to have been drained of all immediacy as it was "legislated" into linguistically orthodox forms as a way of competing with ancient and foreign tongues. And yet, it was precisely this codification that permitted claims for German's authority to be made. Ironically, then, the absolute authority of the society's linguistic standards fell victim to the very rhetoric of consensus that had been its original source of justification. With the passing of the collective came the passing of the fitness of its norms. The historical consciousness built into this irony perhaps explains the emergence of subsequent theories of language; Herder, for example, emphasizes the possibility of a "natural" language in individual utterances. Only by recourse to individual genius, to the standard, that is, of the absolute fitness of individual (rather than collective) insight, could the dichotomy between the historical and the universal be overcome. And yet, in and as texts, the Nuremberg treatises on language theory did celebrate and establish the conditions of possibility for a fully legitimate and competitive vernacular at midcentury. The technical treatises on poetics of the Nuremberg writers fulfilled the same textual function by providing the building blocks of a competitive vernacular poetic tradition in language society texts. It is to the poetics of the Order of Flowers that we now turn.

4   *Institutiones Poeticae*

A Defense of Vernacular Poetics

In the dedication to *Teutsche Rede-bind und Dicht-Kunst* (1679) (hereafter cited as *Art of Poetry*), addressed explicitly to the membership of the Order of Flowers on the Pegnitz as "patron," Sigmund von Birken dwells at length on the place he finds his text, a technical treatise on poetics, inhabiting in a larger narrative about poetry's "history." His depiction of the history of poetry points to the doubled function of poetological theory for the Nuremberg language society: its power to be institutional by both inaugurating and regulating a new literary tradition in and by means of language society texts.

Poetry is the child of pastoral, Birken writes; it was "born and raised in fields and groves," "the daughter of the first golden age" (*Art of Poetry*, iij). This originary age was, however, according to Birken's account, a clearly Judeo-Christian, rather than classical, one. It was Jacob, Moses, and David who were in fact the first singers, the original "shepherds and divine poets" ("HimmelsDichtere"). The Greek Arcadia, the classical locus of both pastoral poetry and poetry's origins in pastoral, merely reproduced this original, Christian model, he writes. The priority of pastoral's and poetry's Christian origins explains why Birken can go on to claim that the "new" version of pastoral represented by the Nuremberg language society, which he calls the "Society of Shepherds on the Pegnitz" (*Art of Poetry*,):(iiij), and by the poetry it was to produce would be more authentic and would have far greater authority than either the classical models or any number of Renaissance texts based on them, by Lope, Sidney, and Montemajor, for example. Precisely because it represented these Christian origins reborn, the new (vernacular) pastoral collective would be able to re-found and to serve as the reincarnation of both the genre's and all of poetry's first moments and purest forms.

> It seems that time, which ought now soon to become a matter of eternity, is like a snake that has curled itself up into a circle, now

returning to its origin (Ursprung) as it approaches its end. [That is,] time is coming to an end in the very same activity with which it made its beginning, [namely,] by making the poets of today into shepherds ... Since we are a society of shepherds who are learned in things poetic, just like the one that emerged at the beginning of the world, who is better able to write of this art [namely, poetry] than we? (*Art of Poetry,*): (iij verso to):(iiij recto) and):(v verso)

Who better, indeed, to do the work of initiating and regulating a new (historical) period of vernacular textuality than a group of shepherd-poets whose identity was linked to the Christian origins of poetry? Where better to do this work than in texts that both describe and claim to instantiate vernacular poetry's privileged origins and standard forms?

The remarks that open Birken's technical treatise on poetics are symptomatic of the instituting and institutionalizing program behind the Nuremberg poetological endeavor. It is a program organized around the development of a discourse about poetry's (new and better) beginnings in the theoretical texts of the order. The poetics of two of the Nuremberg theorists in particular, Harsdörffer and Birken, locate the (absolute) legitimacy of their (historical) effort to "found" a new moment of poetic "history" in the power of language society texts to *supersede* those of the Ancients in the very making present in texts of poetic origins both chronologically prior (i.e., from Old Testament time) and theologically superior (i.e., Christian) to them. As a result, vernacular texts—exemplary poetry as well as the technical poetics themselves—can quite literally replace ancient ones wherever and whenever authoritative textuality is sought (such as in the handbooklike poetics texts that establish rules for composition and set precedents). The textual presence of vernacular poetry in the Nuremberg poetological treatises as well as the very presence of the vernacular poetics themselves was designed to demonstrate *not* vernacular poetry's indebtedness but rather its superiority to ancient poetry. This superiority was legitimated rhetorically by the declaration that this newly created (and thus historically bound) set of theoretical and poetic texts had its roots in nature and the divine. That this superiority and this power to found were ultimately justified by their elucidation in theoretical texts consisting to a large extent in citations of poetic texts by society members themselves reveals the monumental nature of the Pegnitz poetics. They "immortalize" the conventions of the group in texts that, precisely as texts, become absent from their historical, contextual origins as they take on the status of poetological law.

The historical scheme upon which Birken's description of the superior origins of an explicitly Christian vernacular poetry is based can be heard in Harsdörffer's words in part 3 of *Der poetische Trichter* (The poet's funnel) (1653): "The world is like an old man who, as his age increases, grows in experience by virtue of hard work and application. Who would believe that he would have known more or been cleverer in his childhood than in his peaceful and wise age of maturity?" (28). Both Harsdörffer's and Birken's theoretical treatises on poetry demonstrate that precisely by virtue of its "increased age" and nonpresence to poetry's "youthful" origins in classical times, vernacular poetry can "outdo"—and thus do without—the "first forms" of poetry conventionally understood as having occurred in ancient texts. The vernacular poetics thus literally "stand in" for their ancient predecessors and thereby produce new and "better" (Christian) origins for poetry rooted in a new and better time.

The literal displacement of ancient texts (whether cited in whole, in part, or merely by title) by their German-language successors on the pages of the Nuremberg technical treatises on poetics is in fact the most common of the concrete strategies used in these texts to make this instituting and self-legitimating claim. The tendency, moreover, in the Pegnitz technical treatises to dwell upon arguments about vernacular poetry's "closeness to nature" and to emphasize the concept of *inventio* both as a fundamental element of their descriptions of vernacular poetry and as the organizing principle behind the vast prescriptive sections of the treatises themselves reveals the fundamental belief of the Nuremberg theoreticians that vernacular poets will be able to "find" (invent) the "origins" of "natural" poetic creativity or talent in their own (that is, in language society) texts. It is precisely the authority of vernacular poetry as an "original" that the Nuremberg poetological theorists contend their *poetics* can (re)produce as a *textual event* ("without the help of the Latin tongue," as the subtitle of Harsdörffer's poetics reads) in German and in German alone. The two Nuremberg poetics upon which I concentrate here, by Harsdörffer and Birken, like many others in the German Baroque tradition (including those by Stieler, Männling, Kindermann, and Omeis), can thus be understood as *textual institutions*. By their very existence and their having been written as prescriptive poetological texts in German, they formulate an originary logic for vernacular poetry and poetics and provide that poetry's concrete origins—in the form of lists of rules and compositional models, for example—within the borders of their very own texts.

The technical treatises on poetics are thus perhaps the most clearly institutional of all of the Nuremberg language society's texts. They do the work of history by both marking and masking the historical rootedness of the originating and regulatory gestures they make. Much of the substance of these treatises is devoted, for example, to describing the various genres (epic, dramatic, and verse), to explaining and enumerating rhyme schemes and verse forms, and to cataloguing the numerous forms of occasional poetry (*Gelegenheitsdichtung*) that constituted vernacular "literature" at the time. These "catalogues" provide the literal foundations for any future German-language poetic text. As concrete monuments, moreover, to the poetic practice of a particular period, they are signs of the rootedness of vernacular originality in the conventions of the time.[1]

The instituting and institutionalizing gestures that the Nuremberg poetics make explain the only apparently paradoxical claim that these highly schematic poetics quite often make, namely, that the legitimacy of vernacular poetry lies in its ability to be "as-if-inspired" and "artless" art. Behind the competing claims and textual tasks of the poetics—to be prescriptive, on the one hand, and to function as (historical) sources of "original" poetry, on the other—there lies the chiastic logic of the institution, a logic that constructs in the poetological treatises *a foundational discourse* about vernacular poetry's spontaneity and closeness to nature even as it embeds in this discourse *textual models* cited from (historical) society practice. As historical monuments and institutions, the poetics thus testify to their origins in convention, both in postclassical, Christian time and in the particular forms of occasional poetry practised and published by members of the group. At the same time, as concrete textual events, they transcend those origins precisely as prescriptive catalogues designed to ensure the implementation of custom as law.

Constructing a logic of vernacular poetry's superior origins and providing concrete forms for these origins (that is, schematic guides and "model" vernacular texts of all kinds) thus were the main purposes of the handbooklike poetics of the Nuremberg language society. The paradox of institutionalization (the providing of historical origins in a textual form deliberately designed to outlast those origins) helps explain how the prescriptive authority of these schematic texts could be based precisely on their ability to substitute for the Ancients, for spontaneity, and for the "natural talent" described as essential to vernacular creativity. The necessity for treatises to be written that could "teach" (*instituo*) the mechanics of composing creative texts assumes the absence of spontaneity and creativity in the production of new texts.

I focus on this paradox not as a contradiction but rather as productive of the Nuremberg poetics as *institutiones poeticae* and of their power to be the "origins of history" by the very act of their having been written. As a result, I am less interested in their function as prescriptive handbooks either indebted to ancient rhetorical treatises or to be compared to the poetic texts they so carefully describe. Illustrating such indebtedness creates only an imbalance between ancient and vernacular authors and texts, attributing to the Moderns a kind of unthinking appropriation of the authoritative statements of the past.[2] In comparing theoretical descriptions at random to poems written and published at the time, moreover, only the correlation or lack thereof between theoretical prescription and textual performance can be traced;[3] the internal coherence and strategic maneuvering of the poetics themselves are ignored. My analyses focus, then, on the textual strategies of the technical treatises themselves, strategies that defined them and the vernacular poetry that they contain as institutions capable of beginning and regulating a legitimate German-language poetic tradition.[4]

Like the society's language theory, the Nuremberg poetics were designed to fulfill the order's (historical) task of creating "new beginnings" for vernacular poetry in its texts. The turn to history, to context, and to the origins of a "pure" vernacular in locally generated forms that Nuremberg language theory embodies, but elides in its obsession with a metadiscourse of linguistic abundance and fitness, is rendered in the technical treatises on poetry by means of and as a similarly constructed series of textual events. Although these events often occur simultaneously in the Nuremberg poetics, I separate them into two categories in the discussion that follows in order to clarify their instituting and institutionalizing roles. First, a *foundational discourse* about the *internal aptness* of German-language poetry maintains that it is dialectically accurate and rooted not in *imitatio* but, rather, in the *inner nature* of that which it represents. The notion around which this discourse is organized is that of *invention*. The "aptness" of vernacular inventions both to that which they represent and to the context in which they are produced demonstrates the "truth" of the arguments "found" in and by vernacular poetry. German-language poetry is thus defined as competitive with—indeed, even superior to—an imposing literary tradition often equated with nature and often thought of as inspired, universal, and absolute. In turn, the *ars poetica* of the vernacular academy is described as being able to "teach" modern poets what the Ancients were said to "innately" ("naturally") have possessed.[5] Second, the description and construction in society poetics of detailed *compositional models and rules* are designed to both create and ensure easy access to a future orthodoxy of vernacular poetic practice. These descriptive and prescriptive sections are in fact organized in both Birken's and Harsdörffer's treatises around the concept of invention upon which the foundational discourse is based. The models themselves thus also provide a way of "finding" the building blocks of apt arguments and true forms that guarantee the externalization of German poetry's "true insights" into always appropriate textual form. The beginnings of a new and legitimate vernacular tradition can thus be found, as is the case in Nuremberg language theory, in language society texts. The fact that the textual models were also for the most part authored by members of the society increases the strength of this claim.

It is, finally, precisely this emphasis on *textuality* in the Nuremberg poetics and the valorization of whatever becomes *textually present* in German that demonstrates their institutionalizing force, and yet also reveals their limitations in a way that highlights the paradox of institutionalization much more clearly than the language theory texts.[6] In the descriptive sections of the poetics, where the focus is on the origins and thus originality of society poetry, "true" poetic insights (based on the vernacular poet's "natural talent" and imaginative inventiveness, and thus on *inventio* rather than on *imitatio*) can be made present only in *externalized* (the German term is *ausbilden*, literally to "make an external picture") *textual form*; their origins "in nature," spontaneity, and "talent" *must* be absent, in other words, in order for a "true text" in the vernacular to take shape.

The prescriptive sections of the Nuremberg treatises or poetics, whose function was to act as actual *textual origins* for the future production of "inventive" vernacular poetry by providing schematic descriptions of how it should look, do in fact claim to themselves already contain, as I have suggested earlier, proof that these imaginative insights can be made real in vernacular texts. And yet this claim that the future of vernacular poetry is already present and real compromises the institutionalizing task of the treatises because it shuts the compositional mechanism down, so to speak, by already completing, within their own boundaries, the job that the treatises say must be done. Thus the need for and possibility of the ongoing invention of vernacular texts is effectively stopped whenever the monumental function of the *institutiones poeticae* takes the upper hand. And this is often the case. In endowing the actual textual practice of the group (rooted in the historical genres of occasional poetry) with both foundational and normative power by absorbing it into and allowing it to dominate the society's prescriptive texts, both Harsdörffer and Birken in effect limit the usefulness of their treatises as the "beginnings" of a future tradition, because they implicitly suggest that this future is already present in their own texts. By fixing the standard of aptness in a repertoire of model texts (themselves to be imitated) rather than in abstract principles or descriptions of method, the poetics thus ultimately favor rote imitation—both of their own poetic texts and of the text of the poetics—over the possibility of future, potentially different forms of apt practice based on new contextual needs. The possibility of a future of different kinds of poetry in the vernacular is thus effectively denied by the existence of the poetics, texts that, on a conceptual level, make the possibility of difference (from the Ancients) the foundation of their claim to legitimacy.[7]

The doubled institutional nature of the technical treatises and the limitations of the society's institutional endeavor in general begin to become clear, then, in an analysis of their foundational claims, concrete structures, and textual strategies. If the language theory of the Nuremberg order was to redeem the vernacular by associating it with the lost language of the Earthly Paradise and by (re)-creating pure forms of German in society texts, the purpose of the *poetics* of the society was to create in *German-language texts* (1) a foundational discourse about the "originality" of an "as-if-inspired" vernacular poetry based on a description of its "origins" in nature (rather than in imitation)[8] and (2) the patterns and rules (based on *inventio*) for creating that poetry's first (original) forms. These rules are most often made present in the Nuremberg "theoretical" texts in the form of citations of language society poetry and prose. By limiting, however, the literal building blocks of a future of German-language poetry to the forms present in society texts, the poetics—which, as monuments, attempt to outlast their historical moment of origin by defining society usage, as it appears in all society texts, as standard and productive of a new (historical) tradition and of that tradition's norms—remain firmly bound to that origin. The present chapter investigates the strategies that the poetological treatises as texts use to do this instituting and institutionalizing work and assesses the possibility of such a future when its origins and foundations are so firmly located in the conventions of a particular group.

Art, Nature, and Inspiration in the Tradition of Technical Poetics

Since the Ancients, the desire for originality, authenticity, and truthful representation in poetry has been associated less with the rhetoric of individual genius associated with Romantic and post-Romantic poetics than with a discourse of divine inspiration that singled out the poet as a vessel for truths having their origins in myth. One of the earliest moments of divinely sanctioned poetry occurs, moreover, within the framework of a pastoral collective; Hesiod's description of "rude shepherds" inspired by the Muses (*Theogony* 11.26ff.) opens the first account of how "true" knowledge of the origins and ends of the universe was made accessible to humanity in verse. On a symbolic level, it was this account and its authority as a narrative of origins that the theorists associated with the Nuremberg "Order of Shepherds" sought to re-create within their own Christian time.

The fiction of a poetic method capable of guaranteeing inspired, "true insights" was of course omnipresent in many of the technical poetics of the European Renaissance and Baroque. Vida, for example, begs the Muses to inspire him ("inspirate animum") on his "way" to a new (i.e., vernacular) poetry ("novosque ostendite calles"); Ronsard writes of "le Daimon" who presided at his birth, bestowing on the champion of French poetry a "fureur d'esprit" equal to the power of the Hesiodic dream.[9] In defending vernacular writers' ability to produce "true" poetry, the Germans thus followed the general tendency to seek origins for the new vernacular traditions in a narrative of divine spontaneity, a narrative that told of a poetry rooted both in nature and in human history and change. The origins of this poetry would thus imitate the myth of ancient poetry's divine origins while also making clear the myth's inappropriateness to a Christian age and thus the necessity of developing a new definition and moment of nature in vernacular texts.

The originality and legitimacy of vernacular literary forms were defended on the basis of assertions of a proximity to nature and divinity in poetic representation. This proximity allegedly provided insights analogous to those attributed to divine inspiration in ancient myth. The rhetoric of *invention* (in German, *Erfindung*) and of the internal *aptum*, or appropriateness to the "thing itself," that is emphasized in vernacular poetics in general at midcentury was part, then, of a fundamental argumentative strategy that described how to guarantee the presence of just such "true insights" in vernacular texts without resorting to "pagan" explanations. The discussion in the Nuremberg treatises of the necessity for *natural talent* and the ability to write "inspired," insightful poetry can be explained as derived from this powerful subtext of *aptness of word to thing*. This subtext is based on definitions of accurate representation found in ancient and contemporary sources in both the dialectical and rhetorical traditions. Such definitions were mustered to combat mythological explanations of poetry's origins with "scientific" ones more appropriate to a postclassical age. It is to the historical and conceptual origins of this *subtext of aptness* and its relationship to the argument about how a poet's "inspired insight" and "natural talent" can be guaranteed by textual means that I turn first before analyzing its (re)construction in the Nuremberg poetics themselves as the first part of their foundational discourse.

The internal chiasmus upon which many vernacular technical treatises rely, the strategy, that is, of embedding the rules and regulations of prescriptive poetics designed to guarantee aptness in a rhetoric of inspiration and talent, surfaces already in the classical tradition's opposition between *art* and *nature*, between poetic skill as a technique or learned craft, on the one hand, and as the individual's innate or divinely inspired ability to represent accurately, on the other. The claim of divine inspiration had its roots in descriptions of *poetic* identity; the distinction between *natura* and *ars* originally belonged to the *rhetorical* tradition, however, into which the technical aspects of poetological theory had gradually been absorbed; "from the time of its incorporation into the trivium, poetry was conceived as a species of rhetorical excellence."[10] The art-nature dyad was meant to separate in theory what was seldom separate in practice, namely, deliberately situational (i.e., potentially "merely" rhetorical) strategies, on the one hand, and true insights, earnest convictions, and the representation of truth, on the other. Since the time of Plato's attacks on the Sophists as creatures of occasion and his charge in *Republic*, book 10, that nearly all poets were liars, precisely this rivalry between the "philosophical" and the "rhetorical" schools had caused "art" and "nature" to be realigned, even linked, in such a way as to stress the concept of "fitness" (*aptum*) as a measuring stick for the "verbal arts."[11]

Just as random usage of language could compromise its ability to represent accurately, the tradition went, so too could mere circumstance leave poetry at the mercy of the partisan cause; used for random persuasion, both rhetoric and poetry could wander from their ideal office of true representation. In response to this danger, guidelines (*ars*) had to be established to guarantee a fit relationship of *verba* to *res*, reflecting their "natural" accord. Theorists of "philosophical rhetoric"—including Plato, as well as Aristotle and then Theophrastus—picked up on this logic, maintaining that adherence to an "art" would produce reliable speech. Moreover, in the absence of immediate insight into any given subject (i.e., insight based on the speaker's or poet's natural intelligence or talent), a method could be followed (available in schematic, textual form as early as Gorgias and Isocrates in the fifth and fourth centuries B.C.) to guarantee "true" words. Reliable words were thus to be the product not of the individual's personal authority and insight but, rather, of the power of his texts to represent the "nature of things" truly. Guarantees of this power and of immediate and unproblematic access to it could be found in technical instructions and exemplary persuasive texts.

Manley has argued that it was during the medieval period that a discourse began to develop that located "nature" in "art" in this way by explicitly affiliating the so-called verbal arts with the logical tradition. As a result, it became possible to claim that the aptness of words to the nature of things could be "legislated"; both rhetorical and poetical treatises took on the aspect of philosophical commentaries, demonstrating how controlled language could represent truly. "Rhetoric was understood not as an alternative to logic but as a rational science subordinate to it."[12] From this period through the Arab reception of Aristotle, a "virtual identification" of rhetoric and poetics with logic came to account, he suggests, for the criteria of "truth" and "reason" being used in judging poetry.[13]

In later years, it becomes clear, particularly in technical poetics in the vernacular, that an obsession with "proving" poetry's philosophical accuracy developed based on just such logical lines; the crowding of the pages of vernacular technical treatises with elaborate rules and regulations for rhyme and meter and with outlines and schemes for which genres to use when and where was designed to demonstrate the ability of postclassical poetry to represent aptly and truly and thus to rival the technical accomplishments of the Ancients, whose words had often been equated with Nature herself.[14] The dissemination in print of these technical treatises made these regulations and models—and their guarantee of true, apt, and effective speech—widely available in both ornate, court-sponsored and in more economical, "popular" textual form.

Like Socrates' linguistic "legislator," then, whose rational reflection guaranteed insights into the "natural" relationship of word and thing, the orator who followed the sciences of the medieval trivium, namely, grammar and logic, was assured "reasonable" and thus "true" speech precisely by virtue of his adherence to them. Poetry became affiliated with this rational rhetoric by following its procedural model of *invention, disposition,* and *elocution.* "Philosophical poetry"—following schematic outlines of "place logic" (or topics), a tradition that guaranteed accurate representation of that which was understood rationally—was in turn said to come as close to (re)producing nature as was possible without actually being "natural" itself. It purposefully completed a process of composition "on the basis of principle" and rational, repeatable norms.[15] Vernacular "arts of poetry" that articulated these same principles by enumerating the details of *inventio* and *elocutio*, for example, in tabular form could thus claim to enable vernacular poets to produce a new (historical) moment of "nature" by producing poetry capable of true representation, poetry that, without being inspired, achieved an as-if-inspired insight into nature's ways.

Crucial to the foundational logic and bid for authority of many Renaissance technical poetics was, then, the delineation of a strict method of textual production based on the tradition of topics. *Topoi* were, according to the rhetorical tradition, the "places" where arguments could be "found" (invented, hence *inventio*) that would be related in a necessary way to the subject at hand.[16] Here their indebtedness to dialectics becomes clear.[17] Both Cicero and Quintilian describe *topoi* as *loci*, as the "fixed seats" and "homes" of legitimate arguments ("sedes argumentorum," "sedes et quasi domicilia omnium argumentorum"), in which "true" information can be both discovered and stored.[18] The permanence of the places of rhetorical discourse allegedly reflected their rootedness in the logical structures of nature, moreover, a rootedness that guaranteed the aptness of word to thing. Thus rhetorical and poetic images created by means of "inventions" based on topically derived arguments could be said to correspond to the internal nature of the subject being discussed. In this way, the *loci* came to be considered what one recent theorist has called the "elemental building blocks of the imagination."[19] Following a compositional model or method based on topics allowed the vernacular poet to "find" nature's inner logic "on his own" and then to "make it real" in his texts.

The ability to (re)create the inner nature of things in words that such logical methods, or *artes*, guaranteed the vernacular poet could thus be likened to inspiration. Indeed logical methods could replace inspiration because they were capable of providing insights into the first causes of God, humanity, and the world. The authorizing discourse of the mind of the poet as a "mirror of nature" and thus vessel of divine insight has its origins here.[20] This discourse and the immediacy to nature that it promised could, however, be constructed only in and as a *textual event* insofar as the discourse relied, first, on reproducing the rigid outlines and tables of the method books on logic in the technical treatises on poetry and, second, on demonstrating the validity of the method by calling topically derived texts into existence, texts that literally made the inner nature of things present in a convincing way to the minds of vernacular audiences. The internal insights originating in the poet's mind (often itself understood as organized according to "places" much like a treatise on logic) had, then, to become "textualized," externalized into apt words, in order for truth to appear.[21]

Given this tradition, it thus comes as no surprise that the sections of the vernacular poetics on *inventio* (that allowed the poet to "find" apt ideas) and *elocutio* (the articulation of those ideas in proper and convincing form) appear so similar to one another in their schematic arrangement, even though they focus on two different moments of the creative act. The internal *aptum* of logic that was to guarantee the appropriateness of poetic word to thing had merely to be inverted, so to speak, in order to structure the decorum of context, rhetorical expediency, and appropriateness to the external occasion. The poet/orator was inspired and his words were true to the extent that the true insights into nature upon which they were allegedly based were present first in the mind of the poet/orator, then in his speech and texts, and, finally, in the minds of his audience.[22]

Rhetoric, with its primary office of persuasion, had itself of course traditionally had the audience as its judge; accuracy in representation was measured not only by the internal justness of word to thing but also by the successful completion of a specific rhetorical task. But the discourse of external aptness to the situation was related to the discussion of the poet's "natural," even "inspired," ability with words in an additional way. Crucial to successful, poetic representation was the verisimilar mimesis of nature to which Horace said, for example, the "human horse" and "bird woman" did not belong.[23] Fundamental to this mimesis was the development of a discourse of *affective poetics* capable of securing "natural effects" in a specific (historical) context. Here too *ars*, or method, was responsible for producing a standard of natural and as-if-inspired insight and fitness; but the measure of the naturalness of the method was located in this tradition (as in the rhetorical tradition) in the audience rather than in the thing itself. For Horace, as for the German poets of many centuries later, each audience, with its own peculiarities and differences, was to have its own criteria for judging, its own standards of "natural" fitness, and its own methods for producing truth in texts. These were the conventions and methods enumerated in the sections on decorum that filled the pages of treatises on reliable and effective poetry making written for the audiences of classical Athens, imperial Rome, and Renaissance Europe.

In the construction of external aptness of poetic texts to the occasion, "nature" thus continued to be "asserted as the object of artistic expression and the test of artistic fitness" in the theoretical sections of the technical treatises in the vernacular even as convention, historical context, and the "changing expectations, habits, and shared assumptions of men" generated the definitions of what kind of textual representation would be acceptable as "natural" and, hence, would pass as "inspired" poetry at any given time.[24] A contextualist logic thus underlay the foundational one.

Given the importance of this notion of appropriateness to context in the vernacular tradition, it is not surprising that even though any number of vernacular *ars poetica* of the sixteenth and seventeenth centuries agreed with, referred to, and even embedded within themselves sections of ancient rhetorical and poetical treatises, they nevertheless belonged on a conceptual level to what has come to be called the nonimitative trend of anti-Ciceronianism, a movement that preceded the turn in the eighteenth century to a new form of mimesis fully independent of textual imitation as a guarantor of reliable art.[25] Although many scholars of German Baroque poetics have sought to explain the "meaning" of the vernacular technical tradition by demonstrating its indebtedness to classical rhetorical theory, they have underestimated the nonimitative subtext upon which the technical treatises are based. According to this subtext, speech or poetry composed by Moderns according to ancient or foreign standards could not be effective or "inspired," because it ignored the "natural" boundaries of its own audience's horizons and norms. Nevertheless, continuing into the seventeenth century, those ancient theoreticians who had acknowledged the principle of difference and the necessity of contextual accommodation for the production of "natural" effects could still legitimately be cited as guarantors of the principles of vernacular poetry, because they had already argued the very principle of rhetorical fitness upon which vernacular theorists were basing their claim to surpass ancient models.

Among the Germans, Harsdörffer explicitly states that the Ancients can provide good models for poetry making, but only insofar as they supported the production of texts according to "natural," that is, effective norms:

> Thus he [the poet] ought to externalize and paint [out] [ausmahlen] that which does not exist with *natural* word colors, as if it were present before [one's] eyes. It was in this way that the Ancients gave shape to [ausgebildet, literally, "made an external picture of"] the sound and composition of nature and thus bequeathed their wisdom to their descendants in a hidden way. (*Funnel*, 3:105)

The Ancients are considered authoritative here *not* because of their anteriority or age but because they adhered to a standard of fitness to nature indebted to the logical tradition. Their influence is based, then, on the fact that they acknowledged the necessity of making that knowledge present externally and in a "natural" way in poetic texts. Appropriateness to the relative historical context combined with the demands of the logical tradition for internal fitness in representation thus came by the seventeenth century to occupy the place of authority traditionally reserved in the Renaissance for the *ars imitativa*, in which the Ancients were considered the guardians of Nature's laws. And in this "art of aptness," "nature" became a producible, textual event.

Inspired insight into nature was thus historicized in early modern handbooks on poetic method, and its presence guaranteed in texts that followed compositional guidelines based on an earlier, logical tradition and on an increasing attention to circumstance, history, and ethical effect. It is the construction of a narrative about the importance of internal and external *aptum* (*inventio* and decorum) that informed large parts of the descriptive sections of the vernacular technical treatises, parts that have, up until now, been understood as random and insincere repetitions of classical *topoi* about the necessity for natural talent and divine inspiration in the poet. But the very presence of (and necessity for) a discourse about the rootedness in nature of vernacular poetic forms points out the desire to be equal to, yet different from, classical predecessors, to be "original," in other words, and originating within their own context in spite of the implicit acknowledgment of the absence of "natural talent" provided by a tradition in which the details of how to compose these "original" forms were described with such care. It is thus in textual guarantors of aptness—the outlines, tables, and exemplary texts that crowd the pages of the Nuremberg poetics—that new and explicitly Christian foundations of "good poetry" were to be both "invented" and found.

Art Creates Nature: The Nuremberg Poetics as Institutions

The textual coincidence in the Nuremberg poetics of declarations about the necessity of a natural or inspired poetry with the enumeration of rules for the composition of occasional texts produces a conceptual oxymoron, one that describes poetry as the product of a highly derivative and patterned method or "art" and also claims that this poetry is "natural" and "inspired," original and true. To date, the apparently contradictory statements about the "artlessness" of the "art" contained in the Nuremberg poetics have so confused historians and interpreters of these texts that little more than charges of imitative eclecticism have been offered to explain them.[26] However, behind the claim that following the society's technical directives is not inconsistent with the production of inspired vernacular texts lies the desire to invest the poetics themselves with foundational power. The poetics assert their own power to found a new tradition that transcends reliance on prior models by claiming that their method, or art, is linked to nature and divinity in a fundamental way.[27] It is thus to explicit conflations of *ars* and *natura* in the Nuremberg poetics and to statements that identify the monotonously detailed poetological treatises as themselves capable of producing "nature" and inspired song that I turn first. The conceptual apparatus that permits this conflation is the subject of the next section.

The juxtaposition of art and nature in the Nuremberg technical treatises is often embedded in the descriptive sections of the poetics in a narrative about vernacular poetry's origins and offices woven out of a series of citations from both classical and contemporary poetological traditions. These citations are not merely imitative, however. When the Ancients are cited, particularly here, they are cited with a specific intention in mind, namely, to "imitate" prior explanations of the role of "natural" rectitude in the training of orators and poets. It had originally been Quintilian's statement, for example, that art would be to no avail to the young orator if nature had not already provided fertile ground: "nihil praecepta atque artes ualere nisi adiuuante natura." Art—of the sort that catalogued precepts in textual form—would thus merely consummate ("consummerauerit") that to which nature may have predisposed the individual; a fertile "ingenium" had to precede technical instruction.[28] And yet, for Quintilian—as for Cicero and Horace, whom the Baroque writers also copy and quote—the presence of "nature" in rhetoric was to be judged *not* against some mysteriously a priori model of fitness but against the kind of "naturalized art" found in their technical treatises, an art that consisted in a body of rules tested by trial and error, tailored to situational norms, and then learned by every student of poetry and speech.[29] Thus for these classical theoreticians of the verbal arts, producing what would be perceived as "natural" in a specific context was a highly controlled, "artful," and, in all likelihood, textual event. It was this relationship between art and nature for which the Nuremberg poets sought precedents when they cited and elaborated upon earlier theorists.

Assertions in the poetics of the Order of Flowers on the Pegnitz about their ability as technical treatises to produce "closeness to nature" in vernacular poetry are based on rendering the traditional relationship between art (instruction), nature, and inspiration in a number of ways. The "artfulness" of compositional methods such as those outlined in society poetics is often defined, for example, as a reflection of the "art" of "nature" itself. "Natural speech" ("die natürliche Rede") is at a loss, writes Harsdörffer in his section on rhyming, if it does not contain artfully constructed rhymes. The "*art* of rhyming" ("die Reimkunst"), whose techniques and correct forms are then enumerated in great detail, itself possesses a "natural sense of obedience" to the "innate meanings" of words, he writes (*Funnel*, 3:79); this art, as it appears in the principles and models provided in Harsdörffer's book, thus merely externalizes—indeed, (re)creates—nature in speech. Such statements reveal that nature is itself considered to be (re)productive of "art" and itself constituted in an artful way, as is, Harsdörffer claims, human nature ("dess menschen Natur") too. He explains that men have "implanted" ("eingepflantzet") in them an a priori appreciation for the presence of "sameness" that can be found in rhyme. Thus both nature and "natural speech" actually depend on the presence of something like an innate "art" of rhyming in the poet in order to even exist. Harsdörffer concludes:

> Of course this sameness [here, in both internal and end rhymes] must be in accordance with nature; at the same time art (die Kunst) must lie hidden within it. It is for this reason that we [so often] hear:
> Art without (the appearance of) art brings honor and benevolence [i.e., patronage].
> (Ars est quae non sapit artem.) Likewise, everyone knows quite well that whatever nature begins, art can complete and bring to fruition [make useful]. The same can be said of a natural inclination to poetry making. (*Funnel*, 3:81)

Following a logic reminiscent of Castiglione's courtier's *sprezzatura*, it is the "hidden" origins in art of such "natural" effects that come to define what is essential to poetry for the Nuremberg theoreticians. These artful origins guarantee artlessness, or the effect of nature, in rhymed texts. Rather than remaining separate and sequential, as in the tradition, art and nature thus become virtually indistinguishable in statements such as these. Harsdörffer's reworking of the tradition allows him to project agreement onto the classical tradition; the presence of the unattributed Latin quote here acts as a signal of the acquiescence of classical authorities, literally making the Ancients "speak" his (new) words. The final statement that a so-called natural predisposition or talent for poetry, although a crucial ingredient, was also dependent on "art" to produce successful poetry or speech confirms the need for instruction in the production of nature.

The image that introduces Harsdörffer's statement on the role of *ars* in guaranteeing as-if-natural rhyming is one of struggle. We are distressed, he writes, when we witness a grown man beat a young child, since the adult is "by nature" physically stronger than his victim (81). If the combatants are "by nature" "equal" or the same, however, we "pay good money" to see the show. So too must there be "natural" equality in rhyming, an equality that can in fact be created if the suggestions contained in the approximately twenty-five pages of *The Poet's Funnel* concerned with rhyming are followed.

The image of a struggle and of a "natural" preference for equality may apply to the traditional *ars-natura* dichotomy too. Although art and nature, technique and talent, may appear to be rivals, it is when they are conceived of as equals that the poetry produced has any (perhaps literally monetary) worth. Rhymes that have their origins in the "artful" poetics of the order will not just be perceived to be "close to nature" but will actually be "in accordance with nature." The importance of the indistinguishability of art and nature in an economy in which apparently "natural words" will be more readily rewarded suggests that the possibility of using art to produce nature and thus the advisability of following the poetics' instructions to do so would not go unnoticed by the primary audience of the technical treatises, namely, the authors of occasional poetry, whose every act of poetic composition formed the basis of a financial transaction.

The many apparently paradoxical assertions by Nuremberg theorists that art in its embodiment in the *institutiones poeticae* of the society cannot "produce" a "naturally talented" poet and yet contains all that the talented and, indeed, inspired poet needs to know follow the logic of nature's and art's fundamental equality and, indeed, interchangeability embedded in Harsdörffer's discussion of rhyming. It is this logic that endows the poetics with their "scientific" identity, with the ability, that is, to provide "rules" and models for composition. This logic also serves as a source of "originality" for vernacular poetry, since it endows the artfulness of the poetics with origins close to, if not in, nature itself. Schottelius writes, for example, in his *Teutsche Vers- oder Reim-Kunst* (A study of German prosody and rhyme) (1656), of the purpose of his treatise:

> [I do not mean to say] that the science (Wissenschaft) or instructions that I have mentioned could by themselves produce a poet or slowly imbue him with art. For a poetic spirit has witty and charming ideas on its own; it is passionate, soars where no one can follow, and is enterprising and bold. It arms itself with divinelike reason, is inventive in a way that outdoes the merely pedestrian, and surpasses whatever can merely be learned. What I understand by science here is the following, namely, the way in which [this] lively and ingenious nature (gemüht) [and the poetic spirit who possesses it] can invite the sweet Muses to be his fellow travelers [in the production of inspired poetry]. (2–3)

Schottelius's "poetic spirit" is defined as intuitively creative and insightful here; nevertheless, he describes as "inspired" ("accompanied by the Muses") only the poet who, in addition to having ideas "on his own," also follows the methods delineated in the "science" that makes up his poetological text. What seems a confusing causality at first in Schottelius's declaration of purpose is actually based on separating out in theory what is often conflated in practice, namely, "inspired" insights that surpass mere "everyday speech" and the "scientific" method (contained in his text) that ensures that poetry with the appearance of such "inspiration" can be produced upon every occasion.

That the attainment of "divinely inspired" vernacular poetry is made contingent on adhering to method or *ars* goes beyond, I believe, traditional assertions that art must "complete" nature. And yet this added claim is in itself neither illogical nor surprising in the poetological treatises of the Renaissance and Baroque, since the goal of these texts was not just to provide catalogues of the forms of occasional poetry to poets still locked into the patronage system but also to invest these forms with legitimacy by demonstrating their equality with and independence of a learned past, thereby investing them with the authority to begin anew. Johann Klaj appropriates the tradition of the *furor poeticus*, for example, in his *Lobrede der teutschen Poeterey* (In praise of German poetry) (1645) as a way of locating vernacular poetry's origins in a transcendent realm:

> That is: A good poet must be driven by a higher power; he must display divine stirrings and have heavenly affects. It is for this reason that it has been sung:
>
> There is a god in us, a spirit that, when it stirs, incites our spirit too and causes it to act divinely (wie Gott) . . .
>
> And since this poetic spirit has charming and witty insights, soars, in bold enterprises, where none can follow, and arms itself with divinelike reason, outdoing quotidian thoughts, he has been given the name that is reserved only for the highest majesty[, namely, that of a god]. (*Praise*, 388)

If we are not to accuse Klaj of a naiveté based on "mere imitation" here, we must follow his logic of using classical definitions of inspiration to define vernacular autonomy. The presence of a "poetic fury" of the sort of which Ovid writes would allow the poet (here, the vernacular poet) to find the inspiration for his poetry within himself and within the kind of inspiration that had guaranteed the Ancients authority in their own time. The (vernacular) poet could thus be an "original" and initiate (inaugurate) poetry of his own if he could locate the "god in himself" in the same way the Ancients claimed to have done.

There is a clear subtext in Klaj's encomium to poetry in his mother tongue about the role of learnedness and "art" in demonstrating where this divinity is when it is in the vernacular poet; it is a subtext that succeeds in linking inspiration to the "science" contained in the poetological method books and thus in investing them with the power to produce this privileged, inaugural identity in postclassical, Christian time. He elaborates almost immediately:

> The poet must be very learned, must know many languages, and must be experienced in all things. He lifts the weight of his body from the earth, explores the celestial bodies, the paths of the spheres, the locations of the planets, the limits of the stars, the positions of the elements. Yes, he lifts the wings of his senses and seeks the places where it rains and snows, where it is cloudy and where it hails, where there are storms and disputes [?]. He crisscrosses the belly of the earth and winds his way through the ocean's depths. He produces sharp thoughts, apt words, lively descriptions, ponderable inventions, pleasing juxtapositions, notions that are not forced, masterful and ornate speech, rare delights, and reasonable innovations. (*Praise*, 389)

Thus, although the tradition of technical poetics suggests that there is a "contrast . . . between Nature and inspiration on the one hand and Art on the other, between those abilities which are ours from birth and which are 'given' to us, and the skills which we acquire by instruction,"[30] here Klaj in effect equates divine inspiration and the effects of the sciences that permit the poet not only to learn about God's Creation but to capture that knowledge in apt, textual form. According to the quote, the very knowledge that the vernacular poet must have to be inimitable, to soar on the wings of inspiration to places "where none can follow," and thus to himself be an "original" and the origin of vernacular song can only result from "instruction" in languages and literature, in astronomy, geology, chemistry, and the like and thus from access to "universal knowledge" in the humanistic sense.[31] To show that he is under the influence of the divine, moreover, the "good poet" must be able to produce "sharp thoughts," "apt words," and "ornate speech" about the knowledge he has acquired through learning. He must follow, in other words, the "arts" of invention and elocution detailed in rhetorical and poetological method books. In so doing (and here Klaj sounds a great deal like Harsdörffer on rhyming) the poet can know and create "no less than the world and nature themselves" (*Praise*, 390) on his own and is, in this sense, "equal to God":

> It is for this reason that men initially respected the poets and found them noble and marvelous, yes, even equal to God, since they suspected that the poets had a secret arrangement and alliance with the gods, since they could imagine [represent imaginatively] that which had never been present before as if it had existed. (*Praise*, 388)

The poet acts as a *deus secundus*, then, when his texts use "art" to (re)produce "nature." It is logical that the presence of nature and of divinity in the poet can, as a result, be judged only against whether his textual representations are learned, artful, believable, and, most importantly, devout. The techniques that can be said to guarantee learnedness and verisimilitude as they are described here are indebted, of course, to the traditional education and training in the *ars rhetorica* out of which the poetological treatises themselves grew. Thus the artfulness and training found in society poetics can both guarantee and demonstrate the existence of a Christianized, inspired poetry in vernacular texts.

The collapsing of inspiration, nature, and art into a single set of definitions of the Christian poet, of society poetics, and of the "art" of poetry making in a postclassical age yields a foundational logic that enables Nuremberg poetological theory to guarantee the production of vernacular texts that have the (historical) authority to be "originals" and to reflect the poet's divinely inspired nature even though they refer to, and may even be based on, classical texts. The assimilation of divine properties to the vernacular poet (as a "second Maker") identifies him as clearly nonimitative, moreover, by strategically embedding classical references to the "inspired" nature of poetry in a Christian discourse, in "translations," that is, of the pagan formulae of the *furor poeticus* into terms more appropriate to the new time.

This "devotional" aspect of the Nuremberg poetics, clearest in Sigmund von Birken's *Art of Poetry*, written in the 1630s and 1640s but first published in 1679, thus belongs to the necessary conflation of *ars* and *natura* in the Nuremberg technical treatises. In the foreword, for example, Birken gives an elaborate genealogy of poetry that finds the first forms of poetry in Adam's praise of God and the Creation and then describes poetry's development in Old and New Testament hymns of thanks to the Creator, followed by an account, first, of ancient myth and epic and then of the Christian and proto-Christian poets of the Western tradition. Although he casually dismisses pagan stories of poetry's origins in the demigods of springs and fountains as mere "superstition," Birken nevertheless retains the water metaphor in his account of poetry's source in divinity precisely in order to be able to render pagan explanations of inspiration in Christian terms and thus to literally surpass and replace them by "translating" them in a specifically postclassical way:

> But it is another [kind of] water with which the ability to make poetry "flows in," namely, the firey flood of the heavenly spirit, of which Plato said: [human?] nature itself can neither conceive nor give birth to passion [?] except when it is overcome, indeed, inundated with a torrent from heaven. Heaven, or the domicile of the magnificence that is God, is not the abode just of nine, but rather, of 1,000,000 Muses, Muses who strike up one hymn of praise after the other. Here is the authentic Parnassus where this spiritual torrent originates and pours down [on us] . . . [This is why] poetry, since it pours [into us] from heaven, ought to rise up to heaven once again and be used to honor God. (*Art of Poetry*, Foreword,):( ):(iiij verso to):( ):(v recto)

Vernacular poetry that is inspired in this way is clearly original (in the sense of nonimitative of the classical tradition) precisely because its origins lie with a Christian God. Birken capitalizes on the irrefutability of (this sense of) vernacular poetry's originality when he returns to the notion of inspiration as the origin of poetry in part 2 of the *Art of Poetry* and cites a pantheon of ancient authorities (Plato, Cicero, and Ovid) as guarantors of his statements about the inspired quality of vernacular poetry. Appropriating the power of earlier notions of inspiration for vernacular poetry and poetics by citing Plato, for example, he literally transforms the meaning of inspiration in the very act of translating his words: "Poets speak not by virtue of their own ability to make art, but rather, on the strength of a divine urge. It is not they that speak, for their spirits are possessed. Rather, it is God, who speaks through them" (168). Ovid's "est deus in nobis" similarly becomes "God's spirit is in us" (169). This transposition into a Christian discourse—the singularization in German of divinity in God and thus His internalization as the Creator of Man's spirit—allows Birken to identify divine presence and "inspiration" with "natural talent" and subsequently with the necessity of a technical tradition able to guarantee the presence of that talent in texts. He thus demonstrates the ability of (his) vernacular poetry to outdo its pagan predecessors. The typographical manipulation of the citations of classical authors and their relationship to the main, German-language text—the sources are given in the original Greek and Latin and are set off, literally marginalized, on the page—make the Ancients both literally and figuratively subordinate to their German-language successors. The pagan tradition of poetic inspiration is transformed in translation into monotheistic origins for divinely inspired vernacular song and rendered peripheral to the establishment of a vernacular tradition. The "new" period of German-language poetry is thus quite literally the creation of the German language itself.

Birken moves immediately from a discussion of divine inspiration to an explanation of the necessity of a "natural" predisposition to poetry and of art's relationship to that predisposition. The juxtaposition may seem random as it appears in Birken's text, but it indicates that the presence of a "natural talent" for poetry is connected to the presence of divinity in Man:

> But nature prepares the way, as it were, for this kind of divine inspiration. Implanted [in the poet] there is both a nimble spirit and a poised tongue or quill: This is what the Greeks call cleverness [a good nature, disposition, genius]. Above all, a poet must be insightful [astute, scharfsinnig] (*euphantasiotos*). He must be able to imagine all kinds of images [shapes, forms, pictures] of a thing to himself. (Birken, *Art of Poetry*, 170)

The poet's wit and imagination are thus "implanted" in him, Birken explains, and are part of any poetic "nature."[32] It is this nature— the "agile spirit" and talent for giving quick expression to insights— that in turn prepares the way for the inspired or as-good-as inspired song of the poet that praises God's Creation by creating it anew in hymnlike verse. And yet for Birken, as for Harsdörffer and Klaj, the production of inspired poetry is not guaranteed by the presence of a "poetic nature" alone. "It does not follow that a poet by nature is a poet, nor that he does not need any instruction" (171). Rather, a "path" must be followed that can be "marked out" and "learned in an easy way by means of a guide [Wegweiser]." Even Orpheus, the prototype of the inspired poet, needed a "method" or "art" ("Kunstlehre") to produce his inspired song, Birken explains. The individual poet must thus first "ascertain whether God and nature have made him capable of producing poetry" (172). He may possess such a "gift," but it may be hidden, a "spark" of genius that must be coaxed out of the "ashes" by art. Then, Birken writes, even in the absence of talent (regardless of whether this absence is only apparent or real), following a clearly delineated method can lead to the production of as-if-inspired texts. To achieve the transition from a "hidden" talent to the "bright flames" of inspired poetry or to compensate for the absence of either one or both, instruction is necessary:

> One must not despair if at first there appears to be little ability . . . One must allow oneself to be schooled by both living and dead poets. First one must be diligent in reading a prosody, or art of poetry. Upon completing such an instruction, one must produce something and then give it to a good poet to read, and allow oneself to be taken to task for mistakes and learn how gradually to avoid them . . . The [poet who is doing the] instructing must, however, be discrete and praise even poor products at first. By doing so, he will stimulate the [beginner] and spur him on [anfeuern] to rise up higher and higher and to soar [into the realm of inspired poetry]. (*Art of Poetry*, 173)

Birken telescopes the two sides of his foundational project—the construction of a discourse about German poetry's "new" beginnings in nature, inspiration, and devotion, on the one hand, and the provision of instructions about how to find them in a theoretical treatise, on the other—into a single, textual act here. In so doing, he develops a logic whereby the lengthy sections on the classical methods of *lectio*, *selectio*, *translatio*, and *aemulatio* (174–82) that follow in his description of the "art of poetry" can also be said to produce the "fires" of inspiration in a similar way; "one [poetic] spirit will 'light' the next" (178). Indirectly, then, even reading about the *ars poetica* can, in a pseudo-Longinian logic, yield as-if-inspired song.[33] The rest of Birken's treatise in fact usurps the position of ancient texts in this process by synthesizing what it is that one might glean from reading and imitating predecessor texts (descriptions of various genres, for example) and rendering it in vernacular form, thus revealing the institutionalizing logic that his treatise contains as a language society text capable of inspiring young German poets. Vernacular poetological theory is thus given the power not just to complete "nature" but to actually generate "inspired" poetry either with or without the help of nature and the Ancients.

Although Klaj and Birken describe the relationship between *natura* and *ars* in a highly charged language of religious devotion, it is in fact Harsdörffer's discussion of the stylized poetics of the language society that reveals the most about the power of the technical treatise as text to replace both nature and the Ancients and to stand in for divine inspiration in the theoretical writings of the Nuremberg group.[34] Harsdörffer at first seems to follow tradition by paraphrasing Quintilian. A prior disposition to poetry is the minimum requirement for future poetic accomplishments:

> Without nature's help, art is powerless and can achieve as little as a farmer without seed and earth. (*Funnel*, vol. 3, Foreword,)( ))

Indeed, to be a poet, "it is necessary to have both a natural ability and innate skill" (*Funnel*, 2:1). As his argument develops, however, it becomes clear that Harsdörffer is unwilling to state that the individual who is not "naturally" predisposed is therefore necessarily incapable of producing vernacular poetry. With proper instruction, he suggests, even the less-inclined nature can be led into the poetic fold. He uses Quintilian's image to make his point:

> Just as no field can be found that is so poor and ill-mannered [unartig] that one cannot make it productive by means of diligence and constant care, so too is there no impure mind [unreines Hirn] that, through reflection upon a previously acquired instruction (which is at the same time the most prolific), cannot learn to compose verse or a rhymed poem. (*Funnel*, vol. 1, Foreword,)(verso)

Harsdörffer is seeking to do far more than just link nature and art here. If the contemplation of principles can "make the field fertile," then the "art" of society poetics can prompt nature into action, allowing anyone who reads and adheres to them to become "prolific" ("fruchtbar," a term associated with the Fruit-bearing Society is echoed here) in the production of German-language texts. In the logic of vernacular poetics, then, instruction (*ars*) can initiate the production of German-language poetry even (or precisely) in the absence of nature.

"Diligence" and "constant care" can guarantee poetic fertility. Harsdörffer links this fertility to inspiration, first, by pointing out that these are qualities with which no one is born:

> Some people are of the opinion that there is no need for a teachable form [lehrartige Verfassung, "teachable method or constitution"] of poetry (since every task that is undertaken in a reasonable way [mit Verstand] will be limited to artful forms following the instructions of nature). Rather, they can make good verses if they follow the sounds and quantities that they remember after having read a poem. This they take to be possible by virtue of a natural instinct with which they were born. We will leave them and whomsoever else [as agrees with them] to this delusion. (*Funnel*, vol. 3, Foreword,)(verso)

The mere mimicking of model texts is itself not the result of a natural instinct, Harsdörffer makes clear, but, rather, of a complex imitative art. Moreover, the "nature" to which the ignorant appeal in their dismissal of the necessity for training itself turns out to be the projection into the human rational faculty ("Verstand") of a "natural" predisposition to produce "artful forms," a "talent" that can be made accessible, moreover, in "teachable," legalistic ("Verfassung") form. Harsdörffer makes the same point more clearly elsewhere when he points out that a "natural predisposition" to poetry will be found in a mind that is prepared to be artful in a learned, rational way:

> All well-wrought poems that are worthy of being read testify to the fact that especially rare natural talents and familiarity with nearly all sciences are necessary [to write] poetry. The natural ability for such art consists, [then], in a rational faculty [Verstand] devoted to it, so to speak. (*Funnel*, vol. 2, Foreword, Aiiij verso)

Thus, he continues later in the same vein, the poet may be born with a natural predisposition to learn the art, but not with the art itself; "[a]lthough some may well be born [predisposed] to the art which we have been describing, the art [itself] is not something with which they are born. Rather, it must be learned, as must everything that men desire to know" (*Funnel*, 2:2). It is this "reasonable" art, he explains, an art that originates in the "Verstand," that guarantees the production of inspired and devout texts:

> Whatever one might desire to undertake with knowledge and reason must be made into an art. Nature is the mistress who is responsible for igniting the firey spirit. But art [provides] the rich oil, so to speak, by means of which this spirit becomes bright enough to be seen far and wide and to flare up into the heavens. (*Funnel*, vol. 1, Foreword, unpaginated)

The image of "firey" poetry here indicates, as it does for Birken and Klaj, the presence of inspired speech. Although *natura* may provide a predisposition to poetry, then, only the rational *ars* contained in the technical treatise can guarantee that this predisposition will lead to poetic expression that is appropriately devout and has an as-if-inspired effect. And it is this art that is contained in the theoretical "constitutions" that the Nuremberg poetological treatises are designed to be.

The conflation of art and nature in the poetics of the Nuremberg language society provides both the poetry that is produced according to the models contained in the technical treatises and the theoretical discourse of the poetics themselves with origins in nature and with inspired and inspiring effects. By defining the poetic "art" as one that always already respects and produces nature and by describing inspired poetry as the product of a juridically defined method or code, the *ars poetica* of the society effectively dispenses, at least on an explicit, programmatic level, with traditional imitative technique and locates the origins of a competitive vernacular tradition within the very body of the technical treatises themselves. By explaining to the German-language poet that heeding a vernacular poetics can guarantee poetry that will outdo and that can thus do without the poetry of the Ancients, the Nuremberg treatises on poetics are able to insert themselves as texts into the place where the ancient models had been, thus defining themselves as the origins of vernacular song.

It is unfortunate that the German-language poetics of the seventeenth century have come over the last twenty years to be considered as bound in a lockstep relationship with the tropes of the classical rhetorical tradition, reflecting, at best, mere imitativeness of the Ancients, at worst, as one critic has written, no more than unsystematic epigonism bound to occasional, or patron-supported, texts.[35] Critics who fail to interpret as strategic the often paradoxical claims made within the texts themselves, such as those for the simultaneity of inspiration, nature, and art discussed here, ignore the very crucial differences between earlier technical treatises that, although themselves imitative, also recommend *imitatio* as a means to creativity and the Baroque texts, which integrate the use of textual forebears into a larger system whereby the very textual presence of a vernacular *ars poetica* is said to guarantee the production of a legitimate and autonomous poetry. The standard against which the authenticity of this poetry was to be measured became located, moreover, less in prior textual models than in the internal aptness of word to thing and in the justness of expression for a particular audience. Describing and producing a poet rich in inventiveness (*erfindungsreich*) and poetic insights into the inner nature of things formed the second part of the foundational discourse created in the Nuremberg poetics. It is to the discourse about invention and its link to the imagination of the vernacular poet that I now turn.

Invention and the Imagination: Logic, Method, and the Representation of Truth in Vernacular Poetry

Fancy's "wonderful celerity," Thomas Hobbes wrote, "consisteth not so much in motion as in copious Imagery discreetly ordered and perfectly registered in the memory."³⁶ Hobbes's description of the imagination sums up the understanding of that faculty in the early modern period and suggests how *inventio*, the orderly "finding" of "copious" poetic "Imagery," and its externalization into textual form were linked to an understanding of the relationship between "artfulness" and poetic creativity in the tradition of vernacular poetics. It is the development of a discourse about invention (*Erfindung*) and about its reliability as a producer of poetic images based on "true insights" that provided the logic upon which the second part of the foundational claims of the Nuremberg poetological treatises depended. The key ingredient in the vernacular writer's "poetic spirit" was said to be the capacity for imaginative inventiveness, the ability to produce texts that externalized (*ausbilden*) the insights that the imagination (*Einbildungskraft*) invented. If the images that vernacular texts contained could be said to capture in words these true insights into the inner nature of that which they represented, they could no longer be perceived as inferior to or dependent on ancient models, since they would reflect, contain, and produce nature in texts.

At the same time—and here, the necessity of *ars* in the production of nature becomes clear—it was the inventive compositional techniques described in the *ars poetica* of the language society that guaranteed that the poet could create such insightful poetry (and thus produce "copious" imagery) almost upon demand, since they specified exactly what could be said—truly—of whom, in what situation, how, and when (see next section). It is thus a discourse about *inventio* as the primary concern of their poetics that constitutes a second originary discourse in the Nuremberg poetics. By claiming vernacular poetry's rootedness in the nature of things, this discourse created origins for that poetry in a realm equal or prior to ancient poetry. This claim ultimately allowed the poetics themselves to function as the origins of history, as the places, that is, where the foundations of a true poetry in the vernacular could be located and new beginnings made.

Hobbes makes clear that the speed of imaginative thought and thus the possibility of imaginative productivity depend on success in finding carefully stored images and in finding the correct order in which to store perceived images in the memory in the first place. The concept of imaginative storing and finding, or *invention*, played a major role in describing the vernacular "poetic spirit" and the making of original (i.e., true and nonimitative) poetry in the poetological discourse of the Nuremberg group and, indeed, in much of the period's discussion of the imagination as a human faculty.³⁷ Invention belonged to a tradition indebted to dialectics as well as to rhetoric, a tradition that valued the aptness of words to the things they were meant to represent, on the one hand, and to the occasion on which they were to be represented, on the other. The frequent admonition in the Nuremberg poetics that poets must tailor their *verba* to *res* suggests that in their definition of poetic invention, language society theorists were stressing the dialectical tradition and the role of *judicium* in the inventing of poetic images above all. The act of poetic "finding" is described as a process that yields, first, accurate ideas in the properly trained poetic mind and then the proper words to express them.[38] It is clear that the logical and intellectual task of "finding the matter" pertinent to one's poem was thus understood to precede the rhetorical task of elaborating that matter in convincing speech.[39] As a result, whenever it did come to be applied to compositional strategies, *inventio* took on increased authority as a moment of poetic creativity deliberately different from the *ars imitativa* (although descriptions of the "art of inventing" are often indebted to earlier formulations) precisely because it created "new" poetry for new occasions, whose "matter" could be said, moreover, to represent events, occasions, and persons in a "true" (i.e., dialectally derived) way.

The call for internal *aptum* between words and things traditional in rhetorical treatises was designed, then, to signal that maintaining relations of absolute fitness between the matter under discussion and its elaboration in both thought and speech was a priority and could guarantee "truth" in verbal representation. The poetics of the Nuremberg order are tireless in asserting that they themselves, as vernacular "arts" of inventing (*Erfindung*), are responsible for producing this "natural" decorum both in the poet's imagination and in his texts. For Harsdörffer, it was the task of the technical treatise on poetics and of poetry (*Dichtkunst*, as he calls it), for example, to monitor the search for this natural accord. In poetry making, he writes, there is a distinction between the "intention to create a eulogy, a poem of praise, or whatever it may be" and the "invention in the shape of which the content of this intention ought to be constructed." "The latter [namely, the invention] is a matter of instruction by means of the art of poetry [Dichtkunst]" (*Funnel* 1:10). His own *Funnel* provides an example of such an art.

The distinction between the decision to write a text and the method whereby the arguments to be used in that text can be guaranteed to reflect a relationship of "natural fitness" in textual form makes it possible for Harsdörffer to believe in poetic "individuality" (i.e., natural talent) and even "inspiration" as the origin of the "intention" but in "art" (indeed, in the art that his technical treatise contains) as the origin of the "insightful" poetic text. In *Frauenzimmer Gesprächspiele* (Playful colloquies for the ladies), he describes the various genres and the manner in which they can be guaranteed to be used on the appropriate occasions with the same term, thus identifying the office of the *ars poetica* as one of producing apt inventions in texts:

> To give shape to this matter and to other similar ones and to develop and externalize [auszubilden] it with a fitting [zimlichen] invention is what I call the making of [both] poetry and of the art of poetry [too]. (*Colloquies*, 5:132)

The invention must be fitting to the subject at hand; a vernacular poetics provides literal, textual guidelines for the kind of "finding" that guarantees the "natural" appropriateness of thought to thing, thus endowing the invention with origins in "nature."[40]

The rhetoric of propriety (*zimlich*, "fitting, proper") and of internal fitness between the subject and the invention of the poem is a constant presence in the systematic sections of Harsdörffer's poetics. If we are not to dismiss this rhetoric as "inauthentic" but if, instead, we attempt to analyze its place in the founding enterprise of language society texts as a whole, we must turn our attention to the strategic impact such statements make. "The poet forms [bildet] the internal logic [reason] of a thing in the truest way" (*Funnel*, 2:7). "The poet's office of imitation [Nachahmung] consists, then, in the most true description of the thing" (8). The emphasis on the necessity of propriety in the poetic invention that surfaces in the repeated use of the term *true* (*eigentlich*) echoes the insistence upon the literal and proper quality of German words in society language theory. If the poet has the textual representation of historical persons as his theme, for example, they must be depicted "according to their true nature [qualities]" (38). If the substance of his text includes a discussion of particular professions or disciplines, "the poet must consider [using] words that are true and apt to the thing [itself]" (32). Indeed the textual invention is defined in terms of its propriety to the matter under consideration:

> Moreover, the invention must be true to the thing [being represented] and must be apt only to it and to no other occurrence or event . . .
> The invention must proceed from the thing itself; it must not be deformed or far-fetched. (*Colloquies*, 5:136)

If the invention is somehow unfit to the subject or fails to reflect its essential nature, the poet's understanding is said to be at fault, Harsdörffer explains; in cases of such "mistakes in understanding" (136) ("Fehler des Verstandes"), the invention is said to be "untrue" ("uneigentlich") and inept. The fit inventions upon which vernacular poetry relies must thus reproduce on the outside (*ausbilden;* literally, "make an external picture of") the internal and hence "natural" logic of their subjects and cannot be based on either prior textual models or a sponsor's whim.

To understand the manner in which the Nuremberg theoreticians use assertions about the inventive accuracy or truth, pure origins, and thus foundational authority of their own vernacular texts (both their poetry and their poetics), it is crucial that the doubled nature of "inventing" be clear.[41] Traditionally, invention had been understood first as an act of intellection, of internal judgment and thought; in his texts, the poet/orator would then make present that which he had "discovered" following standards of internal fitness. Although second in the process, *textual* inventions could thus be the vessels of "true insight" too, particularly if they followed the *topoi* of the dialectical tradition. The doubledness of invention as an intellectual and textual process was already clear to many classical theorists. "Inventio est excogitatio rerum verarum aut veri similum quae causam probabilem reddant," Cicero wrote.[42] The process of excogitation of accurate thoughts into language (*Ausdenckung;* literally, "thinking out") continued to characterize invention in official definitions of both the Renaissance and the seventeenth century.[43] Harsdörffer relies upon this tradition in explicating the concept of invention in his poetics; he makes explicit that *Erfindung* is first a mental and then an external (verbal, textual) act:

> The invention of the poet consists, then, in the true description of the thing, since his words are, as it were, the paints with which he models forth [vorbildet] everything most clearly . . . The first modeling [Bildung] is in our thoughts, the second in our work, the third in the work of another who imitates ours. It is the responsibility of the poet to complete this last [step]. (*Funnel*, 2:8)

The poet belongs to the class of those who must transfer reliable, internal knowledge into reliable external (linguistic) expression. Harsdörffer comments here indirectly on the Platonic problem of accommodating knowledge, or insight into the true essence of things, to language. Elsewhere he is more explicit:

> Since we are, however, earthly beings, we must convey [vortragen; literally, carry forth] that which is internal by external means and allow our thoughts to be heard by means of clear [vernemlich; literally,

audible] words or to be painted before our very eyes with visible colors. (*Funnel*, 3:30)

Unlike the Platonic critique of art, however, in which external, material art is characterized as irresponsibly distant from the pure Forms of things, Harsdörffer's description of word inventions reveals no privileging of the internal formation of thoughts over their externalization into language. Indeed, word inventions can be as true to their matter as the thought inventions upon which they are based. Thus poetry making is not careless and random but is a rational act: "[T]he content or the invention of a poem must first be examined and 'drawn up' [verfasset, legislated] in the mind, before it can flow out onto paper in verse form" (*Funnel*, 1:5). The discourse of invention present in the Nuremberg treatises works, then, to define the "inventively rich" ("erfindungsreich") vernacular poetry to whose creation it will provide a guide as an externalized form of controlled thought about the subject at hand. If it follows the *ars inventiva* of the technical treatise, in other words, vernacular poetry will find origins in the "inner nature" of things as the verbal rendering of "truth" in textual form.

In the foreword to part 3 of *The Poet's Funnel*, Harsdörffer supplements the argument about vernacular inventions as the verbal materialization of true insights by reiterating his belief that the poet's task is to "bring all of his thoughts into being (zu Werke ... bringen) in a very comprehensible way" ( ) (verso). Shortly thereafter he refers again to poetic thoughts: "Thus the poet ought to externalize [ausbilden] his artful thoughts [Kunst gedanken] with nearly natural colors [words]" ( )(iiij recto). Harsdörffer's choice of vocabulary makes clear that the inventive formation of artful thoughts and their externalization into language depend on the inversion of a prior process of internally imaging "truth" (*phantasia;* in German, *einbilden;* hence, imagination as *Einbildungskraft*).

From Aristotle, Galen, and Aquinas through Pico della Mirandola, Vives, and Huarte, the "inward wits" (*senses internes, innerliche Sinnen*), which included judgment, memory, and the imagination (or fantasy), had been described as organized in the mind in a highly structured way such that sense perceptions could be transformed into the more abstract state of thought through a process of guided "finding," of selection, recollection, retrieval, comparison, and combination.[44] German theorists of the imagination contemporary to the Nuremberg poetic theorists, including Bartholomaeus Keckermann in his *Systema ethica* (1610) and Johannes Micraelius in his *Lexicon philosophicum* (1661), follow this tradition; Micraelius even locates the "vis imaginativa" in the same central area of the brain as the "facultas astimans," or reason. Its images were to link "omnes actiones sensuales" with their "vere cause" and the "genera universalis."[45] In his *Ethica* (1669), Schottelius even offers the term *Bedencken*, "to think or consider," as the German-language equivalent of the Greek *phantasia* and defines the process as one that "immediately considers everything that comes to knowledge, retains [it], and ponders upon it. At the same time, [the fantasy] images it forth and divides it up in order to be able to think about it further." Thoughts are thus the "imagined pictures" ("vorgestellte Bildnisse") of things, internal images that formed the basis of truth in the "speaking pictures" of poetic words.[46] Thus imaging (and imagining) were understood as carefully choreographed processes that relied upon ordering information as it entered the mind and storing it in the proper "places," in much the same way as both the dialectician and the orator/poet relied upon a set of *topoi* to derive and organize their "true" thoughts. It was in the *ars inventiva* of the poetics that this process was described.

This tradition of theories of "orderly imaging" in the mind forms the implicit background of many of the Nuremberg theorists' statements about the externalization of thoughts into words. The orator or poet who controlled the methods of *inventio* could be said to possess a well-disposed ("natural," "innate," and "original") imagination and mind, since "inventing" was defined as the externalization of "true" and insightful thoughts "found" about any given subject into orderly, verbal form. Birken makes the connection explicit:

> He [the poet] must be able, like a painter, to externalize [ausbilden] with the paintbrush of his reason and with word colors all things in both their essence and their form, including all persons, of both sexes, with their gestures and customs, and all of their actions, in such a way that [they] appear present. He must take charge of the person or persons, [for example], about whom he is going to speak or with whom he is going to deal, and must imagine [ihm einbilden] that he saw everything present, as if he saw everything himself... even the internal things. (*Art of Poetry*, 186)

Harsdörffer follows Pierre de Ronsard in explicitly linking invention to the imagination in much the same way: "invention is the *natural ability* to imagine well, when one can grasp [verfassen] the shape of all things well and represent [them] aptly [in a fitting way]" (*Colloquies*, 5:132–33, emphasis added).

The doubled nature of inventing—the virtual indistinguishability of thought inventions from word inventions in the rhetoric of the Nuremberg treatises—allows this "natural ability" to invent to be present in and created by textual form too. Following the traditional rhetorical characterization of the relationship between the things themselves (*res nudae*) and their expression in language as one of clothing (*quasi vestitum*),[47] Schottelius writes, for example, that a "poetic spirit . . . can clothe each of his meaningful concepts and his inventions in German words according to poetic art, decoration, and manner" (*Study of German Prosody and Rhyme*, 3). Harsdörffer also writes that the witty poet ("ein sinnreicher Geist") can "clothe" his thought "inventions" in pleasing words (foreword to Schottelius, *Study of German Prosody and Rhyme*, unpaginated). Thus it is, Harsdörffer writes elsewhere, that inventions either can "flow" "from one's own skill at having pure thoughts" or can be "found" in other poets' "inventions" ("some make use of the inventions of foreign poets") (*Funnel*, 1:102), since thought inventions and word inventions are so intimately related. Such statements indicate that, for Harsdörffer, word inventions go beyond just the *ars imitativa*, since it is the original, internal *insights* of the foreign poets that are being used as a basis for vernacular inventions, and not their words.

This argument recalls the Nuremberg theory of translating. Although Harsdörffer does insist that inventiveness "cannot be reduced to a [certain number of] laws or rules since it concerns the poet's spirit [Geist] and his understanding" (133), if it is not naturally present in the mind (and here the power of the poetics is again stressed), this way of understanding can also be taught "given the fact that all arts . . . can be presented in a clear instructional form" (133). "Good" poets thus know "how to invent [here, ersinnen] many things on their own and on the basis of their own good abilities." But these are things "to which the art of poetry can give rise in an accurate way" (134) too. The "art of finding" ("Erfindungskunst") that the poetological treatises are defined to be can thus provide a method whereby the vernacular poet's "natural" or intuitive ability to make true images out of the true arguments it has found can be (re)produced in textual form.

It is a discourse about *inventio* and about its relationship to the imagination, then, that invests Harsdörffer's and Birken's poetics with the power to "found" a "new" literary tradition. The technical treatises define themselves as texts on which vernacular poets can rely to guide them to the origins of "original" (i.e., true and apt) thoughts and texts precisely when they emphasize their commitment to invention. Harsdörffer writes: "The art of poetry [can be defined] as a skill to invent [erfinden] apt forms for all things, to express [bring forward] them in a moving fashion, and to externalize [ausbilden] them in a well-proportioned [wolständig] way" (*Colloquies*, 5:128). The "good" poet will know (or learn) how to "image" (imagine) inventively both internally and externally, in both thoughts and words. Birken agrees:

> Above all, a poet must be insightful [astute, scharfsinnig] (*euphantasiotos*). He must be able to imagine all kinds of images [shapes, forms, pictures] of a thing to himself [ihme . . . mancherlei Bildungen vorstellen]. For his art and the art of poetry are called [have their name from] thinking. [They] flow from thoughts into words. (*Art of Poetry*, 170)[48]

In connection with the discourse of imagining and inventing, the use of the term *scharfsinnig* here (and of a corollary, *sinnreich*, "full of meaning," elsewhere) to describe the nature of the texts demanded of the vernacular poet may be taken, then, as referring not to irresponsibly witty juxtapositions that delight and impress but, rather, to the link between discussions of poetic imaging and inventing and descriptions of the "true insights" made possible both by the combinatory place logic of the dialectical tradition and by the inventive techniques of the poetological texts.[49] Relying on *topoi* in the derivation of arguments allows the dialectician and the orator/poet, first, to uncover and have "sharp insights" into the internal logic of the subject at hand and, then, to bring that internal logic—not obvious on the surface of things—into being in words that are "full of meaning." Invention, the "finding" of apt arguments and, subsequently, of apt words, was thus a cognitive act that allowed the true "subtilitas rerum" unearthed by the "subtilitas intellectus" of the poet's mind to make its way into textual form.[50] As a result, the texts of the "imaginative" poet that follow the compositional methods of *inventio* can be said to be characterized by wit (*argutia*) *and* to indicate knowledge of the inner nature of (rather than farfetched conceits about) that which they represent. The "astute" and "meaningful inventions" ("scharfsinnige" and "sinnreiche Erfindungen") for which the Nuremberg poets call in vernacular texts are thus presented as a source of revelatory insights rather than as obfuscations of "essences" since they relied on an "art of finding" rooted in dialectics, an art that guaranteed insights first in thought and then in words. In their rhetoric of invention, then, the poetics highlight their commitment to a program concerned with this art, thus appropriating the authority of a discourse about the origins of words in true thoughts for their own cause, namely, the legitimation of vernacular poetry's originality and truth.

"Inventing" Vernacular Poetry: The Theoretical Origins of Texts and the Origins of Theory in Texts

Harsdörffer defines the "art of poetry" as the "skill" of being able "to invent an apt form for all things" (*Colloquies*, 5:128). Against the background of the link between invention and the imaginative externalization of thoughts into words, this description of the "art of finding" as a skill to be found in an "art of poetry" can be read as a description of the role of the technical treatises as the institutors and teachers of how to invent. The clear indication in both Harsdörffer's and Birken's discussions of invention that the poet's "images" can be understood as the "natural" extension of logical thoughts into words provides these books of instruction with their own foundational logic. They can explain why a particular set of (historical) vernacular words, including those contained in the poetics themselves, can claim to provide the origins of a poetry rooted in "nature" rather than in prior texts. Based on this logic, the treatises can, in turn, fulfill their institutionalizing role by themselves functioning as the literal building blocks for (and thus providing textual concretizations of) the standard forms of a new and true German-language poetry.

The foundational discourse about the ability of German-language poetological texts to themselves produce as-if-inspired poetry and the discussion of invention as the ruling concept of the poetics identify the technical treatises as texts with the authority to found. The means whereby these foundations become *concretized in textual form* within the poetics emerges, however, in the internal structuring of their detailed prescriptive sections. Embedded within these sections lie not just theoretical discussions about the "closeness to nature" of the "art of inventing" but also the tediously elaborate, topically organized catalogues of the "correct" forms of rhyming, meter, genres, and so on. These catalogues are based, moreover, not on the simple delineation of general "rules" but on literally filling page upon page of the treatises with exemplary texts authored by members of the language society itself. These examples, many of them texts belonging to the genres of occasional poetry, are defined as "normative" precisely by their strategic placement within the treatises' prescriptive economy. They thus take on a regulatory function as schematic, theoretical discussions are gradually deemphasized (indeed, fail to articulate general rules) and are replaced by fully developed texts as instantiations and sources of norms.

This ceding of the regulatory authority of the poetics to the *textual practice* of the order itself (over the enumeration of rules) reveals the *monumental function* of the *institutiones poeticae*, the tribute they pay, that is, to their own (historical) origins even as they seek, as texts, to outlive them by providing the conditions of possibility for a "new" (future) orthodoxy in the production of vernacular texts. Society texts in general can be said to already contain the "true inventions" described as so crucial to the legitimacy and "originality" of vernacular song.

The act of instituting and institutionalizing vernacular poetic practice and thus of making (a new period of) "history" within the texts of the language society as it is performed by the systematic sections of the Nuremberg poetics is not without drawbacks, however. Indeed, it is in these very sections that the ultimate failure of the logic that produces textual institutions begins to become clear. The bulk of both Harsdörffer's and Birken's poetics is concerned, as I have indicated, not with providing a discourse (in the vernacular) *about* (vernacular) poetry's origin in invention (a discourse produced in the relatively more brief descriptive sections of the treatises) but with providing lengthy catalogues of actual (textual) poetic inventions. Crucial to the institutional identify of the poetics is, then, not just that origins become present in German but that they are already present in language society texts. The argument used in the descriptive sections about the productive nature of the *ars poetica* is thus applicable in the prescriptive sections only to the textual conventions (and conventional texts) contained in their authors' texts. At the same time, then, as the complex and detailed prescriptive sections of the Nuremberg poetics reveal themselves as indebted, on a structural level, to *inventio* (and capitalize on its alleged access to "nature") in their elaborate catalogues of rhymes and metrical schemes, the treatises also claim—by stressing society textuality as exemplary of such inventiveness—that only they themselves can function as the "places" where those "foundations" lie.

As a result of these textual strategies and structures and of their very "having-been-written" in the form of anthologies of language society texts, the poetics thus ultimately cease to serve as the origins of the future production of inventive texts precisely when they reveal themselves to be monuments to the group's practice, to the conventions of Baroque occasional poetry frozen in schematic form.

Organized, then, not just along the lines of a rhetorical "art of topics," an art that other poets could use to invent further "new" texts, but also as compendia of examples, the Nuremberg poetics as texts ultimately occupy the space of the future for themselves by literally becoming the "places" where not just the theory of invention but the inventions themselves may be found.[51] In a way that is symptomatic of the limitations of textual institutionalization, the priority of making German poetry's origins and original forms fully present in the language society's (historical) texts thus ultimately comes to outweigh their stated task of creating a future for vernacular poetry by providing poets with theoretical outlines and instructions as to how to acquire poetic "skill." By offering both themselves and other texts by language society authors as already fully present instantiations of both rule and practice, as both authoritative origin and regulatory code, the Nuremberg technical treatises ultimately short-circuit the process of autonomous poetic production in the vernacular by writers other than themselves as they implicitly call for a reduction of that process to a mere repetition of what they have already done. By making their own poetry into the origins of orthodoxy, the language society poetological theorists succeed in producing in their technical treatises only documents of (and monuments to) a (historical) moment of innovation. This monumentalization actually resists history (in the sense of future production) by resisting the articulation of a usable theory even as they themselves as texts call for the creation of a "new age" of as-if-inspired, imaginative vernacular song. This textual structure of containment appears within the allegedly productive Nuremberg technical treatises in the following form.

While the development of a foundational discourse about invention structures the sections of the Nuremberg poetics devoted to describing poetry's origins, it is the literal "mapping out" of invention as a compositional technique and textual process that at first glance seems to concern the prescriptive sections of the technical treatises. Both Harsdörffer and Birken seem to describe *inventio* (*Erfindung*) in a purely schematic or theoretical way initially, thus appearing to offer only an abstract model for the "invention" of any future vernacular text at first.

> The invention is derived from either the word or the thing itself with which one is concerned. Or [it is derived] from the circumstances [Umständen] of the thing or from appropriate similes [Gleichnissen, comparisons]. (Harsdörffer, *Funnel*, 1:10)

In part 2 of *The Poet's Funnel*, chapters 2 through 4, Harsdörffer elaborates at great length, but in a still general way, the details of how these "derivations" might be produced in texts. They will of course be "true" and "proper" ("eigentlich") if derived from the thing itself in a logical fashion. "The poet must use proper [eigentlich] words that are apt to the things [of which he speaks]" (2:7). The section on "word inventions," or arguments derived from the names of things ("von dem Wort"), might at first seem concerned with unreliable, because merely linguistic, inventions that are not "true" at all. Harsdörffer suggests, for example, that should the name of the thing or person itself not lead to a poetic insight, "one can rearrange the letters and extract another meaning out of them" (*Funnel*, 2:17). Such "linguistic turns" ("Wortgrifflein") (22) seem to verge on a manneristic, merely playful approach to poetry making. Nevertheless, they appear together with more serious attempts to prescribe how to "create" truth in words such as those associated with the Cabbala (25–30) and are grouped under the general rubric of the "apt inventions" ("schikkliche Erfindung"). Thus, even word games are considered part of a general method, discussed as a matter of abstract principle in the quote above, whereby the "aptness" of "arguments" to that which is represented can be guaranteed by following the outline provided by the vernacular, poetological text.

The authority with which Harsdörffer's discussion of the abstract principles of invention endows both the actual text of his poetics as well as his own poetic texts emerges most clearly in the section on "Gleichnisse," a category applied to comparisons of all sorts, from similes and parables to emblems and allegories. It is the proximity of inventions to nature that ultimately allows the sections devoted to cataloguing inventions of all kinds to dominate the more strictly theoretical parts in both Harsdörffer's and Birken's poetics. The emphasis on and delight in "Gleichnisse" in Nuremberg poetics and poetry, the priority given, for example, to the striking inventions associated with "witty juxtapositions" and clever emblems, have been primarily responsible for the charges of mannerism and inauthenticity leveled against the texts of the group.[52] And yet according to Harsdörffer's definition of the principles of such inventions here, "Gleichnisse" were designed to produce *legitimate* arguments about a given subject of a kind that mere observation and description could not. As a method of "inventing," moreover, Harsdörffer writes that the "'Gleichniss' is the very most profound source of inventions that are beautiful and that serve the matter [zur Sache dienliches]" (*Funnel*, 1:12). Later, he describes the "Gleichniss" as derived directly from the poet's privileged insight into the truth of his subject (2:49–50) and subsequently provides, as he had done for the other modes of inventing, a kind of schematic outline of how to "compare":

The [poet's] reason [understanding, Verstand], with its desire to learn, has two means whereby to satisfy this desire: (1) knowledge of the thing

> itself, without considering its properties or constitution in relationship to other things with which it might be associated [united, vereinbaret], (2) [knowledge of the thing] by means of comparing [other] things of equal status [durch die Gegenhaltung gleichständiger Sachen]. When one considers many things at the same time and compares them with one another and considers their similarities and dissimilarities, the knowledge [that results] is more pleasing to the understanding the further that it extends itself, the more completely it sheds light on the thing, and at the same time leads from one truth to another. (*Funnel*, 3:57)

The process of comparison, of a *Gegenhaltung* of one thing to another, is thus designed not to distract a listener or reader from the truth of the poet's matter; rather, it is a cognitive act that represents the work of reason in textual form.

> Accordingly, the "Gleichniss" is the lever or, indeed, the forceps that, when used in an apt and artful way, soars up out of the mud of ignorance, which one is forced to accept without such assistance or aid. Thus Aristotle was correct to say that the invention of an apt comparison was a sign of a wise student, since it meant the linking of the knowledge of two or more things with one another that otherwise might not be easily understood [known, erkennet]. (*Funnel*, 3:57)

The indication here that comparisons produce knowledge that might otherwise not be readily apparent and the fact that this knowledge is said to appear first in textual form become more crucial when Harsdörffer writes of the ability of the "Gleichniss" to represent the "hidden" properties of things in his discussion of the combinatory nature of emblems:

> Emblems, [in German] meaningful pictures [Sinnbilder] mean something else than what they represent [appear to be] and do so in a comparative and explicating way, which is why they are called meaningful. These kinds of pictures capture a hidden and thoughtful meaning. (*Funnel*, 3:102–3)

Texts based on the kind of comparisons designated as central to emblems, we can conclude, also capture a "truth" that can become present for the first time only in textualized form. We are reminded of the strong link between internal images (thought inventions) and poetic images (word inventions) here. Harsdörffer's argument about the power of the "Gleichniss" to "create" truth in texts sheds light, in turn, on the status of the schematic outlines presented in the poetics for all manner of "inventions."

What he has demonstrated in his discussion of "Gleichnisse" is that insights into "true essences" and "nature" can find their origins in texts.

Harsdörffer seems at first to maintain a certain level of abstraction as he articulates general rules for inventing insightful texts in *The Poet's Funnel*, stating in fact in the foreword to part 2 that the purpose of his treatise is to provide the "foundation of the art of poetry" and "instructions" ("Anleitung") on how to produce it. The poets themselves and their texts may be taught in the schools and universities, but, he complains, no attention is paid to the abstract principles of composition behind their poems. His will be the first text ("at this point in time no one has written what may be found here") to do so. As a text sponsored by the language society, it will contain the origins (or foundations, "Grund") of knowledge, a claim that he can make for texts on the basis of the logic of the "Gleichniss" (*Funnel*, pt. 2, Foreword, unpaginated). And indeed, *The Poet's Funnel* is, as I have indicated, organized to provide general precepts "for the first time" on how to "find" vernacular poetry's first and proper forms.

Harsdörffer's emphasis is thus on teaching how to "invent" not just the arguments of a text but apt expressive elements (*elocutio* and *ornatio*) too. The entire first book of the *Funnel* is devoted, for example, to detailing the ways to "find" appropriate meters and rhymes. In part 2, Harsdörffer moves on to explain how to find apt arguments "from the things themselves and from their circumstances" in similarly schematic form. His recommendation here to follow the "beginning, middle, and end of every thing" (2:33) harks back to an Aristotelian concept of closure intended to reflect and represent the "natural" beginnings and ends of things. However, he does go beyond this classical concept.[53] The "Umbstände"—the circumstances or conditions of being of individual subjects or events in the world—may be systematically derived by means of either "beginning, middle, and end" or according to the *loci* of "time, place, and character," he explains (2:33). Although these second three attributes (time, place, person) may seem less "proper" to the internal "true nature" of things than the first triad of internal properties, Harsdörffer clearly understands them as equal, at least in terms of their "apt" relationship to the subject at hand. Existence in the world, which is contingent (time, place, person), is thus equated with the intrinsic, universal properties (beginning, middle, end) of existence itself. A "good" and "true" poem will be based on a model that adheres to the general principles of the "art of inventing" as they are articulated—and thus find their origins in German—here.

Birken's articulation of the general "places" where the "matter" of one's poem can be found seems equally abstract at first. His *Art of Poetry* is also concerned with making the (schematic) origins of vernacular inventions present in a theoretical text.

> Now whosoever desires to write poetry [poetisieren], let him first consider that about which he has to write... The execution (Amplificatio)... is based on [happens by means of] the conditions [Umstände] (a Causa, Effectio, et Fine)... and on what is the same, opposed, or related [to the subject] (A Simili, contrario, et adjunctis:), on the place and time at which it occurs, [and] on its size and constitution. When the opportunity presents itself, an example will also be adduced. In this case, as in the case of similes, the poem becomes especially attractive. (*Art of Poetry*, 187)

The "ways of inventing" are described here, as they are in Harsdörffer's *Funnel*, as abstract principles; they are "made real," that is, only in prescriptive, textual form. The "places" are prescribed in accordance with time, manner, and place, cause, effect, and end. No examples are given. This description of inventing thus seems to provide the concretization of vernacular poetry's "first forms" within the body of the theoretical text only in the most general of terms and to leave the task of filling the "places" with specifics up to others.

As I have indicated, the level of abstraction displayed in these initial descriptions of the "art of inventing" is maintained in the detailed sections of both Harsdörffer's and Birken's poetics most often criticized for their prescriptive insistence, namely, their almost mechanical descriptions of how to "find" appropriate rhymes, meters, poetic figures, and genres. The textual message these sections convey is that the composition of "proper" vernacular poetry is reducible to the obedient following of the schemes and outlines articulated, made present, and institutionalized in the poetics themselves. At the very least, this is work that other poets might also do.

The treatises contain, for example, numerous catalogues of compositional techniques. *The Poet's Funnel* gives rules for proper rhyming: "Final rhymes can consist in either a single syllable, in two syllables, or in three syllables" (1:33). The text of the poetics thus literally legislates "true" rhymes into existence by functioning as an encyclopedia of rules. Birken's treatise follows the same prescriptive strategy, even setting the general precepts about rhyming and meter off typographically on the page from their explanation, as when he writes: "IV. All German prefixes and suffixes (*praefixa et suffixa*) as well as endings (*terminationes*) are short" (*Art of Poetry*, 7).

The delineation of the proper forms for "inventing" the various genres relies on finding the appropriate schematic description in the technical treatise in much the same way. Of pastoral, Harsdörffer explains, for example: "As far as the content is concerned, we have already spoken a bit about it. It generally concerns the pleasures of country living [Lieblichkeit dess Feldlebens] (without speaking of its difficulties), spiritual calm, and respectable love affairs. The pagan idols (of the kind that the Italians introduce) ought to be banned from [such texts]" (*Funnel*, 2:101). And Birken describes the epigram: "An epigram [Gebändling] can consist in 4, 6, 8, 10, 12, or more lines. But it appears that it will lose this name when it is longer than 6 lines, since brevity is its nature and charm" (*Art of Poetry*, 105).

Birken's descriptions of the genres of occasional poetry take this apparently prescriptive strategy and presumably productive function of the poetics as textual models one step further, in fact; they are at once more specific and more general, as if to argue that the actual steps to be taken in the composition of an epithalamium, for example, can be derived from the theoretical text:

> In marriage poems, or epithalamia, there is much out of which one
> can make a poem. One ought to look at the affianced pair and speak
> of them as one would in a poem of praise. One would tell of their noble
> birth, praise their ancestors and parents, and attend to how, when,
> where, and if they have been married more than once, and anything else
> that will serve the subject. One ought to praise the groom on account
> of his spiritual and physical gifts, his studies, trips, his virtue and
> manners, his position of honor and his riches. In the bride one praises
> her beauty and upbringing. (*Art of Poetry*, 203–4)

Birken's description of the epithalamium goes on at great length and in much detail. Theoretically, the vernacular poet reading the treatise would merely have to insert the name of the particular patron or subject of his poem into the sequence of arguments provided here and then follow the steps, thus inventing "on his own" by means of the general outline "found" in Birken's text. The production of metrically correct words, phrases, and lines as well as "apt" rhymes is ensured in a similar way. The treatises thus seem genuinely designed to teach (*instituo*) poets how to produce texts.

Equally as abstract prescriptive models for the rest of the occasional types cover nearly one hundred pages of Birken's *Art of Poetry* (189–292), far outweighing in bulk the descriptive sections of the origins and ends of poetry. On some of the more technical points, both treatises provide general precepts in tabular form, as in Harsdörffer's discussion of meter, which covers nearly twenty pages (1:53–70), and Birken's of letters and syllables that rhyme (41). Although not quite as schematic as Neumark's *A Treatise on Poetry in Schematic Form*, then, whose textual strategy was one of exclusively tabular presentation of all the vernacular poet needed to know, both Harsdörffer's and Birken's technical treatises do indeed at first appear to be manuals, or handbooks. As catalogues of compositional techniques, the poetics have the provision of schemes of classification (for meter, rhyme, genres, and so on) in German as one of their clearest textual goals. On the basis of these schemes and rules, new poetry will continue to be produced.

At the same time, however, as these two Nuremberg poetics seek, as textual events, an instituting and institutionalizing identity for themselves, in the sense that they provide the precepts that any future poetic production in the vernacular must follow, it is obvious that their identity and function as the textual origins of vernacular poetry have another, very different impact. Like all textual institutions, the poetics grew out of the desire not just to legislate randomly but to endow the regular practice of a specific group with regulatory power by articulating it in textual form. In this sense, it is less the repetition in German "for the first time" of ancient dicta about poetry's office and "correct forms" (in Birken, of Horace's "prodesse et delectare" [184], or of Aristotle's "wonder and pity" [335] in connection with a definition of tragedy) or even the enumeration of compositional "rules" that is of interest. What is crucial is the *presentation of a specific kind of German-language text as models* for composition within the body of the poetics. What is so remarkable about the texts of the Nuremberg group (the rhetoric of "invention," natural talent, and inspiration aside) is that they so obviously "find" or locate the origins of vernacular poetry's new and true forms in their very own poetic texts. The desire to present German (rather than ancient or foreign) poetical texts as the origins of "new" and more apt vernacular forms may explain, first, why both Harsdörffer and Birken devote so much attention to enumerating the inappropriateness of, "mistakes" in, and merely preliminary character of both ancient and foreign poetic practice and texts throughout their poetics. Harsdörffer is explicit:

> Whosoever is of the opinion that one must practice German poetry according to the guidelines of Latin poetry is under a completely mistaken opinion. (*Funnel*, 1:18)

Birken is more subtle, even as he devotes an entire chapter to "De Vitiis Versuum" (*Art of Poetry*, 51–73), which he begins by writing: "The custom that the Romans had of transposing words [Wortversetzungen] (*Metatheses*) cannot be imitated in German rhymed speech or poetry" (51). The "mistakes" that he then catalogues are for the most part ones commonly made in vernacular texts; indeed, Birken often uses Latin terminology to explain his corrective suggestions, writing, for example, about the "mistake" of using "Tautologia" (55) or about how to syncopate verse (54). And yet, following the tendency expressed in his first statement about the inadvisability of following the Ancients in matters of transposition, the enumeration of the mistakes themselves reveals a general tendency to recommend avoiding "Latinizing" in the composition of texts (as in the nondeclination of proper names, for example, 56). Foreign terms should not be used (57–58); "natural" German speech and poetry are always preferred. It is no wonder that the poetics are obsessed on a strategic level, then, with literally making more of their own German words and texts present, since it is in their own texts that "nature" must be found.

The desire to avoid everything that is not German gradually matures within Birken's chapter on ancient "mistakes" into a full-scale attack on and literal removal of Ancient and foreign texts and their replacement with German ones. It is this desire that structures numerous sections of his and Harsdörffer's theoretical texts, literally "making room" in the poetics themselves for a "foundational" role for texts authored by language society members. The language society treatises are thus literally structured in such a way as to perform inaugural work.

The second half of Birken's chapter (62–73) on "mistakes," for example, is devoted to a vehement explanation of why it is wrong to use pagan names (of gods, spirits, even place-names) in German-language poetry; the rule is that should the poem call for such usage, Christian substitutes (Sion for Parnassus, for example, 69) can and must always be made. The strategy for explaining this rule is to "translate" two pagan poems into Christian form. Thus, the space of the chapter's "last word" is literally occupied only with German, with translations (71–73). Instead of being asked to memorize more rules, the reader of the chapter confronts, then, two German-language texts—presumably authored by Birken himself—as examples of "good" poetry, of poetry that not only follows the rules but also follows (in the sense of replacing what came before in the reader's mind) the poetry of mistakes. Vernacular poems thus literally supersede and ultimately replace—both on the page and in the mind of the reader and poet-initiate—the rules and the bad models of ancient and foreign texts. It is really only in German-language poetry as found in society-authored texts that the correct forms of poetry can become real.

Harsdörffer relies less often than Birken on such obvious, strategic displacements of the Ancients with his own texts in his pursuit of the goal of founding and finding the origins of the "new poetry." Rather, he periodically makes more general statements in *The Poet's Funnel* such as "Greek and Latin verse forms cannot be imitated [in German] without dissonance" (1:74). Such statements lead the reader to the conclusion that "correct" German-language texts must be composed according to their own rules. Harsdörffer also stresses German-language and society-sponsored poetic practice as the "proper" origins of compositional rules in some more subtle ways, as when he makes explicit in his explanation of imitation, for example, the relative weight and importance of the kinds of texts young poets should read, first in the foreword to part 1, and then, at greater length, in part 3 (36–55). German-language authors and texts should be studied carefully first; writers are enumerated (Luther, Aventinus, Opitz, Schottelius, Rist, 3:52–53) and specific texts named. But, he continues, that is not the end of his teachings on imitating: all (and if not all, then most) of the poets in other traditions should also be read. Harsdörffer lists these traditions in serial form, "the Greek, Latin, French, Italian, Spanish, and Dutch" (3:53); specifics are not considered necessary here. This subtle manipulation of the way in which theoretical advice on *imitatio* is presented, with Harsdörffer's detailed instructions to read specific German authors first and then a general injunction to consider "all the rest" too, indicates the priority that is given to native texts as sources of good poetry. Indeed in the foreword to part 1 of *The Poet's Funnel*, Harsdörffer writes that it is from the "best German poets" that the practice of good German poetry can be learned and not from "Latin and Greek poetry," which can prove to be no more than a blind guide. Moreover, even after reading the German poets named, the young poet is explicitly directed to read the *poetological texts* of language society theorists; Harsdörffer mentions both his own and Schottelius's *Der teutschen Sprach Einleitung* (Introduction to the German language) by name. Language society texts, both poetry and poetics, are thus given priority as the origins of vernacular creativity by means of a literal textual act here. If imitation is to occur, it should be of these texts.

The enumeration of abstract rules or precepts for the production of poetry yields, then, in the Nuremberg poetics to the offering of language society texts (including the technical treatises themselves) as the "places" where poetry's origins can be "found." Harsdörffer's own (poetic) textual practice (as opposed, now, to a mere catalogue of precepts) becomes the *locus* of standards of vernacular creativity early on in *The Poet's Funnel*, for example, even when he is listing the general principles of invention (1:11). The suggestion is that should the precepts somehow not be clear even after he, as theoretician, has inventoried them, Harsdörffer as "poet" can intervene to offer a text of his own as a concrete example of a "witty" (meaningful, "sinnreich") invention based on the form of the simile as he has described it in theory. Although it may appear that the presence of this poem merely "demonstrates" the technical points made, it is the strategic usurping of the place of origin as a concrete textual act that is of interest here. The poem "The Lute Speaks" is nearly two pages long (13–14) and is followed by a second poem that illustrates the same principle of composition but whose "matter" is of a "spiritual" nature (15). Thereupon the chapter ends; no further theoretical statements are made, no precepts explained. Both poems are probably from Harsdörffer's own hand; he had taken special care in the foreword to part 1 of the *Funnel* to state that all of the exemplary texts in his poetics were "of his own invention." (Birken is not quite so explicit about the provenance of the exemplary texts that crowd the pages of his *Art of Poetry*. The presence of a five-page catalogue of all of his printed works just after the foreword to his poetics nevertheless suggests that the reader may consider Birken's texts as the source of many of the examples he goes on to give in the body of the theoretical work.) Thus, it is in fact the already-practiced (and, in many cases, already-published) forms of society poetry that function as the origins of vernacular poetry's "history" rather than the more abstract rules. The only message that poet-initiates can glean from such textual manipulations is that inventiveness can in fact *not* be taught but is a property possessed *only by a particular group of vernacular poets*. The allegedly democratizing function of the technical treatises—namely, that whosoever follows their instructions can participate in the new "republic of letters"—is revealed, then, not as a matter of "class conflict" but of individuals and institutional accessibility. One has to either be Harsdörffer or Birken or possess their most distinguishable trait—namely, language society membership—to be capable of the kind of inventive poetry portrayed as normative here.

Harsdörffer's and Birken's technical treatises thus seek to provide the "foundations" of any future German-language poetry. The poetics work as institutions on two different levels and two very different kinds of textual events. They function as the origins of vernacular song in their provision of catalogues of schematic outlines of compositional technique, on the one hand, and as anthologies of exemplary, society-authored texts, on the other. The strategy of offering his own texts as embodiments of the rules permeates much of Harsdörffer's *The Poet's Funnel*. Citations of his own work often dwarf the theoretical statements in a dramatic way. The final 400 pages of part 3 (114–504) contain an alphabetical "registry" of his own poetic inventions and images and discuss how they are to be developed and in what context they may be used. This section calls attention to the identity of the text of the poetics itself *not* as a compendium of rules but, rather, as the place where the literal building blocks of vernacular poetry can be found. The "registry" provides an encyclopedia of textual fragments authored by Harsdörffer out of which the edifice of a number of original German poems can be built.

In the early and more detailed prescriptive sections on rhyme and meter in part 1, moreover, it had been not just new verse of his own invention, composed on the occasion of the poetics, that was inserted into the theoretical sections but, rather, whole sections of his own previously published texts. Harsdörffer cites, for example, a section from the first part of his own *Pegnesisches Schäfergedicht* (1644) as a model of sixteen-syllable lines, rhymed in couplets (1:73); in the next chapter, he illustrates how to repeat a double rhyme throughout a text by simply reprinting his own poem (1:91). What is interesting here and elsewhere in *The Poet's Funnel* is the process whereby Harsdörffer the theoretician seems pulled by his identity as an "original" poet and by his own textual production to sacrifice a theoretical discussion of various compositional techniques to the bald reprinting of his own poetry as the source of the vernacular tradition's "first forms." The rule of double rhyming leads him to quote not just *Pegnesisches Schäfergedicht* but also his own translation of Montemajor's *Diana;* immediately, on the subject of a further kind of internal rhyming, he reprints from another of "*our* poems of lament on the death of a young man" (1:192–98, emphasis added). In practice, then, even the initial purpose of part 1, the providing, that is, of a repertoire of rhyme forms to which young poets can refer, yields to the stronger desire of the treatise to serve as a vehicle for the anthologizing of its author's own texts as "founding inventions." In the final analysis, then, the poetics seem to place less emphasis on "technique" and instruction than on the cataloguing and thus commemoration of (apparently) already-achieved goals. The possibility of producing such inventions seems in the end to be a privilege restricted to the membership of the language society itself.

This tendency to celebrate his own published works as the origins of vernacular poetry's "first" and "true forms" is clear throughout Harsdörffer's poetics, from the section on *ornatio*, where he cites a selection from his own *Grand Theater of Lamentable Murders* as an example of didactic poetry (1:103–5), to the sections on inventions based on words

(2:18–19) and on the *topoi* of time, manner, and place (2:43–46), where he cites his own *Colloquies* and, again, his translation of Montemajor as sources of both theory and practice. In the lengthier sections on genre toward the end of part 2, moreover, he seems drawn by the very power of his own texts to cite them almost in lieu of providing any theoretical descriptions at all, reciting, for example, the plot of a play, *Die Vernunftskunst* (itself a translation of a British text, *The Sophist*, a fact that goes unmentioned), that was originally printed in part 5 of the *Colloquies* but is referred to here in order to illustrate the principle of "peripetia," a concept whose technical aspects are not discussed at all (2:94). Several pages later, Harsdörffer calls upon his own *Japeta* as an example of "Trago Comoedia" (98) and refers to his *Seelewig*, "[printed] in part 4 of the *Colloquies*" (99), as an example of a pastoral play ("Hirtenspiel").

The derivation of precepts as a moment central to the concept of the poetological treatises is thus increasingly downplayed in Harsdörffer's text, indeed ultimately almost ignored, as young poets are directed to read other of the master's publications and to model their own texts on them. Although Harsdörffer does indicate, finally, that certain foreign texts can also serve as sources for generic rules (such as Sidney's *Arcadia*, 2:103), it is in fact selections of the *German-language versions* of these texts (in his own as well as in other language society translations) that are excerpted in the poetics (a German version of sections of Sannazaro's *Arcadia* on pp. 104–7, for example) as embodiments of generic norms.

From the point of view of this kind of textual strategy, it thus comes as no surprise when part 3 of *The Poet's Funnel* opens with a six-page list of the titles of Harsdörffer's published works similar to the one that opens Birken's *Art of Poetry*. The highlighting of his own publications and the internal structure of the treatise indicate that there is no better place to find (or invent) the origins of German poetry than in the concrete textual presence of language society poetry. The power of his own published works to be "foundational texts" in this way may well explain, finally, a related textual feature of Harsdörffer's *The Poet's Funnel*, namely, his frequent referral to (without actually excerpting or reprinting) his own titles as places where additional examples of certain theoretical points may be found. Made more authoritative precisely in their absence from the prescriptive text, in their identity as "sources," that is, for the rules inventoried in the theoretical texts, Harsdörffer's poetic works themselves come to function as the "origins" of the institutions of a vernacular tradition provided in the handbooklike texts precisely in their exclusion from those texts.

What emerges from the textual performance of regulation that the prescriptive sections of Harsdörffer's *The Poet's Funnel* contain is that society-sponsored, German-language textuality (understood broadly to include both poetic and theoretical writings) is understood to itself possess the "power to found" and thus can itself serve as an "originating" moment in the creation of "inventive" vernacular poetry. Reference to earlier and foreign traditions becomes an unnecessary delay. Against the background of this power, it becomes clear why, in some cases, the poetics' charge to provide poetic "institutions" (that is, rhyme schemes, generic patterns, and so on) must literally invert the schoolbook method of *imitatio* (citing a classical text first, for example, then deriving a precept, and providing, finally, a sample text in the vernacular) and offer instead a pattern of alluding briefly to a theoretical formulation about a certain technique or genre first and then devoting the bulk of the section to the reprinting of an imposing German-language (usually society-sponsored) example that overshadows any precept, precedent, or rule.

Although the net product of this strategy is a technical treatise that has the appearance less of a handbook (although this has been how the poetics have been characterized in the past) than of a publication vehicle for society texts, the textual gesture is one that does more, I would suggest, than merely anthologize. It literally transforms the practice of the society into a source or origin of vernacular norms. This pattern is clear in the case of Harsdörffer's description of the "heroic song" (epic) ("Heldenlied," 2:86–92). The genre is concisely described as being "related" to tragedy; it "describes brave deeds which are too long for a play, [doing so] thoroughly and in verse form" (2:86–87). This pithy (and unproductive) theoretical description is then followed by a nearly six-page, German-language example, admittedly by "Jerome" but presented here in what appears to be Harsdörffer's translation. After this excerpt, the chapter abruptly ends. The textual juxtaposition of definition and example makes clear that it is the poem as it appears here, the literal presence of a German-language text, that is the institution, the beginning; it "makes real" what Harsdörffer says has not been present prior to the publication of his theoretical treatise, namely, the rules of the genre in vernacular form. Both the treatise and the text thus literally define themselves as inaugural and thus as "originals," as creative of the foundations of a vernacular tradition. The statement is a paradoxical one, given that the translation, like so many of the other exemplary texts, had in all likelihood itself been composed prior to the writing of the technical treatise. Thus both the definition and the poem are designed to provide far more than just compositional crutches; they claim to be able to function as the very "origin" of the genre within the textual act that is the technical treatise itself.

Sigmund von Birken's *Art of Poetry* uses many of the same textual strategies as Harsdörffer's *Funnel* to transform society-sponsored (indeed, most often, his own) poetry into the "origins" of a standardized vernacular tradition within the body of the technical treatise, thus restricting creativity to a very limited group. The chapter on lyric genres (101–61), for example, reads like an anthology of his own verse with occasional theoretical asides. Like Harsdörffer, Birken not only uses his own texts to illustrate principles of composition (155) but refers to the texts of other Nuremberg "shepherds" (142) too as the origins of a new and "correct" vernacular poetry above and beyond and yet, precisely by virtue of the allusion to them, somehow already contained within the body of the theoretical text. In his lengthy catalogue of the occasional types (189–293), which range from the celebration of marriages, births, deaths, general poems of praise, and poems in honor of books (!), Birken follows the pattern of briefly outlining the *topoi* that the poet must cover and then inserting a text of his own devising as exemplary of the principles described. The method is inverted in the following section on eclogues, epic, and satire (293–314), in which, for example, Birken's own verse pastorals are listed (293–94) and then a general description is provided (294–96). To flesh out the precept, there follows an *in extenso* citation of a spiritual pastoral by his fellow shepherd Johann Klaj (297–300). Prose pastorals are dealt with more summarily; virtually no "theory" of this genre is articulated at all. Instead, readers are directed to read texts by members of the Nuremberg pastoral Order of Flowers (301) as sources of the genre's rules. Normal becomes normative usage as the institutions—both origins and rules—of vernacular creativity are located in society texts.

Birken's discussion of a wider range of genres, themselves of considerable importance in the production of a "complete" vernacular tradition, is structured in a similar way. Although both ancient and foreign models are alluded to, it is in each case a German-language text that is given priority, even said, as in the case of the "story-poem," or romance ("Geschicht-Gedichte"), to far outstrip even the best of other traditions (303–4). In at least one case, Birken reprints an explanation of an emblem sequence he published some years earlier (213–20). The "last word" is given, moreover, once again in this chapter on invention to a text apparently from Birken's own hand; in lieu of articulating either the principles or purpose of the "serious" poem of warning that he associates with satire in a brief schematic or theoretical way, he simply reprints a poem that he had composed to accompany a text by Schottelius published some years earlier (309–14). The "inventing" (finding) of "true" arguments for a German poetic text of any generic type, arguments previously explained to reflect insights into the inner nature of things, is thus as easy as opening the pages of either this or any of Birken's books.

Society conventions and textual practice are thus quite literally transformed by their place in the regulatory discourse of the poetics into the origins of vernacular song. Birken's final instruction to the reader on the "inventing" of occasional texts is in fact not to go compose "on his own" at all but, rather, to read further examples in a series of his (Birken's) own titles, including a number of the prose-and-verse pastorals for which he later became best known. These further examples can then be "imitated at will by the reader who so desires" (292–93). It is thus in his very own texts and, specifically, in the texts most identified with the pastoral nature of the language society enterprise that the foundations of a new literature can be found. It is only logical, then, that after the end of the theoretical section of the treatise proper, the final 180 pages of Birken's *Art of Poetry* (the continuous pagination indicates that these pages were considered still to belong to the theoretical part of the poetological treatise) consist of full reprints of two of his own texts, one a pastoral, *The Apollo of Nuremberg* (1677), the other a "tragicomedy" (Birken's term) entitled *Psyche* (1652). Here is where the origins of vernacular poetry may be found.

The presence and priority of German-language poetic texts within the poetological treatises reveals the instituting and institutionalizing roles of these "theoretical" texts, their desire to provide both beginnings and regulatory models, to function as both origins and standards. The textual events that were the poetics had an impact, moreover, on their theoretical *content* too, on the power, that is, that the Nuremberg poets were able to attribute to their own, "original" texts to compete with both ancient and contemporary poetic forms. The instituting power that the technical treatises located in the poetic production of society members becomes clearest in the final chapter of Sigmund von Birken's *Art of Poetry*, in which he discusses one last, but certainly not the least important, genre, namely, the drama and its "proper" forms. The literal presence of his own texts in the chapter—both by allusion to their titles and *in extenso*, as exemplary texts are quoted at length—works to endow them with additional originary and regulatory power within the economy of the technical treatise. This empowering of German-language texts has a significant impact on Birken's version of literary history and on his narration of the "origins" of the drama's structural forms and purpose.

What is clearest in Birken's chapter on the drama is that although specific plays by ancient and contemporary dramatists are occasionally mentioned as exemplary for one reason or another, it is in fact Birken's own texts that from the very beginning occupy both his and, as a result, the reader's attention. As examples of the second category of drama discussed, namely, the balletic opera ("DanzSpiele" and "SingSpiel," 315–16), Birken refers to a text by Opitz but goes on to recount, in lieu of providing any technical descriptions, the plots of two of his own texts in increasingly specific detail (315–18), with references to where to find them in published form (317). The pull of his own texts, their literal invasion of the space of the treatise, culminates here in the citation of a lengthy section (317–21) of a text that Birken says will soon appear. The future of vernacular poetry thus literally lies in his hands.

In many of his descriptions of other subgenres of the drama, Birken continues to cite his own work as exemplary. Constant references are made to *Psyche* as a text that is "appended below at the end" (324; see also 332) throughout the prescriptive sections on the drama, indicating that the genre's most perfect example may be found near to hand in a society text. From discussions of the number and arrangement of acts (326) and the function of the chorus (327) to the necessity of certain characters and specific rhymes and speeches appropriate to their social status and place in the play (332–33), it is most often "my *Psyche*" that is used as the embodiment of the generic norm. Indeed, even when Birken most obviously attempts to provide patterns and precepts, he cannot prevent an account of the form that this sequence takes in the *Psyche*—and thus in his own textual practice—from intervening in and occupying the space intended for "theory" (325–26).

The institutionalizing power of Birken's *Art of Poetry* exerts a decisive pressure on the theorist to write a "history" of the drama that locates the genres favored and represented by society-sponsored, German-language texts close to the "origins" of not just the drama but of all poetry as well. Interestingly, it is this history that opens the final chapter of Birken's *Art of Poetry*, as if, almost preemptively, to legitimate the inaugural use of Birken's own texts both in the later prescriptive sections about the genre and in the treatise as a whole. The very first poets were shepherds, Birken explains (314), echoing the description of poetry's first agents that opens the text; once they left their gardens and groves and "came into the city," their songs became "plays" and "satires" ("Satyri"). The generic development into pastoral drama—Tasso's *Amyntas* is cited as an example (315)—followed hard upon this move. Current textual practice, such as can be found in the pastoral ballets and operas written by German-language authors, including Birken, may thus be described as closely related to these "first forms" of the drama. A return to these forms indicates a renewal of the golden age. Thus the particular textual practice favored by language society authors that is highlighted here at great length is literally given "first place" and chronological priority in Birken's history of dramatic forms.

The necessity—and possibility—that it be German-language texts that are close to the origins of drama accounts, I would submit, for both the peculiar sequencing of Birken's history of the drama and for his obvious collapsing of chronological time. "Historically," according to Birken, comedy developed out of the pastoral balletic operas when the "domestic" themes ("vom Häuslichen Stand," 321–22) provided by city life took over from the concerns of the woods and fields (322). The works of Terence, Plautus, and Birken provide examples here. From the cities, drama repaired to the courts, he continues, and thus tragedy was born (322–33). Aeschylus, Euripides, Sophocles, Aristophanes (!), and Seneca are cited as the major authors in this development. Tragicomedy is the last historical development to which Birken refers (323–24); Birken's own *Margenis*, his translation *Androfilo*, and, last, but not least, the *Psyche* are the only exemplary texts named. As Birken tells it, the history of drama thus both originates and culminates in German-language, language society texts.

Not only does Birken ignore the civic origins of Attic comedy and tragedy here in his account of the history of drama, but Greek and Roman model authors appear together out of sequence; the tragic mode is misattributed to Aristophanes, and examples of the final subgenre can be found only in the theoretician's own texts. Yet the effect of Birken's rather chaotic narrative of the genre's "historical" development is to place his own texts—both literally and chronologically—squarely at the beginning and, more importantly, also at the end of literature's normative forms. When Birken turns, then, in the pages that follow to the task of describing the drama's formal characteristics—the number of acts and scenes, for example (324–28)—it is only logical that what he describes in the abstract as paradigmatic for all drama are elements—the prologue; acts consisting in six, seven, or more scenes; choral interludes with allegorical figures; and so on—of the specific kind of play written by German Baroque dramatists. Other generic concerns—such as the kinds of characters, the metric forms, production, and casting (328–35)—are dealt with in a similar fashion. Historically "normal" generic expectations (on the part of Baroque dramatists) thus become normative and obligatory compositional rules; whatever is not practiced by the Nuremberg authors goes unmentioned and is, presumably, not generically significant. It is not surprising, then, that at the very end of the chapter, after describing what was considered in earlier times to be the office of the drama to create "wonder and pity" (335) in the audience, Birken in fact dismisses classical drama as exemplary in no uncertain terms, writing that it is no longer drama's office to either entertain or frighten either audience or players. "In this, the blind heathens, who were not acquainted with the true God, were mistaken in a crass and foolish way" (336). The purpose of drama, as of all poetry, is to "honor God" and to "instruct [one's] fellow man to do good" (336), Birken explains. The only texts that can in fact fulfill this office and thus "follow the rules" are of course postclassical ones, specifically those named in the chapter and excerpted throughout the book. It is, in other words, only in language society texts that the origins and instantiations of the drama's correct forms can be found. The golden age of poetry's origins can in effect be (re)created only in the Nuremberg grove.

Although monuments to themselves and thus to their own (historical) moment of origins, as textual events the poetics attempt to transcend those origins precisely in their claim to provide regulative forms. A strange paradox emerges: the very presence of a vernacular art presumes that poetic technique, for example, is a teachable affair, and yet in these "arts" of poetry, there are very few precepts but rather just sample texts. In their (seemingly deliberate) failure to articulate abstract rules, the poetics thus appear designed to fail as manuals of art (for future production) by favoring the monumental over the inaugural mode. If beginnings are to be made, they can only be made (and have already been made) in language society texts and in the here-and-now. This design makes sense within the discursive economy of the language society enterprise, which of course made claims for the inaugural power of its texts and its texts alone. Were vernacular creativity to *in fact* be, as Attridge has said, "reducible to rule," then the privileged position of the group would be seriously compromised indeed.[54] Thus it is that in the final set of language society texts I analyze here (the prose-and-verse pastorals), the *monumental* task of language society institutions seems effectively to cancel the inaugural gesture of these texts even as, on the surface, the origins of a new and competitive vernacular tradition are sought in the Nuremberg grove. I now turn to an analysis of this institutional self-canceling in the Nuremberg pastorals.

5   Some Versions of Pastoral

In 1644 and in 1645, two prose-and-verse pastoral texts (*Schäffereyen*) were published in Nuremberg. The first was entitled the *Pegnesisches Schäfergedicht* (Shepherd poem of the Pegnitz) and was written by Harsdörffer and Klaj; the second, entitled *Fortsetzung der Pegnitz-Schäferey* (Continuation of the Pegnitz pastoral), was by Birken. In the *Shepherd Poem*, two "shepherds," Strefon and Klajus (Harsdörffer and Klaj under the guise of their society names), wander through a highly localized pastoral grove (details of the Nuremberg landscape and cityscape abound) and are ultimately led by an allegorical figure, Fama, to "discover" an elaborate, commemorative "temple" to three prestigious Nuremberg families whose offspring are about to unite in a double wedding ceremony. The dedication of the text to the houses of Tetzel, Haller, and Schlüsselfelder indicates that it was on the occasion of this wedding that the *Shepherd Poem* was composed. In the temple, on and as a series of celebratory statuary, the backgrounds of the brides and grooms are described, their families are praised, and the promise of their future is celebrated in a series of highly stylized texts. The epithalamic mode of the text continues as the shepherds leave the temple and engage in a singing contest in praise of love, marriage, and fertility. In the *Continuation*, the contest is resolved as Fama awards them a wreath of flowers. Each shepherd picks a flower insignia from the wreath and, in so doing, designates himself as a member of an "Order of Flowers." Other "discovery scenes" ensue. These scenes and parts of the descriptive sections that surround them are textual inventions that find their origins and motivating logic in a series of prior pastoral texts, including Virgil's *Eclogues* and *Georgics*, the *Arcadia* of Jacopo Sannazaro (1503), and Martin Opitz's *Schäfferey von der Nimfen Hercinie* (Shepherd poem of Hercinie the nymph) (1630), even as they are clearly embedded in local contexts and events.[1]

The originating work of the *Shepherd Poem* and of the *Continuation* takes the form of two different kinds of textual events. Their *narratives* provide a moment of origins for the pastoral poet society. Pitted against one another in an amoebean song contest in honor of the wedding pairs, Strefon and Klajus ultimately resolve the "battle" peacefully as befits the occasion by sharing the prize Fama awards them, the wreath of flowers that ultimately becomes a source of collective identity. It is here that the founding mythology of the Nuremberg language society becomes inscribed in the originary realm of the grove. And yet, this resolution—the sharing of the wreath and the establishing of the pastoral poet society to which it leads—occurs not in the *Shepherd Poem* but, rather, in the *Continuation*. The second text nevertheless follows the pattern—celebratory verse embedded within a pastoral narrative frame—established by the first. Within the temple/celebratory scene, however, a group of contemporary heroes associated with the battles of the Thirty Years' War is substituted for the wedding party. Klaus Garber has suggested that more than one hundred texts that followed this model were written by members of the Nuremberg group in the following years.[2] The *provision of a textual model* for future pastorals is the second kind of originating work that the *Shepherd Poem* and the *Continuation* perform.

It may seem curious that as the first text in this peculiarly Nuremberg genre, the *Shepherd Poem* does not in fact end with the founding of the pastoral language society, that this initial text does not contain within its narrative the literal beginning of the language society as a matter of historical "fact." And yet, the fact that the founding moment is put off, left open to be resolved in the imitative, second text, suggests that part of the instituting gesture of this "original" poem was to institutionalize (regulate) a future series of similarly structured textual events.

The *Shepherd Poem* functioned, I would argue, as a textual institution in two ways: it issued a call for future pastorals to be written in the vernacular while offering itself as the genre's first instance and ideal form. This call provided, moreover, the conditions for not just a future of highly stylized texts but for the literal "history" of the language society too, since it was as a pastoral collective and as the sponsor of such celebratory texts that the "Pegnitz shepherds" came into existence and continued to be known. As texts, the *Shepherd Poem* and the *Continuation* served, then, as the origins not only of the *literary* existence of the Order of Flowers in a series of prose-and-verse pastorals but also of its *literal* existence.

Garber has suggested the generic designation of *prose eclogue* for these texts since they do in fact constitute a subgenre of pastoral based on the Virgilian model, a subgenre that, as textual *kind* (the Renaissance term for genre, a literary type defined by specific formal and thematic elements rather than by mode), is associated almost exclusively with the textual conventions of the Nuremberg group.[3] The term may be slightly misleading, however, since the series of pastorals that grew out of these two founding texts (the series referred to by his term) engage, as eclogues, in a very clear dialogue with the *georgic* tradition as well. And it is in this complex *dialogue between the eclogic and the georgic discourses* that the *instituting and institutionalizing work* of the Nuremberg pastorals becomes clear.[4]

As texts, the Nuremberg pastorals begin and structure the enterprise that was the Order of Flowers on the Pegnitz in at least two ways. Their doubled identity as textual events parallels the doubled instituting and institutionalizing nature of Nuremberg language theory and of Nuremberg poetological discourse discussed in chapters 3 and 4. First, the *Schäffereyen* articulate a *poetics of pastoral* based on imitation, commemoration, and renewal formally and conceptually related to the eulogy scene at the center of Virgil's *Eclogue 5* (itself an imitation of Theocritus's *Idyll* 1). This poetics creates origins for and legitimates the vernacular literary tradition represented by the language society's pastoral texts. It does so by allowing each new moment of the genre to be "original" (in the sense of providing legitimate origins for pastoral song in an always new locale and language) and thus inaugural even as it imitates an absent predecessor text. On the basis of this logic, each text is different from and ultimately transcends the tradition to which it is indebted precisely when it uses its past to bring itself and thus a new literary tradition into existence.

Second, this poetics of pastoral takes on a *concrete shape* in the *Shepherd Poem* and the *Continuation* that is both regular and regulating in its provision of a pattern for the production of future vernacular texts. The outlines of this pattern are borrowed from a tradition indebted not to Virgil's *Eclogues*, however, but to his *Fourth Georgic* and to the scene in that text that demonstrates the necessity of organized (institutionalized, ritualized, and repetitive) celebratory work as an integral part of the historical work that pastoral does, namely, the descent to the source of all waters and the discovery of a mythical realm of origins there.[5] The institutionalized functioning—the creation and maintenance of textual orthodoxy—in the Nuremberg shepherd poems relies heavily on the repetition of this scene and its reproduction in stylized texts of praise dedicated to particular patrons. At the same time, it fulfills the poetics of renewal based on the eulogy scene. As texts, the first Nuremberg pastorals thus provide both an inaugural logic and standard forms of text production; as a result, they function as institutions that initiate and regulate a tradition of vernacular poetry in the grove.

The inaugural work that the Nuremberg pastorals do is based, then, on a gesture of renewal motivated by the same kind of logic that informs Virgil's *Eclogue 5*. At the same time, this gesture involves the "always-making-new" of standard (and standardizing) textual elements borrowed from a tradition associated with the *Fourth Georgic*. The simultaneous indebtedness of the Nuremberg pastorals to these two different Virgilian modes may seem ironic; many scholars have interpreted the *Eclogues* and the *Georgics* as two separate discursive events, indeed, as dependent for their existence on being mutually exclusive. On the one hand, the pastoral *otium* of the *Eclogues* has been said to be symbolic of the safety from bloody conflict to be found in a "grove" protected by well-connected sponsors; this mood is echoed in the Nuremberg texts, which are always dedicated to specific patrons, and is that part of the eclogue tradition to which Garber's term refers. On the other hand, the regular and seasonally regulated "rural labor" of the *Georgics* has been considered symbolic of the work that those dispossessed by this bloody conflict and *un*protected by patrons must themselves do in order to survive.[6] The combined presence in the Nuremberg texts of an eclogic poetics of pastoral based on a scene from the *Fourth Georgic* suggests in fact that pastoral *otium* and the survival of any new grove could in fact be produced only by means of the organized, ritualized work of producing a patron for the local grove within and by means of a celebratory or commemorative text.

What the Nuremberg pastorals seem ultimately to say is that there is in effect never a protective spirit "on the outside" of the pastoral text, since it is always the "shepherds" who, by controlling a specific textual tradition of praise, actually do the work of protecting themselves and the grove by engaging in the work of producing a text. The production of sponsorship, protection, and the pastoral leisure of the *Eclogues* thus depends, ultimately, on a kind of self-protective "georgic" labor. It is the textual presence in the Nuremberg pastorals of this combination of eclogic and georgic elements that quite literally "makes history" by providing both the originating space of the language society and the possibility of its members' survival as producers of collective, celebratory texts. Within these texts and by virtue of the promise of sponsorship they contain, the reality—the (literal) founding and continued existence of the language society and its texts—can be guaranteed. It is to the instituting logic and institutionalizing power of the Nuremberg pastorals, to their ability as texts, that is, to provide both the origins of and the possibility of survival for the historical event that was the Order of Flowers, that I turn in this chapter.

It might seem odd to end a book-length analysis of the textual institutions of the Nuremberg language society with an examination of the very texts that did the work of providing the origins (in texts) of "history" (the literal existence of the language society) as it became real "on the outside." However, it is the pastorals themselves that, in their structured existence as texts, produce this ending moment, this moment of closure, even as they engage in their originary work. They do so in the following way. Like the technical poetics, the Nuremberg pastorals telescope the inaugural and monumental functions of textual institutions into a single (their own) textual space. I have shown in chapter 4 that the texts that compose the poetics answer, within their own textual boundaries, the call they themselves issue to begin a "new," vernacular tradition by finding/locating/inventing "true" poetic insights in the texts (and only in the texts) written by members of the group. Ironically, there seems to be no possibility for any textual newness or vernacular inventiveness other than that which the poetics already contains. Similarly, the Nuremberg pastorals engage, like all pastorals, in a poetics of renewal that is, ironically, also self-canceling in the sense that it reduces creativity to a moment of poetic stasis. Pastoral relies, like the eulogy, on an act of commemoration that makes absent predecessors—both shepherds and prior pastoral texts—present in a new shepherd community and in a new, imitative pastoral text. The only possible moment of renewal and innovation is thus restricted to the fullness of the present time. The form that this self-privileging takes in the Nuremberg prose eclogues is one of almost obsessive repetition, of an insistent identification of the Nuremberg grove and of language society texts as the only proper heirs to pastoral tradition. The poetics of renewal articulated in the *Schäffereyen* is thus ultimately based on a gesture of refusal to locate a future for pastoral anywhere but in their own texts and grove. This gesture is of course antithetical to the very structure of renewal and promise of a future upon which pastoral poetics is based.

As in the language society's technical treatises on poetics, then, the foundational gesture and call for a future for poetry are always already answered in the Nuremberg pastorals (as they are answered in most pastoral texts) in and by the very texts and community of authors that issue the call. The future is already contained in and can only be contained in language society texts. This self-totalizing and self-celebratory gesture is characteristic of all textual institutions and helps explain how absence, each new text is itself the originator of the authority of tradition and, as the new guardian of tradition, an authority itself.

Pastorals are thus among the most institutional of texts. Like the poetological discourse of the Nuremberg technical treatises, they refer to and constantly rewrite a narrative of mythic origins, spontaneity, and inspiration as the story of their own origins even as they in fact rely on the (re)production of a recognizable code of predictable textual structures, the *ars pastoralis*, to produce both those origins and themselves. It is precisely because of the conventionalism of the genre in terms of these formal characteristics, moreover, that pastoral seems always to have been relied upon to provide beginnings, to originate, to found. According to the *rota Virgilis*, pastoral traditionally signaled a new start for a poetic career or era for both individuals and nations precisely because its stylized textual structures could be so easily reproduced. Thus pastoral always repeats the past and invokes a tradition of model texts even as it is an original and starts anew.

These aspects of pastoral have caused one recent theorist to define the genre in terms of the very "act of convening" that gives it its shape, the act, that is, of recalling the "absent predecessor" (as both individual shepherd and as earlier pastoral text) into the presence and substance of the new, successor poem.[10] In an instituting and institutionalizing gesture similar to that of the discourse about the *lingua adamica* in Nuremberg language theory, then, the "individual" presence of any given pastoral is made to consist in a commemoration of absence and in the possibility of a renewal of that absence in a new, standardized text. The absence of the authoritative predecessor text is thus the origin of the new text's authority, an absent source that confirms the present's ability to produce its own norms. The chiastic logic of institutionalization thus lies at the basis of the poetics of pastoral as it lies embedded in society language theory and poetics. Substitution of the new text for the absent other of tradition, of the Garden, of inspiration—an absence that is, however, created only in the text and is necessary for it to become present at all—can thus be considered the guiding compositional trope of the grove.

The *structure of substitution* that is so crucial to pastoral's textual conventions (its relationship to the literary tradition) plays an important role in shaping the *eclogic* poetics of pastoral described above, the use, that is, of the space of pastoral as a *space of difference* from that which is "on the outside." This substitution may occur literally, as in Virgil's *Eclogue* 1, where the grove is created as a safe haven (at least for Tityrus) from the circumstances others (namely, Meliboeus) suffer as a result of war. This may be what some theorists of pastoral have suggested is the utopian, nonplace of pastoral in relation to the world.[11]

Pastoral has been offered, however, as a more material substitute for and utopian alternative to "historical" events in other ways too. Javitch identifies British pastoral of the Renaissance, for example, as a vehicle of criticism of the court structured according to a strategy of substitution: "Pastoral poems can be described then as synecdoches writ large . . . the artist furtively discloses only parts of the whole meaning he wants imagined."[12] In Spenser's *Faerie Queene* (book 6), Calidore, the actual ambassador from the court, ultimately proves inadequate to his prescribed knightly tasks. It is the swain Colin Clout, Javitch explains, who is the rustic hero of "Courtesie" and makes real in the grove what the court cannot be. This moment of "narrative indirection"—a digression into pastoral in order to censure the manners of the court by exemplifying its standards in a place and figure where they ought not to exist—suggests that the *locus amoenus* can be used as a positive substitute for direct criticism as well as the location of an impossible better world. A theorist of pastoral contemporary to Spenser describes the genre's surreptitiousness in a similar way: pastoral can "insinuate and glaunce [*sic*] at greater matters," Puttenham writes in his *Arte of English Poesie* (1589), "under the vaile of homely persons."[13] It leaves unsaid what it says and thus says what others cannot. It provides a space for the realization of that which, without pastoral, might otherwise not become real.

Javitch's discussion of Renaissance pastoral under the rubric of *synecdoche*, a trope that substitutes the part for the whole and thus makes the whole present precisely by representing its absence, follows William Empson's famous reading of pastoral as the genre that alludes to great things by means of small by putting the "complex into the simple."[14] In a refined definition of synecdoche, Kenneth Burke suggests that the trope designates a "relationship of convertability" as well; it is the poetic figure that exchanges a present reality for the absent ideal.[15] That which "is" in synecdochic representation "makes real" that which "could" or "should," "was" or "will be," that which must remain absent, in other words, for it to appear in the synecdochic space. Following Burke, we can define the pastoral *poetics of renewal*—in terms that apply to both its ideological function and its formal structures—as a *poetics of transformation;* each pastoral substitutes itself, as the realization of an ideal, for an absent (and lacking) "real" by converting the part (itself as individual text) into the whole (of pastoral tradition). It thus convenes and makes real the ideal forms of pastoral tradition within its own "timeless present."[16] The ideal is made real in a specific grove and pastoral text.

The ability of each pastoral as a conventional textual artifact to substitute presence for absence is represented allegorically in Theocritus's *Idyll* 7 (lines 78–85). The shepherd-poet Comatas has been locked in a cedar chest by his enemies and left to die. The story of his survival centers on the miraculous moment when a swarm of bees, attracted to him in his captivity by the sweetness of his song, feeds him with their honey when all other sources of sustenance are gone.[17] Writers of pastoral follow Comatas in making their own texts—pastoral song—serve as origins and as a means of survival; they do so, moreover, by imitating the bees, by gathering the essence of their texts from other sources of creativity, namely, the pastoral poets and texts that precede them, making them absent so that the new text and poet may become real in their place.[18]

It has been said that Theocritus, in writing *Idyll* 7 and in "inventing" what ultimately becomes a logic of pastoral's origins in *imitatio* in that text, sought to define a kind of poetry that would possess the "vitality of myth and mythic poetry" in a post mythical age.[19] And indeed, the poetics of pastoral does substitute imitation and the (re)production of conventional textual structures at a specific moment in time for the moment of inspiration as the origin of song. The autonomy of the realm of pastoral and its ability to self-(re)produce are figured in other texts in the tradition. Virgil's "regna Saturnia" in his *Eclogue* 4, for example, displays the miraculous fertility and self-sufficiency—"omnis feret omnia tellus"—that had characterized the realm of Comatas's cedar chest even though it is a textual trope.[20] The Christian Garden exemplifies spontaneous pastoral fertility in a similar way. Botanically self-sufficient (all of Eden's plants are self-germinating), both Dante's and Milton's gardens are textual depictions of pastoral self-fulfillment.[21]

This privileging of the textual space of pastoral, the limitation, that is, of the realm of renewal to the realm of imitative textual conventions as a realm of abundant presence (the cedar chest and the Garden), is emphasized, finally, in scenes like that of Colin Clout's vision of the Muses in *Faerie Queene*, book 6 (canto 10, 5–20), where the mythopoetic occasion is restricted to a momentary spectacle in a clearly recognizable, bucolic inner sanctum. It is within the space of pastoral conventions and conventional pastoral, then, that each new (pastoral) text becomes present, substituting itself for a tradition of which it is the most recent member and on whose simultaneous presence and absence it relies.

Although less concerned with this formal aspect of the genre, its origins in textual imitation, Erwin Panofsky's essay "Et in Arcadia ego: Poussin and the Elegiac Tradition" suggests the central role that absence plays in the organization of pastoral.[22] Panofsky points to a series of pictorial representations in which unsuspecting shepherds confront funerary monuments; he suggests—and, in so doing, provides a model for the eclogic poetics of pastoral texts—that the scene defines the *locus amoenus* as a haven from and substitute for temporality and contingency. Analyzing the example of Honoré Fragonard's drawing "The Grave," in which the motto "et in Arcadia ego" engraved on a ruin refers to the reunion of two shepherd-lovers in a celestial bower, Panofsky concludes that because the earthly garden can be said to reproduce itself after death in an eternal form and because one version of pastoral is said, by pastoral, to mimic another and thus to guarantee the presence of a timeless realm, pastoral works privilege the vertical over the horizontal (historical) realm. The continuum that the inscription creates provides a means of resisting mortality.[23] Absence in one realm does not preclude presence in the other; indeed, the absence of the heavenly garden (its difference) from time allows it to serve as the origin of the renewal and eternity of the lovers' bond.

Panofsky's interpretation of the "et in Arcadia ego" motto suggests a textual tradition—that of the *pastoral eulogy*—that parallels but also complicates the pictorial tradition he treats. The scene of eulogy may be read as an *allegory of pastoral poetics*, of the power of the imitative text to be a monument both to the past and to its own origins in that past and in the present as well. In pastoral texts from Theocritus and Virgil to Sannazaro, Opitz, and the Nuremberg poets, the scene of eulogy suggests that renewal (the "making present" of the new) depends on *the commemoration of absence*; generally, a shepherd-poet is represented as lamenting the death of a pastoral leader—usually his direct predecessor as the singer of pastoral song—while also celebrating his achievements. In the process of celebration, supplementary artifacts (commemorative statuary, a monument, or a tomb) are created by the survivor, either literally or in song, in order to compensate for the original poet-singer's demise.[24] Synecdoche is the governing trope of these artifacts as it is of the grove as a whole, since the artifacts for the most part contain or are inscribed with the words of the deceased predecessor and thus substitute for and "remember" him (make his absence present) each time and as often as his successors sing. They are "enduring monuments," then, in more ways than one. As concrete statuary or commemorative tombs, they outlast both the moment of death and the moment of celebration; as textual artifacts created according to generic norms, they belong to a timeless realm of reproducible literary forms.

A celebration of presence—of the new shepherd-leader and of the new pastoral text—thus informs the pastoral eulogy and enables each text to do both inaugural and regulative work. The builder of the monument immortalizes the dead shepherd by creating a new artifact that symbolizes his eternal presence in the collectivity of the grove. At the same time, the builder, as "author" of the eternal monument or tomb, also immortalizes himself as he creates a monument to his own ability to escape (for the moment) the moment of death and to renew the fertility of the grove. The concrete resistance of the commemorative artifact to the passing of time evokes, finally, the timelessness of both the conventional, celebratory rituals that are invoked on each occasion of death and the imitative formal elements of pastoral poetry. As an allegory of the pastoral poetics of renewal, then, the words of the predecessor (shepherd and text) are embedded in and form the body of the new text of lament; this new text depends on but also substitutes for the physical absence of its model and allows pastoral song to continue to be sung.

The pastoral eulogy is thus a figure both of vernacular pastoral and of the genre as a whole. Like the conventional textual structures of pastoral, it identifies every text in which it appears as one in a series, as participating in the tradition. And yet, within the eulogy scene, tradition—represented by the predecessor shepherd-poet (and song of lament)—must be made absent in order for it to continue to be evoked as the originating occasion of the new text. Invoking the generic conventions of the tradition in a new time and place thus also *creates* that new time and place and is thus productive of both tradition and a new moment of "history." It is to the production of pastoral conventions and of a poetics of renewal first within a series of classical eulogy scenes and then in Martin Opitz's *Shepherd Poem of Hercinie the Nymph* (1630) that I turn now before addressing their presence in the Nuremberg shepherd poems.

Theocritus's *Idyll* 1 is the founding text of pastoral eulogy as a subgenre. In the celebratory moment that is central to *Idyll* 1, pastoral's identity as synecdoche becomes clear. The shepherd, Thyrsis, sings a lament, "The Affliction of Daphnis" (lines 64–142), describing how Death overtook his mythical predecessor, the shepherd-singer Daphnis, in the grove. Thyrsis is himself a figure of the instituting and institutionalizing power of pastoral eulogy; even as his song begins the tradition of commemorative song in the grove, it relies for its substance primarily on a highly structured absence, on echoing back what are said to be Daphnis's earlier words. Theocritus thus produces a norm of pastoral lament by "creating" a lineage for both his shepherd and his text within the very matter of the song. At the same time, it is Thyrsis's own words that make Daphnis absent, make his death real, so to speak, so that Thyrsis can succeed to leadership of the grove; the text is thus just as much of a monument to Thyrsis's position and power as successor as to Daphnis's song and death.

Segal has analyzed the internal dynamic of *Idyll* 1, the tensions between the frame story and the lament, between Daphnis and his divine interlocutors, between love and death, between myth and pastoral artifice.[25] More central to the creation of a pastoral poetics, however, is the relationship of successorship between Daphnis and Thyrsis and the dynamic of substitution between their two songs. Whereas Daphnis's song emphasizes the negative aspects of human contingency (history) as he invokes silence and the devastation of the grove, Thyrsis's repetition of his words in a new voice signals belief in history as the source of creativity and in the inevitable production of (new) history precisely as a result of mortality and the passing of time. It is in the space of difference (from earlier shepherds and texts) within the scene of lament that the new (pastoral) grove comes into being, both within the narrative of *Idyll* 1 and as a new, celebratory text.

The substance of Thyrsis's "Affliction of Daphnis" is imitative; it convenes the words of the dead shepherd into its presence as text. Thyrsis relates Daphnis's own prediction of nature's mourning upon his death (132–36).[26] The disarray of the bower Daphnis describes threatens the future of pastoral on both the literal and textual levels. Not only will nature rebel against the conventional norms of productivity, but the future of song itself is threatened since the shepherd-singer will be silenced by the dark river (either Acheron or Lethe, thus either death or the obliteration of memory) that swirls over him (139–40). And yet the threat that Daphnis's death poses to pastoral is softened, even removed, both by the song itself and by the gift that its new singer receives as a reward for his commemorative strains. Recognizing that the "Affliction of Daphnis" reintroduces the dead shepherd into the grove by "quoting" his words, the goatherd of the frame story of *Idyll* 1 bestows an intricately carved cup on Thyrsis. The cup affirms that an imitative song of lament can combat mortality and restore fertility to pastoral by synecdochically reproducing the "original" in a new voice. It is not by chance that the goatherd presents the gift to Thyrsis with the hope that the singer's mouth, "[f]illed ... with honey" (146), will continue to yield poetry like the lament, since his words are possessed of the same substituting substance and productive sweetness as Comatas's self-immortalizing song.

The goatherd's cup represents (is offered in exchange and thus as artifact substitutes for) both Thyrsis's lament in particular and the transforming power signified by the presence of every new pastoral song.[27] The ivy tendrils sculpted around the various scenes on the cup—like the refrain that appears regularly in Thyrsis's lament and frames the scenes of dialogue between Daphnis and his interlocutors—signal the importance of artifice, of convention, in such texts. The vine reveals the careful organization of the symbolic scenes on the cup; the refrain marks the song as an art-song, a dirge. Both signify the only kind of art, namely, the ritualized song of lament, that is capable of renewing pastoral fertility by luring transcendence (both the dead Daphnis's words and the "eternal" forms of pastoral) into the space of difference from death, here, the concrete form of commemorative song.

The prize also testifies to Thyrsis's success as the new singer of pastoral; he overcomes the disarray into which the elder shepherd's death has cast the grove. Indeed, the scenes on the cup can be said to reverse the destructive values represented by Daphnis's words as Thyrsis quotes them in his song.[28] Thyrsis's lament thus holds the dead shepherd's own words—pastoral song at its origins—fast within the imitating, dialogue scenes, thus "convening" (in Alpers's sense) the past into the present even as it confirms Daphnis's absence. It is also itself as "original" and new a poetic artifact as the "deep cup, washed / over with sweet wax, two-handled, and *newly fashioned*, still / fragrant from the knife" (27–28, emphasis added) that Thyrsis receives as a reward for his commemorative work. Incorporating the past while also signaling the necessity that it yield to new creativity, both song and cup "stand in" for the absent Daphnis and, in so doing, stand at the beginning of a tradition of synecdochic (transformatory) and self-celebratory pastoral eulogy. The goatherd even remarks that Thyrsis has already sung the "Affliction" several times before (19–20), suggesting that the canonization of the text as the origin of a genre has begun even as he speaks.

Virgil's *Eclogue* 5 imitates many of the formal elements of Theocritus's *Idyll* 1; it thus elevates the synecdochic moment of the pastoral eulogy as a guarantor of the future within the text into a productive act of literary convention and thus of a future for texts.[29] Just as Virgil's text replaces Theocritus's, so too do his shepherds replace the stylized songs of lament of their predecessor with descriptions of actual funerary monuments and ritualized acts of commemorative celebration. The poetics of pastoral—the replacing of the past with the presence of textual orthodoxy, the substitution of a new and better textual space for whatever is other than (before or beyond) the present—thus enters concrete textual form here.

With *Eclogue* 5, imitation, substitution, and celebration become fixed institutions in the pastoral; capturing the predecessor's words in a commemorative artifact represents the power of the act of convening and of conventional (textual) acts to found a tradition by making it both absent and present at the same time. The form of the future can be legislated on the basis of a monument to its own practice. The crucial third sense of convening—the creation of the community in the very performance of this self-commemorative act—is also addressed here, since beginning with *Eclogue* 5, the celebration of the dead shepherd becomes a collective event. A new community of poet-shepherds—the literal (horizontal) analogue within the text to the literary (vertical) community of "shepherd poets" (Daphnis and Thyrsis, Theocritus and Virgil, for example)—comes into existence each time commemorative song occurs. It is this community that establishes how history (the future of the text) is to look; it is thus within this collective that history, as the space of difference from the past, will be made.

Both the frame story of *Eclogue* 5 and the double-song praise of the dead shepherd (here again, Daphnis) by the shepherds Mopsus and Menalcas create a pastoral dialectic between the past and the present, between absence and presence by means of conventional, commemorative song. The issue of substituting one pastoral song and leader for another is addressed in the opening discussion about which of the two shepherds will sing first. Menalcus, the elder ("tu major," 4),[30] concedes to the younger Mopsus, allowing him to go first, illustrating that allowing the new generation to "start" is central here. A verbal echo underscoring the poetics of succession so central to both pastoral in general and to the eulogy scene in particular is heard as the shepherds enter the cave where they will sing: "sive antro potius succedimus ... successimus antro" ("now we enter into the cave ... we have entered the cave") (6, 19). When Mopsus begins his song of lament and celebration, strategies designed to secure textual inheritances are figured in yet a further scene of renewal. His words describe a scene familiar to us from Theocritus's *Idyll* 1, the grief of nature occasioned by the shepherd-poet's death:

> When fate took you,
> Apollo, god of shepherds, left the fields.
> Furrows where we have buried barley corns
> Grow barren oat straws, darnel, idle weeds;
> Instead of violets soft and gay narcissus,
> Thistles spring up and burdock, spiky thorns. (34–39)

The repetition of the scene of nature's disorder from the Theocritus text indicates how the past is always present in, but also absent from (since the Virgilian "quote" takes its place), the origins of pastoral song. That a new (textual) artifact must literally become present in the place of the past is suggested allegorically as Mopsus commands his shepherd companions to build a tomb and perform funeral rites (40–42) as Daphnis had instructed ("Daphnis calls for rites like these," 41). The tomb itself signals the earlier text's and the dead shepherd's continued presence in Virgil's grove in more ways than one, because the present fulfills the commands of the past as it quite literally convenes Theocritus's text and Daphnis's words into itself. Just as Theocritus's Thyrsis preserved his predecessor's song within the frame of his stylized dirge, so too does Virgil's Mopsus capture his Daphnis's "carmen" as an inscription on the pastoral monument:

> Build him a mound and add this epitaph:
> "I woodland Daphnis, blazoned among the stars,
> Guarded a lovely flock, still lovelier I." (42–44)

For Daphnis to continue to be even synecdochically present in the text, his death must have occurred. It is this absence that enables Mopsus to replace him as the new singer of pastoral lament, as overseer of the construction of the tomb, and thus as director of renewed artistic activities in the grove. The celebration of the deceased shepherd thus quite literally becomes a collective act in Virgil's text for the first time as a pastoral community convenes to help in the construction of the "mound." In the face of mortality, then, the new community becomes just as important as, if not more important than, idealized predecessors (and texts) in maintaining pastoral creativity. The elder Menalcas recognizes the tomb not only as a token of and homage to the dead Daphnis but also as proof, like the goatherd's cup, of Mopsus's ability to succeed him, to be present as the new leader of the pastoral collective: "Piping and singing both, you are his equal, / Fortunate lad, his one and true successor" (48–49). Virgil's text too is the "true successor" to Theocritus's *Idyll* 1; by making it absent in repetition, *Eclogue* 5 takes on the mantle of pastoral song.

Menalcas's reply to Mopsus's song in the second half of *Eclogue* 5 marks the exchange as a traditional (conventional) amoebean singing match. It also abstracts the act of pastoral commemoration into a repeatable and thus timeless pattern of celebratory texts and rites and, in so doing, acts as a bridge to the scene of commemoration in the *Fourth Georgic* that forms the basis of much Renaissance pastoral. In *Eclogue* 5,

Menalcas transforms Mopsus's tomb into an altar to Daphnis by apotheosizing the dead shepherd in song: "I'll sing and raise your Daphnis to the stars, / Yes, to the stars" (51–52). His words thus create a new pastoral deity who, as a personification of tradition, as "deus ille" (64) and *genius loci*, will watch over and protect—perhaps even more effectively than Tityrus's sponsor in *Eclogue* 1—all future groves. The heavenly garden in which Menalcas's words place Daphnis (56–57) is a mirror image of its earthly counterpart but is necessarily different from it, as transcendent spatially (it experiences no change) as its temporal equivalent, the textual tradition.

The synecdochic mechanism behind all pastoral eulogies emerges here; the grove of Mopsus and Menalcas is a representative part of the timeless whole, which, however, can only ever become present as part. Moreover, the continuity of pastoral song that the creation of divinity in the earthly garden represents is given a collective guarantee in the form of the celebratory rituals to the new pastoral deity that Menalcas institutes (65–75). They are to be performed yearly ("quotannis," 79) and forever ("semper," 74). They thus become the essence of pastoral convention in the several senses of the word. By invoking Daphnis's spirit, they "convene" him into the present of the new grove; they also assemble the pastoral community in celebration and become its fixed rites.

Like the refrain of Thyrsis's lament, then, and the imitative structures of the genre of pastoral eulogy as a whole, the presence of the altar/tomb as a concrete artifact and of the annual funeral rites become conventions that ensure a continuing return of commemorative song and the continuing presence of a new shepherd group. The dead shepherd-leader thus gives up his place and his words to a new generation, but he continues to be present (just as Theocritus's poem is present in Virgil's text) as synecdoche, in his song, in the tomb, and, as an immortal version of himself, in the renewed grove of the successor. Death imposes convention on the survivors, who turn to the collective to ensure the enactment of rituals capable of converting loss into renewal.

The Theocritan and Virgilian scenes of pastoral lament and celebration employ the figure of synecdoche to structure both the activities in the text and the text's formal arrangement. They substitute presence (the presence that is the text)—Thyrsis's song, the pastoral tomb, and the annual celebratory rites—for absence, creating ideal origins for that present and for a future (of pastoral song and texts) in the very act of making the new text and grove real. A further Virgilian text, the *Fourth Georgic*, goes on to present an allegory of the power of textual conventions and of ritualism and the structures of celebration per se to do the work of renewing the grove on a regular basis. The *Fourth Georgic* thus locates the protection, "safe space," and future of pastoral song (said in the *Eclogues* to be guaranteed by imitation and patronage) in the poet-shepherd's own ability to produce conventional, celebratory artifacts and texts. The scene of pastoral loss and renewal, of lament and celebration, that comes at the end of the *Fourth Georgic* is in this sense a scene of instruction, of *institutionalizing* the poetics of pastoral embedded in the *Eclogues* as I have analyzed it here; figuratively speaking, the scene teaches shepherd-poets how to set up the (textual) space of self-preservation in a regulated and effective way. It is thus no surprise that a "quote" of the *Fourth Georgic* is in fact employed in many postclassical pastorals to exemplify the work of founding, renewing, and protecting of which pastoral conventions are capable, for the scene encodes many of the same strategies as the poetics of renewal described here.

Although it is not standard to consider the *Georgics* as belonging to the canon of pastoral texts, and, indeed, many have seen the *Eclogues* and the *Georgics* as mutually exclusive and diametrically opposed, Virgil makes clear in the *Fourth Georgic* that the action of the text is pastoral and occurs in Arcadia. He does so by choosing a clearly overdetermined topic as the one that gives rise to the final narrative of the *Fourth Georgic*, namely, bee husbandry. The choice of the apian metaphor is a clear allusion to the tradition of pastoral that dates back to the Comatas myth and to the structure of imitation upon which the production and reproduction of the grove relies.[31] The alleged difference between the bower and the farm, or between the *Eclogues* and the *Georgics*, has been said to lie in the fact that the former yields its fruits "spontaneously" from "untilled earth" and under the sign of patronage, whereas the latter contains a "program of cultivation" based on ritualized acts necessary for the survival of the unprotected and dispossessed.[32] The self-conscious delineation in the *Fourth Georgic* of a program of regular and regulated, artificial and artifice-full renewal of the bees'—and thus of pastoral's—fertility, a program that strives to make present that which is absent in a way similar to *Eclogue 5*, suggests that the shepherd-poet may rely upon celebratory, pastoral conventions and upon his own power to engage with those conventions to produce a new text to protect him as well. Thus when Virgil describes the methods whereby a listless beehive can be made productive again as specifically "Arcadian" (line 283), he is clearly referring to pastoral themes, to Man's "triumph" in renewing Nature's fertility, and to the power of ritualized celebration to protect the future of song.[33]

The *Fourth Georgic* has, then, as one of its main topics the science of bee husbandry. In the event of the death of one's beehive, the production of a new race of bees ("genus unde novae stirpis," 282) is described, in the tradition of the myth of Comatas's miraculous survival, as a moment of apparently spontaneous generation. Nevertheless, as the narrative of the text points out, this moment of renewal depends on the farmer's enactment of a strictly defined rite; Virgil's choice of words ("genus") in describing the "race" of the bees may suggest that his discussion was meant to function as an allegory of the perpetuation of the literary genre of pastoral as well. A bull must be slain, the text explains, in a shrinelike enclosure according to specific procedures and rites ("Choose a narrow place and have it covered for the purpose," 295–96). The tombs and monuments of the *Eclogues* are alluded to here; as in the eclogic tradition, absence and presence, death and renewal, are intertwined.[34] After the appropriate amount of time, the description continues, a new bee colony will emerge from within the putrefying carcass of the bull, out of an enclosed space not unlike Comatas's cedar chest. The problem of an unproductive beehive—and of the future of pastoral—will thus be solved. It is not by chance that the ritualistic procedures that Virgil describes here recall the careful funeral rites for Daphnis at the end of *Eclogue 5*, nor that their origins lie in the mythical story the narrator goes on to tell. The narrative that closes the *Fourth Georgic* is a story with clear references to pastoral infertility, resuscitated by celebration; "vitality . . . cannot be dissociated from death."[35] Both a new race of bees and a family of pastoral poets and texts find their origins in the tale told at the end of the *Fourth Georgic*, a tale that follows the eclogic logic of pastoral by requiring that a dialectic of absence and presence be produced in the text.

In the lore of the *Georgics*, the *bugonia*, or ceremony to which the farmer must resort to restore the activity of listless bees, has its origin in a myth made conventional by its status as embedded narrative in Virgil's text; the inaugural work in which the *Fourth Georgic* engages here—the production of mythic origins for present-day rituals and behavior—is reminiscent of both the language theory of the Order of Flowers and the discussion of the "inspired" quality of vernacular poetry in the Nuremberg poetics. The story of Aristaeus and his bees (318ff.) joins, then, the set piece of Daphnis's death and the lamentation and reproduction of the absent predecessor (shepherd and text) in a new grove as a scene that works as a figure of the genre's poetics. In the *Fourth Georgic*, it is the shepherd figure, Aristaeus, who, like the original Daphnis of Theocritus's text, threatens to call down destruction upon the bower if the secret of restoring his bees is not revealed. He addresses his nymph mother, Cyrene: "With your own hand, lay waste to my beautiful woods" (329). In response to the threat, Cyrene beckons her son to join her in her mythological abode ("umida regna," line 364) and grotto and thus in a closed space of myth not unlike Comatas's box, a "realm of origins" that becomes a textual topos and space of renewal in pastorals throughout the Renaissance and Baroque.

Here, at what is described as the source of all waters (and thus as the source of the creative element itself), the shepherd will learn the secret of renewing his bees, of making pastoral fertility present again within the space of the text.[36] Cyrene seems to be the first in a series of literary nymphs who guide mortals through mythical, subterranean caverns beneath pastoral groves. But she also repeats the words of a Greek ancestor here, Homer's nymph, Eidothea (*Odyssey* 4.365–465), thus relying, like Thyrsis and Mopsus before her, on convening a textual past into her own presence and voice and on making that past absent (in imitation) precisely so she and the text of the *Fourth Georgic* can become present and take its place. Cyrene is thus an emblem of the questions about renewal Virgil poses in this text. Where do unsponsored "shepherds" turn in their efforts to enter the "safe space" of pastoral and to participate in its difference from the destruction around them? How does this *space of difference* and of (literal and literary) renewal of origins come to be in a text that is so heavily indebted to the past? The answers he gives depend on synecdochic logic, on strategies of substitution, and on the ability of a text to generate its own mythic space. It is Cyrene and the acts of commemoration she suggests as the origins of the bees' renewed activity that both begin and organize a future of conventional pastoral texts.

In response to his lament about the absence of productivity in his bees, Cyrene instructs Aristaeus to seek out the mythical Proteus as the only one who can reveal the reasons and remedies for their inactivity. In doing so, she echoes her literary predecessor's advice to Menelaos to seek out the Old Man of the Sea for answers about both his past and his future.[37] Literary imitativeness and synecdochic compositional techniques thus play a role here as they do in the *Idylls* and *Eclogues*. As a figure that celebrates a literary past by making it absent, by her very identity, that is, as a literary convention, Cyrene herself represents the answer to her son's questions as to the return of his bees. The figure of Proteus serves even more literally than Cyrene, however, as an allegory of the temporal transcendence upon which both pastoral and this scene of the *Fourth Georgic* rely. His main gift is omniscience: "For he knows all, the seer, what is, what was, and what will soon be" (392–93). His power is derived from the fact that he embodies past, present, and future all at the same time. The scene in which he appears—a Virgilian version of a Homeric model—also makes the past both absent and present, revealing the present as a source of and substitute for the authority of the past. Like Proteus, moreover, the scene always already participates in pastoral's future too, since it is the scene of descent and the moment of commemoration at its center that are repeated in scores of Renaissance and Baroque texts.

Proteus, in his allegorical identity as convention personified, facilitates the narrative of the myth of origins that ends the *Fourth Georgic* by functioning as the source of knowledge about the infertility of Aristaeus's bees. Cyrene orders her son to lay hold of the seer and to force the secret of the bees' listlessness from him. In so doing, she in effect indicates emblematically where the secret of pastoral fertility and protection is to be found: namely, in the *binding of timeless forms, or conventions, to the present*. Distilling the essential forms, or repeatable formula, out of many changing appearances is the key to the establishing (instituting) of ongoing abundance, of both bees and texts. Cyrene's advice to her son thus merely abstracts the acts of previous pastoral eulogies into a recommendation to derive a single ritual and rule, a "timeless code" of commemorative and celebratory acts that can be repeated in ever-new and always-appropriate forms. Proteus bound represents the power of convention, the power of the present, to renew and protect the grove.

In the scenes of pastoral eulogy from Theocritus to Virgil, sterility in the bower is the result of death and the silence it brings. It is overcome by the presence of commemorative monuments and stylized songs of lament that are always the same but also always tailored to the specific occasion. In the *Fourth Georgic*, Proteus is forced by Aristaeus to reveal that the inactivity of his bees, a sign of pastoral infertility, was in fact caused by *two uncelebrated deaths*, those of the poet Orpheus and his wife, Eurydice (454ff.), at which the gods have taken offense. Thus, although Orpheus is not traditionally portrayed as a shepherd, Proteus's story seems to place him into the lineage of pastoral singers that began with Theocritus's Daphnis; the ritualistic commemoration of Orpheus's death by the surviving shepherd, Aristaeus, will return the bees to the grove, according to the timeless seer.

Orpheus's original lamentation upon Eurydice's death was, Proteus warns, a self-absorbed song that blinded him to the frenzied Bacchae, who eventually destroyed him (495, 520–22). Thus, not only was the dead wife not commemorated correctly in controlled song, but Orpheus the poet also went to his death unsung, a crime against all conventions of pastoral lament. At this point, Cyrene interposes herself between Proteus's tale and her son in order to explicate what he must do; literary tradition must reformulate and make useful the significance of myth for the here-and-now. A new act of celebration, belated funeral rites for Orpheus and Eurydice, will placate the nymphs of the grove and persuade them to return Aristaeus's bees (534–36). Cyrene's explanation of the necessary rituals ("sed modus orandi qui sit prius ordine dicam" ["But as to the manner of prayer and its orderly sequence, I will tell you"], line 537) prepares the way for the bees' return. Her instructions concern the proper ways of commemorating. *Commemorative institutions* must be created to allow Orpheus and Eurydice to become synecdochically present in celebration and to go properly celebrated to their deaths. As institutions, Cyrene's rites can be used to restore Aristaeus's bees and to counter all future threats to the grove. They thus provide both the origins of renewal and the possibility of a future orthodoxy of response.[38]

The rites Cyrene describes capture in prescribed forms both the proper methods of celebrating a specific poetic ancestor (a gesture that traditionally brings fertility to pastoral) and the technical procedures for creating a future of pastoral fertility whenever the productivity of the grove is threatened. Aristaeus must sacrifice four bulls on four altars—here the ritual of the *bugonia* begins—and invoke Orpheus's spirit as he does so; the bees will then be reborn out of the carcasses of the animals, a gift of the placated nymphs. The poetic ceremony of imitation, the feeding of successor poets off their predecessors' corpus by ingesting and synecdochically re-presenting them in new form, is as orderly and prescribed a routine as Cyrene's funeral rites.[39] The bulls' corpses function as vessels of the divine, mysteriously giving birth to a new race of bees even as they mask the mechanical, ritualistic act of reproduction in a moment of mythic spontaneity. Imitative pastorals also appear both new and different even as they feed off (make both absent and present) the texts of the past. The "rural labor" described here as involved in the techniques of bee husbandry suggests that the conventions of celebration—repeated in always new and appropriate contexts—can secure a future of pastoral renewal for the unsponsored shepherd too.

The binding of Proteus and the delineation of codified funeral rites that Cyrene describes attract the bees back to Aristaeus's grove; pastoral fertility is renewed in an act of divine dispensation that appears spontaneous, "inspired," but which is in fact based on the same formulae, or textual conventions ("modus orandi"), with which all future moments of pastoral and poetic sterility can be redeemed. In this and the other pastoral eulogies that I have discussed, song is returned to the grove in the form of ritualistic repetitions of pastoral *topoi* and in the celebration of absent (deceased) shepherds, pastoral poets, and texts. Like the textual artifacts and concrete tombs it contains, the faithfully reproduced eulogy scene is itself a commemorative monument; it marks each pastoral as belonging to the greater literary tradition that the scene, as representative part, makes both absent and present within the new text. It comes as no surprise, then, that it was this highly conventional scene that became the hallmark of many early modern pastoral texts.

The poetics of renewal that guides the idealizing gesture of commemoration and celebration in the genre of the pastoral eulogy finds its origins, then, in the Greek and Latin traditions. This poetics continues to structure pastoral texts written in the vernacular during the European Renaissance and Baroque. Of course many of the guiding principles of *imitatio*, as the internalization of classical forms in vernacular poetry, reproduce the commemorative gesture of the eulogy scene, as the past (ancient tradition) becomes both present and absent, the ideal made real, in localized form. The two texts that form a link between the Theocritan-Virgilian origins of pastoral eulogy and the Nuremberg shepherd poems are Jacopo Sannazaro's *Arcadia* (1503) and Martin Opitz's *Shepherd Poem of Hercinie the Nymph* (1630).[40] In both the *Arcadia* and the *Hercinie*, the celebration of a pastoral *genius loci* continues to act as the central textual rite, growing in both cases into elaborate ceremonies of commemoration in which idealized images are created by means of monuments and collective song. By including implicit and explicit references to the traditional mechanism of eulogization in their texts, vernacular poets endowed themselves and vernacular poetry with the power of pastoral renewal. As successor poets, they pay homage to their classical predecessors while removing them by reproducing them synecdochically within the confines of their own texts. The literary topos of the pastoral eulogy thus comes to serve the same function as the internal mechanisms of the eulogy scene. Both provide a bridge between the past and the present whereby the new shepherd and text move into a position of origins precisely by reproducing the codified forms of earlier pastoral song.

Perhaps even more importantly, however, the scenes of praise that lead in the classical tradition directly and indirectly to the formation (convening) of a textual collective of authors, shepherds, and songs are repeated in the postclassical texts as a means of calling into existence (within the narrative of the text) a "real" pastoral community, a group, that is, of one or more shepherds singing together. This reference to a literal collective voice suggests that the authors of these later texts resorted self-consciously to the metaphor of the eulogy as a means of producing their own history. Sannazaro's scenes of pastoral eulogy, for example, use Virgilian images of pastoral apotheosis to constitute a pantheon of heavenly shepherd-poets that is then quite deliberately mirrored by a pastoral collective below; one of the *Arcadia*'s shepherd protagonists, Sincero, bears Sannazaro's own academy name, an allusion to the Neapolitan academy to which the poet is known to have belonged.[41] The text thus (re)produces history by serving as Sincero/Sannazaro's self-realization as academy poet.

In Opitz's *Hercinie*, the making real in the text of a pastoral collective that was at once historical and literary is even more explicit, since the shepherd protagonists are figures in a narrative that is both a highly imitative, literary occasion and a matter of historical fact.[42] Identified as "three learned poets" who "speak in the guise of shepherds," the shepherds bear the names of Opitz and his historical poet companions.[43] They engage in a series of learned discussions and compose both individual and collective verse, each voice representing a position in the narrative framework and, perhaps, historical viewpoints as well. The shepherds wander first through historical and then through literary landscapes, emerging, finally, from the subterranean grotto of the nymph, Hercinie, where celebratory monuments of all types are discovered and described, to find themselves on the estate of Hans Ulrich von Schaffgotsch, Opitz's patron and the sponsor of the text. The estate is located directly above the mythological realm of the nymph, where his family and he personally had been elaborately praised.

The conflation of the mythical and the historical, of the ideal and the real, in these highly traditional but also contextually specific vernacular texts reveals that it is precisely the synecdochic gesture of pastoral eulogy that governs their content and form. By both referring to (and thus absenting) the tradition in their inclusion of the descent or eulogy scene derived from Virgil's *Fourth Georgic* and by localizing that tradition as they themselves become its newest and perhaps most representative members, vernacular pastoral turns imitation and the genre's literary conventions into the origins of a new "grove" and thus into the same kind of commemorative and foundational ceremony as the eulogy itself. In their imitativeness, the textual forms of vernacular pastoral mirror the events of ritualistic celebration—of both absent predecessors and of their own power to survive—so carefully described in the eulogy scene.

Finally, where mythological and literary figures (Daphnis and Orpheus) had functioned in both Theocritus's and Virgil's texts as the models that future shepherds and readers reproduce, the pastoral protectors in the later texts are often—as in the case of Opitz's *Hercinie*—historical persons and patrons on whom the literal survival of the new tradition of pastoral depends. Here the logic of pastoral poetics derived from *Eclogue* 5 reproduces itself in repetitions of the *georgic* scene of discovery and descent. The most common internalization, or *rendering present*, of what remains of the eulogy scene in these vernacular texts comes in the form of a conversion of the pastoral dirge into an elaborate encomium to a specific patron or protector. And in a concretization of the metaphor of song as artifact, the encomia are often literally inscribed as texts onto commemorative monuments that the shepherds "discover" in local, pastoral caverns, temples, and groves. These monuments are structurally related to the tombs and altars of the eulogy tradition and are produced here by strict adherence to the very same ritualized commemoration called for in Cyrene's celebratory rites. The encomia of vernacular pastoral in the Renaissance and Baroque thus merely literalize the implicit occasionality of all pastoral eulogies, which, like the genre, are designed to follow Aristaeus in his "capturing" of Proteus by laying hold of the fleeting moment of mortality in textual structures that distill what is permanent out of death as a historical "fact."

Beginning with Opitz's *Hercinie*, then, the traditional celebratory gestures of the eulogy scene, although still embedded in a somewhat modified quote of the descent scene from Virgil's *Fourth Georgic*, take on the new and clearly identifiable form of the encomium. In Opitz's pastoral, for example, an elaborate ode to the patron, Hans Ulrich von Schaffgotsch, composed according to the strict pattern of the *genus demonstrativum* as described in many handbooks of rhetoric and poetry, is "discovered" inscribed in a monumental crystal tablet at the center of Hercinie's cavernous abode, a space indebted to Cyrene's watery realm in the *Fourth Georgic*. The tablet itself is located in a kind of subterranean gallery of commemorative artifacts and monuments to the Schaffgotsch family line, of which Hans Ulrich is the culmination and most recent member. The Nuremberg pastorals follow the *Hercinie*'s lead by exploding the poetic conceit of commemoration in the grove into an elaborate demonstrative discourse in which pastoral protectors, their achievements, and their lineage become the focus of massive celebratory monuments and texts. These monuments are based on the pastoral tradition of a *eulogistic artifact* capable of transforming absence into presence, devastation into productivity, pastoral tradition into the substance of vernacular texts.

The gallery scene and description of monuments in the grove thus take the place of the eulogy per se in these texts, which has resulted in the German-language shepherd poems being analyzed as little more than massive, occasional poems. However, these texts articulate the very same poetics of renewal found in their classical predecessors. The Nuremberg pastoral texts follow the strict patterns of textual celebration encoded in the structures of the *genus demonstrativum* (structures not unrelated to the "modus orandi" that Cyrene explains to Aristaeus). The celebratory scenes and the (literal and literary) ability to establish and perpetuate the vernacular grove by creating protectors within the text are central to the Nuremberg pastorals. Like the scenes of eulogy to which demonstrative poetry is both conceptually and structurally linked, the celebratory interludes in the Nuremberg texts signal that the *Schäffereyen* are part of the timeless tradition of pastoral that they both create (in imitation) and surpass (as new texts). This tradition and the new texts that derive their authority from it thus strive to be as timeless as the commemorative statuary that the German shepherds "discover" (invent) in the groves and grottoes in and near Nuremberg itself. The "real" and the local thus become the space of the ideal. Conermann confirms this tendency when he links the monuments of the Nuremberg pastorals to a tradition of humanist topographies and praise of cities, suggesting that the Nuremberg poets use this tradition to "find" Arcadia in the landscape surrounding the city.[44] In both cases, the encomium—both to a local pastoral protector and to a specific geographical location—belongs to a rhetorical and poetic tradition that relies on specific textual structures to invest the real, the local, and the present with mythical, originary, and monumental weight. I examine the transformatory power of encomium's textual institutions briefly now before turning to the use in the Nuremberg shepherd poems of the georgic scene of descent to fulfill the call of pastoral's poetics of renewal.

Textual Monuments: The Institutions of Poetry of Praise

Celebratory texts have always been defended as more than merely occasional, as indebted, that is, to the realization of an (absent) ideal. Indeed, Plato specifically exempted texts of praise (*enkomia*) from his banning of poetry in book 10 of his *Republic*, since they are "beneficial to orderly government and all the life of man" in presenting (making present) idealized images and detailed patterns of exemplary human behavior to wide audiences for imitation.[45] In a reversal, then, of the standard Platonic doctrine that describes the tertiary relationship of art to truth, Socrates describes *enkomia* as separate from reality and thus as dependable in giving shape to the ideal. It is in this way, I would submit, that they provide the same space of difference as both the pastoral eulogy and the genre of pastoral as a whole.

The poem of praise, or encomium, belongs to what in the Latin tradition is called the *genus demonstrativum*, or epideictic speech. Aristotle used the term *epideixis* to describe the kind of oratory that could show a lively linguistic picture of the object or person to be praised.[46] Thus, demonstrative rhetoric or poetry belonged by definition to a public, rhetorical sphere, since "showing" meant providing an example, a visible model for the audience to either emulate or condemn as a standard of viable behavior.[47] In the text of praise in particular, the individual to be praised becomes visible as language "clothes" him in desirable attributes. By adducing an abundance of positive traits through a scheme of *amplificatio* based on Quintilian's description of a rigid textual pattern of praise (*laus hominis*, an eleven-step sequence of textual "discoveries" of the causes, facts, and future reasons for praise not unlike the ritualistic celebrations found in the tradition of pastoral eulogies), the exemplary figure could become "real" in a text, the "reality" of the "description" substituting for the nonpresent referent.[48] In this way, the *genus demonstrativum* fulfilled its Platonic office by providing the space of realization for ideal Forms, the generic equivalent of the eulogy scene.[49]

Like Plato, many Renaissance theorists of the *genus demonstrativum* paid particular attention to another set of historical "facts" susceptible to encomium's power *as text* to make the ideal real, namely, those surrounding the context of reception, or audience. The device of "favorable heightening," of using the facts of an individual's life to create a fictionalized ideal, was meant to stimulate imitation of the exemplary character and his behavior in those who heard, read, or witnessed it.[50] *Aemulatio* of the already-idealized historical figure could thus cause the exemplum, the "composite of perfect features corresponding not to an historical figure, but to an 'idea,'"[51] to become real again in the person of the beholder or listener, in much the same way as the ideal shape of pastoral song becomes real each time a poet-shepherd sings the praise of a deceased predecessor. The ritualistic language of *epideixis* thus became codified according to various subcategories of occasionality and poetic types, since to be effective, it had to be appropriate to the specific moment and audience.[52] These "types" of course had a decorum of their own and were arranged according to both the event and the identity of the person or persons involved. The Romantic and post-Romantic critique that occasional texts were the antithesis of true poetry since they were bound to external causes rather than to the poet's internal "voice" is inappropriate, then, as an accusation that "nature" as the "ideal" could not be heard in poetry of praise. In fact, any particular context—birth, death, arrival, departure, wedding, burial—could become the moment when the ideal could become real both within the text and in its reception. The exchange of past for present, of the absent ideal for its real form in the here-and-now, so central to the classical scene of pastoral eulogy was thus also the guiding mechanism for both the production and reception of poetry of praise.

As a formal genre belonging to the *genus demonstrativum*, the epicedium was a specific kind of laudatory text that relied on the process of idealization.[53] Most similar of all forms of occasional poetry to the pastoral eulogy scene, the epicedium pictures the deceased as immortal and transforms his life into an exemplary (textual) form of itself after and commemorative of his death. Its strict forms mimic the dirgelike aspects of the pastoral eulogy scene, allowing literary tradition to harden into a system of textual institutions (understood here as a set of carefully delineated compositional norms). The epicedium is based on an affective sequence that formalizes the confrontation with death into a carefully orchestrated series of textual cues and emotional responses; praise, a show of sorrow, mourning, consolation, and exhortation to survivors form the steps. The pattern is specific to the occasion but also universally applicable.[54]

Because the *oratio funebris* relies on a fixed code that both arouses and controls emotions and grief, it can be said to participate in both a universal and a particular discourse of mourning based on *convention* as both a textual and a literal fact; it creates a "community" of both mourners and texts. In the tradition, a moment of collective activity, either dancing or song, will follow the completion of the formal epicedium itself, illustrating that the rigid textualization of mortality has had a restorative effect.[55] Thus, the moment of individual death is transformed by a code ("modus orandi") of ritual celebration and lamentation into an occasion of idealization and community formation in a manner not unlike the renewal of the grove in the textual tradition of Theocritus's, Virgil's, and Sannazaro's pastoral eulogies. The ideal figures of both praisers and praised are created in and out of a moment of facticity and serve as its idealized origins; they are transformed by collective lamentation into guiding principles for the community's future well-being.

The *dialectic of absence and presence* that structures the poetics of renewal as it lies embedded in the tradition of classical pastoral eulogy is thus maintained in the vernacular pastorals in the textual institutions of demonstrative poetry. It finds expression within their narrative events as a set of recognizable conventions of commemorative praise (*institutiones poeticae*) that transform specific historical figures and events into ideal versions of themselves. The poetic conceit of ritualized commemorative song thus continues to conventionalize as it founds new communities of pastoral leaders by giving the traditional pastoral scene of praise a local, vernacular shape.

The Nuremberg Pastorals: "Inventing" Origins in the Local Grove

As in Opitz's *Hercinie*, the traditional scene of pastoral eulogy in the Nuremberg shepherd poems is transformed into visits by language society members, under the guise of their shepherd identities, to local, celebratory grottoes and commemorative groves. The monuments discovered there often appear as "fictional architecture," which itself commemorates the tradition of pastoral tombs and altars.[56] Located in temples and palaces that probably did not historically exist (although their environs are often recognizable), these statues, tapestries, and poems nevertheless privilege presence and the power of the text (as concrete artifact) to be an origin. They do so because they follow the poetics of renewal embedded in the genre of pastoral; each new text comes into existence both as a realization in the vernacular of ancient models and as an example of the *genus demonstrativum* hardened into visible form.

As monuments dedicated to preserving the memory of specific, historical pastoral protectors by representing them in idealized form, the Nuremberg pastorals thus found a vernacular literary tradition and secure material support for it by literally making earlier literary traditions both absent and present within the boundaries of their own texts. In turn, the absence of the figures celebrated—either in death or as idealized versions of themselves as "realities" "on the outside" of the space of the text—produces the concrete substance of the shepherd poems. The celebratory interludes occupy most of the space of these texts and are designed to serve as "mirrors" for their recipients and as the origin of "history" in their ability to transform.

The Nuremberg shepherd poems engage in the poetics of pastoral renewal in two ways. They produce a vernacular version of pastoral informed by the logic of Virgil's *Eclogue* 5 and based on the citation of elements from the descent scene in Virgil's *Fourth Georgic*; in so doing, they locate origins for a "new" German literature within the textual practice of language society poets. And they locate the ability to create (found) a safe haven and thus a future for this "original" poetry's literal survival in the pastoral community's control of the highly regulated conventions of celebratory song. It is in the existence and repetition of these highly routinized textual structures, deadening in their appearance, that the renewal of the vernacular grove is able to occur.

At the same time, this structure of renewal is a restrictive one. It must continually repeat itself in order for pastoral to survive, thus allowing for a future not of difference but of reproduction of the same. It also remains restricted to the space of the grove and to the reproduction of textual structures and moral absolutes proper only to the moment and context of founding. As textual monuments to an instituting moment, then, the pastorals become caught in that moment as they attempt to institutionalize its survival.

The versatility of the codes of stylized poetry of praise and the Protean nature of the scene of praise allow for a vast number of occasions and a wide range of figures to be celebrated in the series of pastoral texts written between 1644 and 1677 by members of the Nuremberg language society. Garber has maintained that over one hundred of these shepherd poems were written; I deal with only a select number of them here. The distinguishing characteristic of the three-part typology of these texts that I develop is the identity of the patron figure or figures celebrated in the eulogy-like scene: (1) local patrons, an idealized community of heroes, or the city of Nuremberg; (2) an emperor, local nobility, or patron families; and (3) the language society's own original members or those influential in the group. It is in the very act of writing celebratory texts that these various sponsor figures are transformed into founders and protectors of the local grove. By placing local figures within the scene of eulogy, the scene in the genre that traditionally guarantees the fertility of the grove, the Nuremberg pastorals also demonstrate the *georgic* element of these texts, their symbolic return of the power of protection to the shepherds and to the regular and regulated work of celebration itself.

The acts of group lament and collective celebration described in the narratives of these texts are among the best sources that survive for information about the activities language society members may have performed collectively. Pastoral celebration as an act of convening thus did the work of history on a number of levels in the Nuremberg "prose eclogues." Textual traditions were made into the absent and thus authorizing foundations of local history and into the "reality" of the language society grove by virtue of their synecdochical presence in *imitatio*. And the very act of producing celebratory pastorals literally convened the language society into existence by converting the landscape around Nuremberg into an originary topography in which sacred and timeless, mythological and traditional figures emerged out of and became one with the "reality" of the group's activities. As textual events, the shepherd poems thus created and functioned as the "origin of history"—as the origin of the language society—as they found and organized both the literary and literal conditions of its beginnings and ongoing existence within the boundaries of a citation of the pastoral eulogy tradition structured as occasional poem.

The establishing of a collective, poetic voice in the vernacular is as self-conscious a gesture in the first group of Nuremberg pastorals as are the synecdochical references to the tradition of pastoral texts. This first group of shepherd poems includes the founding text of the type and of the order, the Shepherd Poem of the Pegnitz, written by Harsdörffer and Klaj in 1644. In the text, the poets cast themselves, in the mask of their society names, in the main roles of pastoral protagonists. They carry convention into the local grove. The second text of this first type, Sigmund von Birken's *Continuation* (1645), completes the narrative of the 1644 text by following up the celebratory scene at its center with the establishment of a shepherd community in the grove.

These two shepherd poems present the founding of the Nuremberg Order of Flowers as a stylized, celebratory event in the tradition of the classical pastoral eulogy. They serve both as the origins and as textual reference points and building blocks for much later Pegnitz activity by absorbing the power of both literary history and myth into their own founding moment as a local, authoritative moment of resuscitative pastoral song. The third text in this group, Johann Hellwig's *Die Nymphe Noris* (Noris the nymph) (1650), reproduces the narrative structure and formal organization of the first two, proclaiming itself as the third and fourth installments of the original series. It thus directly canonizes the historical subgenre of the encomiastic shepherd poem as heir to the classical tradition of pastoral eulogy.

The creation of conventional (textual) monuments to contemporary "shepherds" is crucial to the effectiveness of the Nuremberg pastorals. However, their occasional nature shows the limitations of the *Schäffereyen* as textual institutions that attempt to "legislate" their origins into existence. Like the Nuremberg poetics, the Nuremberg shepherd poems rely on a strategy of making the beginnings of vernacular pastoral come to pass in, and only in, a strictly regulated, commemorative textual event (commemorative both of the patron and of their own compositional expertise). The shepherd poems thus produce their own origins and survival in textual form even as they make it impossible to deviate from the scheme.

Harsdörffer's and Klaj's *Shepherd Poem* appropriates the power of pastoral for the Nuremberg group by opening imitating Opitz's *Hercinie*. As if to disarm potential criticism of its highly imitative nature, or, perhaps, to make its readers aware of it, the *Shepherd Poem* capitalizes on its origins in an authoritative tradition by openly examining its heritage ("Theocritus/Virgilius/Ronsard/Tasso/Vega/Sidney . . . Opitz/Flemming/Caesius") in the address to the reader; the most immediate progenitor is later named specifically in a note: "[See] page 59 of the *Hercinie* of The Crowned One [Opitz's society name in the Fruit-bearing Society], which is followed here."[57] The opening lines of this first Nuremberg pastoral are in fact based on the literal convening of a series of quotes from Opitz's pastoral into the presence of the new text:

> There
> Where the Meissen brook flows through the valleys
> [And] the crystal [silver] clear waters mingle with the main provincial stream . . .
> There lies the much praised province of Sesemin, the home of the shepherds' carefree abode, Sanemi . . . In truth it could be called the joyful home, a pleasure palace for the nymphs of the fields, the abode of the sylvan deities, a place of rest for shepherds, a learned retreat for the poets, and a place to tarry for those in love.[58]

The phrases the "shepherds' carefree abode," "learned retreat for the poets," and "place to tarry for those in love" are quoted unchanged from the earlier text and identify the literary provenance of the *Shepherd Poem*. They also make the presence of the earlier text superfluous, because the Nuremberg text literally takes its place. The localization of the grove—Sesemin is an anagram of Klaj's birthplace, Meissen—provides the contextual frame and suggests that a new, clearly recognizable time and place can easily accommodate the authority they have usurped from the predecessor text. The abundance of genealogical information the text gives about itself thus assures the reader that this pastoral is aware of its roots both in the timeless forms of tradition and in the here-and-now of historical fact.

As if to make the simultaneity of the discourses of literary tradition and vernacular origins all the more obvious, the lamentation over the death of a single, mythical shepherd traditional in the pastoral eulogy is replaced in the *Shepherd Poem* (as it had been in Opitz's *Hercinie* too) by a complaint about the nature of mortality specifically within the context of the Thirty Years' War as symbolized by the destruction of the pastoral landscape of "Sesemin" by acts of war:

> The crazed sword, the vengeance of provoked insult, and the raging turmoil of war have most recently harried all art and goodwill out of this place. Shepherds and shepherdesses have been robbed of their dear flocks; the villages, barnyards, adjoining farms, and sheep pastures are desolate. (5)

The literary model of the ravaged eulogy scene is transposed into a specific, historical landscape here. The shepherd Klajus is at once a figure from Sidney's *Arcadia* and the German poet Johann Klaj, who was in fact forced by the war to leave Meissen for Nuremberg, where he met the poet-shepherd Harsdörffer-Strefon soon after his arrival there. This meeting on the banks of the Pegnitz River is reenacted here in the *Shepherd Poem* as the refugee, Klajus, encounters Strefon resting under the cool shade of a tree (10). The two shepherd-poets engage in a further act of convening, moreover, by calling a "more original" literary model into the presence of their own vernacular grove and song, namely, the exchange between Meliboeus and Tityrus in Virgil's *Eclogue* 1, the authorizing scene of pastoral as synecdoche, as the place of difference from war that is the grove.[59] The continuous movement between a literary and a historical landscape (and, indeed, the presence of Strefon and Klajus in both at the same time) thus follows the pastoral poetics of renewal by convening literary predecessors into the present of an actual community of historical poets. The appearance here of Strefon and Klajus as replacements for those predecessors endows them, then, with authoritative origins in a "timeless" grove made real.

The conviction of the Pegnitz shepherd-poets that the local context is capable of taking on the task of making the ideal forms of pastoral discourse present in the "reality" of mid-seventeenth-century German-language poetic forms is obvious as Strefon and Klajus move through the "Neronsburg" (Nuremberg) grove, describing an array of scenes and objects that indirectly celebrate local fertility and its power to absorb such a highly crafted and stylized past. The descriptions seem at first little more than patriotic expressions of local pride; the "cable mill" ("Dratmüle") and the "paper mill" ("Papyrmüle"), the "exercise area" ("Tummelplatz") and the "Haller fields" ("Hallerwiese") are elaborately described in an act characteristic, according to one critic, of Baroque "realism."[60] But it is precisely the relocation of the traditional literary grove on the outskirts of the imperial city of Nuremberg and the recasting of its "natural abundance" in a wealth of early modern technological and urban-development detail that make clear the identity of the local context as a stage upon which, at a specific historical moment, idealizing literary events can occur. The extremely detailed description of the local landscape and backdrop against which the "mythical" pastoral events of the text occur functions as a celebration of local industry (the paper mills), of the bravery of Nuremberg soldiers (the exercise area), and of the richness of the Nuremberg soil (the many crops native to the region are listed in great detail, 21).[61] More than just aspects of the "local color" of the text, these details stress the fertility of the local grove as they emphasize, as so often in the traditional eulogy scene, the idealized exemption of the city of Nuremberg from the devastation brought on by the absence of the protective spirit and, in this case, by war.[62]

The poems of praise to the local landscape are, moreover, themselves celebrations of another sort as well. As examples of vernacular onomatopoeia (*Klangmalerei*) (e.g., p. 20), they link the poetic trademark of the Order of Flowers to the industrial, military, economic, and natural abundance of its actual historical location.[63] Klajus has thus wandered out of a narrative of historical devastation into a local bower of both literal and literary abundance. And yet, for the text to synecdochically re-create the scene of renewal from the eulogy tradition and thus to motivate the abundance that Strefon and Klajus enjoy, it must engage in carefully contrived celebration. And, indeed, the *Shepherd Poem* responds to the call of the genre immediately.

When we recall that the city of Nuremberg was besieged at least one hundred times during the period between 1618 and 1648, the relocation of idealized and highly literary pastoral scenery in a clearly recognizable historical landscape comes as no surprise. Like the death of the shepherd-leader traditional in eulogy texts, the conflict of war presents a grim threat to the continuity of pastoral song. The genre's traditional response of praise and transformatory idealization to the fact of human transience is recalled by the shepherd-poet Strefon. After describing the local landscape, he refers in passing to the noble origins of the great city of Nuremberg (21); Klajus interjects that greater knowledge of these origins, the absent past of the present grove, would serve him and the other shepherds in good stead. Strefon agrees and points out that since the war began, it had become the task of the "noble in spirit," or poets, to save the past and the memory of great deeds from being effaced by the violence of war by inscribing, or textualizing, them in the present:

> [S]ince the Germans have been battling with one another, many of the noble in spirit have concerned themselves and continue to concern themselves with preserving for the annals of eternity everything that has been consumed by fire, washed away from the monuments [stones] by rain and storm, worn away from metal by time; [they have done this] by writing. (22)

Just as when Thyrsis "writes" Daphnis's words into his song in Theocritus's *Idyll* 1, so too is writing seen here as a means of overcoming mortality, of preserving the past while also superseding it. The *Shepherd Poem* is itself a textual monument both to tradition and the past devastation of war, since it uses literary precedents to create a space of difference from the spoilage "outside."

The inscriptions of which Harsdörffer-Strefon speaks have an additional and more specific function as well. Like the funeral monuments erected and celebratory verse sung in earlier eulogy scenes, they are able to immortalize specific historical figures, taking them out of history and bringing them into the present, so to speak, by placing them in the textual position of the deceased *genius loci* of the eulogy tradition, as models for the present to follow, replace, and reenact. It is thus not surprising that the narrative of the *Shepherd Poem* provides at this point for the "Neronsburg" shepherds to encounter a female allegorical figure, Fama ("winged Fame"), modeled on Virgil's, Sannazaro's, and Opitz's nymphs. She leads Strefon and Klajus into a realm that symbolizes a conflation of their literary past with the historical present, namely, a templelike gallery of commemorative statuary (23), which is no more than Virgil's pastoral altars to Daphnis multiplied many times over, no more than Opitz's subterranean grotto now relocated above ground. The artifacts in the temple that honor three Nuremberg families, the Hallers, the Schlüsselfelders, and the Tetzels, to whom the *Shepherd Poem* is dedicated, are enduring monuments beyond time in their reproduction of the standard forms of celebratory textuality and, as the vehicles of occasional poems of praise, are also the origins of a more prosperous future for the shepherds.

The fertility of the Nuremberg grove is thus linked to both an event in the lives of the bourgeois class and to the vernacular shepherd-poets' ability to make literary tradition productive. The localization of the formerly mythical source of pastoral survival in the conventions of a specific community occurs here in the "fictional architecture": "eternal" monuments to those involved in a specific, historical occasion are "found" (invented) in the Nuremberg grove. Thus both the imitative formal elements of the text and its context—the specific occasion of the Nuremberg wedding—internalize and render exemplary a celebratory moment: in the first case, a moment of pastoral tradition, in the second, an event of local note.

As a monument in the grove, the "temple of commemoration" ("Ehrengedächtnis") of the three families recalls Virgil's, Sannazaro's, and Opitz's underground grottoes both literally and allegorically:

> This temple was round in shape and made of variegated red, white, and black marble. There were two grand doors that met in the middle, above them a luminous transom. Ionic columns encircled [the temple]; between them stood those trees; planted many years before, they alternated in offering their boughs as covering for the building. (24)

Although perhaps not quite as elaborate as its literary predecessors, the appearance of the structure "found" by the shepherds is described in terms that suggest its origins in traditions both older than the present context ("many years before") and far from home (the Ionic columns).

Even as the temple imitates a tradition of pastoral artifacts, however, it is much more than simply a monument to its literary past. It also spatializes and literalizes the steps of an encomiastic text—here, of the wedding celebration, or epithalamium—set into motion by the events of a specific time and place. The structure was built by the Muses, it is said, the "daughters of memory" (24). This genealogical detail of the text suggests the "poetic mnemonics," or spatially fixed scheme, according to which demonstrative texts were composed.[64] The interior of the temple houses a gallery of statues, "various sculpture columns," that represent the ancestry of the three family lines to be joined in marriage. The pattern of the *genus demonstrativum* begins with a celebration of the lofty lineage of the persons directly involved. At the same time, however, Fama indicates that each image ("Bildnis") or statue, is meant to act as an exemplum: "consider . . . how Truth has introduced this commemorative temple as a means of encouraging constant emulation of such respected, honest, and much deserving ancient Germans" (24). The fact that these ancestors appear as exemplary figures from a localized past suggests the ability of the present to act as a moment of origins and transformation in more ways than one. The individual histories told by the verses inscribed on the statues become ideal behavioral patterns even as they follow the demonstrative strategy of *aemulatio* at work in the epideictic text; Fama indicates two empty pedestals at the extreme end of the gallery, thus suggesting that the celebratory gesture of the text provides a space of difference for both past and future members of the families:

> Next to the exit to this temple there stood two further pedestals without, however, any statues. Meanwhile Fama explained: "The sons of these last [mentioned] leaders [i.e., those whose statues were in fact there] are still living pillars of their fatherland right now, and it is my most heartfelt desire that they will remain so for a long time to come in blessed prosperity and that this place will not receive their images [for many years]. (27)

As is the custom in pastoral eulogies, then, the descendants of these idealized figures are to emulate and thus convene their more perfect past into the present of the "real" world. The *Shepherd Poem* in fact constitutes that past as the authorizing origin of the power of the present to renew the grove, to make it fertile as the origin of the shepherds' safety and prosperity and of vernacular poetry too. This first half of the first Nuremberg shepherd poem thus relies on conventionalizing strategies as it conflates past and present, real and ideal in a specifically Nurembergian location and text.

The second half of the *Shepherd Poem* contains a series of elaborate encomia dedicated to the three Nuremberg families on the occasion of the double marriage. The dominant conceit of this lengthy collection of celebratory songs is the amoebean singing match between Strefon and Klajus. Fama has instructed them to outsing one another in praise of the historical patrons. A literary past is thus reproduced and superseded in the literal presence of the vernacular text. Here, too, the *genus demonstrativum* plays a role in convening an idealized image of the marriage partners into the presence of the text. Strefon sings, for example, of the studies undertaken by the bridegrooms, who, through "learning all manner of arts, foreign languages, and knightly skills" both at home and abroad, reproduce their lofty ancestors in the here-and-now (44).

Just as importantly, however, the celebratory songs, which take up well over half of the literal textual space of the *Shepherd Poem*, form a kind of anthology of society poetry. Each text represents a new moment of poetic innovation in German; each text is an experiment in a different meter and form of vernacular verse. The epithalamium does much more, however, than merely provide the frame, or vehicle, within which numerous poems can be published together as a single text.[65] It actually participates in an act of convening as it calls together a community of both shepherds and texts that guarantees the creation of new and contextually appropriate poetic forms, thus allowing the present to supersede the past of the pastoral tradition, which the text clearly quotes.[66] Fama's injunction to the shepherd-poets to engage in celebratory verse demonstrates the capacity of the German vernacular, as used by language society poets, to accommodate both traditional pastoral *topoi* and an abundance of new literary forms at the same time as it challenges the patrons to take on the ideal traits of their ancestors as they make their way into the landscape of contemporary Nuremberg. The *Shepherd Poem* is thus a model of institutionalization. It provides mythological foundations and patterns of orthodoxy within the space of a text that commemorates both the past and its (present) power to produce and protect the new grove.

The "original" shepherd poem in the subgenre of the Nuremberg prose eclogue comes to an abrupt end as the singing match is concluded and Fama's decision awaited (47). The moment of postponement is a clue to the form the poetics of pastoral takes in this text. It is a structure whereby a future text, a future of texts, and a separate space of renewal can be called into being within the commemorative moment itself. In direct contradiction to the act of convening as a collective moment, the declaration of a single winner of the contest would give the pastoral a false sense of closure by implying that only one shepherd-poet rather than the society as a whole, of which Harsdörffer and Klaj were to be the founding members, would inherit the mantle of pastoral authority.

Sigmund von Birken's *Continuation* takes up, as its title implies, where the first text has left off, by offering (in place of the elevation of a single shepherd-poet to a position of dominance) a scene in which it is the pastoral poet society as a *collective* moment, a moment of *convening*, that comes to play the decisive role in instituting the language society and providing its textual norms. Fama's decision to declare the poems sung by the poets, rather than one of the poets, as the winners of the song competition recalls that part of the eulogy tradition in which the songs of celebration and lament themselves, rather than the shepherd-survivors, form the "enduring monuments" that represent the presence of immortality in the grove. At the opening of the *Continuation*, Fama hangs a wreath of flowers on a tree in honor of the (absent) promise of vernacular song:

> She [Fame] came back to us and detached that wreath from her silver trumpet. She still did not want to announce to whom of the two of us

it might be due as winner, and so she chose to issue a brief encomium to our poems alone. Then she vanished before our eyes.[67]

The "georgic" gesture of this scene—namely, that the wreath celebrates the work done by poetry itself as the guarantor of the security of the grove—becomes more apparent as Strefon and Klajus each pick a flower out of the wreath as their individual prize, thus instituting (producing the origin in textual form) the language society tradition of individual flower emblems for its members and founding the society as a "flower order": "these flowers will be the mark of our community of shepherds, which from now on will be known as the Society of Flower Shepherds" (32). The wreath is then returned to its place on the tree, marking the grove as the future home of the society; all future shepherds who desire to join the group are enjoined to select a flower from this common, originary wreath. The model of the single singer of the pastoral eulogy is thus modified here, although the synecdochical structure is preserved. The "shepherd society" as a collective is designated as the heir to the tradition of stylized, celebratory, pastoral song. The timeless literary tradition will thus be absorbed into but also adapted to the specific occasion, bringing an idealized past into the historical present within the boundaries of collective pastoral song.

The extension of the scene of song competition from the *Shepherd Poem* into Birken's *Continuation* comes in the form of a partially autobiographical embedded narrative that links the text's mythological and literary origins and its historical frame. Along with Virgil's Meliboeus and the *Shepherd Poem*'s Klajus, the protagonist of the *Continuation*, Floridan (Birken), belongs to a family of dispossessed shepherds looking for a protected grove after he has been driven away from his native Bohemia by the forces of the Counter-Reformation to the safety of the free imperial city of Nuremberg.[68] As he heads for "Neronsburg" and the protection of the new, local Daphnis (Harsdörffer-Strefon), Floridan stumbles upon the very *locus amoenus* for which he searches and upon Klajus, his predecessor in this quest for a safe garden (13). The historical poet, Birken, thus enters onto the stage of Pegnitz mythology as he relates to Klajus how he was accepted into the pastoral order by Harsdörffer.

Klajus rehearses for Floridan the story of the singing contest of the *Shepherd Poem* and the sharing of the prize of the wreath, thus engaging in pastoral poetics by using the earlier text as an origin of local mythology and replacing references to an older tradition with a new, authoritative textual source. The story of the flower emblem selection ceremony and of the origins of collective pastoral song ("and thus did this Society of Shepherds take its beginning," 33) includes a reference to Birken's own choice of a flower and thus to his own formal initiation into the group.

The literal collection of blooms that make up the wreath is endowed, finally, with a more figurative meaning as a florilegium-anthology; each shepherd obligates himself to compose vernacular verse ("for our mother tongue wishes fervently to be well served with useful practice, with verse that is a model of and for ornament, and with witty inventions," 32) after he chooses an emblem and thus promises to celebrate the expanding membership of the society and of its textual production. Floridan and Klajus proceed to compose a series of songs in fulfillment (within the narrative of the *Continuation*) of the obligation to produce pastoral song (34–41). The anthology of poems that the entire text includes also "remembers" and is a monument to the community of poets, a living florilegium, who form the membership of the vernacular language society.

The song competition that began on the occasion of the double wedding of local citizens is resolved, then, in the founding of a local pastoral community and in the establishing of the outlines of a new genre of literary texts (both the prose eclogue and the numerous lyric and song forms). Each occasion represents the opportunity for idealized figures and textual predecessors to become "real" in historically appropriate form and thus to replace the past even as it is honored as origin and model.

The founding of a pastoral language society with a goal of creating a vernacular literature with the authority of myth is itself celebrated here in such a way as to link it to a timeless, authoritative realm precisely because the *Continuation* is constructed as a *textual monument* of commemoration. Soon after the reference to the founding of this new community of shepherd-poets, the narrative shifts to a new level in order to integrate the historical occasion of the beginnings of the Order of Flowers on the Pegnitz into the literary tradition by recalling the subgenre of the eulogy scene as it appeared embedded within a narrative frame based on Virgil's *Fourth Georgic*. As "quote," the scene "remembers" the past and is a literal monument to it even as it celebrates the power of the present to replace (substitute for) that past in a new voice. Klajus and Floridan encounter a mythological figure (the heir to Cyrene, Hercinie, and Fame), here, a "satyr... whom they quickly recognize as the god Pan" (41). Emerging quite literally from both a mythological (and textual) past and the local landscape, Pan leads them into a cave that opens onto elaborate, subterranean sculpture galleries reminiscent, once again, of Cyrene's underground realm. The presentation of architectural detail in this section, together with extensive marginalia indicating textual sources (Ovid, Lucan, Livy) for the "many stories and ancient histories" (42), calls attention to the text itself as monument and suggests the extent to which the Nuremberg poets depended on fixed textual patterns (such as the descent scene) and a variety of ancient model texts to generate their local mythology. Further galleries contain monuments to Pan and pastoral life (46–47) as well as to other mythological figures. The shepherds are joined by a band of satyrs, who guide them through the pastoral museum. The monuments are described collectively by two of the founding members of the Nuremberg Order of Flowers, thus confirming the story told them by their guide, namely, that Pan had come to Nuremberg from Arcadia, assured of a good reception because of the founding of the local "shepherd society" there (47). There is poetry in Nuremberg, in other words, because the pastoral language society and its texts exist. Thus literary history and myth are literally convened into the presence of the Nuremberg landscape as the local "shepherds" wander through a pastoral monument, which, as text, commemorates the pastoral tradition and celebrates the ability of the Pegnitz shepherds to (re)produce it in local form.

Central to this section of Birken's *Continuation*, as I have suggested, is the literary quote that confirms the text's membership in the tradition of celebratory pastoral. At this point in the narrative, the shepherds enter a vast gallery of statues where they discover monuments inscribed with demonstrative verse dedicated to commemorating a series of historical figures (48–56). Here, in the "cave of heroes" ("Heldenhöle"), the text provides the space of difference from history (as facticity) in which the ideal can become real in a most graphic manner, because those represented by the monuments discovered by the shepherd-poets in the cave are the heroes of the Thirty Years' War, the conflict so often said in the Nuremberg shepherd poems to have destroyed local pastoral groves. The scene exploits the figure of synecdoche and the notion of exchange—of part for whole and real for ideal—central to all pastoral song. Up above, in the nonsacred world of the real, war had been the cause of Floridan-Birken's despair. And yet, down below, in an idealized and idealizing realm of pastoral celebration, the perpetrators of this war are transformed into a community of peaceful and cooperative leaders.

The array of historical figures is remarkable, above all, for its variety of both status and confessional ties; the Calvinist Christian of Anhalt appears alongside the Catholic Ferdinand Infant; Louis XIII of France stands next to "Gabriel Betlem, Prince in Siebenbürgen." Although the celebration of war heroes would seem antithetical to the desire for stability and for the cessation of war, Pan interprets the moment of praise, especially praise of virtue, in a positive way: "Virtue is present in weaponry too, [for] it is with weapons that we must secure peace" (41). Designed to be productive of a "reality" more desirable than the devastation above, the synecdochical mechanism of pastoral motivates the celebratory statuary in an overtly didactic way here. Only in epideictic representation can these all-too-human heroes become exempla of good warriors, whose goal is peace. The shepherd-"readers"—those within and outside the narrative—are challenged by the genre's implicit command to emulate these irenically disposed figures in such a way as to be able to take their place on one of the empty pedestals (49) at the end of the gallery. A call for transformation of the devastated grove into a protected realm is both issued and answered by the re-presentation that is the vernacular pastoral text.

The striking artificiality of the underground community of exemplary heroes demonstrates the conventionality of Birken's text in a special sense. Klajus's and Floridan's satyr guides inform them that the commemorative "tablets" will hang in the grotto only as long as war rages up above; when peace comes, each monument will return to a "commemorative temple" (56) in the country or territory where it rightly belongs. Were the heroes not "captured," however, in the patterns of idealization that the encomium provides and were they not assembled within the confines of a well-defined literary quote (the grotto scene), the peaceful company could hardly exist. Their "coming together" is possible only as exemplum, as a convention, only as a part of the visionary whole made real in the text. It comes as no surprise that as the shepherds pass out of the "cave of heroes," they enter a neighboring gallery of pastoral monuments (57) where Pan's pipes are discovered as the centerpiece of a shrine to bucolic mythology. The juxtaposition suggests that it is only within the confines of the pastoral code that such transformatory representation can occur. At the same time, however, as myth emerges in local garb, it must become absent as origin in order to become present as text. The shepherds of the Order of Flowers are thus told by Pan that he is well-disposed toward their "brotherhood" and are given the sacred panpipes to take back with them into the Nuremberg grove (57).

The mythic sacralization of the language society represented by the transferral of the ancient panpipes into local hands explains the disappearance of myth and its simultaneous reconstitution within the formal conventions of language society texts. The transfer is achieved, figuratively speaking, as the shepherd members pass out of the sacred, subterranean realm and leave it behind for a historical landscape. They view a miniaturized version of the origin of all waters (58) imitated from Virgil's *Fourth Georgic* and are informed about the relationship of their own Pegnitz River, an individual and historical river, to the waters present in this mythic realm. Once back in the Nuremberg grove and together with Strefon (Harsdörffer), the shepherds "christen" their grove as part of the tradition by hanging the mythic "Pan pipes" on a tree as a symbol (like the original wreath of flowers) of a collective harmony ("the shepherds' organ piece," 67) on the local level that has its origins, like the Pegnitz River, deep within the absent, sacred realm of a literary quote.

In the pages that follow, the shepherd company discovers a tree where the names and emblems of additional society members are inscribed. The society thus quite literally writes itself into a local landscape with roots in a timeless pastoral realm. The verses of the various members then fill the final 30 pages of this 100-page text with displays of poetic virtuosity not unlike the ending poems of the original *Shepherd Poem*. In a third act of convening, the discovery of verses written or attached to trees (itself a convention of pastoral) quite literally calls a poet community into existence; as a collective publication, the subsequent collection of poems identifies society members (the poems' authors) as part of a single enterprise. The power of the mythological realm and its idealized inhabitants thus reemerges, becomes "real," in the founding of the language society and in the writing of this language society text.

By 1650, Birken had retold his version of the founding myth of the Order of Flowers a second time in a text entitled *Der Pegnitz-Schäfere Gesellschaft-Weide und Frülings-Freude: Beschrieben durch Floridan* (The springtime revels of the Pegnitz shepherds in their fields: as described by Floridan) (1645). He had, moreover, reworked the cave of heroes scene into an independent text of its own, the *Schäferey: Behandelt durch Floridan* (Shepherd poem: as rendered by Floridan) (1649),[69] thus establishing the norms of the subgenre in a textual code and series of scenes as fixed as Cyrene's "modus orandi" of ritualized celebration, in textual institutions, that is, capable of founding and giving ongoing form.

In *Noris the Nymph* (1650), a shepherd poem that follows the pattern defined by Birken's text, Johann Hellwig (1609–74) follows the implicit injunction for society members to continue to compose stylized, celebratory pastoral song, writing in his introduction that the text is the result of his efforts "to increase my practice of the heroic German language, as I promised in a solemn vow to do."[70] Hellwig's shepherd poem *Noris the*

Nymph is the third and final text of the first group of Nuremberg pastorals.

In Hellwig's *Noris the Nymph*, it is the city of Nuremberg, together with its architecture and inhabitants, that migrates into the central position of celebration, thus transforming the local landscape quite literally into a *locus* of pastoral protection and survival. The choice of "patron" seems obvious given the function of the imperial city in the lives of the language society poets during these last years of the Thirty Years' War. The shepherd poets Montano and Periander (Hellwig himself and the poet Friedrich Lochner[71]) meet two nymphs, who report the invitation of the famous nymph Noris, protector of the local Nuremberg grove, to visit a commemorative temple. Although the descent scene and description of originary waters are not repeated here, the "discovery" motif persists. The local bower, a replica of the Nuremberg *locus amoenus* as described in earlier texts, is depicted as a kind of glorified graveyard, a collection of architectural celebrations (altars and commemorative monuments) to the memory of members of notable Nuremberg families deceased in the recent past. Following the pattern of the *genus demonstrativum*, the celebration of the glorious past and notable achievements of its citizens elevates the city as a whole to the status of a kind of illustrious progenitor.

Hellwig's text itself is structured as an epicedium, a text of lament, and idealizes historical individuals whose importance as sources of patronage for language society poets was quite real. The altars and artifacts, as evidence of the literary quote and as concrete monuments in the text, thus serve the traditional synecdochic function of the eulogy as they assimilate historical events, locations, and individuals into a well-ordered, pastoral present with roots in a well-respected literary past. It is precisely this gesture of commemorative celebration and substitution that, in the past, had been the origin of renewed fertility in the grove. For this reason, Hellwig is fully justified in calling his text the "third and fourth installments . . . of the Pegnitz Shepherd Poem," since it absorbs the mythological origins of the Nuremberg bower into an even more explicitly historical present and, by casting the city and its citizenry into the role of protector, transforms that present into a source of support at the same time.[72] Once again, the ideal realm of literary tradition and exemplary behavior is represented as "real" in an extremely localized text and grove.

Hellwig's version of the pastoral eulogy scene ends with the performance of celebratory rites, which calls attention to the importance of the collective in the shepherd-poem subgenre. In the classical scene of eulogy and in the series of imitative texts, a shepherd community—both in the text and as texts—is formed whose task it is to engage regularly in ritualized acts dedicated to preserving the memory of all that is past and, in so doing, to create the origins of the present. In *Noris the Nymph*, this convening is the result of performing ritualistic acts of commemoration that culminate in a song of praise:

> Montano approached the altar in deepest prayer and placed some of the burnt offering (Rauchwerck) upon the flame as a token of his obligation and obedience. Such a delightful and sweet scent rose up that both Montano and Helianthus were sent into a rapturous state, and with a single heart and mind struck up the following ode in honor of Noris the nymph. (54–55)

The vision of an altar to local history, combined with the submerged presence of the descent/discovery scene from the *Fourth Georgic* in the text, thus "inspires" the shepherds to engage in collective, commemorative song. As in the tradition of pastoral eulogies, a poetic community is literally brought into existence here as the result of an imitative, textual act.

Hellwig's use of the standard scene of celebration is even more explicit about its didactic intentions, and thus about its power to make the ideal real in the text, than some of the earlier Nuremberg shepherd poems perhaps precisely because of the radical move into facticity that the glorification of the city of Nuremberg as pastoral patron represents. Because the historical present absorbs and stands in for the idealized forms of the pastoral in so immediate a way, it is essential that the emulative process (the reproduction of pastorals of the past in the present text) be emphasized within the narrative of the text. Thus the arching roof of the "commemorative temple" is studded with "tablets of sapphire [and] stars cut out of diamond" that bear the names of those being celebrated. Literally inscribed into this artificial "heaven," a figure of the transcendent realm made real on Nuremberg soil, the "stars" will quite literally "light the way" for those who wish to follow:

> And, upon careful examination, one could discern a variety of letters glimmering forth out of these [stars]. The two nymphs reported that these ought to be the names of such persons as had particularly recommended themselves above all others in both word and deed and whose memory would now light the way for those to come as luminous model[s] of virtue. (27)

In the second half of Hellwig's text, where the extravagant praise of Nuremberg continues within the frame of the discovery scene, the idealization of historical figures that belongs to celebratory genres is repeated. The shepherds of part 1, now accompanied by Strefon and Klajus, enter the temple once again, "a place where the pictures and monuments to our much-praised late leaders are preserved with much splendor [and our late leaders] incorporated into a realm of immortality [even though they are physically deceased]" (54). Absorbed into the niches of immortality, these individuals become models, like the classical eulogy scene in which they are themselves inscribed, for the local shepherds to follow. In an unusual passage, the process of commemoration is described as a concrete event. A recently deceased Nuremberg citizen, Lucas Friderich Böheim, is to be inducted into the monument gallery:

> An elderly man, carrying a winged hourglass . . . was holding a newly crafted plaque made out of cedar upon which there was an image . . . The Most Honest Lucas Friderich Böheim 1648 . . . other nymphs took the plaque and coated it with a special oil to protect it from decay and then [added] it to the other images on the wall of the oft-mentioned chapel, where there were other empty places as well. (135–36)

Noris explains to the shepherds that this process of commemoration transforms the worthy deeds and virtues for which the individual was celebrated in life into exemplary patterns after death:

> They are "caught" upon the cedar plaques after their departure from this earthly life to be celebrated and permanently remembered . . . there, [upon the plaques] the persons portrayed are honored and serve to encourage others. (137)

Each figure in the gallery becomes "a lively example and model which [his] descendants are to follow" (139). The monuments in Hellwig's temple are thus not only the patterns of encomiastic poetry in concretized form but the imitative imperative of the classical pastoral eulogy scene made literal in the Nuremberg grove.

The three "original" Nuremberg prose eclogues thus locate a timeless pastoral tradition in the local grove. They associate the founding of the pastoral language society and the practice of its special brand of stylized, celebratory song with the radical contextualization of the classical eulogy scene, thus investing their own collective practice with the power of ancient models to make the grove a safe and fertile realm for vernacular song. A second set of Nuremberg texts uses the device of the central celebratory interlude in a pastoral grotto or temple to praise more specific patrons and their families, thus following Opitz's model in the *Hercinie* much more exactly. This second set of texts follows the generic norm by raising individuals from a wide range of classes, from the imperial family and local princes to illustrious members of the Nuremberg bourgeoisie, into the position of pastoral protector and source of both literal and literary renewal.

Sigmund von Birken most often adapted the pattern of the pastoral eulogy based on the descent/discovery scene to a specific encomiastic occasion, leading nineteenth- and twentieth-century literary historians to identify the poetic production of the Nuremberg language society in general with the subgenre of the pastoral poem of praise.[73] Birken's two most elaborate prose eclogues, *Ostländischer Lorbeerhayn* (Eastern laurel grove) (1657), in celebration of the House of Habsburg, and *Guelfis oder Nider sächsischer Lorbeerhayn* (Guelfis; or, laurel grove of Lower Saxony) (1669), dedicated to the House of Brunswick-Lüneburg, are typical of this middle group of Nuremberg pastorals. Both families had acted as patrons to the Nuremberg poet on different occasions.[74] In Birken's texts, the family trees of these two ruling houses are transformed into galleries of monuments to their lineage, thus using the structures of the *genus demonstrativum* to fulfill the imperative of the pastoral eulogy to represent the real as an idealized form of itself while recognizing the literal importance of patronage for the local production of pastoral song.

The *Eastern Laurel Grove* is dedicated to Leopold I, heir apparent to the Habsburg imperial crown in 1657, when Birken wrote the text. In the dedication, Birken makes explicit the comparison between his relationship to Leopold and that of the shepherd Tityrus to his benefactor in Virgil's *Eclogue* 1 ("You see / How he allows my flock to graze in safety"[75]), thus casting himself once again in the role of the disenfranchised shepherd in search of a secure grove. Indirectly, of course, the "monuments" Birken's text erects to Leopold and the Habsburgs in the pastoral poem are themselves emblems of stability and testify to the poet's power to create his own safe space; they not only repeat the traditional celebratory scene and family of texts but evoke an ancient and exemplary political lineage as well. They are explicitly conventional, moreover, because the *Eastern Laurel Grove* openly exploits its identity as a group text to function as a vehicle for securing publication of poems by members of the language society. Thus the Nuremberg prose eclogue continues to rely as a genre on conventions of several kinds—from the repetition of textual *topoi* to the act of composing collective song in the grove—to represent the very real circumstances of midcentury poetic life in textual forms borrowed from an idealized and idealizing pastoral discourse of praise.

In Birken's 1657 text, a band of shepherds engaged in learned conversation wanders through a local *locus amoenus* and meets the indigenous nymph, Noris, who indicates to them that the language society's goals and texts are well known in this grove. Noris of course represents the earlier Nuremberg pastorals by her very appearance in this encomiastic text. She thus makes the order's own mythology present to the group of shepherds gathered to praise Leopold's line.

Noris leads the shepherd poets to a sequestered "commemorative temple" in a celebratory cave where she describes—and, in describing, makes present as *ekphrasis*—a vast series of genealogical monuments to Frederick III, Rudolf I, and other, more recent members of the House of Habsburg preserved in that mythical space. An appendix ("Anhang") to the text is filled with page after page of celebratory verse, dedicated to other members of the Habsburg line not included in the temple scene as well as to other lesser or nonnoble families who had been instrumental in securing imperial patronage for Birken.[76] (The juxtaposition of the anthology of celebratory poems to the series of monuments to patrons in the traditional cave scene makes explicit the parallel between two ways of "publishing" and disseminating celebratory texts in the early modern world.) Idealizing images that represent the addressee-patron as a product of an illustrious past and thus as a timeless, immortal form of himself can be found in both the subterranean statuary and in the demonstrative texts. The Nuremberg shepherds gathered to admire the monuments "created" by their own collective song thus represent a community of poets whose task it was to commemorate both the past and their own power to use it to secure their own future within the boundaries of celebratory texts. In so doing, they also celebrate the mythical and literary historical realm of texts and caves that Noris represents, the realm of literary pastoral, that is, of which their vernacular songs form a synecdochical part.

Birken's second, explicitly panegyrical prose eclogue, *Guelfis* (1669), expands the grotto-temple scene even further. Dedicated to Birken's former pupil and current duke of Brunswick-Lüneburg, Anton Ulrich, the text begins with a lengthy autobiographical lament by the shepherd Birken-Floridan concerning his separation from Nuremberg and the

Pegnitz River on whose banks the pastoral poet society thrives. This autobiographical section—Birken had in fact traveled to Wolfenbüttel in his capacity as tutor—thus quickly makes plain the historicity of the "story" to be represented in the highly conventional text.

The customary lament nevertheless soon turns into praise, as Birken celebrates the generosity of the patron's family, whose support had begun in 1645/46 and was to continue throughout the poet's life.[77] The specific events that concern the poet-shepherd here nevertheless continue to be integrated into a literary and mythological world. The shepherds discover a "grotto or cave whose floor is of whitest marble" in this quite recognizable pastoral grove; celebratory statues to the house of Brunswick-Lüneburg are housed there.[78] A series of initiated nymphs, who identify themselves as "the daughters of the great Hercinie," explain the monuments to the shepherds. Birken includes engravings of the various rooms, galleries, and statues described in the text, thus allowing the architectural solidity with which these "enduring monuments" were conceived to become quite literal even as they are constituted as textual events. Their literary heritage dates back to Opitz, if not beyond, and is as "immortal" as their apparently timeless presence in the local grove.

The architectural layout of the subterranean temple in *Guelfis* follows the patterns of the *genus demonstrativum* in exact detail. The grotto contains a series of monuments that form a personal museum celebrating the patron, Anton Ulrich, as well as descriptions of his family's funeral vault ("the residence of heroes and the crypt in honor of this same house," 174). The bejeweled caverns contain emblematic statuary and "pictures upon the walls" that follow the genealogy of the family from the first mythological "Welf" (Guelph) up to Duke August, the famous father of Birken's patron and a supporter of the arts. A special monument to Duke August is located in a separate grotto:

> In yet another crypt, fashioned in the round in the style of an ancient temple and equal to the first one in decoration (except that the place was illuminated by two golden chandeliers with crystal lamps instead of columns of crystal) . . . there stood a low pedestal . . . with a hero's image [upon it] crowned with a laurel wreath. (194–95)

The idealized past "discovered" (or invented) in the grotto by the poet-shepherds is to function as the source and basis of the current patron's behavior.[79] Plaques affixed to the base of the statue of his father depict the family line, August's education and other accomplishments, as well as his offspring, including Anton Ulrich. An etching of the monument is included to render the reality of the statuary described in the text all the more plausible. The origins of these descriptive passages in *ekphrasis* are clear; thus, textuality is still considered a key factor in the process of celebration and idealization.

The importance of texts both in the world *in* this text and in the world *of* this text (namely, the world of the language society) is emphasized in the section that follows. Because the shepherds are fearful of forgetting the subterranean wonders they have seen, they are given a scroll by their nymph guide, Guelfis; the scroll contains copies of all the genealogical verse discovered on the grotto walls (224). The shepherds are thus able to carry the idealized artifacts of the mythological realm back with them into the local Wolfenbüttel grove in textualized form, allegorically extending the realm of perfection into the "reality" beyond the confines of the quoted scene. The emphasis on their own specific brand of celebratory poetry as the vehicle best able to mediate such truths and make them real is most clear in the anthology-like appendix to *Guelfis*, which is said to contain the very poetry given to the shepherds by the nymph. The fifty pages of celebratory verse (*Ehrengedichte*), collected here with seventy pages of family trees, reveal that the eulogistic elements of the tradition—praise as a means of tradition building—inform this prose eclogue too. As an anthology of occasional verse by language society members, these pages also emphasize the collective and thus conventional nature of praise. Moreover, the appendix is also entitled a "Laurel Grove" (271ff.), the textual equivalent in the world-of-the-text to the grotto of celebratory statuary in the world-in-the-text. The ideal realm of concrete textual acts is realized in encomiastic texts by society poets.

Birken makes clear that it is his privileged status as a vernacular successor to a divine or semidivine tradition of shepherd-singers that guarantees the "truth" of his idealizing representation of the patron. In a "georgic" gesture of laboring to secure his own leisure, Birken, under the guise of his identity as Floridan, recounts a dream in which he had been crowned a poet laureate: "I remember a similar vision in which, on my twenty-first birthday, hoping against hope, I was awarded the poet's crown" (61). Birken actually received the title of poet laureate much later than his twenty-first birthday. But as the shepherds come together in a collective interpretation of the dream that implicitly condemns the blood nobility for passing over the noble-in-spirit in awarding the laureate title, their leader, Floridan, goes on to remind them in a song entitled "The Awarding of the Laurel Wreath" that the much more important elevation into a community of poets occurs on quite a different level:

> How now? Am I become immortal?
> Or do I just hover as a spirit?
> It is another manner of order that has received me here.
> ... Wait! Who is snatching me up from the earthly seat?
> Alas! Where am I then?
> I am become one of the stars. (61)

The language of the song echoes the scene of pastoral eulogy in Virgil's *Eclogue* 5 in which commemorative song and the building of altars and tombs raise the poet-shepherd into the ranks of a celestial order, here "another order" in the creation of a community of shepherd gods. Although Floridan's words may seem to suggest a vision of Christian salvation, they almost certainly also refer to the ceremony by means of which poets joined the Nuremberg group. And, indeed, much later in the text, Floridan-Birken composes a song of celebration that elevates his Daphnis, the poet Martin Opitz, to the level of the mythical progenitor-shepherd. The literary and mythological mechanism of pastoral apotheosis is thus drawn into the here-and-now of the Nuremberg text:

> Daphnis! O jewel and prize of poets!
> Judge of those who would spoil our language!
> Defender of our purest rhymes!
> Sweet Orpheus of German songs!
> O Opitz, who now inhabits the chambers of the heavenly realm!
> O German Amphion, rewarded now in eternity with much desired praise! (162)

Celebration thus occurs on several levels in Birken's *Guelfis*. The patron as *genius loci* is integrated by means of demonstrative poetry into a lofty lineage that defines him as the result of an idealized past, as a transformation of history into myth that literally provides him with models for behavior. Moreover, poet figures are praised as members of the "divine order" of literary tradition in much the same way as the "immortal" words of Opitz's *Hercinie* are commemorated within the very body of a new celebratory text. The shepherds and their texts are thus as much representative parts of the whole of pastoral tradition as Anton Ulrich is of his celebrated dynastic past. They portray the ideal made real in local, immediate form by means of a textual monument both to that moment of immediacy and to that moment's ability to create a future of pastoral texts and shepherd leaders.

Another set of explicitly panegyrical texts within this second group of prose eclogues uses the same grotto-temple scene in a series of encomiastic texts to celebrate local Nuremberg families belonging to the patriciate. The shift in class orientation is partially explained by the shifting power basis and struggle for prestige that was occurring in Nuremberg. Since the late sixteenth century, Hirschmann reports, the landed nobility in the countryside surrounding the imperial city had sought to usurp the position and influence of the princely courts; in turn, the urban patriciate, many of whom were sponsors of the language society, took on the role of a local aristocracy, acquiring estates, for example, that sometimes served as the site of increasingly localized groves in subsequent Nuremberg texts.[80]

As sources of support for the collective pastoral enterprise moved ever closer to home, the renewing power of myth became present in ever more specific and circumscribed contexts, producing idealized forms of literature and patrons of pastoral repose in ever more local form. It is thus no surprise that textual occasionality and historical (even geographical) specificity are stressed in these texts more than they were in the earlier texts. Specific persons and occasions are endowed with the power to protect the grove, thus revealing that it is in fact the *genus demonstrativum* itself that, in the hands of the poet-shepherds, will produce a secure future.

It is interesting that the specific moment of celebration and commemoration in these texts is most often the funeral; the demonstrative form followed is that of the epicedium. It may be more than coincidence that the structures of the stylized funeral lament apparent in these texts most closely recall the original form and function of commemorative song in the eulogy to the dead shepherd, since in these texts the Nuremberg pastorals move even closer to a recognition of the overwhelming importance of local support for the survival of their pastoral cause. Mortality signals the presence of facticity or history in the otherwise apparently timeless realm of pastoral. The ideal forms of textual structuring must intervene in the disorder caused by death and convert it into a moment of renewal by transforming loss into an occasion for the production of vernacular song.

Martin Limburger's *Kressischer Ehrentempel* (Temple honoring the House of Kress) (1663) is an epicedium-prose eclogue dedicated to preserving the memory of the most recently deceased member of an old Nuremberg family, Jobst Christof Kress of Kressenstein, in an elaborate celebratory text. Following the established ritual, the pastoral narrative calls earlier textual traditions and personnel into its presence even as it relies on conventional patterns of demonstrative poetry to bring a literal shepherd community together in a collaborative commemorative song. A lamenting shepherd is accosted by the mythological figure, Noris, from earlier texts, who leads him to a commemorative temple located in a familiar pastoral grove; the temple commemorates and extends the tradition of literary monuments as it transforms the moment of death into an occasion of renewal.[81]

In Limburger's text, the nymph, Noris, wears a headdress—"a tiny crown in the shape of the battlements of the city wall"—that marks her as an indigenous spirit whose ancestors nevertheless lie in ancient, literary realms. The temple itself is located deep in a dark "cypress-tree forest" (8) surrounded by cliffs, foreshadowing the occasion, death, upon which it was built. Here as before, the architectural detail of the temple reflects the textual categories of the epicedium. Elaborate genealogical artifacts, "memorials to the blessed ancestors of our late master" (16), hang in the temple; they testify to the patron's lofty past. Additional plaques detail his personal qualities and accomplishments, such as his "learnedness," his travels, and his military and civic achievements. Just as Birken had done in *Guelfis*, Limburger includes etchings of various aspects of the temple in his text, detailing the layout of its interior, the arrangement of each gallery, and the physical appearance of each celebratory artifact. The conflation of linguistic and architectural patterns in the text indicates that celebratory words can be just as "enduring" as monuments of stone. In fact, Limburger compares his text not only to the tombs and altars customary in pastoral eulogies but also to established celebratory rites that, in their codification, outlast even architectural artifacts:

> It was in order to testify to the immortality of such honorable virtue that the heathens [the Ancients] created the gods Virtue and Honor and, in an effort to recommend themselves to them most effectively, made constant votive offerings to them in temples built in their honor. ( )o(iij)

Even such ongoing rites of celebration, although both timeless and always appropriate to specific occasions of death, are neither as "immortal" nor as specific as textual celebration: "written memorials [outlast] even bronze and marble." Poetry and the ritualistic composition of epicedia to specific patrons bestow an immortality that is both individual and transcendent upon both Kress of Kressenstein and the *Schäfferey* in which he is celebrated.

In two prose eclogues of a slightly later date, Birken uses even more "realistic" (localized) versions of the standard commemorative scene to structure epicedia to Nuremberg patrons in an attempt to invest the specific context of his pastoral enterprise with the power of an immortal literary and mythological past. Although marked as belonging to a lengthy literary tradition by the inclusion of the standard celebratory scene, the two texts are also quite deliberately "Norimbergian." Their titles encode both their "otherness" (rootedness in the forms of the past) and their indigenous "sameness" (their embeddedness in the discourses of the present): *Der norische Metellus oder Löffelholzisches Ehrengedächtnis* (Metellus of Nuremberg; or, memorial in honor of the House of Löffelholz) (ca. 1675) and *Der norische Parnass und irdische HimmelGarten* (Parnassus in Nuremberg and the earthly paradise) (1677); each is a combination of foreign- or ancient-sounding names with the specificity of the localizing adjective, "norisch." Following the doubledness of their titles, both texts rely on the by-now-standard celebratory scene to integrate transparent references to the patrons and shepherds as real-life individuals and to their experiences in the local grove into a textual continuum of timeless literary forms. At the same time as this continuum is in fact created and extended by means of the repetition of the scene, it is also effaced, replaced by the realization of the tradition in the immediate present.

In Birken's *Metellus of Nuremberg*, the grotto-temple scene unfolds "in a large hall" in the "noble residence at Steinach," where a group of twelve shepherds takes refuge from bad weather; the group convenes there in order to enact standard rituals of commemoration and praise. At Steinach, on the estate of the recently deceased Burkhardt Löffelholz of Coburg, members of the pastoral language society find a collection of monuments ("tapestries" and a "panel of paintings"—b iiij) to the former patron. The contents of this commemorative gallery are augmented and given specific textual form as the shepherds challenge one another to devise emblems in honor of Löffelholz's life and death. The emblems represent the patron as "He Who Is Nobly Born," "He Who Is Well Brought Up and Schooled," "He Who Is Well Respected," "He Who Is Well Traveled," "He Who Is Well Married," "He of the Noble Offspring," "He Who Rules Well," each a step in the epicedian text, created jointly here as the result of collective song.[82]

Although the convention of the descent/grotto scene and of the predecessor texts in which the scene is found is the unspoken model to which this scene of eulogy in *Metellus of Nuremberg* refers, the domination of the patterns of the *genus demonstrativum* on the surface indicates that textual rituals and generic patterns take over where imitation of a classical, textual past once appeared. The formation of a living collective of historical shepherd-poets who, with the support of Löffelholz's family, will continue to create ideal representations in pastoral song as part of their common task illustrates that convention rather than imitation is the dominant textual strategy here.

Birken's *Parnassus in Nuremberg* is a more complex text with an episodic narrative that absorbs the description of several commemorative groves in Nuremberg into a sequence of references to a "heavenly" garden beyond the specifics of any given time and place. The historical occasion of the text is the death of Georg Sigismund Fürer, a member of the Nuremberg patriciate who had supported the activities of the Order of Flowers during his life. The grotto-temple interlude is once again relocated in a recognizable scene, a small chapel on the Fürer estate, where the commemorative monuments take the form of textual inscriptions upon an elaborate parchment scroll. Text and commemorative monument are thus once again brought into direct proximity to one another.[83] A hermit-monk takes on the role of the initiated nymph; he leads the band of shepherds to the chapel and hands them the scroll describing the genealogical decorations on its walls.

> When the shepherds then considered the names on the wall, the monk handed them a scroll upon which the most distinguished tales of the Fürer family were inscribed. In order to leave behind some testimony to their desire to honor the family, each of the shepherds chose one or two of the family's members and composed a brief poem of praise to set under their names. These follow here. (10)

New poems by the Nuremberg shepherds are thus added to an already preexisting commemorative collection, recalling the textual imperative that each new shepherd-poet must literally inscribe his new words into traditional, pastoral patterns of celebration and lament. The texts that are composed follow the Fürer family from the thirteenth century up through the recently deceased Georg Sigismund. They thus represent not only the "spontaneous" generation of the vernacular epicedium text at the moment of death but also the integration of the newly deceased member of the clan into his own immortal past. Both the prose eclogue and the patron are thereby associated with more perfect forms of themselves by being cast in the role of fulfilling the promise of earlier texts and generations in a new, historical moment and place.

The tradition of the grotto scene is not exhausted, however, by the initial chapel scene in Birken's *Parnassus in Nuremberg*. The facticity of Fürer's life and death are not allowed to distract from the idealized forms this localized pastoral is obliged to represent. The shepherds leave the chapel and are led to the gardens on the Fürer estate; "After they had departed from the deepest reaches of the mountain, they saw stretching out in front of them the noble estate, Haimendorf" (16). The reference to the real estate acquisitions of the Nuremberg patriciate thus embeds the mythological parts of the text that follow in a highly specific historical locale.

The bowers and grottoes through which the shepherds pass have ancient literary and religious origins that are symbolized by the central monument they discover in a cave or grotto just off an "open clearing" near the woods adjoining the palace:

> They then entered a crevice or grotto through the lowest arch; there were thirty subdivided niches on each side . . . is there any place in the world that is more similar than this to the Parnassus of the ancient Greeks? (17)

Decorated with emblematic plaques and learned inscriptions, the "Parnassian" niches and grotto stand for the origins of this extremely localized pastoral in classical groves and texts. As the shepherds make their way out of the cave onto a grassy hill, they find the fulfillment of this ancient past in the formal gardens of the historical Fürer estate, appropriately designated by Floridan-Birken as a "heavenly garden," or paradise on earth (24). Like any one of the many historical and mythological gardens listed here in the text, the Fürer gardens thus participate in a continuum of ideal and real pastoral settings; the historical individuality of both the text and the literal surroundings is distinguished, ironically, by its capacity to be mistaken for the genre's and the garden's absolute form.

The final section of Birken's *Parnassus in Nuremberg* is devoted to a full-scale epicedium to the late Georg Sigismund Fürer, who had fulfilled in recent times the family line's promise as mapped out in the chapel scene. The explanation of his death and the vision of his life in a celestial kingdom are based on the garden metaphor and on the notion of an exchange of the earthly for a divine grove:

> All too recently he has exchanged the Parnassus at Nuremberg for paradise, the earthly for the heavenly Garden . . . it has pleased God to draw him unto himself in eternity and to set him among the stars. (33)

The image of pastoral apotheosis here is the same as that used by Virgil in the immortalization of Daphnis; the former leader and protector of the earthly grove moves on into a heavenly garden and is replaced by new singers of pastoral song in the local grove. The hermit-monk who is the shepherds' guide locates Fürer in this lineage by pointing out that his name signifies leadership; his garden was the local "Parnassus," he himself "the Apollo of Nuremberg, the leader of muses" (13). The verses that the shepherds compose to commemorate Fürer's demise are conventional in the sense that they follow the traditional pattern of the epicedium in describing his birth, schooling, civic accomplishments, marriage, and offspring. Perhaps more importantly, however, they also signify yet another instance of collective pastoral song; taken down by the shepherd Macarius on a parchment scroll, they represent an anthology of Nuremberg poetry, a testimony to the power of the celebratory moment to form a new community of poets and language society texts.

In a third and final set of Nuremberg pastoral encomia, the identity of the protective spirit, or *genius loci*, celebrated in the central grotto-temple scene becomes ever more specific as Harsdörffer and Birken themselves become the focus of the central eulogy scene. The attention paid to imperial and noble houses and to local patrician supporters in the two earlier sets of shepherd poems is focused here on figures of relatively minor social status—none higher than a patrician—who are nevertheless distinguished by their direct affiliation with the Order of Flowers. The locating of individuals capable of inspiring or resuscitating pastoral conventions of all sorts specifically within society circles acknowledges that the source of all standards lies within the local language society, which was to take on the responsibility of providing mythical or naturelike norms to the local, vernacular poetic community.

It is not by chance, then, that the celebratory statuary described in these texts was, in some cases, also quite real in the sense that it actually existed in a literal Nuremberg grove. Like the "self-cultivated, commemorative graves of six of our flower comrades" that the twelve shepherds of Birken's *Metellus of Nuremberg* discover in the local grove (a iij), the artifacts described in this last set of texts seem to have been based on monuments actually located in the Maze, or grove, in the Nuremberg suburb of Kraftshof, where members of the language society are said to have met, discussed, and composed joint texts just as they are pictured doing in countless prose eclogues. Johannes Herdegen, the historian of the society, describes the Kraftshof grove in the following way:

> A small hut [cottage] shall be available to each member, opportunity permitting... He may devise an emblem, which is usually painted and attached to the door of the structure, according to his own pleasure and

of his own invention ... in the case that another member of the society had possessed the hut previously and had then passed away, his emblem and nameplate should, in honor and memory of the deceased, either be taken inside the hut, hung on a door, or stored in some other area. And when he should [himself] die, his survivors ought to erect a votive plaque in a specific place in the Maze to preserve his memory and to give rise to future fond remembrance.[84]

Here the literary conceit central to the pastoral eulogy, namely, the gesture of erecting commemorative monuments to deceased shepherd companions, became as real in the historical Nuremberg grove as it did in the prose eclogue texts. In both cases, the reference to monuments functioned quite literally as a community-building device. The collection of actual monuments at Kraftshof stood for the collectivity of poets and texts whose task it was to represent and make real a timeless pastoral tradition in the immediate context of vernacular song. The Nuremberg pastorals that refer indirectly to the Kraftshof Maze by filling the central grotto-temple scene with descriptions of funerary monuments to particular society members also draw the mythical and literary powers of pastoral song into the here-and-now of Nuremberg life.

The first of the pastoral encomia dedicated to a member of the poet society was written by Sigmund von Birken in celebration of one of the founders of the language society, Georg Philipp Harsdörffer, in a text dedicated to celebrating the engagement of Harsdörffer's son in 1667. The prose eclogue is entitled *SchäferSpiel der Ehre des ruhmseligen Spielenden ... gewidmet* (Pastoral play dedicated to the memory of the much honored Playful One). The title emphasizes the importance of language society connections by using the name given to Harsdörffer in the Fruit-bearing Society ("Der Spielende") in the title.

Although there is no explicit descent into a grotto or cave in Birken's *Pastoral Play*, the sequence of events is strongly reminiscent of the other prose-and-verse pastoral texts. The visit to a commemorative monument is replaced by the collective composition of a sequence of songs, texts, and emblems that, following the pattern of the epicedium, re-create in epideictic form Harsdörffer's family history, education, civic accomplishments, and, most importantly, the texts he wrote under society sponsorship. As the shepherds wander through a clearly recognizable, historical grove, they "invent" (discover) a series of emblems representing each of Harsdörffer's major works (95ff.). The garden is filled with commemorative pastoral texts that, as an anthology of celebratory poetry, function as much as a monument to Harsdörffer's memory as the altars or tombs of earlier texts. Indeed, the entire grove through which the shepherds are said to meander as they compose their songs is itself a kind of living testimony to the founder's importance; the group revisits many of the specific Nuremberg locations mentioned in the founding texts of the Order of Flowers, the *Shepherd Poem* and the *Continuation*, including the blacksmith's forge and the waterwheel that signal the technical sophistication of the local grove.

Birken's *Pastoral Play* of 1667 thus confers an originating and authorizing power upon local Nuremberg scenery and textuality by locating the sources of his commemorative song in the earlier *Shepherd Poem* of 1644. The *Pastoral Play* also refers indirectly to the ancient tradition of pastoral eulogy by following the rigid patterns of the epicedium in a pastoral text. Harsdörffer is thus transformed in and by Birken's text into the source, so to speak, of his own immortalization in two ways: his personal history provides the building blocks of an idealized picture of the leader of pastoral song; and his own work quite literally provides his successors with the words with which the commemorative grove can be described. Although the ancient, timeless tradition of pastoral eulogy is implicit in Birken's *Pastoral Play*, it becomes clear that the local context and, specifically, the historical occasion of Harsdörffer's activities in behalf of the vernacular have come to outweigh the importance of referring to ancient or foreign sources or norms. The (historical) founding moment itself becomes the "enduring monument" and regulator within the grove.

If Birken's *Pastoral Play* in memory of Harsdörffer almost literally substitutes the part (the Nuremberg grove itself) for the whole of the pastoral eulogy tradition, thus reversing the synecdochic gesture by making the real the model for (indeed, the only available form of) the ideal, his final prose eclogue in honor of Johann Michael Dilherr revives the explicit use of funerary monuments in the grove as a vehicle for commemorative song. Although Dilherr was himself not a member of the Order of Flowers, he participated in its activities, supported its members, and wrote poetry himself.[85] When Floridan-Birken calls for a group of his fellow shepherds to devote a pastoral to the memory of their deceased companion in the *Dilherrisches EhrenGedächtnis* (Memorial in honor of Dilherr) (1679), he invokes the tradition of the pastoral eulogy as a convention, as both a standardized textual pattern and a community-building device.[86]

The ritually composed epicedium takes the form of a design for a funerary monument "with columns in twelve sections" sketched on a piece of bark that is then ceremoniously hung from a tree. The twelve spaces will be filled with twelve emblems designed by the shepherd clan, each giving symbolic expression to the stages of Dilherr's life ("noble birth," "early youth," "schooling," "profession," "wit," 161–97). Just as important, however, is the fact that the sounds of lament that fill the grove when the news of Dilherr's death is received are turned into a series of joyous songs at the prospect of his arrival in a more perfect grove:

> He is passed away here from the mortal realm . . . in order to be all the more present in eternity. He has merely exchanged places and has set here, like the sun, in order to rise in the other world. (197)

The entire epicedium to Dilherr is thus explicitly oriented toward *consolatio*, toward the depiction of the deceased in a more perfect, transcendent realm as a means of easing the grief of those left behind. Although also a traditional feature of the pastoral eulogy, this consolatory aspect points to the text's function as a vehicle for convening a shepherd community into the presence of the text and into the present of history. Indeed, the final, elaborate song sequence of the *Memorial in Honor of Dilherr* uses the language society's wreath of flower emblems as a device for generating an anthology of society song:

> And then Floridan and Myrtillus sang an eclogue in which they glossed all of the society flowers in terms of our dear late Dilherr's demise . . . and therewith brought this pastoral play to its close. (201)

The florilegium, or collection of verse generated out of the "society flowers," celebrates both Dilherr and the power and presence of the group of shepherd-poets in uniting in commemorative song. His death thus occasions the renewed coming together of the community of shepherds, who, like their immortal predecessors, transcend the specific occasion of mortality by uniting in collective song. Unlike their mythical and literary predecessors, however, this group of shepherd-poets also represents a historical community of poets capable of embodying the ideal in textual form in the here-and-now.

The final prose eclogue in this series of localized pastorals based on the classical eulogy model celebrates Sigmund von Birken himself, one of the most important figures in the history of the Nuremberg Order of Flowers. Written by Johannes Georg Pellicer in 1677 and entitled *Lob des Floridans, besungen in zimbrischen Lustgefilden/von dem ausländischen Pegnitz Schäffer Thyrsis* (Balthis, in praise of Floridan, sung in the delightful pastures of Cimbria, by the Pegnitz shepherd who lives abroad, Thyrsis), the text goes to extraordinary lengths not only to celebrate Birken, under whose leadership the language society had expanded far beyond its original size, but also to provide a textual monument to the literary tradition upon which the subgenre of prose eclogue was founded. *Balthis* both follows the encomium pattern and contains multiple versions of the grotto-temple scene. It thus identifies itself with the textual tradition as a vernacular version of the pastoral eulogy; its main function is, like its classical predecessors, to preserve the memory of those whom it honors ("to save those much honored persons from the clouds of obscurity") by literally inscribing their names and deeds into the pastoral landscape ("it is the constant task of the shepherds to carve the names of heroes into the bark of trees").[87] The "good names" of those celebrated—members and leaders of the Nuremberg language society—will thereby become as "impervious to decay" as the literary tradition itself, the equivalents to the immortal community of shepherd-heroes from Theocritus and Virgil to Opitz in textual form.

Balthis both begins and ends by identifying itself as a member of the tradition of pastoral eulogy. The nymph Balthis greets a band of shepherds headed by Thyrsis-Pellicer, the local shepherd leader. Together they discover a secluded mountain reminiscent of Helicon ("an overgrown and wild mountain"), where they visit a temple of monuments and inscriptions to the famous shepherd-poet Floridan. There they find (as textual invention) "a straight line of marble columns and pyramids, each of which displayed an emblem with its inscription engraved next to it" (20). Of the seventeen "commemorative columns" to Birken, twelve are inscribed with celebratory emblems; the five remaining monuments carry inscriptions to other shepherds—some mythical, some local—as if to re-create in the local grove the very immortal community of which the Nuremberg poet is said to be a part. The emblems are identified as the work of the Muses, thus endowing the statuary with a mythological origin befitting the pastoral locale.

Pellicer's "quote" of the grotto-temple tradition is not only much more elaborate but also far more suggestive of the figural importance of the celebratory scene than equivalent scenes in many of the other prose eclogues. The shepherds in *Balthis* discover a further grotto where they find commemorative monuments to language society members whom they had thought still alive; they pause at each grave to lament the companion commemorated there (52–53). These funerary grottoes seem to literally grow one out of the other as a further "grotto ... with many paintings and inscriptions most worth seeing" is discovered nearby. But this grotto and its monuments go undescribed as the shepherds leave the grove and return home. Having been united in collective pastoral lament, they already constitute a community in place of the deceased shepherds described in the text.

The proliferation of funerary artifacts in Pellicer's *Balthis* and the impossibility of describing them all offers an indirect commentary on the function of the grotto-temple scene: the community formed by the tradition of prose eclogues and thus by the German-language singers of pastoral is more than capable of creating "timeless" groves with local and mythological inhabitants. The mechanism, or "modus orandi," is so clear that Pellicer need not discuss or enact it at length. Thus Birken, second president of the Order of Flowers and perfector of the pastoral genre in its native, Nuremberg form himself plays Daphnis to a younger shepherd-poet in providing both the occasion and the words with which to perpetuate pastoral song. He is in fact called "another Virgil" (26–27) and said to stand second to none, to no ancient poet, in the production of inspired song.

The almost divine capacity of the grove to reproduce both the tradition and itself is thus relocated in a specific, historical, clearly "vernacularized" setting. The prose eclogue is thus an individualized rendering of apparently timeless literary forms. The synecdochic replacement of the part for the whole, of the real for the ideal, of the local for the ancient version of pastoral, now appears to be complete.

Pastoral is a figure of conventionalism in literature. As the genre favored by the Nuremberg language society, the prose eclogue functions as a textual transition from mythic authority to contextual and historical standards. The act of convening the past into the present, of calling ancient sources and texts into the presence of occasional vernacular poems that, in turn, often include the backgrounds of those celebrated in the body of their texts, allows for a double confirmation of the power of the historical moment to found a new literary tradition and to develop standards for it. The historical individual or individuals and groups celebrated and their conventions come to be defined as the culmination and representation of a set of both textual and ethical qualities and norms. In combining the standards of nature and culture, of inspiration and contextualization, of internal and external aptness, the Nuremberg pastorals never violate the doctrine of difference. They acknowledge the need to establish definitive standards for the community at large while remaining relevant to the moment of their creation. They cull these standards from both the tradition of pastoral eulogy and the demonstrative rhetorical tradition.

By localizing the scene of pastoral celebration in the here-and-now of the Nuremberg grove, the Pegnitz "shepherds" draw the power of literary history and myth into their own textual creations and thus into historical time, making it possible to "begin" a new era of vernacular poetry by relying on apparently timeless textual structures. Precisely in capturing these "ideal" structures, however, precisely by making them textually present and "real" within the confines of the Nuremberg grove, the pastorals of the Order of Flowers in effect close off the possibility of their texts doing anything more than making this inaugural gesture for the group. It is thus no wonder that the commemorative or monumental aspect of the Nuremberg pastorals as textual institutions outweighs the inaugural function of these texts since as monuments they make the poetics of renewal a matter of exclusivity, available not to every poet or political and social group but only to those belonging to and supporting the Nuremberg language society. The extreme localization of the eulogy scene performed by these texts resists their theoretical thrust, because it clearly limits the future to a continual reproduction of the present and its norms. Aware of the power of texts as institutions to commemorate, but also to dispense with, their moment of origins, the Nuremberg poets produced texts predicated on a principle of closure, on the restriction, that is, of the moment of renewal to the Nuremberg grove alone.

6 The Limits of Institutional Practice and the Resistance of the Text

The analyses in the preceding chapters have shown that the texts of the Nuremberg language society, the Order of Flowers on the Pegnitz, may be interpreted as institutions insofar as they are productive of (historical) origins and orthodoxies. In each of three sets of texts—language theory, technical treatises on poetics, and the prose-and-verse pastorals (or prose eclogues)—two different institutional identities emerge: (1) the *instituting* moment of foundations, origins, and authenticity; and (2) the *institutionalizing* moment of regulation, standardization, and concretization of linguistic and poetic norms. The foundational narratives and logic provided by the Nuremberg texts are organized around concepts of originary authority (closeness to nature, proximity to the divine, inspiration, and renewal); it is this authority—in its simultaneous absence and presence as a narrated or theorized "lost" but renewable original moment of authentic language or poetry—that endows the (historical) moment of the language society's beginnings with an "openness" to history, with the power to initiate, or institute, a new period of linguistic and literary time. The institutionalizing power of the Nuremberg texts is based, in turn, on the premise that they represent textual concretizations of a linguistic and literary law whose authority is rooted in this inaugural moment and logic. However, these regulatory texts also resist this "openness" to history at some more fundamental level, as I have shown, by restricting the moment of renewal to the historical moment of the language society itself. By strategically displacing and replacing any prior or other forms of linguistic or poetic authority (in the language or literature of the Ancients, for example, or in nature and the divine) with the textual production of society members, language society texts endow their own historically apt forms with effectively absolute and immutable legislative power by articulating them in institutionalizing and institutionalized shape. Ironically, then, the claim to inaugurate, to produce the possibility of a new and different literary and linguistic space, is characterized by a structure of sameness and closure.

The Nuremberg Institutionalization of Textuality

What emerges from an analysis of the Nuremberg texts as institutions (and from an institutional analysis of these texts) is thus the following paradox. The principle of historical difference upon which the legitimacy of the instituting moment of the Nuremberg texts is based articulates a counterhegemonic logic. In principle, no prior or "other" (textual or historical) instance can serve as the origin or regulator of the German language's new and true "first forms"; only within the language society texts themselves can this historical moment take shape. And yet this powerful confirmation of community autonomy (and thus of the principle of difference) is radically challenged by the essentially hegemonic gesture of the language society's regulatory texts at the very same time. Because they are monuments to a particular group's normal linguistic and poetic practice, the textual institutions of the Order of Flowers act, as do all textual institutions, to arrest the play of difference by formalizing habitual behavior into law.

The openness to history and to the principle of the self-generated standards of individual communities that the Nuremberg texts represent and explicitly confirm thus necessarily closes in upon itself and is negated in practice, because any absolute confirmation of radical specificity or difference would in fact deny the capacity of the collective and its texts to function as regulatory for anyone else. If new and authoritative origins can be found(ed) or invented by any collective or community, then the privileged legislative power of language society linguistic and poetic codes in particular would be "democratized" out of existence whenever new communities, even ones internal to the founding collective, emerge. It is for this reason that the regulatory texts of the Nuremberg language society ultimately fail as manuals for the future production of texts in spite of themselves. Instead they become the "places" where writings by Nuremberg theorists and poets (rather than catalogues of abstract rules) are enshrined as poetic and linguistic "truths." The doubled institutional identity of the Nuremberg texts—their simultaneous instituting and institutionalized functioning—thus asserts a kind of democratizing power even as it refuses the implications of this democratization by imposing clear limits on it.

The significance of the German Baroque for a theory of the autonomy and historical power of texts has been obscured by its position between the two equally imposing ages of the Renaissance and the Enlightenment. Often measured by standards more appropriate to the periods that border it—in terms of the Other of ancient textuality or of an individualized, rational Self—the texts of the Baroque fall short of the idealized model and have been dismissed as manneristic or obscure as a result. But these categories fail to address the difference of the fundamental project of many of these texts from both the imitative and the rational modes, a project that, I have suggested, seeks to enact a mode of self-fashioning whereby authority emerges in the form of explicit identification with the collective identity of a historical community. The texts of the Order of Flowers on the Pegnitz rely implicitly on eliding the paradox of their insistence on the specific (their own Difference) and their appeal to the general (the Sameness of collective opinion) as the origin of absolute standards and truth. This elision is reflected in the contextualizing strategies behind their instituting and institutionalizing claims, strategies that claim that appropriateness to a given historical (vernacular) moment (occasion) can serve as a universal norm when fixed in textual form.

My analyses of the textual practice of the Nuremberg order suggest, moreover, a potentially more general critique of any program of institutionalization and of the principles upon which it relies. To formulate this critique as a paradox in advance: When a specific, historical "interpretive community" derives what it claims are natural or near-natural norms from its own conventions of poetic, linguistic, and, implicitly, moral behavior and institutionalizes them in textual form, it in fact obscures the very principle of contextualism that it so desires to champion, namely, the notion of difference on which its own claims to validity are based. By universalizing or totalizing its own collectively based practice as law, the specific interpretive community thus effectively limits its own authority, disallowing the contingent moment to function as a source of absolutes. It does so by creating the logical necessity for a "more authoritative" (even if only provisional) universal sphere opposed to and separate from itself. This is the sphere created by the presence of the regulatory text. The embedding of the standards of the specific interpretive community in texts thus undermines the authority and truth value of its own contingent claims by converting habitual into necessary practice, by distancing that practice from its (historical) moment of origin.

An analysis of the process of textual institutionalization thus reveals the limitations of, even a moment of resistance to, claims for proximity to nature, inspired wisdom, and objective authority. In the textual economy of the claims made in the Nuremberg texts that the group's conventional practice could inaugurate and regulate a new and pure moment of linguistic and literary time, the text itself, in its concrete existence as object and thus as other than either its origin or reception, can and does resist the conversion of habit into law by resisting any such hypostatization of a single time as the origin of truth. Precisely in its otherness from its moment of conception, the text guarantees a future other than that moment (a future with different and equally binding, community-derived norms) by means of the interpretations always virtual in it. It is this otherness and future orientation, the future of difference (and thus resistance to sameness) always within the text, that the Baroque poets and language theorists fail to acknowledge as they attribute normative power to their claims.

It is with this contradiction in mind that the Nuremberg program of textual institutionalization can be understood as providing a historical example of a larger theoretical issue, namely, the limitations and potential dangers inherent in contextualist thinking and practice, in the claim, that is, that a particular community can function as the arbiter of behavior and origin of law. Even as the Nuremberg texts themselves attempt to elevate a particular community's linguistic and poetic norms to universal status, they contain within themselves, precisely as texts, the moment that compromises their power to do so. As a historical example, then, the phenomenon of the Nuremberg language society and its texts points to a larger philosophical debate about the relationship between the individual, history, and the absolute, between opinion, mediation, and truth. This debate has been elaborated with particular force in the theoretical and critical program known as pragmatism. The critique of the limitations of conventionalism that has emerged in the preceding analyses of the Nuremberg texts provides the terms of my investigation of pragmatism, the philosophical agenda that I would contend lies behind it. In turn, this investigation and its focus on questions of the conventional origins of textual meaning will provide a final commentary on the issues of history and literature, context and text, addressed at the opening of this study.

The Limits of Pragmatism and the Resistance of the Text

According to Richard Rorty, the main spokesman for what has come to be known as the new pragmatism, debates central to contemporary critical theory posit an opposition between two primal moments or positions as they swing back and forth between "Western metaphysics," on the one hand, and deconstruction, on the other. In other periods and traditions, these positions have been variously described by means of dichotomies between nature and human culture, between Realism and Nominalism, between Platonism and sceptical Sophism, between, finally, absolute or transcendental Idealism and Empiricism. In his book *Philosophy and the Mirror of Nature*, Rorty originally continued to think in oppositions such as these by contrasting what he calls epistemology with hermeneutics. The first of these two "ideal opposites," epistemology, assumes the reality of absolutes as it assumes the "existence" of a true "common ground" that could ultimately unite all speakers in a universal "rationality"; the second, hermeneutics, "refrains from epistemology" by acknowledging that it is "civility" and the particulars of a given social or communicative situation rather than any metaphysical principle that makes any exchange possible.[1]

Rorty the pragmatist originally championed the hermeneutic pole of this opposition because epistemology assumes the existence of an all-encompassing rationality (the "absolutist" side of the basic philosophical opposition) and thus necessarily privileges what he calls "foundationalist" thought, creating a hierarchy out of the opposition. The hermeneutic model, however, conceives of "culture as a conversation rather than as a structure erected upon foundations" (319), a conversation in which all participate equally. For Rorty, to be antifoundationalist was thus to support the antihierarchical and pragmatic position that different communities have different truths and different ways of establishing their validity.

In exploring this dichotomy further, however, Rorty has come to see the opposition between epistemology and hermeneutics as an uninteresting and fruitless one, since it must posit, for the sake of balance in the equation, the potential existence of an absolute or "rational" standard of "Truth" that is not and could never have been possible if culture and its standards are in fact the products of a conversation in the way he describes. In his article "Deconstruction and Circumvention," Rorty questions the attack of contemporary applied theory on the so-called fundamental problem of philosophy—the dilemma of choosing between the "Way of Truth" and the "Way of Opinion," between nature and history, between the general/absolute and the specific/particular—because it has set up the absolutist pole as a "straw man." Derrida has claimed (mistakenly, according to Rorty) that there is a "dream at the heart of philosophy" of a "language which can receive no gloss, requires no interpretation" and whose "vocabulary ... is intrinsically and self-evidently final" in representing "Truth" to a world dominated by "Opinion." Derrida is obsessed, according to Rorty, with "deconstructing" this language and its claims for immediacy by pointing out its inadequacy and chronic "interpreted-ness," its indebtedness to rhetoric or culture. And yet, also according to Rorty, this "dream" of being able to mask mediation and to cover up the limitation of universalist claims was never really at the "heart of philosophy"; this has never really been what the history of philosophy was about.[2] Foundationalist sounding words like *scientific*, *objective*, and *truth*, when used to designate the conditions of universal intelligibility, rationality, and agreement, "have been worn down to the point," Rorty says, "where most people are content to let them mean 'the way we do things around here' " (16).

Interpreting texts while keeping in mind Rorty's critique of deconstruction and his explication of the principles of pragmatism in turn "deconstructs" Derrida's own concern, then, that the primal texts of Western philosophy cover up the provisionalness of their language by claiming to describe the conditions for absolute knowledge and philosophical closure. Such a concern is misplaced, indeed, is somewhat of a farce, Rorty writes. Everyone is perfectly aware that there is no such thing as philosophical closure, no such thing as Truth clothed in historical garb; "nobody even tries to pretend there is," Rorty summarizes, "except as an occasional and rather ineffective rhetorical device" (15). The pragmatist is constantly aware of the contextual and conventional limitations of rhetorical claims, then, even as he permits them to be made, indeed, sometimes cannot help but make them himself.

The alternative to Derrida's program of pointing out what Rorty conceives of as obvious, namely, that philosophical closure has not been and cannot be attained, would therefore be to embrace pragmatism by accepting as outmoded the notion that historical individuals can know Truth and represent it adequately. When one uses "absolutist"-sounding words, according to Rorty, one is always already aware of the conventionality and contextual limitations of one's discourse. And yet—and here the crucial turn in Rorty's argument occurs—when one refers to the limited nature of one's own discourse, one does so with an implicit understanding that *within* those limits, concepts take on an "absolute" status. What pragmatists really do then when they point out that we are always only "telling stories" about the "universe" instead of pretending to make "true statements" about it is merely make explicit what everyone already knows. For the pragmatist, the only issue is consistency, "whether describing the planets in one language or the other lets us tell stories about them which will fit together with all the other stories we want to tell."[3]

Accordingly, "true" knowledge about objects is less a "relation" between "mind and object" than a kind of collective agreement between minds as to the consistency of these various stories, a consensus reached by effective telling or persuasion. It is, in other words, a convention, the product of a particular context. In the pragmatist's view, finally,

> the notion of reality as having a "nature" to which it is our duty to correspond is simply one more variant of the notion that the gods can be placated by chanting the right words. The notion that some one among the languages mankind has used to deal with the universe is the one the universe prefers—the one which cuts things at the joints—was a pretty conceit. But by now it has become too shopworn to serve any purpose. (3)

Thus Rorty, the pragmatist philosopher, can agree with Stanley Fish, the pragmatist literary critic and theorist, that all "facts" are conventional rather than evidence of some original correspondence. Fish believes that facts are true only because of the prior institution of socially conceived dimensions of assessment within the "interpretive community."[4] Interpreting texts from a pragmatist point of view necessitates, as a result, an acceptance of the fact that this conventional, provisional, always limited and limiting moment of consensus is essential to the interpretive task.

According to Rorty, the assertion that "contextual agreement can produce 'truth'" is flawed by an internal logical contradiction unless one considers it from a nonpragmatist point of view. Although a community might suggest that its "story" is in fact the one "the universe prefers," that story is actually only being made to do exactly the kind of explanatory work for the community it was always meant to do, namely, to endow a limited, historical frame with universal status and validity. And yet I would argue, differently from Rorty and Fish, that these claims have a very different effect when they are used to do the work of interpreting texts. Indeed, in spite of the fact that theories of pragmatism have begun to be used to develop theories about the production of textual meaning, it is precisely the move into textuality that provides the basis for, and indeed makes inevitable, some form of resistance to the concept of a community's "pragmatic" laws. A final look at and critique of the implications of some pragmatist notions of intersubjectivity and of the production of textual meaning by any given interpretive community may suggest why.

In implicit concert with Rorty's effort to explain away what he believes to be deconstruction's more radical assertions and thus to claim, ironically, the universal applicability of the pragmatist approach, David Bleich has analyzed the model of intertextuality as an extension of what reader-response criticism originally conceived of as the structure of interpretive acts. The investigation of reception on both the phenomenological and sociological levels has gradually become, according to Bleich, only so much "speculation" as to how people actually read and concerns itself increasingly with texts, with "blanks," "gaps," and "concretizations," and thus with the textuality of texts rather than with the readers themselves.[5] This concern with textual analysis and the "self-removal" of the critic from the "community of readers" has given rise, Bleich asserts, to claims about the "ludic priority of language," to the notion, that is, that language is autonomous, that the text stands alone (407), and that interpretive communities cannot be described. Theorists who champion such textual or linguistic games—and here Derrida is intended—downplay the importance of the "critic's subjectivity"; in a betrayal of its origins in hermeneutics (but in support of its indebtedness to phenomenology), Bleich claims that reader-response criticism has in fact come to ignore the rootedness of the reader in particular traditions, contexts, and communities.

Thus the "game" of intertextuality, Bleich asserts, "supervenes the purposes, intersubjectivity, and historicity of . . . reading communities" (407) and denies what he perceives to be the "social origins and social character of knowledge" (410). In support of his project of establishing a theory of intersubjective reading, Bleich cites the historian of science Ludwik Fleck, who, according to Bleich, explained that "*any* facts, scientific or humanistic, bec[a]me so only by virtue of their embeddedness in a thought collective—a community of real people with common interests" (411). Epistemologically speaking, then, facts cannot be facts from an "individualistic" point of view, since both "facts" and "truth" are always already "stylized solutions" to local problems and "are always collectively held." It is merely in the reporting of "facts," in this case, of scientific facts, that the "original collective experience" of their constitution tends to be omitted and the "facts" represented as "absolute" and "true" (411).

Like Rorty, then, Bleich, following Fleck and others, thinks that the "truth of the matter" is that there is no "Way of Truth" other than the "Way of Opinion." In fact, the opposition of necessity dissolves since the dichotomy can be said not to exist. Bleich reports that in the so-called hard sciences, "the idea of the origin of knowledge in individuals has been gradually replaced by the belief in its origins in groups, in history, and in social purposes" (412). He goes on to relate this "growing sense of the social determination of knowledge" (412) to various other fields, including psychology and linguistics, with the ultimate goal of establishing the "fact" that reading and literary interpretation, the "construing" of knowledge about texts, must also be understood as a social or community act. Bleich labels his pragmatics of reading with knowledge of the historical collective "intersubjective reading"; intersubjective reading "starts with recognizing the community ('thought collective') in which individual readings take place" (418). Thus Bleich's concept of the "social constitution of knowledge" is indebted to the notion that facts are conventional rather than natural. In turn, interpretations are provisional solutions to questions of meaning posed by specific, historical communities. They are thus functional (rather than "premature") absolutes. The text, in turn, is no more than the catalyst for community formation.

What both Rorty and Bleich consistently downplay in their articulation of multiple locations of standards and meaning is the effective exclusion of the *object of interpretation* from the process of interpretation as they describe it. They neglect to account for the fact that the absence of the object of interpretation ultimately makes possible a radical unaccountability to the text on the part of the community in its formation of meaning. Of course, this absence and subsequent unaccountability are in fact necessary for the community's assumption of the effective irreducibility of its readings, since in the absence of the object, these readings cannot be challenged or proved "wrong" by reference to any "outside."

At the same time, moreover, the absence of the object effectively limits the possibility of future interpretations by other communities in an even more final way, since the absence of the text also renders absent the virtuality of interpretation always present in the text, a virtuality that at the most fundamental level resists the notion of interpretative closure of any kind (community based or otherwise).

And yet, given the power of the historical collective to function as the source of absolutes in a model like Bleich's, we must step back and analyze pragmatic theory's denial of the community's implicitly hegemonic claims. How is it that precisely that community which asserts the necessity of heterodoxy and difference in an act of self-legitimization can itself come to function as the source of universalizing and thus implicitly exclusionary norms? A critique of Rorty's and Bleich's allegedly "democratic" notions of the "conversation" and their theories of pragmatism and intersubjective interpretations of texts will point out the origins of this contradiction between an acceptance and a denial of difference and will offer a solution to it in the form of a recommendation to return to the text.

While Rorty and Bleich are probably correct in asserting that there are no absolutes but rather only socially constituted, pragmatic solutions to questions of "how we do things around here," their analyses of the internal functioning of such pragmatist strategies are nevertheless based on a series of problematic assumptions. Rorty, for his part, conceives of pragmatist "storytelling" as a benign community activity; knowledge is not an absolute relation between mind and object, but "roughly . . . the ability to get agreement by using persuasion rather than force."[6] Bleich, in turn, considers endorsing a process of self-objectification unproblematic in light of his belief in the importance of dialogue on both the theoretical and practical levels. "Self-objectification is the key to understanding subjective experience as intersubjectively grounded" (415); individuals do and always will identify the community to which they belong—and thus the limitation of their claims—when a given reading occurs.

Both the persuasive power of community opinion and the notion of self-objectification, however, carry within themselves a denial of the concept—and reality—of difference that they are, at least implicitly, designed to permit. That is, both Rorty's and Bleich's suggestions of replacing assertions of the existence of Truth with pragmatic and intersubjective standards, with agreements among equals about which Opinion shall currently prevail, are in fact based, first, on the absence of the object of interpretation as a limiting instance and, second, on a belief in an enlightened community of likeminded people who will dispassionately agree on what has functioned or is to function as the social basis of truth. Accordingly, individuals must and will gladly give up any aspiration or claim to autonomy and individual claims on the truth and meaning of the text since, according to this definition, it is only within the collective—and, in effect, not at all in the text—that truth can be said to exist.

The limits of such arguments emerge on several fronts. The assumption of a paradoxically "universal" orthodoxy of opinion within a contingent community out of which a "story" emerges and within which it is told is exclusionary on a number of levels. The very existence of an "interpretive" or "reading community" is based on a standard of collective legitimization. And this legitimization needs the existence both of nonmembers on the margins and of a homogeneous core in order to exist. As Elizabeth Meese has written, the very notion of a community or collective is predicated on an "insider-outsider dynamic" that necessarily excludes and homogenizes even as it offers a fiction of inclusiveness and plurality.[7] According to the pragmatists, in order to tell a story or to offer an interpretation that is at all "credible," the storyteller or critic *must* belong to such a collective, to something like Fish's "interpretive community," and must be a member of the club. But the "club preserves and affirms control," Meese writes, "while offering the illusion of admissibility" to those on the "outside" (8), on the one hand, and the illusion of universal agreement within, on the other. Moreover, an interpretive community, precisely as one of many interpretive communities, needs a belief in its own superior singularity as an organized community to be effective. Hayden White writes:

> Any appeal to the "interpretive community" must fail for the more fundamental reason that there is no such thing as *the* interpretive community but rather a hierarchy of such communities, each with its own conventions and all more or less antagonistic to the rest.[8]

Thus the notion of a single and unified body that dictates any standards at all must collapse from within, since if it were to truly open itself up to difference—as its identity as an interpretive community would suggest it must—it would open itself up to both internal disagreement and to the possibility of equally as legitimate standards in other communities "on the outside." As a result, there would be no point in claiming its standards to be any more universal or binding than those of any other community. In the absence of any underlying logic of equality in heterogeneity or difference, hierarchies must thus be established—Foucault's "regime of truth"—in which some communities of opinion can be said to take precedence over others.[9]

In spite of the fact, then, that both Rorty's pragmatism (as a provisional agreement as to "the way we do things around here") and Bleich's "thought collectives" seem to unmask the constituted (social, political, historical) and thus plural nature of knowledge, they do not challenge the fundamental gesture of exclusion and homogenization upon which even their attempts to broaden the basis of "knowledge" are implicitly based. The "pretenses to equality . . . and universality" to which their concepts of convention and intersubjectivity appeal allow hierarchy and a hegemony of homogeneity to evolve in the guise of a "limited plurality."[10]

Finally, in their search for a logic of community, Rorty and Bleich elide the concrete existence of the text as a moment that combats this hierarchization in its ontological separateness from any specific community and thus its potential openness to all communities. What in fact guarantees an effective notion of pluralism in interpretation is not so much the existence of further, alternative interpretive communities, as Meese might suggest, but the existence of the text as artifact and object of interpretation. Not only do interpretive communities include and exclude according to hierarchical principles, but they tend to hypostasize their readings and methods for attaining these principles as well. They thus lose sight of the text and effectively replace it with a meaning they have constituted for and by themselves. And yet precisely because the text is always objectively other than its reception (as well as its origin), it cannot be locked or coopted into coinciding with any particular reception, interpretation, or collective stance. Its openness to interpretation cannot be "closed down" or restrained within any particular interpretive act. The resistance to the hegemony of the moment ultimately lies embedded, then, in the resistance of the text as concrete artifact to interpretation and in the virtuality of interpretation present in its concrete existence.

Conclusion

Pragmatism ultimately confirms the autonomy of the text even as it tries to deny it by locating the origin of meaning and truth outside the text in the collective. It was the power of this autonomy that the Nuremberg language theorists and poets—perhaps all too intentionally—recognized and sought to harness, *not* by attempting to efface the historical limitedness of their foundational and universalizing claims, but precisely by linking the absolutes invoked in their texts firmly to the historical phenomenon that was the urban-bourgeois language society itself. Thus, even as the origins of many of the Nuremberg principles in historical contexts and collective experience are constantly presented in language society texts, the status of the community as historical and provisional is elided, "forgotten," and omitted in order for its principles, in their textualized forms, to be identified as absolute and true.

The members of the vernacular poet society at Nuremberg thus attempted to yoke the power of the text into the service of their particular enterprise, allowing their texts to give expression to the absolute in the here-and-now. Their conventions aspired to a kind of foundationalist (inaugural and original) status rooted in appeals to a series of discourses about the organic, dialectical, and transcendent realm. By associating the intersubjective standards of the community with discourses related to nature and the divine, the Nuremberg shepherds made clear, however, that they considered their "stories" about the origins of the German language and its poetic forms in a realm beyond the here-and-now to be "true" ones. By textualizing these stories, by endowing them with "truth value" in institutionalized form, the language society theorists attempted to invest their "pragmatic" claims with regulatory power.

Nevertheless, precisely this strategy of hypostatization created one of the first cases in German literary history in which the collapse of the standards of the group and of collectively derived norms occurred under the burden of those standards' own double logic. The High German of the group was forced, for example, as a result of its historicity and community identity, to give way to a new language once a new historical community of linguistic "legislators" with their own texts emerged. Of course, the regulatory texts of the order survived the passing of the community that produced them and thus also marked that passing and ultimately the nonuniversality and nonapplicability of the community's historically derived norms to a new age. Texts both "made history" and became historical at one and the same time.

The present study has offered an analysis of the textual strategies by which a specific interpretive community developed a set of poetic and linguistic conventions and in turn created the conditions of possibility for a new era of historical time. Its critical purpose has been to expose the role of the text in the creation of collective authority and to highlight the ability of the text to resist that authority once it has been created by outliving it. As Meese writes, only in naming and analyzing—indeed, only in deconstructing—incidents of normalization and standardization in history do we prepare the ground for transforming them (16). For even though certain structures and strategies are based on "mere convention," they are "fully motivated" and "designed to work [as effectively absolute] in a specifiable rhetorical function."[11] Thus collective standards may be relative to context, but within that context, they can be made to serve specific ideological ends. During the crucial period of the Baroque, authority migrated from the Ancients to the present, from nature to culture, from the nonpresent Other of tradition to a collective, contemporary Self. The texts of the pastoral language society at Nuremberg provide evidence of how conventions come to be constituted and universalized by means of texts. In understanding the genealogy and structural limitations of these conventions, we can begin to understand the origins, implications, and limitations of our own interpretive communities.

Notes

1 Interpreting Conventions: History, Literature, and Textual Institutions

1. For a summary of the new historicism, see Cohen, "Political Criticism of Shakespeare," 32–38; and Newton, "History as Usual? Feminism and the 'New Historicism,'" 87–121. There are clear theoretical differences in the approaches the various new historicists take. See Erickson, "Rewriting the Renaissance, Rewriting Ourselves," esp. 331–36. The following titles could be considered central to understanding the new historical approach: Greenblatt, "Introduction"; idem, *Renaissance Self-fashioning*; Goldberg, *James I and the Politics of Literature*; Helgerson, *Self-crowned Laureates*; idem, "The Land Speaks"; Montrose, "Shaping Fantasies"; idem, "The Elizabethan Subject and the Spenserian Text"; Mullaney, "Strange Things, Gross Terms, Curious Customs"; and idem, *The Place of the Stage*.
2. See Hans-Georg Gadamer, *Wahrheit und Methode*, 4th ed. (Tübingen: J. C. B. Mohr/Paul Siebeck, 1975), 367.
3. I am indebted here to Professor Benjamin Bennett (University of Virginia) for the formulation.
4. On Giambattista Vico's *New Science*, see Berlin, *Vico and Herder*, 27. Auerbach explains his Vichean method in *Literatursprache und Publikum in der lateinischen Spätantike und im Mittelalter*, 11–12. I am grateful to Juliet Flower MacCannell (University of California, Irvine) for drawing my attention to the parallels between Vico and Auerbach.
5. Greenblatt, *Renaissance Self-fashioning*, 5.
6. See Edward Pechter, "The New Historicism and Its Discontents," 297.
7. See Jean E. Howard, "The New Historicism in Renaissance Studies," esp. 19, 31; and Cohen, "Political Criticism of Shakespeare," 34. As an initial response to charges of a lack of self-reflection, see Montrose, "Renaissance Literary Studies and the Subject of History."
8. See Goldberg, "The Politics of Renaissance Literature," 533; and Pechter, "The New Historicism and Its Discontents," 300–301. For an excellent critique of Pechter's argument, see Holstun, "Ranting at the New Historicism."
9. Montrose, "Elizabethan Subject and the Spenserian Text," 305. Emphasis is in original.
10. Greenblatt, "Introduction," 6.

11. Hunt, "States of Theory," 4. I am grateful to Hunt for sharing her manuscript with me.
12. Greenblatt, *Renaissance Self-fashioning*, 5.
13. Goldberg, *James I and the Politics of Literature*, xi.
14. On the distinction between the real and the imaginary and the need to break it down in analyzing culture, see Geertz, *Negara*, 136.
15. Greenblatt, *Renaissance Self-Fashioning*, 5.
16. See Erickson, "Rewriting the Renaissance, Rewriting Ourselves," 333.
17. See Greenblatt, *Renaissance Self-fashioning*, 4.
18. See Pechter, "The New Historicism and Its Discontents," 298.
19. See Greenblatt, "Capitalist Culture and the Circulatory System"; and *Shakespearean Negotiations*.
20. See, e.g., Fineman's fascinating "Shakespeare's 'Perjur'd Eye,'" which is more or less about "Shakespearean subjectivity," which, I would submit, is "history" of a very different sort than Montrose might accept.
21. Lima, "Social Representation and Mimesis," 447.
22. Ibid., 449.
23. See Martin Heidegger's *What Is a Thing?* (1935–36), as quoted in Bennington and Young, "Introduction: Posing the Question," 8.
24. See, e.g., the catalogue *"Gebt uns den Frieden": Aus den Anfängen des Pegnesischen Blumenordens* for the exhibit of the same name, which locates the order's activities squarely in the context of the Thirty Years' War. Many literary histories follow this trend.
25. See Garber, "Der Hirten- und Blumenorden an der Pegnitz," 2–5. I am grateful to Garber for having made this manuscript available to me. See also Garber, "Sigmund von Birken," for an example of his methodology. Reinhart has followed Garber in his "An Annotated Edition of Johann Hellwig's *Nymphe Noris* (1650)" and his "Literary and Historical Synchronism in the Utopian Project of Hellwig's *Noris*." I am grateful to Reinhart for sharing his manuscript with me.
26. The formulation is Montrose's in "Elizabethan Subject and the Spenserian Text," 304.
27. The term *feeble form* is used by Macherey in his "The Problem of Reflection," 11. On what is in fact the "boundless-ness" of context, see Culler, "Convention and Meaning," 24.
28. On this kind of monological approach to early modern texts, see Greenblatt, "Introduction," 5.
29. I am indebted to Juliet Flower MacCannell (University of California, Irvine) and to Alex Gelley (University of California, Irvine) for their comments on figuration.
30. Carroll, "Representation or the End(s) of History," 201. Emphasis is in original.
31. See Carroll, *Paraesthetics: Foucault, Lyotard, Derrida*, 131.
32. The term *reflex theory* is Lima's in his "Social Representation and Mimesis," 448–49.
33. See Fineman, "Shakespeare's 'Perjur'd Eye,'" 152–53, in particular.
34. I am indebted to Benjamin Bennett, who pointed out these specific texts as examples of the notion of texts with the power to "be history."

35. See Hegel, *Vorlesungen über die Philosophie der Geschichte*, 114. I am again grateful to Bennett for pointing out the Hegel parallel.
36. See Hohendahl, *The Institution of Criticism*, 14; and Peck, "The Institution of *Germanistik* and the Transmission of Culture," 308–19.
37. Culler, "Criticism and Institutions," 82–98; and Graff, *Professing Literature*.
38. On Heidegger, see Jonathan Arac, "Introduction," in *Postmodernism and Politics*, ed. Jonathan Arac, xxviii.
39. Hauriou, "The Theory of the Institution and the Foundation," 99.
40. Giddens, "Action, Subjectivity, and the Constitution of Meaning," 163.
41. Marsch, "Institution," col. 783.
42. Manley, "Concepts of Convention and Models of Critical Discourse," 32.
43. For the terms *bounded* and *unbounded*, see Krieger, "The Figure in the Renaissance Poem as Bound and Unbounded," in *A Reopening of Closure*.
44. See Williams, *Keywords*, 139.
45. Godzich, "Afterword: Religion, the State, and Post(al) Modernism," 155.
46. See *Oxford Latin Dictionary*, ed. P. G. W. Glare (Oxford: Clarendon, 1982); and Eduard Bonnell, ed., *Lexicon Quintilianeum* (1838; Hildesheim: Georg Olms Verlagsbuchhandlung, 1962), 435.
47. See Cave, *The Cornucopian Text*, 37.
48. Claude de Sainliens, *A Dictionary of French and English* (1593) (Alston, ed., *English Linguistics, 1500–1800*); Guillaume Budé, *G. Bvdaei operum tomys III in quo commentarii lingvae Graecae habentur*. . . . (Basileae, 1557); and Randle Cotgrave, *A Dictionarie of the French and English Tongues* (1611; Hildesheim: Georg Olms Verlag, 1970). See also Edmond Huguet, *Dictionnaire de la langue française du sizième siècle*, vol. 4 (Paris: Didier, 1950).
49. See A. W. Pollard et al., eds., *A Short Title Catalogue of Books Printed in England, Scotland and Ireland and of English Books Printed Abroad, 1475–1640*, 2 vols. (London: Bibliographical Society, 1969, 1976); and A. F. Allison et al., eds., *Titles of English Books (and of Foreign Books Printed in England)*, vol. 1. On Calvin, see Bouwsma, *John Calvin*, esp. 17, on the title of Calvin's major text.
50. See Bennett, "Texts in History," 75.
51. Grafton, *Joseph Scaliger*, 15–17; quotations, 14.
52. Ibid., 17.
53. See Gilbert, *Renaissance Concepts of Method*, 66; and Kahn, "Humanism and the Resistance to Theory," 383.
54. These are just two of the titles listed by Gilbert in his appendix "*Methodus* in Titles of Books in the Late Renaissance," in *Renaissance Concepts of Methods*, 233–35.
55. Saussure, *Course in General Linguistics*, 66.
56. Umberto Eco writes that the referential fallacy is based on the "belief that an actual state of the world must underwrite the functioning of every semiotic entity . . . Every attempt to establish what the referent of a sign is forces us to define the referent in terms of an abstract entity which moreover is only a cultural convention" (*Theory of Semiotics*, 66).
57. See Culler, *Structuralist Poetics*, 8.
58. Saussure, *Course*, 14.
59. Steven Mailloux, *Interpretive Conventions*.

60. See Williams, *Keywords*, 70–71.
61. The example is Mailloux's in *Interpretive Conventions*, 128–29.
62. See Manley, *Convention, 1500–1750*.
63. I am indebted to Robert Montgomery (University of California, Irvine) for the suggestion of the "every-man" formulation.
64. Manley, "Concepts of Convention and Models of Critical Discourse," 32.
65. As quoted in Manley, *Convention, 1500–1750*, 3.
66. This of course does not mean that there had been no literature written in German prior to this time. Apparently, the deliberate ignoring of earlier vernacular texts other than those that had been recuperated by the language societies was one of the self-justifying strategies of the Nuremberg texts.
67. Jacques Derrida, "Difference," 141.
68. For the term *premature ultimates*, see Wimsatt, *Day of the Leopards*, as quoted in Manley, "Concepts of Convention and Models of Critical Discourse," 40.

2 Academic Conventions

1. The description can be found in Carl Gustav von Hille's history of the Fruit-bearing Society, *Der teutsche Palmbaum*, 8. Page references refer to pagination of original text.
2. On Ludwig's relationship to the Italian academy and on his efforts to re-create the Italianate model in his homeland, see Bircher, "The Fruchtbringende Gesellschaft and Italy"; Conermann, "Die Fruchtbringende Gesellschaft und ihr Köthener Gesellschaftsbuch," 2:21–127 (cited hereafter as Conermann, "Einleitung"). Also see Dünnhaupt, "Die Übersetzungen Fürst Ludwigs von Anhalt-Köthen," 513–29, esp. 515, for a description of Ludwig's background and his trip to Italy.
3. Hille, *Der teutsche Palmbaum*, 8, 10.
4. On the botanical imagery in all aspects of the Fruit-bearing Society, see Otto's description of the society in his *Die Sprachgesellschaften des 17. Jahrhunderts*, 7–9, 14–33.
5. Hille, *Der teutsche Palmbaum*, 9.
6. See chap. 3 for a more detailed argument on the primarily symbolic role of Luther's language. An argument for understanding Luther's translations as symbolic may be found in Ebert, "Verb Position in Luther's Bible Translation and in the Usage of his Contemporaries."
7. Manley, "Concepts of Convention and Models of Critical Discourse," 32.
8. See Conermann, "War die Fruchtbringende Gesellschaft eine Akademie? Über das Verhältnis der Fruchtbringenden Gesellschaft zu den italienischen Akademien," 113–14 (cited hereafter as Conermann, "Verhältnis").
9. See Conermann, "Einleitung," passim, and idem, "Verhältnis," passim.
10. Conermann uses the term *institutionelle Ähnlichkeiten* to describe these similarities in his "Verhältnis," 111.
11. See Conermann, "Verhältnis," 123. Conermann in fact uses the term *academy* when discussing the Fruit-bearing Society in the more recent "Einleitung."
12. On anti-Ciceronianism, see Cave, *The Cornucopian Text*, 36–48, 60–76.
13. Erasmus, *Ciceronianus*, col. 992 c–d, as quoted and translated in Gilmore, "*Fides et Eruditio*: Erasmus and the Study of History," 104–5.

14. See Quint, *Origin and Originality in Renaissance Literature*, x-xi. I am indebted to Quint for introducing me to questions of history and originality in early modern literature in always innovative, always fascinating ways.
15. On the "internal coherence" of humanism and the shift away from imitation to convention, see Manley, *Convention, 1500–1750*, 231–40. On historical self-consciousness and the competing claims of eloquence and history, see also Struever, *The Language of History in the Renaissance*.
16. Quint, *Origin and Originality in Renaissance Literature*, xi.
17. Bouwsma, *John Calvin*, 114.
18. For an overview of the Italian academies, see Buck, "Die humanistischen Akademien in Italien"; and Pevsner, *Academies of Art, Past and Present*, 14ff.
19. See Cochrane, "The Renaissance Academies in their Italian and European Setting," 24–25. Also see Conermann, "Verhältnis," 119.
20. Cochrane, "Renaissance Academies in their Italian and European Setting," 28.
21. Ibid., 31.
22. The statute is quoted in Parodi, "L'Accademia della Crusca interprete della coscienza linguistica nazionale," 114: "interpretando, componendo, e da ogni altra lingua ogni bella scienza in questa nostra riducendo."
23. See Pevsner, *Academies of Art, Past and Present*, 15.
24. See Parodi, "L'Accademia della Crusca," 114.
25. Quoted in ibid., 115: "seguitando il nome di Crusca e vivendo allegramente, ... con piu saldezza, si palesasse il lor valore," they will be able to show "all'altre Adunanze il modo e la via del tenere Accademie scrivendo e leggendo ... con piacevolezza."
26. On the philosophical endeavors of the Florentine academy, see Buck, *Italienische Dichtungslehren vom Mittelalter bis zum Ausgang der Renaissance*, "Humanismus und volkssprachliche Dichtung," esp. 98 and 108.
27. Josten, in his *Sprachvorbild und Sprachnorm im Urteil des 16. und 17. Jahrhunderts*, discusses and documents the numerous "sprachlandschaftliche Prioritäten" and the status of dialects as normative during the period of the Baroque.
28. See Haas, *Rhetorik und Hochsprache*, 21ff.
29. See Buck, *Italienische Dichtungslehren vom Mittelalter bis zum Ausgang der Renaissance*, 129, on Speroni. For an excellent edition of Speroni, see Speroni, *Dialogo delle lingue*.
30. See Buck, *Italienische Dichtungslehren vom Mittelalter bis zum Ausgang der Renaissance*, 132–33, on the desire for local ascendancy. Machiavelli, states Buck, considered "das Florentinische" to be the "Grundlage der italienischen Volkssprache."
31. Conermann uses the term *Kulturpolitik* in describing Cosimo's plans for the academy ("Verhältnis," 119).
32. See Du Bellay, *La déffence et illustration de la langue françoyse*, chap. 12, "Exhortation aux Françoys d'écrire en leur langue: auecques [sic] les louanges de la France."
33. Du Bellay often acknowledges other ancient sources, but he suppresses the fact that he actually used Speroni as a model for the majority of the *Déffence*. The dependence on Speroni is clear in Henri Chamard's excellently annotated edition of the *Déffence* in Du Bellay, *Oeuvres poétiques*.
34. See Yates, *The French Academies of the Sixteenth Century*, 19–35.

35. See Stackelberg, "Die Académie française," 29.
36. Puttenham, *The Arte of English Poesie*, 157.
37. See Grayson, "The Growth of Linguistic National Consciousness in England," 168.
38. Quoted in ibid., 169.
39. Quoted in Pevsner, *Academies of Art, Past and Present*, 15. Pevsner is himself quoting here from J. Hunter, *Archeologia* 32 (1846).
40. See Pevsner, *Academies of Art, Past and Present*, 20.
41. See Woodhouse, "The Reluctant Academicals," 176.
42. On the commitment to translation by the academies, including the German language societies, see Conermann, "Verhältnis," 120–21.
43. The translation of "unvorgreiflich" is difficult; literally it means "not anticipatory," or perhaps "right on schedule." Hence my translation of "timely."
44. Leibniz, *Unvorgreifliche Gedanken*, 525.
45. See Stammerjohann, "The *Vocabolario* and German Lexicography," 64.
46. On the history of German dictionaries, see Henne, "Deutsche Lexikographie und Sprachnorm im 17. und 18. Jahrhundert"; and Ising, *Die Erfassung der deutschen Sprache des ausgehenden 17. Jahrhunderts in den Wörterbüchern Matthias Kramers und Kaspar Stielers.*
47. For this perspective on language theory during this period, see Grazia, "The Secularization of Language in the Seventeenth Century."
48. I am indebted to Aarsleff for having allowed me to consult his manuscript "Language, Man, and Knowledge in the Sixteenth and Seventeenth Centuries," here lecture 4, p. 4. Also see Aarsleff, "Leibniz on Locke on Language."
49. See Aarsleff, "Leibniz on Locke on Language," 173–74, n. 28.
50. See Aarsleff, "Language, Man, and Knowledge," lecture 4, p. 18.
51. See ibid., lecture 2, p. 7. In his lectures "Language, Man, and Knowledge," Aarsleff sorts out the various strands of language theory in the sixteenth and seventeenth centuries and differentiates among doctrines of an Adamic *Ursprache*, a scientific natural language, and a philosophical character. He suggests, however, that all were fundamentally related.
52. On the isomorphic character of language and reality, see Greenblatt, "Learning to Curse: Aspects of Linguistic Colonialism in the Sixteenth Century," 572.
53. See Evans, "Learned Societies in Germany in the Seventeenth Century," 130.
54. See ibid., 133; and Aarsleff, "Language, Man, and Knowledge," lecture 2, pp. 24ff. Also see Berns, "Zur Tradition der deutschen Sozietätsbewegung im 17. Jahrhundert," on parallels between the Rosicrucians and the language societies.
55. See Evans, "Learned Societies in Germany in the Seventeenth Century," 133.
56. General introductions to the German language societies may be found in Otto, *Sprachgesellschaften des 17. Jahrhunderts*, and in Stoll, *Sprachgesellschaften in Deutschland des 17. Jahrhunderts*. Ferdinand van Ingen has written three interpretive articles on the language societies: "Die Sprachgesellschaften des 17. Jahrhunderts: Versuch einer Korrektur" (cited hereafter as "Versuch"); "Überlegungen zur Erforschung der Sprachgesellschaften" (cited hereafter as "Überlegungen"); and "Die Erforschung der Sprachgesellschaften unter sozialgeschichtlichem Aspekt" (cited hereafter as "Erforschung").

57. Hille, *Der teutsche Palmbaum*, 10.
58. Hille explains that society members are obligated to act "erbar/weiss/tugendhaft/höflich/nutzlich/und ergetzlich" as well as to defend the mother tongue (*Der teutsche Palmbaum*, 16–17).
59. See van Ingen, "Überlegungen," 86.
60. On the *Ritterakademien* and their relationship to the *Sprachgesellschaften*, see Conrads, "Ritterakademien und Sprachgesellschaften," esp. 89–90 and 95. Conrads also discusses some overlap in membership between some *Ritterakademien* and some *Sprachgesellschaften*, which he explains as natural, because the two institutions addressed the same class.
61. Harsdörffer, *Frauenzimmer Gesprächspiele*, 5:97–99.
62. Johannes Herdegen, *Historische Nachricht*, 46.
63. See van Ingen, "Versuch," 17.
64. See van Ingen, "Erforschung," 18–19.
65. Conermann suggests that a study of the *Sprachgesellschaften* in connection with the *Ordenswesen* and *Brüderschaften* of the period would be revealing ("Verhältnis," 123). For a lengthy passage on the Fruit-bearing Society as the "Teutscher Sprache Ritterplatz," see Hille, *Der teutsche Palmbaum*, 73. Conrads ("Ritterakademien und Sprachgesellschaften," 84–85) points out that Hille goes to great lengths to juxtapose the numerous *Ritterorden* of the period with the Fruit-bearing Society in his description of the statutes of the society in *Der teutsche Palmbaum*, 48–56.
66. See Bircher, "The Fruchtbringende Gesellschaft and Italy," passim; and Hartung, *Geschichte der Stadt Cöthen bis zum Beginn des 19. Jahrhunderts*, 73ff.
67. On the humanist concept of the Fruit-bearing Society, see Bircher, "The Fruchtbringende Gesellschaft and Italy," 124.
68. See Hille, *Der teutsche Palmbaum*, 138, on the allegedly "democratic" practice of publishing under society names: "[It was] for that reason usual practice, on the one hand, that equality and communality would be found between and among people of unequal [social] rank, on the other, that under [the mask of] such titles [namely, titles highlighting society membership] they would publish their texts without ambition or personal renown, and that they would [thereby] hope to witness [a contribution] to the general good rather than proud praise [of themselves individually] by readers." The society names were in fact designed, another historian of the academy remarks, to prevent "occurrences of disputes over honor" in "society meetings"; "society members can be instructed [to attend to] unity according to the dates of admission and not according to the privilege of [social] rank" (Neumark, *Der Neu-Sprossende teutsche Palmbaum*, 68).
69. See Neumark, *Der Neu-Sprossende teutsche Palmbaum*, 77–78.
70. For a similar argument about the textual availability of compositional principles and its impact upon the class identity of poets and rhetoricians, see Attridge, "Puttenham's Perplexity"; and Kahn, "Humanism and the Resistance to Theory."
71. Hille, *Der teutsche Palmbaum*, 73.
72. Ibid., 14.
73. Ibid., 6–7.
74. Ibid., 7.

75. See Conermann, "Einleitung," 31.
76. For a discussion of the meetings (*Tagungen*) of the Fruit-bearing Society, see Otto, *Sprachgesellschaften des 17. Jahrhunderts*, 28–29; for a description of the membership history of the Fruit-bearing Society, see ibid., 22.
77. The documents from the archives of the Fruit-bearing Society are collected in Krause, *Der Fruchtbringenden Gesellschaft ältester Ertzschrein*. For Conermann's discussion of the level of "community" involved in the activities of the Fruit-bearing Society, see his "Einleitung," esp. 35, on the exchanging of letters.
78. For a discussion of the necessity of social connections in being accepted into the Fruit-bearing Society, see Martin Bircher, *Johann Wilhelm von Stubenberg (1619–1663) und sein Freundeskreis*, 229ff. On the hierarchical implications of these connections, see Sinemus's description of the exchange between Prince Ludwig and Philipp von Zesen in his *Poetik und Rhetorik im frühmodernen deutschen Staat*, 210–14.
79. Georg Neumark in a letter to Sigmund von Birken, 17 Aug. 1659, as cited in Burkhart, "Aus dem Briefwechsel Sigmund von Birkens und Georg Neumarks, 1656–1669," 28.
80. According to Krebs, the formation of the more intimate group in Nuremberg was deliberate, since Harsdörffer was disappointed in the Köthen group (Krebs, *Harsdörffer*, 1:29–41, esp. 38).
81. The following is based on an analysis of the biographies of the twenty-seven members of the Blumenorden, who are listed in Spahr's "The Pastoral Works of Sigmund von Birken," 29–30. Information was collected by Gary Campbell (University of Wisconsin—Madison) from the *Allgemeine deutsche Biographie* and Jöcher's *Allgemeines Gelehrten-Lexikon*.
82. On the presence of *Exulanten* in Nuremberg and on contact with them by members of the Order of Flowers, see Garber, "Sigmund von Birken," 226.
83. See Jöns, "Literaten in Nürnberg und ihr Verhältnis zum Stadtregiment in den Jahren 1643–1650 nach den Zeugnissen der Ratsverlässe," 87–89.
84. See Spahr, "Nürnbergs Stellung im literarischen Leben des 17. Jahrhunderts," esp. 81–83.
85. See van Ingen, "Überlegungen," 92; and Jöns, "Literatur und Stadtkultur in Nürnberg im 17. Jahrhundert," 218.
86. See Böttcher's "Der Nürnberger Georg Philipp Harsdörffer," 291.
87. See ibid.
88. See Garber, "Sigmund von Birken," 228; and Böttcher, "Der Nürnberger Georg Philipp Harsdörffer," 291–92.
89. See Otto, *Sprachgesellschaften des 17. Jahrhunderts*, 46–47, for data on the membership of the Order of Flowers. On possibly exclusionary behavior by members of the Order of Flowers themselves, see van Ingen, "Erforschung," 14–15. The Order of Flowers in fact still exists today.
90. See van Ingen, "Überlegungen," 91–98. Van Ingen points out the differences between the Fruit-bearing Society and the Order of Flowers on the Pegnitz but neglects to mention the simple fact of the more limited membership of the Nuremberg group.
91. Spahr even suggests that some members only joined in order to please Birken and

to win his favor so that he would promote them at the various courts with which he was affiliated ("Nürnbergs Stellung im literarischen Leben des 17. Jahrhunderts," 81). Böttcher suggests that even Harsdörffer was more concerned with the Fruit-bearing Society than with the welfare of his own group ("Der Nurnberger Georg Philipp Harsdörffer," 325). Krebs's analysis would obviously contradict Böttcher's statements.

92. See Otto, *Sprachgesellschaften des 17. Jahrhunderts*, 48–50; and Herdegen, *Historische Nachricht*, passim, for details of society lore and activities.
93. For a general description of the Nuremberg group as a collective event, see Wölfel, "Barockdichtung in Nürnberg," 338–44.
94. See Spahr, "Nürnbergs Stellung im literarischen Leben des 17. Jahrhunderts," 81.
95. On the "kleiner Rat" and the neutrality it enforced, particularly during the Thirty Years' War, see Jöns, "Literaten in Nürnberg," 86 and 89–90. I have derived much of my information of the historical context in Nuremberg from the excellent collection of essays in Pfeiffer's volume *Nürnberg: Geschichte einer europäischen Stadt* and from Moeller, "Imperial Cities and the Reformation."
96. Pfeiffer, *Nürnberg*, 268.
97. Ibid., 272. There is an interesting footnote to this discussion. As a reward for returning to the imperial fold, the academy at Altdorf (not far from Nuremberg) was raised to the status of a university by the Crown. As of 1622, then, there was a full university that could draw intellectuals to the Nuremberg area. See Spahr, "Nürnbergs Stellung im literarischen Leben des 17. Jahrhunderts," 74. For additional information on the university at Altdorf, see Kunstmann, *Die Nürnberger Universität Altdorf und Böhmen*.
98. Pfeiffer, *Nürnberg*, 269.
99. Ibid., 272.
100. See Jöns, "Literaten in Nürnberg," 89–92; and Paas, "Poeta Incarceratus."
101. See Conrad Wiedemann's *Nachwort* to his edition of Johann Klaj's *Friedensdichtungen und kleinere poetische Schriften*, 20–27; and Fähler, *Feuerwerke des Barock*, 149–78.
102. See Spahr, "Nürnbergs Stellung im literarischen Leben des 17. Jahrhunderts," 73.
103. See Bircher, *Johann Wilhelm von Stubenberg*, 225ff. and 244ff.
104. See van Dülmen, "Sozietätsbildungen in Nürnberg im 17. Jahrhundert," 178.
105. See Hirschmann, "Das Nürnberger Patriziat," 265.
106. See in particular Breuer, "Gibt es eine bürgerliche Literatur im Deutschland des 17. Jahrhunderts?"; Martino, "Barockpoesie, Publikum und Verbürgerlichung der literarischen Intelligenz."
107. On Harsdörffer, see Bischoff, "Georg Philipp Harsdörffer"; Böttcher, "Der Nürnberger Georg Philipp Harsdörffer"; Ferschmann, "Die Poetik Georg Philipp Harsdörffers"; Narciss, *Studien zu den "Frauenzimmer Gesprächspielen" G. P. Harsdörffers*; and Zeller, *Spiel und Konversation im Barock*.
108. Many of the details of the *Pegnesisches Schäfergedicht* (1644) are taken from Klaj's own life. See Garber, "Vergil und das 'Pegnesisches Schäfergedicht,'" 180.
109. See Garber, "Sigmund von Birken," 230.
110. See Kröll, "Der Bayreuther Hof zwischen 1660 und 1670."
111. See Lee, "Justus Georg Schottel and Linguistic Theory." Schottelius is men-

tioned as a significant figure in both Haas's *Rhetorik und Hochsprache*, 72–77, and Josten's *Sprachvorbild*, passim, esp. 175ff. and 200ff.

112. Dilherr is mentioned as a significant figure in Böttcher, "Der Nürnberger Georg Philipp Harsdörffer," 293; Jöns, "Literaten in Nürnberg," 92–93; Spahr, "Nürnbergs Stellung im literarischen Leben des 17. Jahrhunderts," 78–79.

113. See Bischoff, "Georg Philipp Harsdörffer," 206; and Wietfeldt, *The Emblem Literature of Johann Michael Dilherr (1604–1669)*.

114. See Newald, *Die deutsche Literatur vom Späthumanismus zur Empfindsamkeit, 1570–1750*, 211.

3 Redemption in the Vernacular: From the Garden to Society Texts

1. For a detailed analysis of the many language theorists in this period working within the Judeo-Christian tradition, see Borst, *Der Turmbau von Babel*, vol. 3, pt. 1, esp. pp. 1150–1394 (cited hereafter as Borst, *Turmbau*); and Allen, "Some Theories of the Growth and Origin of Language in Milton's Age." For an introduction to the *phusei/thesei* distinction, see Kayser, *Klangmalerei*, esp. 137–67.
2. See Kayser's critique of Paul Hankamer's thesis in *Klangmalerei*, 167–76, for example. Krebs also explores the relationship between the two traditions in his *Harsdörffer*.
3. See Kayser, *Klangmalerei*, 156–86.
4. See ibid., 177–86, e.g., on the emphasis placed on a doctrine of "natural meaning" in words in those places in Harsdörffer's language theory where he seeks to distinguish between writing and painting.
5. G. P. Harsdörffer to Philipp von Zesen, 23 Dec. 1644, in Dissel, *Philipp von Zesen und die Deutschgesinnte Genossenschaft*, as quoted in Stoll, *Sprachgesellschaften im Deutschland des 17. Jahrhunderts*, 48.
6. On the concept of "unboundedness," see Krieger, *A Reopening of Closure*.
7. Luther, "Sendbrief vom Dolmetschen" in the *Weimarer Ausgabe*, 30.2:637.
8. Harsdörffer, *Poetischer Trichter* (Darmstadt: Wissenschaftliche Buchgesellschaft, 1975), book 1, p. 18 (cited hereafter as *Funnel*, book number, and page).
9. There had been other German Bibles prior to Luther's translation, of course (see Heimo Reinitzer, *Biblia deutsch: Luthers Bibelübersetzung und ihre Tradition* [Wolfenbüttel: Herzog August Bibliothek, 1983], 57–86), but Luther's work was seen as a watershed.
10. The edition of the Bible cited here is the Jerusalem Bible. I have given additional citations from Luther's *Biblia: Das ist: Die gantze Heilige Schrifft: Deudsch*, when the German formulation is significant.
11. Krebs sees a place for Christian language theory within the classical language theory of the period but does not explore it fully. "Or il existe au XVIIe siècle, entre l'arbitraire aristotélicien et l'identité cratylienne—mystique ou humaniste— la place pour un langage analogique, constitué de signes, mais fidèles et transparents. C'est le langage du croyant et du poéte, qui engage plus profondement que les prises de position nationalistes ou rationelles" (*Harsdörffer*, 1:253).
12. Plato, *Cratylus*, 421–74. Other references to this edition will be included parenthetically in the text.
13. See Kayser, *Klangmalerei*, 168–69.

14. On Plato's theory of convention in both law and language, see Manley, *Convention, 1500–1750*, 25–31.
15. See Plato, *Laws*. On *techne*, see Jaeger, *Paideia*, 2:129–30.
16. Krebs emphasizes the linkage between the language theories of Schottelius and Harsdörffer in particular (*Harsdörffer*, 1:27).
17. Klaj, *Lobrede der teutschen Poeterey* (In praise of German poetry), 397 (cited hereafter as *Praise*; page references are to the reprint edition).
18. Fürst Ludwig von Anhalt-Köthen, Brief vom 15. Mai, 1648, in Krause, *Der Fruchtbringenden Gesellschaft ältester Ertzschrein*, 113.
19. Schottelius even goes so far as to claim elsewhere that the German speaker's "soul" ("Gemüt") is naturally structured in such a way that he can almost automatically understand the inner workings of this ancient and privileged language (*Account*, 1:13). Thus German words are intimately connected with the German speaker's physical and moral constitution. For a further discussion of the linkage of linguistic and moral attributes, see chap. 2.
20. See Borchardt, *German Antiquity in Renaissance Myth*, 177–81.
21. Krebs speaks of "l'identité fondamentale de la langue nationale et du langage originel donné par Dieu aux hommes" (*Harsdörffer*, 1:44).
22. On Becanus, see Borst, *Turmbau*, 1215–17; Krebs, *Harsdörffer*, 1:47–51; and Brink, "Goropius Becanus and the Movement to Establish a Written Standard for Dutch in the 16th Century." I am grateful to Brink for sharing his paper with me.
23. See Hille, *Der teutsche Palmbaum*, 91–92.
24. See Birken, *Königlich Polnischer Chur- und Fürstlich Sächsischer Helden-Saal*, 208; and Klaj, *Praise*, 391.
25. For a description of Harsdörffer's "théorie des racines," see Krebs, *Harsdörffer*, 1:51–54.
26. See Harsdörffer, *Model*, 141; Klaj, *Praise*, 397; and Schottelius, *Account*, 1:62.
27. The simplest and most reliable account of the origins of the Cabbala may be found in Gershem Scholem's *Sabbatai Sevi*, 15–93. Also see Yates, *Occult Philosophy in the Elizabethan Age*, 2.
28. See Harsdörffer, *Lessons*, 2:517. Wolfgang Kayser refers to the Cabbalistic origins of the *Denckring* only in passing in his *Klangmalerei*, 185, n. 101. Zeller discusses Harsdörffer's "language ring" in more detail in her *Spiel und Konversation im Barock*, 163ff. Zeller also discusses similar constructs developed by Schottelius and Quirinus Kuhlmann. On the language ring, also see Krebs, *Harsdörffer*, 63.
29. Schottelius, *Introduction*, G iij.
30. On the background of the *phusei-Lehre*, see Kayser, *Klangmalerei*, 138–58. On "Grundrichtigkeit," see Josten, *Sprachvorbild*, 170, 178–79, and 211–14; and Haas, *Rhetorik und Hochsprache*, 75.
31. See Kayser, *Klangmalerei*, 176, on this passage as illustrative of Harsdörffer's allegiance to the *phusei-Lehre*.
32. For this definition and on the interest in a "philosophical character," see Aarsleff, "Language, Man, and Knowledge in the Sixteenth and Seventeenth Centuries," lecture 4, pp. 4, 18.
33. See Krause, *Der Fruchtbringenden Gesellschaft ältester Ertzschrein*, 247: "The German language rests solid and unmovable in its principal foundations, implanted in

it by God. These [foundations] are the pure, clean, clear, and for the most part monosyllabic radicals that, in most beautiful purity, continuous certainty, and unmeasurable abundance, reach their little shoots, their veins, and boughs rich in branches far and wide, in such a way that it is not necessary to mix the sounds of strange peoples among them."

34. See Schottelius, *Teutsche Vers- oder Reim-Kunst* (A Study of German Prosody and Rhyme) (Lüneburg, 1656; rpt. Hildesheim: Olms, 1976), 43–44. Elsewhere Schottelius writes: "Yes, it is so that whosoever should reflect on its [German's?] ability [will discover] that he will reach the innermost properties of all natural activity in [by means of] German words" (*Introduction*, 104). Thus, while Kayser is correct in identifying the Nuremberg preference for the poetic figure of onomatopoeia as part of a seventeenth-century indebtedness to humanist poetic technique, he errs on the side of caution—as these quotations indicate—in concluding that the Nuremberg interest in *Klangmalerei* was unrelated to the natural language theories of the period. See his *Klangmalerei*, 126, n. 86.
35. See Krebs, *Harsdörffer*, 1:42: "Le développement de la langue nationale apparaît encore indissociable de l'oeuvre poétique par laquelle elle manifeste sa précellence."
36. See Neumark, *Der Neu-Sprossende teutsche Palmbaum*, 52.
37. See Krause, *Der Fruchtbringenden Gesellschaft ältester Ertzschrein*, 424. Ludwig does Zesen some injustice here (perhaps for other than merely linguistic reasons) in attributing the confusion to his habit of "making up" German words. See Sinemus, *Poetik und Rhetorik im frühmodernen deutschen Staat*, 210–12.
38. Others used the same discourse. In 1656, Martin Zeiller writes of German as "a virgin . . . who [ought] not to receive the brand of subservience to Rome" (*606 Episteln oder Sendschreiben von allerhand Politischen Historischen und anderen sachen gestellt und verfertiget*, 685, as quoted in Dyck, *Ticht-Kunst*, 71). Georg Neumark also speaks of careless writers who "dirty the pure 'dialect' of our noble High German language" (*Der Neu-Sprossende teutsche Palmbaum*, 51–52).
39. See Dyck, *Ticht-Kunst*, 71: "The metaphorics of language as metal admits the imperfection of language and casts the necessary work still to be done as a process of purification through fire."
40. The choice of the Saxon and the Meissen area dialects seems to have been associated with the notion of Luther's language as a model. See Josten, *Sprachvorbild*, 19–58.
41. Opitz, *Buch von der deutschen Poeterey*, vol. 2.1, p. 371.
42. Birken, *Teutsche Rede-bind- und Dicht-Kunst*, 48 (cited hereafter as *Art of Poetry*).
43. Harsdörffer, "Schutzschrift/für die teutsche Spracharbeit/und Derselben Beflissene: Zu Einer Zugabe/den Gesprächspielen angefüget. durch [sic] den SPIELENDEN," (On protecting work on behalf of the German language), in Harsdörffer, *Colloquies*, 1:339–95, here 346.
44. This formulation is Meyfart's in his *Teutsche Rhetorica*, 2.
45. *Consuetudo* was originally one of Quintilian's categories according to which spoken language could be standardized; it was defined as usage documented in the writings of the educated few: "Ergo consuetudinem sermonis vocabo consensum eruditorum." See his *Institutio oratoria* 1.6.1 and 45. Harsdörffer has a marginal note

in *Colloquies*, 3:289, referring to Quintilian's concept. Krebs, *Harsdörffer*, 58, claims that for Harsdörffer, the authority of the learned is to take over only when natural reason falls short of adequate standards. Haas, *Hochsprache*, 22–25 and 74, discusses the notion of *consuetudo* in connection with Schottelius.

46. See Schottelius's letter as reproduced in Krause, *Der Fruchtbringenden Gesellschaft ältester Ertzschrein*, 384–85: "The One Who Searches has informed the One Who Plays [Harsdörffer] that he cannot complete the promised word-book [Dictionarium] on account of [his] many official duties and other affairs. Should, however, someone else want to undertake such a useful, necessary, and complex task, he, The One Who Searches, would be abundantly willing, if asked, to make available the complete notes that he has been making for years."
47. The discussion of Harsdörffer's project for a dictionary may be found in his letter to Prince Ludwig in ibid., 387–97; quotation, 387.
48. The phrase is Schottelius's in a letter to Prince Ludwig in 1645. See ibid., 296.
49. On Goldast, see the *Allgemeine Deutsche Biographie* 9:327–30.
50. For a fascinating treatment of the centenary celebrations in 1617, see Kastner's *Geistlicher Rauffhandel*. Conermann has recently discussed the founding of the Fruit-bearing Society as associated with, even a direct reflection of, a "Protestant coalition" ("evangelische Koalition"). It might well have been for this reason that the association with the important Lutheran year of 1517 was emphasized. See Conermann, "Die Fruchtbringende Gesellschaft und ihr Köthener Gesellschaftsbuch," 24.
51. Martin Luther, "An die Ratherren aller Städte deutsches Lands, dass sie christliche Schulen aufrichten und halten sollen" (To the members of the city councils of all cities . . .), 37. On Luther's theory of translation as a Pentecostal act, see Meinhold, *Luthers Sprachphilosophie*, 31.
52. See Hankamer, *Die Sprache*, 43.
53. See Krebs, *Harsdörffer*, 1:24: "Autour de la langue nationale, c'est l'Allemagne luthérienne qui cherche son identité."
54. On the lack of influence of the language of the Luther Bible, see Baeumer, "Luther and the Rise of the German Literary Language"; and Ebert, "Verb Position in Luther's Bible Translation and in the Usage of his Contemporaries." Nevertheless, Luther was cited as a standard setter almost immediately. See Georg von Anhalt as cited in Johann Olearius's *Biblische Erklärung* (1678) as quoted in Dyck, *Ticht-Kunst*, 153, n. 8; and Erasmus Alberus, *Wider die verfluchte Lehre der Karlstadter* (1556) as quoted in Hankamer, *Die Sprache*, 69.
55. The identification of Luther's German as exemplary is by Fabian Frangk, *Orthographia* (1531), published as the *Anhang* to his *Cantzlei- und Titelbüchlein*. Frangk is quoted in Josten, *Sprachvorbild*, 106.
56. See Luther, *Tischreden* (Table talk), vol. 1, no. 1040, in the *Weimarer Ausgabe*, 2.1:525.
57. On "Gemeindeutsch" in relation to Luther, see Werbow, "'Die gemeine Teutsch.'"
58. See Luther's "Sendbrief vom Dolmetschen" in the *Weimarer Ausgabe*, 30.2: 637.
59. See Klaj, *Höllen- und Himmelfahrt Jesu Christi nebenst darauf erfolgter sichtbarer*

Aussgiessung Gottes dess Heiligen Geistes (Christ's journey to heaven and hell . . .), "Überreichungsschrift," A 2.

60. See, e.g., Tscherning, *Tschernings unvorgreiffliches Bedencken über etliche missbräuche in der deutschen Schreib- und Sprach-Kunst/insonderheit der edlen Poeterey* (Timely thoughts on some abuses . . .), 38.
61. Schottelius, *Brevis et fundamentalis manductio ad orthographiam et etymologiam in lingua Germanica* (A short and thorough guide . . .), A iij v to A v r.
62. For a history of the reception of Opitz as the "father of German poetry," see Garber, *Martin Opitz—"Der Vater der deutschen Dichtung."*
63. German dictionaries had been published prior to the seventeenth century. See Franz Claes, *Bibliographisches Verzeichnis der deutschen Vokabulare und Wörterbücher bis 1600* (Hildesheim: Georg Olms Verlag, 1977). It is commonly agreed that no complete, German-German dictionary was published until several centuries hence. See Helmut Henne, *Deutsche Wörterbücher des 17. und 18. Jahrhunderts: Einführung und Bibliographie* (Hildesheim: Georg Olms Verlag, 1975).
64. See Herdegen, *Historische Nachricht von dess löblichen Hirten- und Blumen-Ordens an der Pegnitz Anfang und Fortgang/biss auf das durch Göttl. Güte erreichte Hunderste Jahr* (Historical report on the praiseworthy shepherd and flower order on the Pegnitz . . .), 46, 47.
65. Manley, *Convention, 1500–1750*, 62.
66. See Steiner, "Precursors to Dryden."
67. See Dünnhaupt, "Die Übersetzungen Fürst Ludwigs von Anhalt-Köthen"; idem, *Bibliographisches Handbuch der Barockliteratur*, 2:1106–15.
68. Dünnhaupt, "Übersetzungen," 517.
69. Dünnhaupt, *Bibliographisches Handbuch*, 3:1913–27.
70. Ibid., 1780–91; and Bircher, *Johann Wilhelm von Stubenberg (1619–1663) und sein Freundeskreis.*
71. Dünnhaupt, *Bibliographisches Handbuch*, 3:1922.
72. Ibid., 1781, 1784.
73. On Birken, see Garber, "Sigmund von Birken," 242; on Neumark, Dünnhaupt, *Bibliographisches Handbuch*, 2:1283–1301; on Schottelius, see Dünnhaupt, *Bibliographisches Handbuch*, 3:1676–93. The analysis of Harsdörffer's translating work is based largely on Dünnhaupt's list of titles and editions in *Bibliographisches Handbuch*, 2:776–820, which is the most complete inventory of Harsdörffer's work to date.

4 *Institutiones Poeticae*: A Defense of Vernacular Poetics

1. On the pervasiveness of occasional poetry during the Baroque, see Segebrecht, *Das Gelegenheitsgedict.*
2. On this kind of "intellectual condescension," see Margaret Ferguson, "Sidney's *A Defence of Poetry*: A Retrial," *Boundary 2* 7.2 (1979): 61–95, esp. 61.
3. For examples, see Dyck, *Ticht-Kunst*, 47–48.
4. There were German-language literary texts written prior to those of the Nuremberg language society. Here I am investigating the foundational logic within the Nuremberg discourse about poetic origins, not its historical accuracy in asserting that its texts were the first.

5. On the equivalence between nature and the Ancients in Renaissance poetics, see Wilson, "Some Meanings of 'Nature' in Renaissance Literary Theory."
6. I am indebted here to suggestions made by Professor Benjamin Bennett (University of Virginia) concerning the power of textual presence in vernacular poetological discourse.
7. I base this argument on the suggestion made by Victoria Kahn that British technical treatises were "antitheoretical" precisely because their authors did not want to make themselves dispensable by providing theoretical models for "correct" behavior to be used indiscriminately. The Nuremberg technical treatises are antitheoretical in a similar way in that they foreground their own (language society) practice as the only possible correct practice. See Kahn, "Humanism and the Resistance to Theory," 382–83.
8. In posing the question, I am indebted, here as elsewhere, to David Quint, *Origin and Originality in Renaissance Literature*, for his insights on the "problem of how Renaissance culture was to define its own individual creativity with respect to the classical tradition that it at once posited and sought to displace as a source of authority and value" (1).
9. Vida, *De arte poetica*, as reprinted in Cook, ed., *The Art of Poetry*, 77. Pierre de Ronsard, "Hymne de l'Autonne," in *Oeuvres complètes*, 12:46.
10. Manley, *Convention, 1500–1750*, 141.
11. See ibid., 138; and Wesley Trimpi, *Muses of One Mind: The Literary Analysis of Experience and Its Continuity* (Princeton: Princeton UP, 1983), xiv.
12. Manley, *Convention, 1500–1750*, 142.
13. Ibid., 140. On the reception of Aristotle and on poetry as a part of logic, see Hardison, *Enduring Monument*, 11–18.
14. See Hardison, *Enduring Monument*, 9. Hardison suggests that the elaborate creation of an *ars metrica* in vernacular poetic treatises, for example, was designed to show that "great poetry" was also possible in those postclassical languages that could reproduce classical rules of prosody.
15. See Manley, *Convention, 1500–1750*, 34–35, on Aristotle's *Poetics*, in which, according to Manley, "the art of poetry ... receive[d] the same analysis as any natural process" (34).
16. This is of course not the Curtian understanding of *topoi*, which is in fact a form of historical *Motivik*. See Curtius, "Zum Begriff einer historischen Topik," 3–20; and Jehn, "Ernst Robert Curtius," vii–lxiv.
17. See Manley, *Convention, 1500–1750*, 142–46.
18. [Cicero?], *Rhetorica ad herennium* 3.17.31; Quintilian, *Institutio oratoria* 3.5.10–20; Cicero, *De oratore* 2.2.39.162.
19. The phrase is Lothar Bornscheuer's ("Zehn Thesen zur Ambivalenz der Rhetorik und zum Spannungsgefüge des Topos-Begriffs," 210).
20. See Rorty, *Philosophy and the Mirror of Nature*, chap. 1.
21. On the tradition of the "art of memory," in which the *topoi* were conceived of as permanent "places" in the mind, see Yates, *Art of Memory*, 1–50; and Rossi, *Clavis universales*.
22. Quintilian identifies the capacity to image first in the mind of the orator/poet and then in the mind of the audience as reciprocal in his *Institutio oratoria* 6.2.29.

23. Horace, *Ars poetica*, lines 1–4. See Manley, *Convention, 1500–1750*, 36–39, on Horace's *Ars poetica*.
24. See Manley, *Convention, 1500–1750*, 139, 137.
25. On anti-Ciceronianism, see Cave, *Cornucopian Text*, 36–48, 60–76; and Williamson, *The Senecan Amble*.
26. See, e.g., Dyck, *Ticht-Kunst*, 14. According to Dyck, the method of Baroque poetics is no more than an "eclectic collection of preexisting archetypes from the literary tradition."
27. See Krebs, *Harsdörffer*, 10, on Harsdörffer's "refus de la valeur absolue du modèle antique."
28. Quintilian, *Institutio oratoria* 1.1.26–27, 2.1.17–19.
29. See Manley, *Convention, 1500–1750*, on Cicero (39–41, 44–45), Quintilian (45–46), and Horace (46–53).
30. See Castor, *Pléiade Poetics*, 41.
31. On the notion of *Universalbildung*, see Dyck, *Ticht-Kunst*, 123.
32. See Krebs, *Harsdörffer*, 95: "L'enthousiasme surnaturel est transposé dans le caractère de l'individu qui porte en lui-même son ressort poétique."
33. See the Loeb edition of "On the Sublime," in Pseudo-Longinus, *On the Sublime*, ed. and trans. W. F. Fyfe (Cambridge: Harvard UP, 1965), 13.2.
34. See Krebs, *Harsdörffer*, 96–97, on the predominance of *ars* over *natura* in Harsdörffer.
35. Dyck, *Ticht-Kunst*, 14. In this tradition of reception of Baroque poetics, also see studies by Ludwig Fischer, Elke Haas, Renate Hildebrandt-Günther, and Reiner Schmidt.
36. Thomas Hobbes, "Answer to Davenant's Preface to *Gondibert*" (1650), 59–60.
37. See Krebs, *Harsdörffer*, 214–18, on the importance of invention in Harsdörffer's poetics.
38. For background on this tradition, see Beetz, *Rhetorische Logik*; Plett, "Der Affektrhetorische Wirkungsbegriff in der rhetorisch-poetischen Theorie der englischen Renaissance"; Wilhelm Risse, Foreword to Agricola, *De inventione dialectica*, 8–16.
39. See Dyck, *Ticht-Kunst*, 42, on *inventio*.
40. On the notion of aptness or appropriateness ("Angemessenheit") in Harsdörffer, see Krebs, *Harsdörffer*, 111–13.
41. See Castor, *Pléiade Poetics*, 103–13, for a similar conflation of the two senses of invention in the French tradition.
42. Cicero, *De inventione* 1.7.9.
43. See, e.g., the German/French/Latin *Dictionarium* (1669), s.v. "inventio," where "Ausdenckung" is the German synonym given for the French "invention."
44. Here I follow Castor's excellent survey of the tradition of physiological accounts of the imagination in *Pléiade Poetics*, 137ff. See also Bundy's *Theory of Imagination in Classical and Medieval Thought*; Harvey, *Inward Wits*; Robinson, *Shape of Things Known*; Levi, *French Moralists*. Baxter Hathaway deals with the Italian tradition in his *Age of Criticism*. On the later tradition, see Engell, *Creative Imagination*.
45. See Keckermann, *Systema ethica*, 66; and Micraelius, *Lexicon philosophicum terminorum philosophis usitatorum*, s.v. "imaginatio" and "phantasia."

46. Schottelius, *Ethica*, bk. 2, Capitel 1, pp. 5–6. For the tradition of the "speaking picture," see Lee, *Ut pictura poesis*, 9–16.
47. See Melanchthon, *Elementorum rhetorices libri duo*, bk. 1, col. 420.
48. The use of the Greek term *euphantasiotos* here to designate the fantasy first appears in the German-language tradition in Martin Opitz's *Buch von der deutschen poeterey* (1624) and was derived from Quintilian's use of the term in *Institutio oratoria* (6.2.29) to link the artist's or orator's compositional method and the internal activity of the mind.
49. Herrmann, in his *Naturnachahmung und Einbildungskraft*, emphasizes that inventions were meant to be new and astounding but links them with the logical tradition: "Die delectatio bleibt sachlich dem docere untergeordnet" (48). Also see Lange, *Theoretiker des literarischen Manierismus*. Verweyen (*Apophthegma und Scherzrede*, 53) criticizes Manfred Windfuhr's oversimplification of *Scharfsinn* as mere "Entlegenheitsstil und Concettismus" (Windfuhr, *Die barocke Bildlichkeit und ihre Kritiker*).
50. See Hermann, *Naturnachahmung und Einbildungskraft*, 79 (after Wundt, *Die deutsche Schulmetaphysik des 17. Jahrhunderts*). Also see Verweyen, *Apophthegma und Scherzrede*, 52 (Verweyen is citing Gracian here). Also see Funke, *Gewohnheit*, 247.
51. In this sense, the Nuremberg poetics do more than just repeat the catalogues of topics to be found in classical rhetorical treatises. For an investigation of some technical treatises as "arts of topics," see Dyck, *Ticht-Kunst*, 40–65.
52. See Beetz, *Rhetorische Logik*, 135, 148–49.
53. See Manley, *Convention, 1500–1750*, 32–36, on classical notions of invention.
54. See Attridge, "Puttenham's Perplexity," 270.

5 Some Versions of Pastoral

1. Blake Lee Spahr has defined the genre of the *Schäfferey* to which the *Shepherd Poem* belongs in purely formal terms. "A 'Schäfferey' is that genre of pastoral writing which consists of both prose and poetry, of which the action is portrayed dramatically rather than descriptively, with a rigid but open plot within a fixed schema of dualistic nature, leading to a eulogy which is usually not organic but independent" ("The Pastoral Works of Sigmund von Birken," 41). Klaus Garber mentions the occasional pastorals in his *Der Locus amoenus und der Locus terribilis*, 18–19, but does not really analyze them as a genre there. Krebs discusses the various pastoral forms available to and composed by the Nuremberg poets (*Harsdörffer*, 401–21).
2. See Garber, "Forschungen zur deutschen Schäfer- und Landlebendichtung des 17. und 18. Jahrhunderts," 240 (cited hereafter as "Forschungen").
3. On the prose eclogue, see Garber, "Forschungen," 229. On the definition of genre as "kind," see Barbara K. Lewalski, "Introduction: Issues and Approaches," in *Renaissance Genres*, ed. Lewalski, 5.
4. For a discussion of the inherent connectedness of the two modes in a different historical context and set of texts, see Annabel Patterson, "Pastoral versus Georgic: The Politics of Virgilian Quotation," in *Renaissance Genres*, ed. Lewalski, 241–67, passim.
5. Although I highlight different aspects of the text, I am indebted to David Quint's

discussion of the *Fourth Georgic* in his *Origin and Originality in Renaissance Literature*.
6. See Patterson, "Pastoral versus Georgic," passim; and Miles, *Virgil's Georgics*.
7. See Garber, "Forschungen," 240–42; and Reinhart, "Literary and Historical Synchronism in the Utopian Project of Hellwig's *Noris*."
8. For an example of such a method, see Eberhard Mannack, "'Realistische' und metaphorische Darstellung im 'Pegnesischen Schäfergedicht,'" 156.
9. Charles Segal has made the point that the highly stylized forms of pastoral seem at odds with the "cowherd-slave, *boukolos doulos*" who is described in *Idyll* 7 ("Poets and Goatherds," 8). Renato Poggioli speaks of this same moment as the "artistry" of "pastoral's artlessness" (*The Oaten Flute*, 157).
10. See Paul Alpers's innovative approach to pastoral poetics in his essay "Convening and Convention in Pastoral Poetry." Thomas G. Rosenmeyer also defines tradition, imitation, and continuity of artistic purpose as the main characteristics of pastoral (*Green Cabinet*, 4).
11. See, e.g., Garber, "Forschungen," 237.
12. See Javitch, *Poetry and Courtliness in Renaissance England*, 82.
13. As cited in ibid, 79.
14. See Empson, "Proletarian Literature," in *Some Versions of Pastoral*, 23.
15. See Burke, "The Four Master Tropes," 508.
16. See Segal, "Poets and Goatherds," 3.
17. See *Theocritus*, ed. and trans. Gow, 2d ed. (1952). All further references to Theocritus's *Idylls* are to this edition.
18. On the bee metaphor in imitative poetry, see Seneca, *Epistolae morales*, no. 84, in Seneca, *Ad Lucilium epistolae morales* (1962). Also see Stackelberg, "Das Bienengleichnis." An excellent introduction to the history of literary imitation and its many metaphors may be found in Pigman, "Versions of Imitation in the Renaissance."
19. Segal, "Theocritus' Seventh *Idyll* and Lycidas," 165.
20. See Virgil, *Eclogue* 4.39, in *Eclogues, Georgics, Aeneid I–VI*, ed. Fairclough (1978). All references are to this edition.
21. See John Milton, *Paradise Lost*, ed. Christopher Ricks (1968), bk. 4, lines 236–56; and Dante Alighieri, "Purgatorio," in *The Divine Comedy*, trans. Singleton (1973), canto 28, lines 91ff.
22. Panofsky, "Et in Arcadia ego," 271–304.
23. The relationship between mortality (history) and timelessness as it is reflected in the tensions between the grove and the city has been one of the main topics of discussion on the subject of pastoral. See Garber, "Vergil und das 'Pegnesische Schäfergedicht'"; Alpers, *The Singer of the "Eclogues,"* chap. 3.
24. For a discussion of the poem of praise as both a literal and a figurative monument, see Hardison, *The Enduring Monument*.
25. See Segal, "Since Daphnis Dies."
26. The text is: "Now violets bear, ye brambles, and ye thorns, bear violets, / and let the fair narcissus bloom on the juniper. Let all be / changed, and let the pine bear pears since Daphnis is dying. / Let the stag worry the hounds, and from the mountains let the owls cry to nightingales . . . So much he said, and ended."

27. See Segal, "Since Daphnis Dies," 27.
28. See ibid., 33–34.
29. On the relationship between Theocritean and Virgilian pastoral, see Alpers, *The Singer of the "Eclogues,"* 96–113; and Rosenmeyer, *Green Cabinet*, 122ff.
30. I follow the Latin text and Alpers's new translation of the *Eclogues* in Alpers, *The Singer of the "Eclogues,"* in what follows.
31. See Quint, *Origin and Originality in Renaissance Literature*, 32–42.
32. On the "program of cultivation" in the *Georgics*, see ibid., 33.
33. On the notion of Man's "triumph," see ibid. See Miles, *Virgil's Georgics*, for a reading of the poem that concentrates on Virgil's "political and philosophical, not agricultural" concerns (xii). Miles suggests that the *Georgics* are "structurally and conceptually analogous with the *Eclogues*" (xiii). I refer in the following discussion to the Oxford edition of the *Georgics* in P. Vergili Maronis, *Opera*, ed. F. A. Hirtzel (Oxford: Clarendon, 1956). All translations are my own following Miles.
34. See Miles, *Virgil's Georgics*, 254.
35. See ibid., 256.
36. On the tradition of the source of all waters and for an interpretation of the source as a figure of poetic creativity, see Quint, *Origin and Originality in Renaissance Literature*, 34–35.
37. Of course the *Odyssey* episode has the theme of inheritance at its center as well, since it concentrates on the son, Telemachos, as he asks Menelaos about the whereabouts of his father, Odysseus. Menelaos responds by relating Proteus's story of Agamemnon and Aigisthos, a story about false inheritances and about the trials of another son, Orestes, in securing his proper patrimony. Quint (*Origin and Originality in Renaissance Literature*, 35–36) sees the Virgilian descent here in relation to Odysseus's other descent as well, namely, the descent to Hades in *Odyssey* 4.
38. Quint interprets the Orpheus section of the *Fourth Georgic* as a "failure" and as a figure of "inconsolable human mortality," as opposed to the distinct "success" of the Aristaeus myth (ibid., 36–42). Miles interprets the *bugonia* as being about the necessity to forget the past (*Virgil's Georgics*, 281). He is working from a strictly political interpretive stance, however, positing that it was necessary for the new Roman emperor to forget the immediate past—one of civil war—in the interest of beginning anew. My interpretation of the significance of the *bugonia* for the poetics of pastoral does not conflict with Miles's interpretation.
39. See Cave, *The Cornucopian Text*, 37, 45, 71, on imitation as ingestion.
40. On the German pastorals, including Opitz's *Hercinie*, as imitative of the Italian pastoral tradition, see Huebner, "Das erste deutsche Schäferidyll und seine Quellen"; and Meyer, "Der deutsche Schäferroman des 17. Jahrhunderts."
41. See Sannazaro, *Arcadia*, eclogue 5. On Sannazaro, see Quint, *Origin and Originality in Renaissance Literature*, 43–80.
42. On the historical background of the *Hercinie*, see Garber, "Martin Opitz' *Schäferei von der Nymphe Hercinie*." On the relationship between "history" and literature in the *Hercinie*, see my "Et in Arcadia Ego"; and Wiedemann, "Bestrittene Individualität."
43. See the edition of Opitz's *Schäfferey von der Nimfen Hercinie* found in vol. 2, pp.

397–464, of Opitz, *Weltliche Poemata* (1644), ed. Erich Trunz (Tübingen: Niemeyer, 1975), here p. 400.
44. See Conermann, "Der Poet und die Maschine," 173–74.
45. Plato, *Republic*, in *The Collected Dialogues of Plato*, ed. Hamilton and Cairns (1961), 10.607a–d.
46. Aristotle, *Rhetoric*, in *Basic Works of Aristotle*, ed. McKeon (1941), 1.3.1358b.
47. See [Cicero?] *Rhetorica ad herennium*: "Demonstrativum est quod tribuitur in alicuius certae personae laudem vel vituperationem" (1.2.2). See Lausberg, *Handbuch der literarischen Rhetorik*, vol. 1, paragraphs 239–54, for further ancient sources on the *genus demonstrativum*.
48. See Quintilian, *Institutio oratoria* 3.7.6–19 and 5.10.24–30.
49. See Buchheit, *Untersuchungen zur Theorie des Genos Epideiktikon*. Buchheit explains that *amplificatio* allows the *genus demonstrativum* to fulfill its Platonic office of idealization: "das Wahre eines Gegenstands zu erkennen ... und in passender Form auszusagen" (106).
50. See Hardison, *Enduring Monument*, 52–56.
51. See ibid., 55, on the idealizing exemplum. Hardison is citing the Italian theorists Minturno and Cinthio here.
52. See Hardison's appendices of the "occasional types" listed in Menander's and Scaliger's treatises (ibid., 195–98). For references to similar lists in treatises used by early modern German-language writers, see Maria Fürstenwald, "Letztes Ehren = Gedächtnüss und Himmel-klingendes Schäferspiel," 49. Also see Segebrecht, *Das Gelegenheitsgedicht*.
53. For a detailed description of the epicedium, see Fürstenwald, "Letztes Ehren = Gedächtnüss," 38; and Krummacher, "Das barocke Epicedium." For a sampling of Baroque epicedia, see Fürstenwald, ed., *Trauerreden des Barock*.
54. Descriptions of the epicedium vary slightly. Krummacher, for example, suggests a "fünf- oder sechsteiliges Aufbauschema: (etwa: Begründung des tröstenden Zuspruchs, *laudatio* des Toten, Beschreibung der Krankheit und des Todes, Beschreibung der Bestattung, Aufnahme des Toten in der Unterwelt, Trostgründe)" ("Das barocke Epicedium," 101). Fürstenwald describes a four-step outline: "Mitteilung des Trauerfalls, Lob des Verstorbenen, Klage um seinen Verlust und Trost für Familie und Freunde" ("Letztes Ehren = Gedächtnüss," 38). The pattern is nevertheless fixed in such a way that it can be applied to all persons.
55. Compare Fürstenwald's analysis of several "Trauerschäferspiele" in which the community listening to the praise of the dead shepherd is restored to activity after the epicedium is completed ("Letztes Ehren = Gedächtnüss," 46–47).
56. On the "Beschreibung fiktiver Architektur," see Conermann, "Der Poet und die Maschine," 174.
57. Harsdörffer and Klaj, *Shepherd Poem*, reprinted in Harsdörffer, Birken, and Klaj, *Pegnesisches Schäfergedicht, 1644–1645*, ed. Garber (1966), 12. Page references are to the pagination of the original text.
58. *Shepherd Poem*, 5. Compare Opitz, *Hercinie*, 402, 455.
59. See Garber, "Vergil und das 'Pegnesisches Schäfergedicht,'" 180.
60. See *Shepherd Poem*, 17, 19. Compare Garber's Nachwort to the reprint edition of the *Shepherd Poem* (1966), 12, on these details as well as Mannack, "'Realistische'

und metaphorische Darstellung im 'Pegnisischen Schäfergedicht,'" passim; and Krebs, *Harsdörffer*, 425–26. For a critique of reading the *Shepherd Poem* for its "realistic details," see Conermann, "Der Poet und die Maschine," 175. For a standard interpretation of "realism" in the German Baroque, see Alewyn, *Johann Beer*.

61. See Conermann, "Der Poet und die Maschine," 176–79, for a lengthier interpretation of some of these details as signals of a specifically patrician identity.
62. For these details as signifying the "Örtlichkeit" of the text, see Mannack, "'Realistische' und metaphorische Darstellung im 'Pegnisischen Schäfergedicht,'" 160.
63. Conermann, "Der Poet und die Maschine," 180–81, following Kayser (*Klangmalerei*), speaks of a certain "Sprachpatriotismus" here.
64. For the architectural metaphors often used in mnemonic systems, see Yates, *Art of Memory*, chaps. 1–5.
65. Spahr belittles the function of the poem as publication vehicle, calling it the "display case" aspect of the *Schäffereyen* ("Pastoral Works of Sigmund von Birken," 31).
66. Conrad Wiedemann comments on the extravagant display of poetic virtuosity in many of the Nuremberg texts, explaining that the Nuremberg poets felt it was a "duty of the poet . . . to demonstrate what the German language was capable of. The attempt to try out all possible metrical and verse forms distinguishes the poetry of this period" (*Johann Klaj und seine Redeoratorien*, 158).
67. Birken, *Continuation* (1645), reprinted in Harsdörffer, Birken, and Klaj, *Pegnisisches Schäfergedicht, 1644–1645*, ed. Garber (1966), 28. Page references are to the pagination of the original text.
68. See Garber, "Vergil und das 'Pegnesisches Schäfergedicht,'" 180.
69. The first text was published in Birken, *Pegnesis*. The second text was published in Birken, *Krieges und Friedensbildung*.
70. See Hellwig, *Noris the Nymph*, Vorrede (unpaginated).
71. Compare Spahr's index of society names in the index to his "Pastoral Works of Sigmund von Birken," 29–30.
72. See the Vorrede to Hellwig, *Noris the Nymph* (unpaginated), and Conermann's explanation of the topographical tradition ("Der Poet und die Maschine," 173).
73. See, e.g., Garber, "Sigmund von Birken," 245.
74. See ibid., 226–27.
75. Birken, *Eastern Laurel Grove*, Überreichungsrede (unpaginated).
76. Among those celebrated in the "Anhang von Ehrengedichten an Fürsten/Grafen und Herren" are several individuals well connected at the Habsburg court. One, Johann Wilhelm von Stubenberg, had helped Birken gain entrance to the Fruitbearing Society. (Bircher, *Johann Wilhelm von Stubenberg [1619–1663] und sein Freundeskreis*, 244). Also see Klaus Garber, "Der Nürnberger Pegnesische Blumenordern" (manuscript, 1980), 119.
77. See Garber, "Sigmund von Birken," 226.
78. Birken, *Guelfis*, 169–70.
79. On Birken's *Guelfis* as a source of criticism of the court and thus as a source for how behavior could be modified, see Garber, "Der Nürnberger Pegnesische Blumenorden," 88ff.; and Spahr, "Dogs and Doggerel in the German Baroque."

80. See Hirschmann, "Das Nürnberger Patriziat," 269.
81. Limburger, *Kressischer Ehrentempel,* 6.
82. Birken, *Metellus of Nuremberg,* b iiij and following.
83. Birken, *Parnassus in Nuremberg,* 19.
84. Herdegen, *Historische Nachricht von dess löblichen Hirten- und Blumen-Ordens an der Pegnitz Anfang und Fortgang,* 60–61.
85. On the Dilherr pastoral, see Fürstenwald, "Letztes Ehren = Gedächtnüss," 43ff.
86. Birken, *Memorial in Honor of Dilherr,* 161–97.
87. Pellicer, *Balthis,* 15.

6 The Limits of Institutional Practice and the Resistance of the Text

1. Rorty, *Philosophy and the Mirror of Nature,* 318.
2. See Rorty, "Deconstruction and Circumvention," 5, 14.
3. See Rorty, "Texts and Lumps," 5–6.
4. Fish, *Is There a Text in This Class?* 198.
5. Bleich, "Intersubjective Reading," 401.
6. See Rorty, "Texts and Lumps," 11.
7. See Meese, *Crossing the Double-Cross,* 7.
8. White, "Conventional Conflicts," 155.
9. Foucault, *Power/Knowledge,* 133.
10. Meese, *Crossing the Double-Cross,* 12, 10.
11. See Reeves, "'Conveniency to Nature,'" 799.

Bibliography

Primary Sources

Agricola, Rudolph. *De inventione dialectica.* 1515. Rpt. Ed. Wilhelm Risse. Hildesheim: Olms, 1979.

Aquinas, St. Thomas. *Summa theologiae.* 61 vols. New York: Blackfriars in conjunction with McGraw-Hill, 1964.

Aristotle. *De anima. Aristoteles.* Ed. Walter Bröcker. Frankfurt: Vittorio Klostermann, 1964.

———. *De anima. On the Soul, Parva Naturalia, On Breath.* Trans. W. S. Hett. Loeb Classical Library. Cambridge: Harvard UP, 1957.

———. *On Memory and Recollection. On the Soul, Parva Naturalia, On Breath.* Trans. W. S. Hett. Loeb Classical Library. Cambridge: Harvard UP, 1957.

———. *Rhetoric.* Trans. W. Rhys Roberts. *Basic Works of Aristotle.* Ed. Richard McKeon. New York: Random House, 1941. 1317–1451.

Birken, Sigmund von. *Dilherrisches EhrenGedächtnis: Aufgestellet durch Floridan.* Birken, *Pegnesis Zweyter Theil.*

———. *Fortsetzung der Pegnitz-Schäferey/behandlend/unter vielen andern reinneuen freymuhtigen Lust-Gedichten und Reimarten/derer von Anfang des teutschen Krieges verstorbenen Tugend-berümtesten Helden Lob-Gedächtnisse; Abgefasset und besungen durch Floridan/den Pegnitz-Schäfer. mit Beystimmung seiner andern Weidgenossen.* Nürnberg, 1645. Rpt. in Harsdörffer et al. *Pegnesisches Schäfergedicht, 1644–1645.*

———. *Guelfis oder Nider Sächsischer Lorbeerhayn: Dem HochFürstlichen uralten Haus Braunsweig und Lüneberg gewidmet/auch mit dessen Alten und Neuen StammTafeln bepflanzet: Durch Sigismund von Birken/der Hochlöb. Fruchtbring. Gesellschaft den Erwachsenen.* Nürnberg, 1669.

———. *Königlich Polnischer Chur- und Fürstlich Sächsischer Helden-Saal....* Nürnberg, 1677, 1718.

———. *Krieges und Friedensbildung: In einer/Bey hochansehnlicher Volkreicher Versammlung/offentlichen vorgetragenen Rede/aufgestellet/Nebenst einer Schäfferey.* Nürnberg, 1649.

———. *Der norische Metellus oder Löffelholzisches Ehrengedächtnis des Glückhaften Vördesten Regentens der Weltberühmten Norisburg.* . . . Nürnberg, ca. 1675.

———. *Der norische Parnass und Irdische HimmelGarten. Welchen der norische Föbus/als deren Besitzer/verwechselt mit dem Himmelischen Sion und Ewigem Paradies.* . . . Nürnberg, 1677.

———. *Ostländischer Lorbeerhäyn/Ein Ehrengedicht/von dem Höchstlöbl. Erzhaus Oesterreich: Ein Fürstenspiegel/in XII. Sinnbildern/und eben sovielen Keyser- und Tugend-Bildnissen/Neben dem Oesterreichischen Stam- und Zeit-Register.* . . . Nürnberg, 1657.

———. *Pegnesis: Oder der Pegnitz Blumgenoss-Schäfere FeldGedichte in Neun Tagzeiten: Meist verfasset/und hervorgegeben/durch Floridan.* Nürnberg, 1673.

———. *Pegnesis Zweyter Theil: Begreifend Acht Feldgedichte der Blumgenoss-Hirten an der Pegnitz/geistliches Inhalts: Meist verfasset/und hervorgegeben/durch Floridan.* Nürnberg, 1677.

———. *SchäferSpiel der Ehre des Ruhmseligen Spielenden und seines Wol-Edlen Stamm- und Nam-Erbens in dem Pegnitz-LindenThal gewidmet durch die Pegnitz-Hirten.* In Birken, *Pegnesis Zweyter Theil.*

———. *Teutsche Rede-bind und Dicht-Kunst/oder Kurze Anweisung zur teutschen Poesy/mit Geistlichen Exempeln: Verfasset durch ein Mitglied der höchstlöblichen Fruchtbringenden Gesellschaft den Erwachsenen.* Nürnberg, 1679. Rpt. Hildesheim: Olms, 1973.

Charron, Pierre. *De la sagesse.* Amsterdam, 1662.

Cicero. *De inventione.* Ed. H. M. Hubell. Loeb Classical Library. Cambridge: Harvard UP, 1960.

———. *De oratore.* Ed. Edmond Courbaud. 3 vols. Paris: Les Belles Lettres, 1967.

[Cicero?] *Rhetorica ad herennium.* Ed. Harry Caplan. Loeb Classical Library. Cambridge: Harvard UP, 1977.

Dante Alighieri. "Purgatorio." *The Divine Comedy.* Trans. C. S. Singleton. Bollingen Series 80. Princeton: Princeton UP, 1973.

Dilthey, Wilhelm. "Die Funktion der Anthropologie in der Kultur des 16. und 17. Jahrhunderts." *Gesammelte Schriften*, vol. 2. 19 vols. Leipzig: B. G. Teubner, 1921. 416–92.

Du Bellay, Joachim. *La déffence et illustration de la langue françoyse.* 1549. Ed. Fernand Desonay. Textes littéraires français. Geneva: Librairie Droz; Lille: Librairie Girard, 1950.

———. *Oeuvres poétiques.* Ed. Henri Chamard. Paris: Société d'Editions d'Enseignement Supérieur, 1961.

Du Vair, Guillaume. *La saincte philosophie.* Rouen, 1617.

Ficino, Marsilio. *Theologia platonica sive de immortalitate animorum.* 1576.

Galen. *On the Natural Faculties.* Ed. A. J. Brock. Loeb Classical Library. London: Loeb, 1916.

Gueintz, Christian. *Die deutsche Rechtsschreibung.* Halle, 1645.

———. *Deutscher Sprachlehre Entwurf.* Cöthen, 1641.

Harsdörffer, Georg Philipp. *Delitiae mathematicae et physicae: Der mathematischen und philosophischen Erquickstunden . . . zweyter und dritter Theil*. Nürnberg, 1651, 1653.

———. *Frauenzimmer Gesprächspiele*. 8 vols. 1641–49. Rpt. Deutsche Neudrucke, Reihe: Barock 13. 8 vols. Ed. Irmgard Böttcher. Tübingen: Niemeyer, 1968–69.

———. *Poetischer Trichter: Die teutsche Dicht- und Reimkunst/ohne Behuf der lateinischen Sprache/in VI. Stunden einzugiessen*. 1648–53. Rpt. Darmstadt: Wissenschaftliche Buchgesellschaft, 1975.

———. *Specimen philologiae Germanicae, continens disquisitiones XII. de linguae nostrae vernaculae historia, methodo & dignitate. Praemissa est porticus virtutis, serenissimo atque celsissimo principi, ac Domino, Domino Augusto, Brunssvvcensium atq Lünaeburgensium Duci potentissimo &c. sacra*. Norimbergae, 1646.

Harsdörffer, Georg Philipp, and Johann Klaj. *Pegnesisches Schäfergedicht in den Berinorgischen Gefilden/angestimmet von Strefon und Clajus*. 1644. Rpt. in Harsdörffer, Birken, and Klaj. *Pegnesisches Schäfergedicht, 1644–1645*.

Harsdörffer, Georg Philipp, Sigmund von Birken, and Johann Klaj. *Pegnesisches Schäfergedicht, 1644–1645*. Ed. Klaus Garber. Deutsche Neudrucke, Reihe: Barock 8. Tübingen: Niemeyer, 1966.

Hellwig, Johann. *Die Nymphe Noris in Zweyen TagZeiten vorgestellet: Darbey mancherley schöne Gedichte/und wahrhafte Geschichte/nebenst unterschiedlichen lustigen Rätzeln/Sinn- und Reimbildern/auch artigen Gebänden mitangebracht durch einen Mitgenossen der Pegnitz-Schäfer*. Nürnberg, 1650.

Herdegen, Johannes. *Historische Nachricht von dess löblichen Hirten- und Blumen-Ordens an der Pegnitz Anfang und Fortgang/biss auf das durch Göttl. Güte erreichte Hunderste Jahr*. Nürnberg, 1744.

Hille, Carl Gustav von. *Der teutsche Palmbaum: Das ist/Lobschrift von der hochlöblichen Fruchtbringenden Gesellschaft Anfang/Satzungen/Vorhaben/Namen/Sprüchen/ Gemählen/Schriften und unverwelklichem Tugendruhm. . . .* Nürnberg, 1647. Rpt. as *Die Fruchtbringende Gesellschaft: Quellen und Dokumente in vier Bänden*, vol. 2. Ed. Martin Bircher. München: Kösel, 1970.

Hobbes, Thomas. "Answer to Davenant's Preface to *Gondibert*." (1650). *Critical Essays of the Seventeenth Century*, vol. 2. Ed. J. E. Spingarn. 3 vols. Oxford: Clarendon, 1908. 54–67.

Horace. *Ars poetica*. Trans. H. Rushton Fairclough. *Horace: Satires, Epistles and Ars Poetica*. Loeb Classical Library. Cambridge: Harvard UP, 1978.

Huartes, Juan. *Examen de Ingenious*. 1575. *The Tryal of Wits . . . Made English from the Most Correct Edition of Mr. Bellamy*. London, 1698.

Keckermann, Bartholomaeus. *Systema ethica: Tribus libris adornatum et publicis praelectionibus traditum in gymnasio Dantiscano a Bartholomaeo Keckermanno Dantiscano, philosophiae ibidem professore*. Hannover, 1610.

Klaj, Johann. *Friedensdichtungen und kleinere poetische Schriften*. Ed. Conrad Wiedemann. Deutsche Neudrucke, Reihe: Barock 10. Tübingen: Niemeyer, 1968.

———. *Höllen- und Himmelfahrt Jesu Christi nebenst darauf erfolgter sichtbarer Aussgiessung Gottes dess Heiligen Geistes. . . .* Nürnberg, 1644. Rpt. in *Redeorato-*

rien. By Johann Klaj. Ed. Conrad Wiedemann. Deutsche Neudrucke, Reihe: Barock. Tübingen: Niemeyer, 1965. 57–127.

———. *Lobrede der teutschen Poeterey*. 1645. Rpt. in *Redeoratorien*. By Johann Klaj. Ed. Conrad Wiedemann. Deutsche Neudrucke, Reihe: Barock. Tübingen: Niemeyer, 1965. 377–416.

Krause, Gottlieb. *Der Fruchtbringenden Gesellschaft ältester Ertzschrein . . . und anderweitigen Schriftstücke*. Leipzig: Verlag der Dyk'schen Buchhandlung, 1855.

Leibniz, Gottfried Wilhelm. *Unvorgreifliche Gedanken, betreffend die Ausübung und Verbesserung der teutschen Sprache*. *Hauptschriften zur Grundlegung der Philosophie*, vol. 2. Ed. Ernst Cassirer. Philosophische Bibliothek 108. Hamburg: Meiner, 1966.

Limburger, Martin. *Kressischer Ehrentempel: Nach dem Seeligen Ableiben/ . . . Herrn Jobst Christof Kressens/von Kressenstein/ . . . in einem teutschen Gedicht Sinnbildweis gezeiget. . . .* Nürnberg, 1663.

Lipsius, Justus. *Manuductionis ad Stoicam philosophiam libri tres*. Paris, 1604.

Luther, Martin. "An die Ratsherren aller Städte deutsches Lands, dass sie christliche Schulen aufrichten und halten sollen." 1524. *Werke (Weimarer Ausgabe)*, vol. 15.1. 9–53.

———. *Biblia: Das ist: Die gantze Heilige Schrifft: Deudsch*. 1545. Ed. Hans Volz. München: Deutscher Taschenbuch, 1974.

———. *D. Martin Luthers Werke: Kritische Gesamtausgabe (Weimarer Ausgabe)*. Weimar: Hermann Böhlaus Nachfolger, 1883; Graz: Akademische Druck- u. Verlagsanstalt, 1964–.

———. "Sendbrief vom Dolmetschen." *Sendbriefe*. *Werke (Weimarer Ausgabe)*, vol. 30.2. 627–46.

———. *Tischreden*. 6 vols. *Werke (Weimarer Ausgabe)*, vols. 2.1–2.6.

Melanchthon, Philipp. *Commentarius de anima*. Wittenberg, 1548.

———. *Elementorum rhetorices libri duo*. 1531. Rpt. Halle: Bretschneider, 1846.

Meyfart, Johann Matthäus. *Teutsche Rhetorica/oder Redekunst/Darinnen von aller Zugehör/Natur und Eygenschafft der Wohlredenheit gehandelt. . . .* Coburg: 1634. Rpt. Deutsche Neudrucke, Reihe: Barock 25. Ed. Erich Trunz. Tübingen: Niemeyer, 1977.

Micraelius, Johannes. *Lexicon philosophicum terminorum philosophis usitatorum*. . . . Stettin, 1661. Rpt. *Instrumenta Philosophica, Series Lexica I*. Ed. Lutz Geldsetzer. Düsseldorf: Stern-Verlag Janssen, 1966.

Milton, John. *Paradise Lost*. Ed. Christopher Ricks. New York: Signet Classics, 1968.

Montaigne, Michel de. "De la force de l'imagination." 1580. *Essais de Montaigne*. Ed. M. Rat. Paris: Éditions Garnier Frères, 1962.

Neumark, Georg. *Der Neu-Sprossende teutsche Palmbaum. Oder Ausführlicher Bericht/Von der Hochlöblichen Fruchtbringenden Gesellschaft Anfang/Absehn/Satzungen/Eigenschaft/und deroselben Fortpflanzung. . . .* 1668. Die Fruchtbringende Gesellschaft, Quellen und Dokumente in vier Bänden, 3. Ed. Martin Bircher. München: Kösel, 1970.

———. *Poetische Tafeln, oder Gründliche Anweisung zur teutschen Verskunst.* Jena, 1667. Rpt. Ed. Joachim Dyck. Heppenheim: Athenäum, 1971.

Opitz, Martin. *Buch von der deutschen Poeterey. Gesammelte Werke.* 1624. Ed. Georg Schulz-Behrend. 3 vols. Bibliothek des literarischen Vereins in Stuttgart 295, 297, 300. Stuttgart: Hiersemann, 1968–78.

———. *Schäfferey von der Nimfen Hercinie.* 1630. Vol 2 of *Weltliche Poemata (1644).* Ed. Erich Trunz. Deutsche Neudrucke, Reihe: Barock 3. Tübingen: Niemeyer, 1975. 397–464.

Pellicer, Johann Georg, et al. *Balthis oder Etlicher an dem Belt weidenden Schäffer des Hochlöbl. Pegnesischen Bluhmen Ordens. Teutsche Gedichte Drey Theile In sich haltend Allerhand zuschrifften/Glükwunschungen/Anbindungen/Lobreden/Ehre- Traur- Lust- Hochzeit- und FreudenGedichte nebst Hundert im dritten Theile befindlichen Sonneten oder Klingreimen nach Alexandrinischer/Jambischer/Trochaischer/Daktylischer/Pindarischer/Anapaestischer usw. Art entworffen. Und allen der teutschen Poesie Liebhabern anitzo zum Nutzen und Ergötzen mitgetheilet.* Bremen, 1677.

Pico della Mirandola, Gianfrancesco. *De imaginatione.* 1500.

Plato. *Cratylus.* Trans. Benjamin Jowett. *The Collected Dialogues of Plato.* Ed. Edith Hamilton and Huntington Cairns. Bollingen Series 71. Princeton: Princeton UP, 1961. 412–74.

———. *Laws.* Trans. A. E. Taylor. *The Collected Dialogues of Plato.* Ed. Edith Hamilton and Huntington Cairns. Bollingen Series 71. Princeton: Princeton UP, 1961. 1225–1513.

———. *Republic.* Trans. Paul Shorey. *The Collected Dialogues of Plato.* Ed. Edith Hamilton and Huntington Cairns. Bollingen Series 71. Princeton: Princeton UP, 1961. 575–844.

Puttenham, George. *The Arte of English Poesie.* 1589. Facsimile reproduction, introduced by Baxter Hathaway. Kent: Kent State UP, 1970.

Quintilian. *Institutio oratoria.* Ed. Jean Cousin. 7 vols. Paris: Les Belles Lettres, 1975.

Ronsard, Pierre de. *Oeuvres complètes.* 19 vols. Ed. Paul Laumonier. Paris: Librairie Marcel Didier, 1903–75.

Sannazaro, Iacopo. *Arcadia.* Ed. Michele Scherillo. Torino: Ermano Loescher, 1888.

Scaliger, Julius Caesar. *Poetices libri septem.* 1561. Rpt. Ed. A. Buck. Stuttgart: Frommann, 1964.

Schottel[ius], Justus Georg. *Ausführliche Arbeit von der teutschen HaubtSprache/ Worin enthalten Gemelter dieser HaubtSprache Uhrankunft/Uhralterthum/Reinlichkeit/Eigenschaft/Vermögen/Unvergleichlichkeit/Grundrichtigkeit. . . .* Braunschweig, 1663. Rpt. Deutsche Neudrucke, Reihe: Barock 11. 2 vols. Ed. Wolfgang Hecht. Tübingen: Niemeyer, 1967.

———. *Brevis et fundamentalis manductio ad orthographiam et etymologiam in lingua Germanica.* Braunschweig, 1676.

———. *Ethica: Die Sittenkunst oder Wollebens-Kunst/In teutscher Sprache vernehmlich beschrieben.* Wolfenbüttel, 1669.

———. *Teutsche Vers- oder Reim-Kunst.* Lüneburg, 1656. Rpt. Hildesheim: Olms, 1976.

———. *Teutsche Sprachkunst/Darinn die Allerwortreichste/Prächtigste/reinlichste/ vollkommene/Uhralte Haupsprache . . . Abgetheilet in Drey Bücher.* Braunschweig, 1641.

———. *Der teutschen Sprach Einleitung/Zu richtiger Gewisheit und grundmessigen Vermügen der teutschen Haubtsprache/samt beygefügten Erklärungen.* Lübeck, 1643.

Seneca. *Ad Lucilium epistolae morales.* 3 vols. Trans. Richard Grummel. Loeb Classical Library. Cambridge: Harvard UP, 1962.

Speroni, Sperone. *Dialogo delle lingue.* Trans. and ed. Helene Harth. Humanistische Bibliothek, Reihe 2: Texte 2. München: Fink, 1975.

Theocritus. *Idylls. Theocritus.* Ed. and trans. A. S. F. Gow. 2d ed. 2 vols. Cambridge: Cambridge UP, 1952.

Tscherning, Andreas. *Tschernings unvorgreiffliches Bedencken über etliche missbräuche in der deutschen Schreib- und Sprach-Kunst/insonderheit der edlen Poeterey.* Lübeck, 1659.

Vida, Marco Girolamo. *De arte poetica.* Romae, 1527. Rpt. in *The Art of Poetry: The Poetical Treatises of Horace, Vida, Boileau.* Ed. Albert S. Cook. Boston: Ginn and Co., 1892.

Virgil. *Eclogues. Eclogues, Georgics, Aenead I–IV.* Ed. H. Rushton Fairclough. Loeb Classical Library. Cambridge: Harvard UP, 1978.

———. *Georgics. Opera.* Ed. F. A. Hirtzel. Scriptorum Classicorum Bibliotheca Oxoniensis. Oxford: Clarendon, 1956.

Vives, Johannes Ludovicus Valentinus. *De anima et vita libri tres. . . .* Basel, n.d.

Zeiller, Martin. *606 Episteln oder Sendschreiben von allerhand Politischen Historischen und anderen sachen gestellt und verfertiget.* Marburg, 1656.

Secondary Sources

Aarsleff, Hans. "Language, Man, and Knowledge in the Sixteenth and Seventeenth Centuries." Five lectures given under the auspices of the Program in the History of Philosophy and Science. 10, 17, and 24 Mar., 7 and 14 Apr. 1964. Princeton U.

———. "Leibniz on Locke on Language." *American Philosophical Quarterly* 1 (1964): 165–88.

Alewyn, Richard. *Johann Beer: Studien zum Roman des 17. Jahrhunderts.* Leipzig: Mayer und Müller, 1932.

Allen, D. C. "Some Theories of the Growth and Origin of Language in Milton's Age." *Philological Quarterly* 28 (1949): 5–16.

Allgemeine deutsche Biographie. Leipzig: Duncker und Humbolt, 1875.

Allgemeine Gelehrten-Lexicon. Leipzig: Gleditschens Buchhandlung, 1750.

Allison, A. F., et al., eds. *Titles of English Books (and of Foreign Books Printed in England).* Vol. 1, *1475–1640.* Folkestone, Kent, England: Dawson, 1976.

Alpers, Paul. "Convening and Convention in Pastoral Poetry." *New Literary History* 14 (1983): 277–304.

———. *The Singer of the "Eclogues": A Study of Virgilian Pastoral.* Berkeley and Los Angeles: U of California P, 1979.
Alston, R. C., ed. *English Linguistics, 1500–1800: A Collection of Facsimile Reprints.* Menston, England: Scholar Press, 1970.
"Anatomy and Physiology." *Oxford Classical Dictionary.* 1961.
Arac, Jonathan, ed. *Postmodernism and Politics.* Minneapolis: U of Minnesota P, 1986.
Attridge, Derek. "Puttenham's Perplexity: Nature, Art, and the Supplement in Renaissance Poetic Theory." Parker and Quint, eds., *Literary Theory/Renaissance Texts.*
Auerbach, Erich. *Literatursprache und Publikum in der lateinischen Spätantike und im Mittelalter.* Bern: Francke, 1958.
Baeumer, Max L. "Luther and the Rise of the German Literary Language: A Critical Reassessment." *The Emergence of National Languages.* Ed. Aldo Scaglione. Ravenna: Longo Editore, 1984.
Barner, Wilfried. *Barockrhetorik: Untersuchungen zu ihren geschichtlichen Grundlagen.* Tübingen: Niemeyer, 1970.
Beetz, Manfred. *Rhetorische Logik: Prämissen der deutschen Lyrik im Übergang vom 17. zum 18. Jahrhundert.* Tübingen: Niemeyer, 1980.
Bennett, Tony. "Texts in History: The Determinations of Readings and Their Texts." *Post-Structuralism and the Question of History.* Ed. Derek Attridge et al. Cambridge: Cambridge UP, 1987.
Bennington, Geoff, and Robert Young. "Introduction: Posing the Question." *Post-Structuralism and the Question of History.* Ed. Derek Attridge et al. Cambridge: Cambridge UP, 1987.
Berlin, Isaiah. *Vico and Herder: Two Studies in the History of Ideas.* New York: Random House, 1976.
Berns, Jörg Jochen. "Zur Tradition der deutschen Sozietätsbewegung im 17. Jahrhundert." Bircher and van Ingen, *Sprachgesellschaften.*
Bircher, Martin. "The Fruchtbringende Gesellschaft and Italy: Between Admiration and Imitation." *The Fairest Flower.*
———. *Johann Wilhelm von Stubenberg (1619–1663) und sein Freundeskreis: Studien zur österreichischen Barockliteratur protestantischer Edelleute.* Quellen und Forschungen zur Sprach- und Kulturgeschichte der germanischen Völker 25. Berlin: de Gruyter, 1968.
Bircher, Martin, and Ferdinand van Ingen, eds. *Sprachgesellschaften-Sozietäten-Dichtergruppen: Arbeitsgespräch in der Herzog August Bibliothek Wolfenbüttel 28. bis 30. Juni 1977.* Wolfenbütteler Arbeiten zur Barockforschung 7. Hamburg: Hauswedell, 1978.
Bischoff, Theodor. "Georg Philipp Harsdörffer: Ein Zeitbild aus dem 17. Jahrhundert." *Festschrift zur 250jährigen Jubelfeier des Pegnesischen Blumenordens.* Nürnberg: n.p., 1894.
Bleich, David. "Intersubjective Reading." *New Literary History* 17 (1986): 401–21.
Böttcher, Irmgard. "Der Nürnberger Georg Philipp Harsdörffer." *Deutsche Dich-*

ter des 17. Jahrhunderts: Ihr Leben und Werk. Ed. Harald Steinhagen and Benno von Wiese. Berlin: Schmidt, 1984.

Borchardt, Frank L. *German Antiquity in Renaissance Myth.* Baltimore: Johns Hopkins UP, 1971.

Bornscheuer, Lothar. "Zehn Thesen zur Ambivalenz der Rhetorik und zum Spannungsgefüge des Topos-Begriffs." *Rhetorik: Kritische Positionen zum Stand der Forschung.* Ed. Heinrich Franz Plett. München: Fink, 1977.

Borst, Arno. *Der Turmbau von Babel: Geschichte der Meinungen über Ursprung und Vielfalt der Sprachen und Völker.* 4 vols. Stuttgart: Hiersemann, 1957–63.

Bouwsma, William J. *John Calvin: A Sixteenth-Century Portrait.* New York: Oxford, 1988.

Breuer, Dieter. "Gibt es eine bürgerliche Literatur im Deutschland des 17. Jahrhunderts? Über die Grenzen eines sozialgeschichtlichen Interpretationsschemas." *Germanisch-Romanische Monatsschrift* 30 (1980): 211–26.

Brink, Daniel. "Goropius Becanus and the Movement to Establish a Written Standard for Dutch in the 16th Century." First Biennial Interdisciplinary Conference on Netherlandic Studies. 11–13 June 1982. College Park, Maryland.

Buchheit, Vinzenz. *Untersuchungen zur Theorie des Genos Epideiktikon von Georgias bis Aristoteles.* München: Hueber, 1960.

Buck, August. "Die humanistischen Akademien in Italien." Hartmann and Vierhaus, eds. *Der Akademiegedanke im 17. und 18. Jahrhundert.*

———. *Italienische Dichtungslehren vom Mittelalter bis zum Ausgang der Renaissance.* Beihefte zur Zeitschrift für Romanische Philologie 94. Tübingen: Niemeyer, 1952.

Bundy, Murray Wright. *The Theory of Imagination in Classical and Medieval Thought.* Urbana: University of Illinois, 1927.

Burke, Kenneth. "The Four Master Tropes." *A Grammar of Motives.* New York: Braziller, 1955.

Burkhardt, C. A. H. "Aus dem Briefwechsel Sigmund von Birkens und Georg Neumarks, 1656–1669." *Euphorion* 3 (Supplement) (1897): 12–55.

Carroll, David. *Paraesthetics: Foucault, Lyotard, Derrida.* New York and London: Methuen, 1987.

———. "Representation or the End(s) of History: Dialectics and Fiction." *Yale French Studies* 59 (1980): 201–29.

Castor, Grahame. *Pléiade Poetics: A Study in Sixteenth-Century Thought and Terminology.* Cambridge: Cambridge UP, 1964.

Cave, Terence. *The Cornucopian Text: Problems of Writing in the French Renaissance.* Oxford: Oxford UP, 1979.

Cochrane, Eric. "The Renaissance Academies in Their Italian and European Setting." *The Fairest Flower.*

Cohen, Walter. "Political Criticism of Shakespeare." *Shakespeare Reproduced: The Text in History and Ideology.* Ed. Jean E. Howard and Marion F. O'Connor. New York and London: Methuen, 1987.

Conermann, Klaus. "Die Fruchtbringende Gesellschaft und ihr Köthener Gesellschaftsbuch: Eine Einleitung." *Der Fruchtbringenden Gesellschaft Geöffneter Erzschrein: Das Köthener Gesellschaftsbuch Fürst Ludwigs I. von Anhalt-Köthen, 1617–1650.* Ed. Klaus Conermann. 3 vols. Weinheim: VCH Verlagsgesellschaft, 1985. Vol. 2:21–127.

———. "Der Poet und die Maschine—Zum Verhältnis von Literatur und Technik in der Renaissance und Barock." *Teilnahme und Spiegelung: Festschrift für Horst Rüdiger.* Ed. Beda Allemann and Erwin Koppen. Berlin: de Gruyter, 1975.

———. "War die Fruchtbringende Gesellschaft eine Akademie? Über das Verhältnis der Fruchtbringenden Gesellschaft zu den italienischen Akademien." Bircher and van Ingen, *Sprachgesellschaften.*

Conrads, Norbert. "Ritterakademien und Sprachgesellschaften. Ein Vergleich." Bircher and van Ingen, *Sprachgesellschaften.*

Cook, Albert S. *The Art of Poetry: The Poetical Treatises of Horace, Vida, Boileau.* Boston: Ginn, 1892.

Culler, Jonathan. "Convention and Meaning: Derrida and Austin." *New Literary History* 13 (1981): 15–30.

———. "Criticism and Institutions: The American University." *Post-Structuralism and the Question of History.* Ed. Derek Attridge et al. Cambridge: Cambridge UP, 1987.

———. *Structuralist Poetics: Structuralism, Linguistics, and the Study of Literature.* Ithaca: Cornell Paperbacks, 1975.

Curtius, Ernst Robert. "Zum Begriff einer historischen Topik." *Toposforschung: Eine Dokumentation.* Ed. Peter Jehn. Frankfurt: Athenäum, 1972.

Derrida, Jacques. "Differance." *Speech and Phenomena, and Other Essays on Husserl's Theory of Signs.* Trans. David B. Allison. Evanston: Northwestern UP, 1973.

Dissel, Karl. *Philipp von Zesen und die Deutschgesinnte Genossenschaft.* Hamburg: Wissenschaftliche Beilage zum Osterprogramm des Wilhelm-Gymnasiums in Hamburg, 1890.

Dülmen, Richard van. "Sozietätsbildungen in Nürnberg im 17. Jahrhundert." *Gesellschaft und Herrschaft: Forschungen zu sozial- und landesgeschichtlichen Problemen vornehmlich in Bayern. Eine Festgabe für Karl Bosl zum 60. Geburtstag.* München: Beck, 1969.

Dünnhaupt, Gerhard. *Bibliographisches Handbuch der Barockliteratur.* 3 vols. Stuttgart: Hiersemann, 1980.

———. "Die Übersetzungen Fürst Ludwigs von Anhalt-Köthen." *Daphnis* 7 (1978): 513–29.

Dyck, Joachim. *Ticht-Kunst: Deutsche Barockpoetik und rhetorische Tradition.* Ars Poetica 1. Bad Homburg: Gehlen, 1966.

Ebert, Robert Peter. "Verb Position in Luther's Bible Translation and in the Usage of His Contemporaries." *Monatshefte* 75 (1983): 147–56.

Eco, Umberto. *A Theory of Semiotics.* Bloomington: Indiana UP, 1976.

Empson, William. *Some Versions of Pastoral.* New York: New Directions, 1974.

Engell, James. *The Creative Imagination: Enlightenment to Romanticism.* Cambridge: Harvard UP, 1981.

Erickson, Peter. "Rewriting the Renaissance, Rewriting Ourselves." *Shakespeare Quarterly* 38.3 (1987): 327–37.
Evans, R. J. W. "Learned Societies in Germany in the Seventeenth Century." *European Studies Review* 7 (1977): 129–51.
"Evidenz." *Historisches Wörterbuch der Philosophie*. Ed. Joachim Ritter. 6 vols. to date. Bern: Schwabe, 1971–.
Fähler, Eberhard. *Feuerwerke des Barock: Studien zum öffentlichen Fest und seiner literarischen Deutung vom 16. bis 18. Jahrhundert*. Stuttgart: Metzler, 1974.
The Fairest Flower: The Emergence of Linguistic National Consciousness in Renaissance Europe. International Conference of the Center for Medieval and Renaissance Studies, University of California, Los Angeles. 12–13 Dec. 1983. Firenze: Presso l'accademia, 1985.
Ferschmann, Siegfried. "Die Poetik Georg Philipp Harsdörffers: Ein Beitrag zur Dichtungstheorie des Barock." Diss. U of Vienna, 1964.
Fineman, Joel. "Shakespeare's 'Perjur'd Eye.'" *Representing the English Renaissance*. Ed. Stephen Greenblatt. Berkeley and Los Angeles: U of California P, 1988.
Fish, Stanley. *Is There a Text in This Class? The Authority of Interpretive Communities*. Cambridge: Harvard UP, 1980.
Forschner, Maximilian. *Die stoische Ethik: Über den Zusammenhang von Natur-, Sprach- und Moralphilosophie im altstoischen System*. Stuttgart: Klett-Cotta, 1981.
Foucault, Michel. *Power/Knowledge: Selected Interviews and Other Writings, 1972–1977*. Ed. Colin Gordon. New York: Pantheon, 1980.
Frühsorge, Gotthardt. *Der politische Körper: Zum Begriff des Politischen im 17. Jahrhundert und in den Romanen Christian Weises*. Stuttgart: Metzler, 1974.
Fürstenwald, Maria. "Letztes Ehren-Gedächtnüss und Himmel=klingendes Schäferspiel: Der literarische Freundschafts- und Totenkult im Spiegel des barocken Trauerschäferspiels." *Daphnis* 2 (1973): 32–53.
———, ed. *Trauerreden des Barock*. Beiträge zur Literatur des XV. bix XVIII. Jahrhunderts 4. Wiesbaden: Steiner, 1973.
Funke, Gerhard. *Gewohnheit*. Vol. 3 of *Archiv für Begriffsgeschichte, Bausteine zu einem historischen Wörterbuch der Philosophie*. Bonn: Bouvier, 1958.
Garber, Klaus. "Forschungen zur deutschen Schäfer- und Landlebendichtung des 17. und 18. Jahrhunderts." *Jahrbuch für internationale Germanistik* 3 (1971): 226–42.
———. "Der Hirten- und Blumenorden an der Pegnitz." Unpublished manuscript, 1980.
———. *Der Locus amoenus und der Locus terribilis: Bild und Funktion der Natur in der deutschen Schäfer- und Landlebendichtung des 17. Jahrhunderts*. Literatur und Leben 16. Köln: Böhlau, 1974.
———. "Martin Opitz' *Schäferei von der Nymphe Hercinie*: Ursprung der Prosaekloge und des Schäferromans in Deutschland." *Daphnis* 11 (1982): 547–603.
———. *Martin Opitz—"Der Vater der deutschen Dichtung": Eine kritische Studie zur Wissenschaftsgeschichte der Germanistik*. Stuttgart: Metzler, 1976.
———. Nachwort. *Pegnesisches Schäfergedicht, 1644–1645*. By Georg Philipp

Harsdörffer, Sigmund von Birken, and Johann Klaj. Ed. Klaus Garber. Deutsche Neudrucke, Reihe: Barock 8.

———. "Sigmund von Birken: Städtischer Ordenspräsident und höfischer Dichter: Historisch-soziologischer Umriss einer Gestalt-Analyse seines Nachlasses und Prolegomenon zur Edition seines Werkes." Bircher and van Ingen, *Sprachgesellschaften*.

———. "Vergil und das 'Pegnesisches Schäfergedicht': Zum historischen Gehalt pastoraler Dichtung." *Deutsche Barockliteratur und europäische Kultur*. Zweites Jahrestreffen des Internationalen Arbeitskreises für deutsche Barockliteratur in der Herzog August Bibliothek Wolfenbüttel 28. bis 31. August 1976. Ed. Martin Bircher and Eberhard Mannack. Dokumente des Internationalen Arbeitskreises für deutsche Barockliteratur 3. Hamburg: Hauswedell, 1977.

"Gebt uns den Frieden": Aus den Anfängen des Pegnesischen Blumenordens. Catalogue of an exhibition of the Institut für fränkische Literatur der Bibliothek Nürnberg im Rahmen der Veranstaltungsreihe "Barock in Franken." 1968.

Geertz, Clifford. *Negara: The Theatre State in Nineteenth Century Bali*. Princeton: Princeton UP, 1980.

Geisenhof, Erica. "Die Darstellung der Leidenschaften in den Trauerspielen des Andreas Gryphius." Diss. U of Heidelberg, 1957.

Giddens, Anthony. "Action, Subjectivity, and the Constitution of Meaning." *The Aims of Representation*. Ed. Murray Krieger.

Gilbert, Neal W. *Renaissance Concepts of Method*. New York: Columbia UP, 1960.

Gilmore, Myron P. "*Fides et Eruditio*: Erasmus and the Study of History." *Humanists and Jurists: Six Studies in the Renaissance*. Cambridge: Harvard UP, 1963.

Godzich, Wlad. "Afterword: Religion, the State, and Post(al) Modernism." *Institution and Interpretation*. Ed. Samuel Weber. Theory and History of Literature 31. Minneapolis: U of Minnesota P, 1987.

Goldberg, Jonathan. *James I and the Politics of Literature: Jonson, Shakespeare, Donne and Their Contemporaries*. Baltimore: Johns Hopkins UP, 1983.

———. "The Politics of Renaissance Literature: A Review Essay." *English Literary History* 49.2 (1982): 514–42.

Graff, Gerald. *Professing Literature: An Institutional History*. Chicago: U of Chicago P, 1987.

Grafton, Anthony. *Joseph Scaliger: A Study in the History of Classical Scholarship*. Vol. 1, *Textual Criticism and Exegesis*. Oxford: Clarendon, 1983.

Grayson, Cecil. "The Growth of Linguistic National Consciousness in England." *The Fairest Flower*.

Grazia, Margreta de. "The Secularization of Language in the Seventeenth Century." *Journal of the History of Ideas* 41 (1980): 319–29.

Greenblatt, Stephen. "Capitalist Culture and the Circulatory System." *The Aims of Representation*. Ed. Murray Krieger.

———. "Introduction." *Genre* 15 (1982): 3–6.

———. "Learning to Curse: Aspects of Linguistic Colonialism in the Sixteenth

Century." *First Images of America: The Impact of the New World on the Old*, vol. 2. Ed. Fredi Chiappelli. Berkeley and Los Angeles: U of California P, 1976.

———. *Renaissance Self-Fashioning: From More to Shakespeare*. Chicago: U of Chicago P, 1980.

———. *Shakespearean Negotiations: The Circulation of Social Energy in Renaissance England*. The New Historicism: Studies in Cultural Poetics 4. Berkeley and Los Angeles: U of California P, 1988.

Haas, Elke. *Rhetorik und Hochsprache: Über die Wirksamkeit der Rhetorik bei der Entstehung der deutschen Hochsprache im 17. und 18. Jahrhundert*. Europäische Hochschulschriften. Series 1: Deutsche Sprache und Literatur 349. Frankfurt am Main: Lang, 1980.

Hankamer, Paul. *Die Sprache: Ihr Begriff und ihre Deutung im 16. und 17. Jahrhundert*. Bonn: Cohen, 1927.

Hardison, O. B. *The Enduring Monument: A Study of the Idea of Praise in Renaissance Literary Theory and Practice*. Chapel Hill: U of North Carolina P, 1962.

Hartmann, Fritz, and Rudolf Vierhaus, eds. *Der Akademiegedanke im 17. und 18. Jahrhundert*. Wolfenbütteler Forschungen 3. Bremen: Jacobi, 1977.

Hartung, Oskar. *Geschichte der Stadt Cöthen bis zum Beginn des 19. Jahrhunderts*. Köthen: n.p., 1900.

Harvey, E. Ruth. *The Inward Wits: Psychological Theory in the Middle Ages and the Renaissance*. London: Warburg Institute, 1975.

Hathaway, Baxter. *The Age of Criticism: The Late Renaissance in Italy*. Ithaca: Cornell UP, 1962.

Hauriou, Maurice. "The Theory of the Institution and the Foundation: A Study in Social Vitalism." 1925. *The French Institutionalists: Maurice Hauriou, Georges Renard, Joseph T. Delos*. Trans. Mary Welling. Cambridge: Harvard UP, 1970.

Hegel, Georg Wilhelm Friedrich. *Vorlesungen über die Philosophie der Geschichte*. Stuttgart: Reclam, 1961.

Helgerson, Richard. "The Land Speaks: Cartography, Chorography, and Subversion in Renaissance England." *Representations* 16 (1986): 50–85.

———. *Self-Crowned Laureates: Spenser, Jonson, Milton, and the Literary System*. Berkeley and Los Angeles: U of California P, 1983.

Henne, Helmut. "Deutsche Lexikographie und Sprachnorm im 17. und 18. Jahrhundert." *Deutsche Wörterbücher des 17. und 18. Jahrhunderts: Einführung und Bibliographie*. Ed. Helmut Henne. Hildesheim: Olms, 1975.

Herrmann, Hans Peter. *Naturnachahmung und Einbildungskraft: Zur Entwicklung der deutschen Poetik von 1670 bis 1740*. Bad Homburg: Gehlen, 1970.

Hirschmann, Gerhard. "Das Nürnberger Patriziat." *Deutsches Patriziat, 1430–1740*. Ed. Helmuth Rössler. Limburg: Starke, 1968.

Hohendahl, Peter Uwe. *The Institution of Criticism*. Ithaca: Cornell UP, 1982.

Holstun, James. "Ranting at the New Historicism." *English Literary Renaissance* 19 (1989).

Howard, Jean E. "The New Historicism in Renaissance Studies." *English Literary Renaissance* 16 (1986): 13–42.

Howard, Jean E., and Marion F. O'Connor, eds. *Shakespeare Reproduced: The Text in History and Ideology.* New York and London: Methuen, 1987.

Huebner, Alfred. "Das erste deutsche Schäferidyll und seine Quellen." Diss. U of Königsberg, 1910.

Hunt, Lynn. "History beyond Social Theory." *The States of Theory: History, Art, and Critical Theory.* Ed. David Carroll. New York: Columbia UP, 1990.

———. "States of Theory: History and Social Theory." Paper presented at States of Theory conference. 24–25 Apr. 1987. U of California, Irvine.

Ingen, Ferdinand van. "Die Erforschung der Sprachgesellschaften unter sozialgeschichtlichem Aspekt." Bircher and van Ingen, *Sprachgesellschaften.*

———. "Die Sprachgesellschaften des 17. Jahrhunderts: Versuch einer Korrektur." *Daphnis* 1 (1972): 14–23.

———. "Überlegungen zur Erforschung der Sprachgesellschaften." *Internationaler Arbeitskreis für deutsche Barockliteratur. Erstes Jahrestreffen in der Herzog August Bibliothek Wolfenbüttel 27. bis 31. August 1973. Vorträge und Berichte.* Dokumente des Internationalen Arbeitskreises für deutsche Barockliteratur 2. Hamburg: Hauswedell, 1976. 82–106.

Iser, Wolfgang. "The Interplay between Creation and Interpretation." *New Literary History* 15 (1984): 387–95.

Ising, Gerhard. *Die Erfassung der deutschen Sprache des ausgehenden 17. Jahrhunderts in den Wörterbüchern Matthias Kramers und Kaspar Stielers.* Deutsche Akademie der Wissenschaften zu Berlin. Institut für deutsche Sprache und Literatur 7. Berlin: Akademie, 1956.

Jaeger, Werner. *Paideia: The Ideals of Greek Culture.* Trans. Gilbert Highet. 1944. New York: Oxford, 1965.

Javitch, Daniel. *Poetry and Courtliness in Renaissance England.* Princeton: Princeton UP, 1978.

Jehn, Peter. "Ernst Robert Curtius: Toposforschung als Restauration." *Toposforschung: Eine Dokumentation.* Ed. Peter Jehn. Frankfurt: Athenäum, 1972.

Jöns, Dietrich. "Literaten in Nürnberg und ihr Verhältnis zum Stadtregiment in den Jahren 1643–1650 nach den Zeugnissen der Ratsverlässe." *Stadt-Schule-Universität-Buchwesen und die deutsche Literatur im 17. Jahrhundert.* Ed. Albrecht Schöne. München: Beck, 1976.

———. "Literatur und Stadtkultur in Nürnberg im 17. Jahrhundert (Bericht über ein Forschungsprojekt an der Universität Mannheim)." Bircher and van Ingen, *Sprachgesellschaften.*

Josten, Dirk. *Sprachvorbild und Sprachnorm im Urteil des 16. und 17. Jahrhunderts.* Bern: Lang, 1976.

Kahn, Victoria. "Humanism and the Resistance to Theory." Parker and Quint, eds., *Literary Theory/Renaissance Texts.*

Kastner, Ruth. *Geistlicher Rauffhandel: Form und Funktion der illustrierten Flugblätter zum Reformationsjubiläum 1617 in ihrem historischen und publizistischen Kontext.* Frankfurt: Lang, 1982.

Kayser, Wolfgang. *Die Klangmalerei bei Harsdörffer: Ein Beitrag zur Geschichte der*

Literatur, Poetik, und Sprachgeschichte der Barockzeit. Leipzig: Mayer und Müller, 1932. Palaestra 179. Göttingen: Vanderhoeck und Ruprecht, 1962.

Krebs, Jean-Daniel. *Georg Philipp Harsdörffer (1607–1658): Poétique et poésie.* 2 vols. Publications universitaires européennes. Series 1: Langue et littérature allemandes 642. Berne: Lang, 1983.

Krieger, Murray. *A Reopening of Closure: Organicism against Itself.* New York: Columbia UP, 1989.

———, ed. *The Aims of Representation: Subject/Text/History.* Irvine Studies in the Humanities 2. New York: Columbia UP, 1987.

Kröll, Joachim. "Der Bayreuther Hof zwischen 1660 und 1670: Eine Bestandsaufnahme." Bircher and van Ingen, *Sprachgesellschaften.*

Krummacher, Hans-Henrik. "Das barocke Epicedium: Rhetorische Tradition und deutsche Gelegenheitsdichtung im 17. Jahrhundert." *Jahrbuch der deutschen Schillergesellschaft* 18 (1974): 89–147.

Kunstmann, Heinrich. *Die Nürnberger Universität Altdorf und Böhmen: Beiträge zur Erforschung der Ortbeziehungen deutscher Universitäten.* Köln: Böhlau, 1963.

Lange, Klaus-Peter. *Theoretiker des literarischen Manierismus: Tesauros und Pellegrinis Lehre von der "Acutezza" oder von der Macht der Sprache.* München: Fink, 1968.

Lausberg, Heinrich. *Handbuch der literarischen Rhetorik: Eine Grundlegung der Literaturwissenschaft.* 2 vols. München: Hueber, 1960.

Lee, Mary Elizabeth. "Justus Georg Schottel and Linguistic Theory." Diss. U of Southern California, 1968.

Lee, Rensselaer W. *Ut pictura poesis: The Humanist Theory of Painting.* New York: Norton, 1967.

Levi, Anthony. *French Moralists: The Theory of the Passions, 1585 to 1649.* Oxford: Clarendon, 1964.

Lewalski, Barbara Kiefer, ed. *Renaissance Genres: Essays on Theory, History, and Interpretation.* Cambridge: Harvard UP, 1986.

Lewis, Thomas E. "Notes toward a Theory of the Referent." *PMLA* 94 (1979): 459–75.

Lima, Luiz Costa. "Social Representation and Mimesis." *New Literary History* 16 (1985): 447–66.

McCoy, Dorothy Schuchman. *Tradition and Convention: A Study of Periphrasis in English Pastoral Poetry from 1557–1715.* The Hague: Mouton, 1965.

Macherey, Pierre. "The Problem of Reflection." *Sub-stance* 15 (1976): 6–20.

Mailloux, Steven. *Interpretive Conventions: The Reader in the Study of American Fiction.* Ithaca: Cornell UP, 1982.

Manley, Lawrence. "Concepts of Convention and Models of Critical Discourse." *New Literary History* 13 (1981): 31–52.

———. *Convention, 1500–1750.* Cambridge: Harvard UP, 1980.

Mannack, Eberhard. "'Realistische' und metaphorische Darstellung im 'Pegnesischen Schäfergedicht.'" *Jahrbuch der deutschen Schillergesellschaft* 17 (1973): 154–65.

Marsch, W.-D. "Institution." *Religion in Geschichte und Gegenwart*, vol. 3. Ed. K. Galling. 3d ed. Tübingen: Mohr, 1957.

Martino, Alberto. "Barockpoesie, Publikum und Verbürgerlichung der literarischen Intelligenz." *Internationales Archiv für Sozialgeschichte* 1 (1976): 107–45.

Mauser, Wolfram. *Dichtung, Religion und Gesellschaft im 17. Jahrhundert: Die "Sonnete" des Andreas Gryphius.* München: Fink, 1976.

Meese, Elizabeth A. *Crossing the Double-Cross: The Practice of Feminist Criticism.* Chapel Hill: U of North Carolina P, 1986.

Meinhold, Peter. *Luthers Sprachphilosophie.* Berlin: Lutherisches Verlagshaus, 1958.

Meyer, Heinrich. "Der deutsche Schäferroman des 17. Jahrhunderts." Diss. U of Freiburg i. B., 1928.

Meyer-Kalkus, Reinhardt. "Wollust und Grausamkeit: Affekttheorie und argute Affektdarstellung in Lohensteins' Dramatik am Beispiel von 'Agrippina.'" Diss. U of Göttingen, 1980.

Miles, Gary B. *Virgil's Georgics: A New Interpretation.* Berkeley and Los Angeles: U of California P, 1980.

Moeller, Bernd. "Imperial Cities and the Reformation." *Imperial Cities and the Reformation: Three Essays.* Ed. and trans. H. L. E. Midelfort and M. U. Edwards. Philadelphia: Fortress, 1972.

Montrose, Louis Adrian. "The Elizabethan Subject and the Spenserian Text." Parker and Quint, eds., *Literary Theory/Renaissance Texts.*

———. "Renaissance Literary Studies and the Subject of History." *English Literary Renaissance* 16 (1986): 5–12.

———. "Shaping Fantasies: Figurations of Gender and Power in Elizabethan Culture." *Representations* 2 (1983): 61–94.

Mullaney, Steven. *The Place of the Stage: License, Play, and Power in Renaissance England.* Chicago: U of Chicago P, 1988.

———. "Strange Things, Gross Terms, Curious Customs: The Rehearsal of Cultures in the Late Renaissance." *Representations* 3 (1983): 40–67.

Narciss, Georg Adolf. *Studien zu den "Frauenzimmer Gesprächspielen" G. P. Harsdörffers.* Leipzig: Eichblatt, 1928.

Newald, Richard. *Die deutsche Literatur vom Späthumanismus zur Empfindsamkeit 1570–1750.* 4th rev. ed. Vol. 5 of *Geschichte der deutschen Literatur von den Anfängen bis zur Gegenwart.* 7 vols. to date. Ed. Helmut de Boor and Richard Newald. München: Beck, 1963–.

Newman, Jane O. "Et in Arcadia Ego: Pastoral Poetics, or Imitation as Survival in Theocritus, Virgil and Opitz." *Deutsche Vierteljahresschrift für Literaturwissenschaft und Geistesgeschichte* 59 (1985): 525–50.

———. "The Word Made Print: Luther's 1522 *New Testament* in an Age of Mechanical Reproduction." *Representations* 11 (1985): 95–133.

Newton, Judith. "History as Usual? Feminism and the 'New Historicism.'" *Cultural Critique* 9 (Spring, 1988), 87–121.

Orgel, Stephen. *The Illusion of Power: Political Theater in the English Renaissance.* Berkeley and Los Angeles: U of California P, 1975.

Otto, Karl. *Die Sprachgesellschaften des 17. Jahrhunderts.* Stuttgart: Metzler, 1972.
Paas, John Roger. "Poeta Incarceratus: Georg Philipp Harsdörffers Zensur-Prozess, 1648." *Literatur und Gesellschaft im deutschen Barock: Aufsätze.* Ed. Conrad Wiedemann. Beiheft 1 of *Germanisch-romanische Monatsschrift.* Heidelberg: Winter, 1979. 155–64.
Panofsky, Erwin. "Et in Arcadia ego: Poussin and the elegiac tradition." *Europäische Bukolik und Georgik.* Ed. Klaus Garber. Darmstadt: Wissenschaftliche Buchgesellschaft, 1976.
Parker, Patricia, and David Quint, eds. *Literary Theory/Renaissance Texts.* Baltimore: Johns Hopkins UP, 1986.
Parodi, Severina. "L'Accademia della Crusca interprete della coscienza linguistica nazionale." *The Fairest Flower.*
Pechter, Edward. "The New Historicism and Its Discontents: Politicizing Renaissance Drama." *PMLA* 102.3 (1987): 292–303.
Peck, Jeffrey M. "The Institution of *Germanistik* and the Transmission of Culture: The Time and Place for an Anthropological Approach." *Monatshefte* 79.3 (1987): 308–19.
Pevsner, Nikolaus. *Academies of Art, Past and Present.* Cambridge: Cambridge UP, 1940.
Pfeiffer, Gerhard, ed. *Nürnberg: Geschichte einer europäischen Stadt.* München: Beck, 1971.
Pigman, George. "Versions of Imitation in the Renaissance." *Renaissance Quarterly* 1 (1980): 1–32.
Plett, Heinrich Franz. "Der Affektrhetorische Wirkungsbegriff in der rhetorisch-poetischen Theorie der englischen Renaissance." Diss. U of Bonn, 1970.
Poggioli, Renato. *The Oaten Flute: Essays on Pastoral Poetry and the Pastoral Ideal.* Cambridge: Harvard UP, 1975.
Quint, David. *Origin and Originality in Renaissance Literature: Versions of the Source.* New Haven: Yale UP, 1983.
Raith, Werner. *Die Macht des Bildes: Ein humanistisches Problem bei Gianfrancesco Pico della Mirandola.* Humanistische Bibliothek. Series 1, Proceedings 3. München: Fink, 1967.
Read, M. K. *Juan Huarte de San Juan.* Boston: Twayne, 1981.
Reeves, Charles Eric. "'Conveniency to Nature': Literary Art and Arbitrariness." *PMLA* 101 (1986): 798–810.
Reinhart, Roland Max. "An Annotated Edition of Johann Hellwig's *Nymphe Noris* (1650)." Diss., Ohio State U, 1987.
———. "Literary and Historical Synchronism in the Utopian Project of Hellwig's *Noris.*" Unpublished manuscript.
Robinson, Forrest G. *The Shape of Things Known: Sidney's "Apology" in the Philosophical Tradition.* Cambridge: Harvard UP, 1972.
Rorty, Richard. "Deconstruction and Circumvention." *Critical Inquiry* 11 (1984): 1–23.

———. *Philosophy and the Mirror of Nature.* Princeton: Princeton UP, 1979.
———. "Texts and Lumps." *New Literary History* 17 (1985): 1–16.
Rosenmeyer, Thomas G. *The Green Cabinet: Theocritus and the European Pastoral.* Berkeley and Los Angeles: U of California P, 1969.
Rossi, Paolo. *Clavis universales: Arti mnemoniche e logica combinatoria da Lullo a Leibniz.* Milano: Riccardo-Riccardi, 1960.
Rotermund, Erwin. *Affekt und Artistik: Studien zur Leidenschaftsdarstellung und zum Argumentationsverfahren bei Hofmann von Hofmannswaldau.* München: Fink, 1972.
Saussure, Ferdinand de. *Course in General Linguistics.* Trans. Wade Baskin. New York: McGraw-Hill, 1959.
Scholem, Gershom. *Sabbatai Sevi: The Mystical Messiah, 1626–1676.* Bollingen Series 93. Princeton: Princeton UP, 1973.
Segal, Charles. "Poets and Goatherds, Forests and Consuls: Art, Imagination, and Realism in Ancient Pastoral." *Poetry and Myth in Ancient Pastoral.* Ed. Charles Segal. Princeton: Princeton UP, 1981.
———. "Since Daphnis Dies: The Meaning of Theocritus' First *Idyll.*" Segal, ed., *Poetry and Myth in Ancient Pastoral.*
———. "Theocritus' Seventh *Idyll* and Lycidas." Segal, ed., *Poetry and Myth in Ancient Pastoral.*
Segebrecht, Wulf. *Das Gelegenheitsgedicht: Ein Beitrag zur Geschichte und Poetik der deutschen Lyrik.* Stuttgart: Metzler, 1977.
Sinemus, Volker. *Poetik und Rhetorik im frühmodernen deutschen Staat: Sozialgeschichtliche Bedingungen des Normenwandels im 17. Jahrhundert.* Palaestra 269. Göttingen: Vandenhoeck und Ruprecht, 1978.
Spahr, Blake Lee. "Dogs and Doggerel in the German Baroque." *Journal of English and Germanic Philology* 54 (1955): 380–86.
———. "Nürnbergs Stellung im literarischen Leben des 17. Jahrhunderts." *Stadt-Schule-Universität-Buchwesen und die deutsche Literatur im 17. Jahrhundert.* Ed. Albrecht Schöne. München: Beck, 1976.
———. "The Pastoral Works of Sigmund von Birken." Diss. Yale U, 1952.
Stackelberg, Jürgen von. "Die Académie française." Hartmann and Vierhaus, eds. *Der Akademiegedanke im 17. und 18. Jahrhundert.*
———. "Das Bienengleichnis: Ein Beitrag zur Geschichte der literarischen *imitatio.*" *Romanische Forschungen* 68 (1956): 271–93.
Stammerjohann, Harro. "The *Vocabolario* and German Lexicography." *The Fairest Flower.*
Steiner, Thomas R. "Precursors to Dryden: English and French Theories of Translation in the Seventeenth Century." *Comparative Literature Studies* 7 (1970): 50–81.
Stoll, Christoph. *Sprachgesellschaften im Deutschland des 17. Jahrhunderts.* Literatur als Geschichte: Dokument und Forschung 1463. München: List, 1973.
Struever, Nancy S. *The Language of History in the Renaissance: Rhetoric and Historical Consciousness in Florentine Humanism.* Princeton: Princeton UP, 1970.

Tuve, Rosemund. *Elizabethan and Metaphysical Imagery: Renaissance Poetic and Twentieth-Century Critics.* 1947. Chicago: U of Chicago P, 1972.
Verweyen, Theodor. *Apophthegma und Scherzrede: Die Geschichte einer einfachen Gattungsform und ihrer Entfaltung im 17. Jahrhundert.* Linguistica et Litteraria 5. Bad Homburg: Gehlen, 1970.
Weber, Samuel. *Institution and Interpretation.* Theory and History of Literature, vol. 31. Minneapolis: U of Minnesota P, 1987.
Weiner, Andrew. *Sir Philip Sidney and the Poetics of Protestantism: A Study of Contexts.* Minneapolis: U of Minnesota P, 1978.
Wells, Susan. *The Dialectics of Representation.* Baltimore: Johns Hopkins UP, 1985.
Werbow, Stanley N. "'Die gemeine Teutsch': Ausdruck und Begriff." *Zeitschrift für deutsche Philologie* 82 (1963): 44–63.
White, Hayden. "Conventional Conflicts." *New Literary History* 13 (1981): 145–60.
Wiedemann, Conrad. "Bestrittene Individualität: Beobachtungen zur Funktion der Barockallegorie." *Formen und Funktionen der Allegorie.* Ed. Walter Haug. Symposion Wolfenbüttel 1978. Germanistische Symposien Berichtsbände 3. Stuttgart: Metzler, 1979.

———. "Heroisch-Schäferlich-Geistlich. Zu einem möglichen Systemzusammenhang barocker Rollenhaltung." *Schäferdichtung: Referate der fünften Arbeitsgruppe beim zweiten Jahrestreffen des Internationalen Arbeitskreises für deutsche Barockliteratur vom 28. bis 31. August 1976 in Wolfenbüttel.* Ed. Wilhelm Vosskamp. Dokumente des Internationalen Arbeitskreises für deutsche Barockliteratur 4. Hamburg: Hauswedell, 1977.

———. *Johann Klaj und seine Redeoratorien: Untersuchungen zur Dichtung eines deutschen Barockmanieristen.* Erlanger Beiträge zur Sprach- und Kunstwissenschaft 26. Nürnberg: Carl, 1966.

———. "Kosmischer Gleichklang: Beobachtungen zum Romananfang im deutschen Barock." Literatur und Kosmos, 1500–1700. Conference held 28–30 Mar. 1986, at Washington U, St. Louis.

———. Nachwort. *Friedensdichtungen und kleinere poetische Schriften.* By Johann Klaj. Ed. Conrad Wiedemann. Tübingen: Niemeyer, 1968.
Wietfeldt, Willard James. *The Emblem Literature of Johann Michael Dilherr (1604–1669).* Schriftenreihe des Stadtarchivs Nürnberg 15. Nürnberg: Stadtarchiv, 1975.
Williams, Raymond. *Keywords: A Vocabulary of Culture and Society.* New York: Oxford UP, 1976.
Williamson, George. *The Senecan Amble: A Study in Prose Form from Bacon to Collier.* London: Faber and Faber, 1951.
Wilson, Harold S. "Some Meanings of 'Nature' in Renaissance Literary Theory." *Journal of the History of Ideas* 2 (1941): 430–48.
Wimsatt, W. K. *Day of the Leopards: Essays in Defense of Poems.* New Haven: Yale UP, 1976.
Windfuhr, Manfred. *Die barocke Bildlichkeit und ihre Kritiker: Stilhaltungen in der deutschen Literatur des 17. und 18. Jahrhunderts.* Stuttgart: Metzler, 1966.

Wölfel, Kurt. "Barockdichtung in Nürnberg." *Nürnberg: Geschichte einer europäischen Stadt.* Ed. Gerhard Pfeiffer. München: Beck, 1971.

Woodhouse, John. "The Reluctant Academicals: Linguistic Individualism in England after the Crusca." *The Fairest Flower.*

Wundt, M. *Die deutsche Schulmetaphysik des 17. Jahrhunderts.* Tübingen: n.p., 1939.

Yates, Frances A. *The Art of Memory.* Chicago: U of Chicago P, 1966.

———. *The French Academies of the Sixteenth Century.* London: Warburg Institute, 1947.

———. *The Occult Philosophy in the Elizabethan Age.* London: Routledge and Kegan Paul, 1979.

Zeller, Rosemarie. *Spiel und Konversation im Barock: Untersuchungen zu Harsdörffers "Gesprächspielen."* Quellen und Forschungen zur Sprach- und Kulturgeschichte der germanischen Völker 58. Berlin: de Gruyter, 1974.

Index

Aarsleff, Hans, 49–50, 272n.32
Académie de poésie et de musique, 44
Académie des sciences et belles lettres, 48
Académie française, 44
Academies: and botanical imagery, 36; British, 44–46; classical, 39; European, 30, 32, 40, 68; French, 43–44; and history, 36; Italian, 9, 33–43; Leibniz on, 47–48; and nationalism, 40, 44; and politics, 37, 48–51; of Renaissance compared with Enlightenment, 49; and translation, 37, 40; and vernacular, 37
Accademia degli intronati, 53–54
Accademia degli umida, 39–41
Accademia della crusca, 41
Accademia fiorentina, 39–41, 43
Accademia platonica, 39
Adamic languages, 62, 69, 70, 73, 74–78, 93, 104–5, 106; and Dutch, 91; and German, 75, 83–84, 88, 89, 93–102, 112, 130; and Hebrew, 90, 92, 93–102; and natural language, 100, 101, 103–4; and pastoral, 193
Adolf, Gustav, 63
Alpers, Paul, 199, 280n.29, 280n.30
Altdorf, 60, 66, 270n.97
Anthropology, and new historicism, 5–6, 7
Aristotle, 78, 140, 141, 162, 170, 171, 174, 212
Attridge, Derek, 185
Auerbach, Erich, and Vico, 4
August, Duke, 234
Aventinus, 176

Babel, 76, 91–93, 95, 105–6, 107, 108, 109
Barth, Caspar von, 129

Becanus, Goropius, 91, 101
Beer, Johann, 64
Bennett, Benjamin, 262n.3, 263n.34, 264n.35, 276n.6
Birken, Sigmund von, 59–60, 61, 63, 65, 66, 122, 134, 156, 166–69, 245–46, 247, 269–70n.91, 282n.76; *Androfilo*, 184; *The Apollo of Nuremberg* (Der norische Föbus), 182; *Dilherrisches EhrenGedächtnis* (Memorial in honor of Dilherr), 244–45; *Fortsetzung der Pegnitz-Schäferey* (Continuation of the Pegnitz pastoral), 8–9, 186–87, 188, 216, 223–28, 244; *Guelfis oder Nider sächsischer Lorbeerhayn* (Guelfis; or, laurel grove of Lower Saxony), 232, 233–36, 238; *Königlich Polnischer Chur- und Fürstlich Sächsischer Helden-Saal* (The heroes' gallery of the royal Polish Electorate and Saxon princes), 92; *Margenis*, 184; *Der norische Metellus oder Löffelholzisches Ehrengedächtnis* (Metellus of Nuremberg; or, memorial in honor of the House of Löffelholz), 238–40, 242; *Der norische Parnass und Irdische HimmelGarten* (Parnassus in Nuremberg and the earthly paradise), 238–39, 240–42; *Ostländischer Lorbeerhäyn* (Eastern laurel grove), 232–33; *Der Pegnitz-Schäfere Gesell schaft-Weide und Frülings-Freude: Beschrieben durch Floridan* (The springtime revels of the Pegnitz shepherds in their fields, as described by Floridan), 228; *Psyche*, 182, 183, 184; *Schäferey: Behandelt durch Floridan* (Shepherd poem, as rendered

Index

Birken, Sigmund von (*cont'd*)
by Floridan), 228; *SchäferSpiel der Ehre des Ruhmseligen Spielenden... gewidmet* (Pastoral play dedicated to the memory of the much honored one), 243–44; *Teutsche Rede- bind- und Dicht-Kunst* (Art of Poetry), 111, 126, 132–34, 136–37, 151–54, 163, 165, 171–72, 173–75, 177, 181–85
Bleich, David, 255–59
Boccaccio, and vernacular, 41–42
Bohemia, 224
Böhme, Jacob, 50
Bolton, Edmund, 45
Borde, Andrew, 45
Böttcher, Irmgard, 269–70n.91
Bouwsma, William, 39
Budé, Guillaume, 20
Burke, Kenneth, 194

Cabbala: and German, 90, 95–98, 108; and poetics, 169
Calvin, John, 20
Carroll, David, and figuration, 11–12
Castiglione, Baldassare, 147
Charles II, 45, 46
Christian of Anhalt, 226
Cicero, 125, 142, 146, 152, 161; and "anti-Ciceronianism," 37–38, 144; and institutions, 19; Luther as German, 120, 121
Cochrane, Eric, 40
Cohen, Walter, 262n.1
Community: and difference, 27; and institutions, 4; and interpretation, 255, 256–60; and language, 23, 24; in Order of Flowers, 61, 250, 251–52; and pastoral, 200, 201, 208–9, 213, 215, 220, 225, 228, 230, 233, 235, 242, 243, 244, 246, 247; and reception theory, 256; and story of the Pentecost, 77; and textuality, xii–xiii
Conermann, Klaus, 36, 37, 211, 268n.65
Conrads, Norbert, 268n.60, 268n.65
Conventions: and absolutes, 254; and authority, 39; combined with history and sacred, 89–90; and community, 251, 255; in *Cratylus*, 79–81; and facts, 255, 256–57; and institutions, 16, 23, 25, 261; and language, 23–28, 69; and language

societies, 36, 58; and law, 26; Mailloux on, 25–26; and pastoral, 193, 195, 199, 203, 206, 207–8, 213, 222, 227, 232–33, 235, 242, 244, 247; and poetics, 135, 167; and synchronic analysis, 25; and texts, 26; and vernacular, 143
Culler, Jonathan, 13–14, 16, 24

Dante, Alighieri: *Commedia*, and vernacular, 41–42; and pastoral, 195
Deconstruction, 252–54
de Man, Paul, 17
Derrida, Jacques, 12, 28–29, 253–54, 256
de Sainliens, Claude, 19
Dictionnaire françaises, 44, 47
Dictionaries: 69, 70, 83; German, 113–23; Johnson's, 46; Leibniz on, 47–48; and vernacular, 41–42, 44, 46–48
Différance, 28–30
Dilherr, Johann Michael, 66, 122
Dorothea Maria, Duchess of Weimar, 33
Dryden, John, 46
Du Bellay, Joachim, 44; *La déffence et illustration de la langue françoyse*, 43, 57
Dünnhaupt, Gerhard, 127
Dürer, Albrecht, 63

Eco, Umberto, 264n.56
Elizabeth, Queen of England, 5
Elyot, Sir Thomas, *Governour*, 45
Empson, William, 194
Epic, 180, 181
Epistemology, 253, 256
Erasmus, 37–38
Erickson, Peter, 7, 262n.1
Evelyn, John, 46

Ferdinand II, 64, 226
Ficino, Marsilio, 39
Figuration, and history-textuality relationship, 11–12
Fineman, Joel, 263n.20
Fish, Stanley, 255, 258
Fleck, Ludwik, 256
Foucault, Michel, 4–5
Frederick I, 48
Frederick II (the Great), 48
Frederick III, 233
Fragonard, Honoré, 196

Fruit-bearing Society (Fruchtbringende Gesellschaft), 33–35, 36, 41, 52–59, 91, 217, 274n.50, 280n.76; compared to Order of Flowers, 60, 61, 64, 65, 87, 117; *Kurtzer Bericht der Fruchtbringden Gesellschaft Zweck und Vorhaben* (Short report on the purpose and plans of the Fruit-bearing Society), 56; and language theory, 88; and Luther, 115; Order of Palms, 54; and poetics, 155; and translation, 127–28, 129
Freud, Sigmund, 29
Fürer, Georg Sigismund, 240

Gadamer, Hans-Georg, and history, 2
Galen, 20, 162
Garber, Klaus, xi, 9–10, 187–88, 191
Garin, Eugenio, 38
Geertz, Clifford, 263n.14
Gelley, Alex, 263n.29
Genre: as "kind," 187–88; and pastoral, 204; in poetics, 180–82
George, John, of Saxony, 63
German, xi; as Adamic language, 62, 75, 83–84, 88, 89, 93–102, 112, 130; as "ancient" (*uralt*) language, 82–83, 87–89, 91, 99, 100, 101, 108, 115, 118, 121; and Cabbala, 90, 95–98, 108; combining natural and sacred discourses, 69, 104–9, 130, 249; and Germanic languages, 91; High German, 83, 111, 112, 120, 122, 130, 261; and history, 86–89; linked to Hebrew, 93–102, 108; monosyllabism of, 93–95, 98, 101, 103, 121–22; as natural language, 67, 100–104; as philosophical character, 85, 95, 101–2, 125, 130; and poetry, 134, 136, 153, 155, 157, 160, 166, 167, 168, 171, 180–85, 191; purity of, 34, 54, 56–57, 107, 273n.38; as sacred language, 116; and textual institutions, 22–23, 28, 32–33, 70–71, 93; and Thirty Years' War, 105; and translation, 127–30. *See also* Vernacular
German-minded Association (Deutschgesinnete Genossschaft), 64, 71
Giddens, Anthony, and institutions, 15–16
Godzich, Wlad, 17–18
Goldast, Melchior, 115, 122
Goldberg, Jonathan, 1, 6, 262n.8
Graff, Gerald, 13–14, 16

Grafton, Anthony, 20–21
Greek, 21, 80, 90, 92, 96, 99
Greenblatt, Stephen, 1, 6, 10
Greiffenberg, Catharina Regina von, 64

Hardison, O. B., 276n.14
Harsdörffer, Georg Philipp, 53–54, 59–60, 61, 63, 65, 66, 70, 71–74, 128–29, 133, 134, 153, 167, 242, 244, 269n.80, 271n.4, 272n.16; *Diana*, 178; *Frauenzimmer Gesprächspiele* (Playful colloquies for the ladies), 53–54, 96, 97, 101, 103–4, 106, 110, 112, 113, 123, 124–25, 127, 159–60, 163, 164–65, 166, 179, 273–74n.45; "Fünffacher Denckring der teutschen Sprache" (Fivefold ring for thinking in the German language), 97, 122; *Der grosse Schauplatz/ jämmerlicher Mordgeschichte* (Grand Theater of Lamentable Murders), 129, 178; *Japeta*, 179; Letter to Prince Ludwig, 114, 117; *Poetischer Trichter* (The poet's funnel), 72–73, 85, 86, 96, 107–8, 110, 112, 113, 119, 120–21, 124–26, 133–34, 136–37, 144, 146–48, 154–56, 159–62, 164, 168–71, 172–73, 174, 176–81; *Seelewig*, 179; *Specimen philologiae Germanicae* (A model for a German study of words), 91–92, 95, 99, 101–2, 103
Harsdörffer, Georg Philipp, and Johann Klaj: *Pegnesisches Schäfergedicht* (Shepherd poem of the Pegnitz), 8–9, 178, 186–87, 188, 216, 217–25, 228, 244, 278n.1
Hart, John, 45
Hauptsprache. *See* Principal tongue
Hauriou, Maurice, 14–16, 18
Hebrew, 96; as Adamic language, 90, 92, 93–102; linked to German, 93–102, 108
Hegel, Georg Wilhelm Friedrich, 48; and history, 13
Heidegger, Martin: and Derrida, 28, 29; and history, 8; and institutions, 14
Helgerson, Richard, 1
Hellwig, Johann, 66; *Die Nymphe Noris* (Noris the nymph), 216, 228–32
Herdegen, Johannes, 54, 123, 242–43
Herder, Johann Gottfried, 131

308 Index

Hermeneutics, 253, 256
Herrmann, Hans Peter, 278n.49
Hesiod, *Theogony*, 138–39
Hille, Gustav von, *Der teutsche Palmbaum* (The German palmtree), 33, 34, 35, 36, 52–53, 56, 88, 90–91, 92, 105–6, 115, 122–23, 268n.65, 268n.68
Hirschmann, Gerhard, 65, 237
History: and contextualism, 84–89; and difference, 27; and Erasmus, 38; and Hegel, 13; and Heidegger, 8; and individual, 252; and institutions, 14, 15–23, 31; and language, 1, 24, 25, 45, 49, 71, 86, 89, 110, 116, 119, 127, 249–52, 260–61; and literature, 252; as "made event," 4; and myth, 209; as "Other," 2, 12–13, 17; and pastoral, 187, 188, 189–91, 192, 197, 200, 208, 210, 214, 215–16, 217, 219–20, 221–22, 224, 226, 229, 230, 234, 237, 247–48, 249–52, 260–61, 279n.23; and poetics, 132, 134–36, 145, 158, 167, 168, 177, 183–85, 249–52, 260–61; and "reflection theory," xiii, 10; and science, 43, 256; and textuality, xii–xiv, 1–13, 28, 30, 33, 39, 52, 70–71, 73, 256; and translation, 127
Hobbes, Thomas, 157–58
Hochsprache. See German, High
Hohendahl, Peter Uwe, 13–14, 16
Holstun, James, 262n.8
Homer, 27; and Virgil, 205–6, 280n.37
Horace, 143, 146, 174
Humanism: 20–21; and language, 39; and literacy, 40
Hunt, Lynn, 5–6

Ingen, Ferdinand van, 54, 269n.90
Ingolstetter, Andreas, 61
Institutions: 3, 13–23; academic, 13–14; and agency, 14, 15; and Cicero, 19; classical, 19; and community, 4; and convention, 16, 23, 25; and dictionaries, 41–42; French institutionalists, 14; and Heidegger, 14; and history, 14, 15–23, 31; and individual, 15, 16; and language, 24, 82; and law, 14–15, 18, 19; and method books, 21–22; and Order of Flowers, 23, 69, 100; and pastoral, 187–92, 197, 199, 203, 207, 211, 214, 224–25, 236, 244, 248; and Quintilian, 18–19; Renaissance, 19–23; and vernacular, 73–74. See also Academies; Language societies; Textual institution
Irenic movement, 50

James I, 45
Javitch, Daniel, 194
Johnson, Samuel, 46

Kahn, Victoria, 276n.7
Kayser, Wolfgang, 70, 273n.34
Keckermann, Bartholomaeus, *Systema ethica*, 162
Klaj, Johann, 53, 59–60, 63, 64, 65, 66, 87, 107, 122, 153, 154, 156, 181; *Lobrede der teutschen Poeterey* (In praise of German poetry), 92, 98, 103, 106, 112, 117–18, 149–51
Klaj, Johann, and Georg Philipp Harsdörffer: *Pegnesisches Schäfergedicht* (Shepherd poem of the Pegnitz), 8–9, 178, 186–87, 188, 216, 217–25, 228, 244, 278n.1
Krause, Gottlieb, 272–73n.33
Krebs, Jean-Daniel, 269–70n.91, 271n.11, 272n.16, 272n.21
Kress, Jobst Christof, 237
Krieger, Murray, 264n.43, 271n.6

Language societies (*Sprachgesellschaften*): 8, 48–51; and class, 55; and conventions, 36, 58; and European academies, 30; and ethics, 54, 57, 107; and Italian academies, 33–43; and knightly academies, 53–56; Leibniz on, 47–48; as Platonic legislator, 107, 112, 117, 261; and politics, xi, 48–51, 54, 57, 117; statutes of, 122–23; and textual institutions, 32–33, 36, 51, 55–56, 57, 59, 61, 66–68. See also Fruit-bearing Society; German-minded Association; Order of Flowers on the Pegnitz; Order of Swans on the Elbe
Language theory: and Cabbala, 95–98; and Catholic church, 118; chancery language, 114, 117–20; and class, 57, 58, 110; classical, 78–82; classical compared with Christian, 78, 81–82, 83, 271n.11;

Index   309

classical compared with Renaissance and Baroque, 81; and community, 23, 24; contextualism in, 77, 79–80, 83–89, 110, 124, 126, 129, 130; and conventions, 23–28; deconstruction, 252–54; foreign influence on, 106, 107, 108, 109; inspirational theories, 98; and institutions, 24, 82; and knowledge, 46, 161–62; language and history, 1, 24, 25, 45, 49, 71, 86, 89, 110, 116, 119, 127; and language societies, 53, 88; and law, 70, 109, 119; and militarism, 56, 105–6; and nationalism, 42, 43–44, 46–50, 75; and national languages, 71, 272n.21, 273n.35; and new historicism, 4, 6–7; and Order of Flowers, xi, 30, 68, 69–74, 82–131, 249–52, 260–61; and ontology, xiii; origins of, 35; and pastoral, 188; and Pentecost, 75–78, 106; Plato's, 72; Protestant, 116; Saussure's, 23–25; speech vs. writing, 109, 115, 120, 123; universal language, 49–51. *See also* Adamic languages; Natural language; Philosophical character
Latin, 21, 40, 90, 92, 96, 99
Law: and conventions, 26; and custom, 135; and institutions, 14–15, 18, 19, 249–52, 260–61; and language theory, 70, 109, 119; and semiotics, 25; and vernacular, 39
Leibniz, Gottfried Wilhelm: *Unvorgreifliche Gedanken, betreffend die Ausübung und Verbesserung der teutschen Sprache* (Timely thoughts on the use and improvement of the German language), 47–48
Leopold I, 232
Limburger, Martin, 66; *Kressischer Ehrentempel* (Temple honoring the House of Kress), 237–38
Locke, John, *Essay concerning Human Understanding*, 50
Löffelholz, Burkhardt, 239, 240
Ludwig, Prince of Anhalt-Köthen, 33–34, 37, 41, 57, 58, 87, 105, 106, 127, 128, 273n.37
Luther, Martin, 27, 83, 176; "Sendbrief vom Dolmetschen" (Letter on translating), 72, 73; and vernacular, 33, 35–36, 46, 70, 74, 114, 115–20, 121, 122, 273n.40

MacCannell, Juliet Flower, 262n.29
Machiavelli, *Dialogo intorno alla nostra lingua*, 43
Mailloux, Steven, 25–26
Manley, Lawrence, 16, 26–27, 36, 141
Maximilian of Bavaria, 63
Medici, Cosimo de', 39
Medici, Cosimo II de', 39, 43
Meese, Elizabeth, 258–60, 261
Meissen, 65, 217, 218
Method books, 21–22, 150–51
Micraelius, Johannes, *Lexicon philosophicum*, 162
Milton, John, and pastoral, 195
Mimesis, 8, 11
Mirandola, Pico della, 162
Montemayor, 128, 132, 178, 179
Montgomery, Robert, 265n.63
Montrose, Louis A., 1, 5, 6, 262n.7
Mullaney, Steven, 1

Nationalism, 40; and language, 42, 43–44, 46–50, 75
Natural language (*Natursprache*): and Adamic languages, 100, 101, 103–4; and contextualism, 102–3; and onomatopoeia, 103–4; and science, 102; and vernacular, 100–104
Neumark, Georg: *Der Neu-Sprossende teutsche Palmbaum* (The newly budding German palm tree), 57, 273n.38; *Poetische Tafeln, oder Gründliche Anweisung zur teutschen Verkunst* (A treatise on poetry in schematic form), 174
New historicism, xiii; and anthropology, 5–6, 7; and Foucault, 4–5; and language, 4, 6–7; and mimesis, 8; and politics, 6–7; and reception theory, 1–2; and representation, 1–13; and semiotics, 4
Newton, Judith, 262n.1
Nietzsche, Friedrich, 29
Nuremberg, xii, 9, 30, 61, 62–65, 186, 211, 215, 216, 218–19, 229, 230–31, 242–43

Onomatopoeia: and natural language, 103–4, 273n.34; and pastoral, 219
Opitz, Martin, 111, 119, 176, 183, 191, 196, 210, 234, 236, 246, 278n.48; *Schäfferey von der Nimfen Hercinie* (Shepherd poem

Opitz, Martin (cont'd)
of Hercinie the nymph), 186, 197, 208, 209, 214, 217, 218, 220, 221, 232, 236
Order of Flowers on the Pegnitz (Pegnesischer Blumenorden), 1, 2, 3, 22–23, 35, 52, 59–68; and Accademia degli intronati, 53–54; community in, 61; compared with Fruit-bearing Society, 60, 61, 64, 65, 87, 117; and historical study, xi–xiv, 8–10; institutionalizing function of, 13, 23, 27–28, 28–29, 249–52, 260–61; and language theory, xi, 30, 69–74, 82–131, 249–52, 260–61; and pastoral, xi, 30–31, 59, 186–95, 214–48, 249–52, 260–61; and poetics, xi, 30, 68, 132–39, 145–85, 249–52, 260–61; textual institutions of, 59, 61–62, 249–52, 260–61; and translation, 128–29, 164. *See also* Language societies
Order of Swans on the Elbe (Elbschwanenorden), 64
Ovid, 149, 152, 226

Panofsky, Erwin, on pastoral, 195–96
Paracelsus, 50
Pastoral, 67–68, 173, 181, 182; and Ancient-Modern debate, 214, 231–32; *aptum* in, 247; architecture in, 214, 220–21, 226, 234, 238; British, 194; and class, 191, 220, 232, 236; combining eclogic and georgic discourses, 188, 210, 214; combining sacred and historical discourses, 192; community, 200, 201, 208–9, 213, 215, 220, 225, 228, 230, 233, 235, 242, 243, 244, 246, 247; conventions, 193, 195, 199, 203, 206, 207–8, 213, 222, 227, 232–33, 235, 242, 244, 247; eclogue, 193, 197, 199–202, 204, 215, 240, 246; *Ehrengedichte*, 235; ekphrasis in, 233, 235; encomium in, 191, 211–12, 215, 216, 222, 227, 231, 232, 235, 243, 246; epicedium in, 191, 212–14, 229, 237, 238, 241, 244–45; epithalamium in, 186, 221, 222–23; eulogy, 188–89, 190, 196–211, 212, 213, 214, 215, 216, 218, 219, 220, 222, 224, 225, 229, 231, 232, 236, 237, 239–40, 243, 244, 246; *genius loci* in, 202, 208, 220, 236, 242; and *genus demonstrativum*, 191, 212–14, 221, 222, 229, 232, 234, 237, 239; georgic, 215, 224, 235; and history, 187, 188, 189, 192, 197, 200, 208, 210, 214, 215–16, 217, 219–20, 221–22, 224, 226, 229, 234, 237, 247–48, 279n.23; and imitation, 188, 191, 192, 195, 197, 198, 200, 205, 207, 208, 211, 212, 216, 221; institutional logic of, 187–92, 197, 199, 203, 207, 211, 214, 224–25, 236, 244, 248; and invention, 188, 195; labor in, 189, 203, 207, 235; and language theory, 188, 193, 204; models for, 187; and myth, 195, 207, 211, 224, 227–28, 233, 234, 237, 246, 247–48; Nuremberg in, 211, 215, 216, 218–19, 229, 230–31, 236; and occasional poetry, 191, 211, 213, 235; onomatopoeia in, 219; and Order of Flowers, 214–48; origins of, 201; patrons of, 189, 215, 217, 220, 222, 229, 230, 232, 233, 234, 235, 238–40, 242; and poetics, 188, 190, 193, 204, 216; and realism, 219, 238; and renewal, 191, 192, 194, 200, 202–3, 205, 208, 211, 213, 219, 223, 237, 238, 248; and substitution, 193, 200; synecdoche in, 194, 196, 201, 202, 207, 208, 209, 216, 219, 224, 226–27, 244, 247; and Thirty Years' War, 218, 219–20, 226–27, 229; and transformation, 194, 199, 211; and vernacular, 59, 187, 191, 192–93, 197, 209–11, 216–18, 222, 225, 227, 228, 231–32, 237, 240, 242, 246, 247–48. *See also* Birken; Harsdörffer; Limburger; Opitz; Pellicer; Theocritus; Virgil
Pechter, Edward, 7, 262n.7
Peck, Jeffrey M., 13–14, 16
Pellicer, Johannes Georg: *Lob des Floridans, besungen in zimbrischen Lustgefilden/von ausländischen Pegnitz Schäffer Thyrsis* (Balthis, in praise of Floridan, sung in the delightful pastures of Cimbria, by the Pegnitz shepherd who lives abroad, Thyrsis), 245–47
Petrarch, and vernacular, 41–42
Phenomenology, 256
Philosophical character, 46, 48–50, 85, 95, 101–2, 125, 130
Piccolomini, Octavio, 63
Plato, 8, 152, 161–62; *Cratylus*, 72, 78–82, 95–96; *Republic*, 140, 211–12

Pléiade, La, 44
Poesis, 7–8
Poetics: and Ancient-Modern debate, 133–38, 144–45, 146, 147, 150, 153–55, 157, 158, 175, 181, 182, 249; and *aptum*, 136, 139–45, 150, 158–65, 168–69, 171, 174; and Cabbala, 169; Christian origins of, 132–34, 145, 152–53; classical, 132, 138, 143, 146, 152, 175, 176, 184–85; combining art and nature, 146–57, 158, 166; combining natural and sacred discourses, 143, 145, 146, 151, 153, 249; contextualism in, 143; and convention, 135, 167; and dialectics, 158–59, 161, 165; and drama, 182–85; examples in, 166–69, 177–85; foundational logic of, 135, 142, 143, 145–46, 151, 154, 157, 158, 161, 164, 166–67, 171, 174–76, 177–78, 180, 275n.4; and history, 132, 134–36, 139, 158, 167, 168, 177, 183–85; and humanism, 150; and imitation, 137, 149, 157, 159, 164, 176; and inspiration, 140, 142, 149, 150, 151, 152–53, 154, 156, 159, 166, 174, 204; and invention, 134, 136–38, 139, 141–45, 150, 157–65, 166, 167–70, 172–74, 176–77, 181–82; and knowledge, 171; occasional poetry, 173; and pastoral, 132, 173, 181, 182, 188, 193, 204, 216; and print, 141; producing nature, 146–57; Renaissance, 132, 139, 143, 149; and representation, 140; and rhetoric, 140–45, 150–51, 157, 158–59; rules of, 135, 136–37, 138, 140–45, 146, 148, 153–54, 156–57, 166, 171, 172, 174–78, 179–83, 276n.14; and satire, 181–82, 183; textuality of, 142, 166; and translation, 164; and truth, 161–65; vernacular origins of, 132–38, 139, 141, 142, 145, 148–57, 158, 161, 165, 166, 167, 168, 171–72, 174, 180–85
Pope, Alexander, 27
Power: and conventions, 31; and institutions, 23, 30, 249–52, 260–61; and language, 39, 45, 49, 84; and New Historicism, 4–5, 6–7; and pastoral, 192; and poetics, 145–46; and textuality, xi, 2, 3, 13, 24, 33, 109, 154, 164, 212, 214, 228, 248
Pragmatism, 252–60
Principal tongue: German as, 69, 71, 73, 99, 101, 111; Greek as, 90, 96, 99; Hebrew as, 96; Latin as, 90, 96, 99; Slovanic as, 91
Printing: and dictionaries, 115; and literacy, 40; and Nuremberg, 64; and textuality, 20–21; and translation, 125, 127; and vernacular, 33, 72, 119, 128
Prussia, 48
Pseudo-Longinus, 154
Puttenham, George, *Arte of English Poesie*, 45, 194

Quint, David, 38, 265–66n.14
Quintilian, 43, 142, 146, 154–55, 212, 273n.45, 276n.22, 278n.48; and institutions, 18–19

Ramus, Petrus, *Dialecticae institutiones*, 22
Ratichius, Wolfgang, 127
Reception theory, xiii, 1, 255–56
Reformation, 62; Counter-Reformation, 224
Reinhart, Max, 9–10, 191
Representation: and history, 1; and new historicism, 1–13; and poetry, 140, 191; reception theory, xiii, 1
Rhetoric: and nature, 146; and poetry, 140–45, 157
Richelieu, Cardinal, 44
Rist, Johann, 64, 176
Ronsard, Pierre de, 44, 139, 163, 217
Rorty, Richard, 252–55, 256, 257–59; "Deconstruction and Circumvention," 253; *Philosophy and the Mirror of Nature*, 253; "Texts and Lumps," 254
Rosicrucians, 51
Rossi, Basiano de', *Trattato dell'agricoltura*, 34
Royal Society, 45–46, 50–51
Rudolf I, 233

Salviati, Leonardo, *Orazione*, 41
Sannazaro, Jacopo, 196; *Arcadia*, 186, 208, 209, 213, 220, 221
Satire, 181–82, 183
Saussure, Ferdinand de, 23–25, 26, 29
Schäfferey, 67, 186, 216, 278n.1. *See also* Pastoral
Schaffgotsch, Hans Ulrich von, 209, 210

Schottelius, Justus Georg, 65–66, 70, 88, 182, 272n.16, 272n.19; *Ausfürliche Arbeit von der teutschen HaubtSprache* (A detailed account of German as a principal tongue), 69, 90, 93–95, 98–99, 100–101, 102, 103, 105, 107, 108, 110, 111–12, 114, 120–22, 123, 126; *Ethica*, 163; *Der teutschen Sprach Einleitung* (Introduction to the German language), 97, 112, 176, 273n.34; *Teutsche Sprachkunst* (Art of Language), 102, 107, 110, 119; *Teutsche Vers- oder Reim-Kunst* (A study of German prosody and rhyme), 148–49, 164

Science: and history, 43, 256; and natural language, 102; and new pragmatism, 254, 256; and Order of Flowers poetics, 148–50; and vernacular, 38, 43, 46–47, 49–51

Segal, Charles, 198

Shakespeare, William, and new historicism, 7

Sidney, Sir Philip, 132, 217; *Arcadia*, 179, 218

Society of Sciences (Societät der Wissenschaften), 48

Socrates, 79–82, 112, 212

Spahr, Blake Lee, 60, 61, 269–70n.91, 278n.1

Spenser, Edmund, *Faerie Queene*, 194, 195

Speroni, Sperone, *Dialogo della lingue*, 42–43

Stubenberg, Johann Wilhelm von, 127, 128, 282n.76

Sturm, Johann, 22

Tasso, 217; *Amyntas*, 184

Text: and Cabbala, 97; and convention, 26; and history, xii–xiv, 1–13, 28, 33, 39, 52, 70–71, 73; and interpretive community, 259–60; intertextuality, 255–56; materiality of, 27–28; mediating action and object, 17; and poetics, 141, 142, 166; power of, xi, 2, 3, 13, 24, 109, 154, 164, 212, 214, 228, 248; pragmatism and textuality, 255; and printing, 20–21; producing nature, 145, 146, 175; and reception theory, 256

Textual institution: xii–xiv, 3–4, 12–13, 16–23, 28–29; and dictionaries, 42, 44, 47, 48; and German, 22–23, 28, 32–33, 70–71, 93; and historical criticism, 13; and language societies, 32–33, 36, 51, 55–56, 57, 59, 61, 66–68, 87, 109, 120, 249–52, 260–61; and Luther, 33; and pastoral, 187–93, 213, 216, 228, 248; and poetics, 133, 134–35, 137, 167–68, 174, 180; and translation, 127, 128, 129; and vernacular, 28, 33. *See also* Institutions

Theocritus, 191, 196, 210, 213, 217, 246; *Idyll 1*, 188, 197–99, 220; *Idyll 7*, 192, 195; and Virgil, 199, 201, 204–5

Thirty Years' War, xi, xii, 9, 30, 51, 56, 59, 62–64, 88, 105, 218, 219–20, 226–27, 229

Tragedy, 180, 184

Translation, 69, 83, 113; and academies, 37, 40, 45; contextualism in, 124; and history, 127; and language societies, 123–30; and Luther, 70, 72, 73; and poetics, 151–53, 164; and printing, 125, 127; and vernacular, 46–47, 116, 127–30, 179

Ulrich, Anton, 233, 234, 236

Ursprache. *See* Adamic languages

Vega, Lope de, 132, 217

Vernacular: and Ancient-Modern debate, 37–46, 49–51, 66–68, 133–38, 141, 144–45, 249; combining sacred and historical discourses, 71, 73, 74; combining sacred and natural discourses, 36, 38, 69, 97–98, 99–100, 104–9, 113, 130, 249; common vs. society usage, 109–13, 114–15, 117, 130; and consensus, 26, 27–28; and convention, 143; and dictionaries, 41–42, 44, 46–48; and European academies, 32; and history, 73–74; and Leibniz, 47–48; and Luther, 33, 35–36, 72, 73; and natural languages, 100–104; and pastoral, 59, 187, 188, 191, 192–93, 197, 204, 209–11, 214–15, 216–17, 217–18, 222, 225, 227, 228, 231–32, 237, 240, 242; and poetics, 134–38, 139, 141, 142, 145, 148–57, 165, 166, 167; and politics, 39, 44, 57; and printing, 21, 33, 72, 116, 119, 128; purification of, 40, 41, 43, 45;

and science, 38, 43, 46, 49–51; and translation, 46–47, 116, 179. *See also* German

Vico, Giambattista, and history, 4; and mimesis, 8

Vida, Marco Girolamo, 139

Virgil, 21, 187, 191, 193, 196, 210, 213, 217, 220, 221, 241, 246, 247; *Eclogue 1*, 202, 218, 232; *Eclogue 4*, 195; *Eclogue 5*, 188–89, 199–202, 203, 204, 214, 236; *Eclogues*, 186, 188, 204; *Fourth Georgic*, 188–89, 201–8, 209, 210, 214, 225, 228, 230; *Georgics*, 186, 224; and Homer, 205–6; 280n.37; and Theocritus, 199, 201

Vives, Johannes Ludovicus Valentinus, 162

Vocabolario della Accademia della crusca, 41, 44, 47

Weber, Samuel, 17
Wells, Susan, 1
Werder, Diederich von dem, 127, 128
White, Hayden, 259
Wiedemann, Conrad, 282n.66
Wilhelm IV, of Sachsen-Weimar, 58
Wilkins, John, 50
Williams, Raymond, 17
Woodhouse, John, 46

Zeiller, Martin, 273n.38
Zesen, Philipp von, 64, 71, 73, 106, 119, 273n.37

Designed by Martha Farlow

Composed by Village Typographers, Inc., in Janson Text with Luther Fraktur display

Printed by BookCrafters, Inc., on 50-lb. BookText Natural and bound in Holliston Roxite A with Rainbow Texture endsheets